MW01152287

ALL · IN · ONE

CompTIA Strata™ IT Fundamentals

EXAM GUIDE

(Exam FC0-U41)

ALL·IN·ONE

CompTIA Strata™ IT Fundamentals
EXAM GUIDE

(Exam FC0-U41)

Scott Jernigan
Mike Meyers

New York • Chicago • San Francisco • Lisbon
London • Madrid • Mexico City • Milan • New Delhi
San Juan • Seoul • Singapore • Sydney • Toronto

McGraw-Hill is an independent entity from CompTIA. This publication and CD may be used in assisting students to prepare for the CompTIA Strata IT Fundamentals Exam. Neither CompTIA nor McGraw-Hill warrants that use of this publication and CD will ensure passing any exam. CompTIA is a registered trademark of CompTIA in the United States and/or other countries.

The McGraw·Hill Companies

Cataloging-in-Publication Data is on file with the Library of Congress

McGraw-Hill books are available at special quantity discounts to use as premiums and sales promotions, or for use in corporate training programs. To contact a representative, please e-mail us at bulksales@mcgraw-hill.com.

CompTIA Strata™ IT Fundamentals All-in-One Exam Guide (Exam FC0-U41)

Copyright © 2011 by The McGraw-Hill Companies. All rights reserved. Printed in the United States of America. Except as permitted under the Copyright Act of 1976, no part of this publication may be reproduced or distributed in any form or by any means, or stored in a database or retrieval system, without the prior written permission of publisher, with the exception that the program listings may be entered, stored, and executed in a computer system, but they may not be reproduced for publication.

Trademarks: McGraw-Hill, the McGraw-Hill Publishing logo, and related trade dress are trademarks or registered trademarks of The McGraw-Hill Companies and/or its affiliates in the United States and other countries and may not be used without written permission. All other trademarks are the property of their respective owners. The McGraw-Hill Companies is not associated with any product or vendor mentioned in this book.

1234567890 DOC DOC 10987654321

ISBN: Book p/n 978-0-07-176019-5 and CD p/n 978-0-07-176020-1 of set 978-0-07-176022-5
MHID: Book p/n 0-07-176019-9and CD p/n 0-07-176020-2 of set 0-07-176022-9

Sponsoring Editor Timothy Green	**Technical Editor** Chris Crayton	**Production Supervisor** James Kussow
Editorial Supervisor Jody McKenzie	**Copy Editor** Bob Campbell	**Composition** Apollo Publishing
Project Editor Emilia Thiuri	**Proofreader** Paul Tyler	**Illustration** Ford Pierson, Lyssa Wald
Acquisitions Coordinator Stephanie Evans	**Indexer** Jack Lewis	**Art Director, Cover** Jeff Weeks

Information has been obtained by McGraw-Hill from sources believed to be reliable. However, because of the possibility of human or mechanical error by our sources, McGraw-Hill, or others, McGraw-Hill does not guarantee the accuracy, adequacy, or completeness of any information and is not responsible for any errors or omissions or the results obtained from the use of such information.

The logo of the CompTIA Authorized Quality Curriculum Program and the status of this or other training material as "Authorized" under the CompTIA Authorized Curriculum Program signifies that, in CompTIA's opinion, such training material covers the content of the CompTIA's related certification exam. CompTIA has not reviewed or approved the accuracy of the contents of this training material and specifically disclaims any warranties of merchantability or fitness for a particular purpose. CompTIA makes no guarantee concerning the success of persons using any such "Authorized" or other training material in order to prepare for any CompTIA certification exam.

I dedicate this book to my wife, Katie.
Thank you for your love, support,
and laughter through the years.
You're simply the best.

—Scott Jernigan

ABOUT THE AUTHOR

Scott Jernigan wields a mighty red pen as Editor in Chief for Total Seminars. With a Master of Arts degree in Medieval History, Scott feels as much at home in the musty archives of London as he does in the warm computer glow of Total Seminars' Houston headquarters. After fleeing a purely academic life, he dove headfirst into IT, working as an instructor, editor, and writer.

Scott has written, edited, and contributed to dozens of books on computer literacy, hardware, operating systems, networking, and certification, including *Computer Literacy— Your Ticket to IC³ Certification*, and co-authoring the best-selling *All-in-One A+ Certification Exam Guide, 5th edition*, and the *A+ Guide to Managing and Troubleshooting PCs* (both with Mike Meyers).

Scott has taught all over the United States, including stints at the United Nations in New York and the FBI Academy in Quantico. Plus, Scott teaches numerous online courses, ranging from "Introduction to Microsoft Expression Web" to "Intro to PC Troubleshooting." Practicing what he preaches, Scott is a CompTIA A+ and CompTIA Network+ certified technician, a Microsoft Certified Professional, a Microsoft Office User Specialist, and Certiport Internet and Computing Core Certified. And of course, Scott has the CompTIA Strata certificate.

E-mail: scottj@totalsem.com
Web forums: www.totalsem.com/forums

About Mike Meyers

Mike Meyers is the best-selling author of numerous books on computer literacy and certifications, including the *Introduction to PC Hardware and Troubleshooting*, the *All-in-One CompTIA A+ Certification Exam Guide*, the *All-in-One CompTIA Network+ Certification Exam Guide*, and the *CompTIA Network+ Guide to Managing and Troubleshooting Networks*. Most consider Mike the leading expert on computer industry certifications. He is the president and founder of Total Seminars, LLC, a major provider of PC and network repair seminars for thousands of organizations throughout the world.

About the Technical Editor

Chris Crayton (CompTIA A+, CompTIA Network+, MCSE) is an author, editor, technical consultant, and trainer. Chris has authored several print and online books on PC repair, CompTIA A+, and CompTIA Security+. He has served as technical editor on numerous professional technical titles for leading publishing companies, including the *All-in-One CompTIA A+ Certification Exam Guide*, the *All-in-One CompTIA Network+ Certification Exam Guide*, and the *Mike Meyers' CompTIA Network+ Certification Passport*.

CompTIA.

CompTIA Strata IT Fundamentals

CompTIA Strata IT Fundamentals is designed for

- Individuals seeking a new career in IT
- Students new to the IT and technology job market
- Professionals in technology sales careers
- Individuals considering CompTIA A+ or other IT industry certifications
- Certified or seasoned IT career professionals who want to enhance their credentials

It Pays to Get Certified

In a digital world, digital literacy is an essential survival skill. Certification proves you have the knowledge and skill to solve business problems in virtually any business environment.

Certification makes you more competitive and employable. Research has shown that people who study technology get hired. In the competition for entry-level jobs, applicants with high-school diplomas or college degrees who included IT coursework in their academic load fared consistently better in job interviews—and were hired in significantly higher numbers. If considered a compulsory part of a technology education, testing for certification can be an invaluable competitive distinction for professionals.

How Certification Helps Your Career

Learn new skills to get a job	Retain your job and salary	Want to change jobs	Stick out from the resume pile	IT is everywhere
Certifications are essential credentials that prove you have the knowledge and skills to perform.	Make your expertise stand above the rest. Competence is usually retained during times of change.	Certifications qualify you for new opportunities, whether locked into a current job, see limited advancement or need to change careers.	Hiring managers can demand the strongest skill set.	IT is needed in most companies across the industries. There aren't enough trained professionals to fill jobs.

Why CompTIA?

- **Global recognition**   CompTIA is recognized globally as the leading IT nonprofit trade association and has enormous credibility. Plus, CompTIA's certifications are vendor neutral and offer proof of foundational knowledge that translates across technologies.

- **Valued by hiring managers**   Hiring managers value CompTIA certification because it is vendor- and technology-independent validation of your technical skills.

- **Recommended or required by government and businesses**   Many government organizations and corporations either recommend or require technical staff to be CompTIA certified (e.g., Dell, Sharp, Ricoh, the U.S. Department of Defense, and many more).

- **Three CompTIA certifications ranked in the top ten**   In a study by DICE of 17,000 technology professionals, certifications helped command higher salaries at all experience levels.

CompTIA Career Pathway

CompTIA offers a number of credentials that form a foundation for your career in technology and allow you to pursue specific areas of concentration. Depending on the path you choose to take, CompTIA certifications help you build upon your skills and knowledge, supporting learning throughout your entire career.

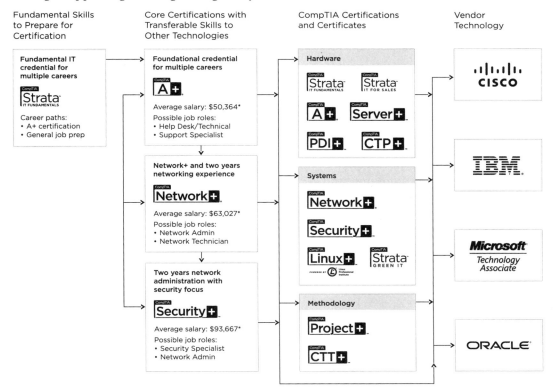

*Source: *Computerworld* Salary Survey 2010—U.S. salaries only

Four Steps to Getting Certified

1. **Review exam objectives.** Review the certification objectives to make sure you know what is covered in the exam:

   www.comptia.org/certifications/testprep/examobjectives.aspx

2. **Practice for the exam.** After you have studied for the certification, take a free assessment and sample test to get an idea of the type of questions that might be on the exam:

   www.comptia.org/certifications/testprep/practicetests.aspx

3. **Purchase an exam voucher.** Purchase exam vouchers on the CompTIA Marketplace:

   www.comptiastore.com

4. **Take the test!** Select a certification exam provider and schedule a time to take your exam:

   www.comptia.org/certifications/testprep/testingcenters.aspx

Join the Professional Community

The free IT Pro online community provides valuable content to students and professionals.

Career IT job resources include

- Where to start in IT
- Career assessments
- Salary trends
- U.S. Job Board

Join the IT Pro community and get access to

- Forums on networking, security, computing, and cutting-edge technologies
- Access to blogs written by industry experts
- Current information on cutting-edge technologies
- Access to various industry resource links and articles related to IT and IT careers

 **AUTHORIZED**

Content Seal of Quality

This text bears the seal of CompTIA Approved Quality Content. This seal signifies this content covers 100 percent of the exam objectives and implements important instructional design principles. CompTIA recommends multiple learning tools to help increase coverage of the learning objectives. Look for this seal on other materials you use to prepare for your certification exam.

How to Obtain More Information

Visit Us Online

Visit www.comptia.org to learn more about getting a CompTIA certification. And while you're at it, take a moment to learn a little more about CompTIA. We're the voice of the world's IT industry. Our membership includes companies on the cutting edge of innovation.

Contact CompTIA with Any Questions or Comments

Please call 866-835-8020, ext. 5 or e-mail questions@comptia.org.

Explore Social Media

Find us on Facebook, LinkedIn, Twitter, and YouTube.

CONTENTS AT A GLANCE

CONTENTS

ACKNOWLEDGMENTS

My acquisitions editor, Tim Green, worked his usual motivational magic and helped get this book out in a timely fashion. Thanks for being there when I needed you.

Aaron Verber was my go-to guy when it came to keeping all the pieces of this book in order and rolling along. Great editing, and thanks for laughing at (and fixing) some of my really bad prose.

Ford Pierson did a marvelous job with the frequently funny and always creative illustrations. His personality is clearly stamped on this work. And he did a great job with editing as well.

Michael Smyer helped this book greatly. His gorgeous photographs grace most pages of this book. Plus his technical knowledge and research abilities came into play many times.

Chris Crayton caught every little technical error and kept me honest. His knowledge and attention to detail were invaluable.

On the McGraw-Hill side, I had an equally excellent team. Everyone was unfailingly polite, helpful, and pushy when it was needed.

Stephanie Evans, my acquisitions coordinator, managed to keep me sending in chapters. She didn't even need to fly to Houston to pry them out of my fingers (although there were a few times when I thought she was about to board the plane). Nice working with you!

Jody McKenzie, my editorial supervisor, did her usual fabulous work. It's always fun doing a project with you.

Emilia Thiuri did a great job running the team that turned copyedited chapters into a final book. I enjoyed working with you on this, our first project together, and look forward to the next project as well.

To the copy editor, Bob Campbell, proofreader, Paul Tyler, indexer, Jack Lewis, and layout folks at Apollo Publishing—superb work in every facet. Thank you for being the best.

INTRODUCTION

The people who build and fix personal computers and the computer networks most of us have used—the *techs*—have many specific skills. To become a good tech takes time, thought, hard work, and a handy screwdriver.

To prove his or her skills, a tech earns industry certifications. This generally means that the tech takes and passes a certification exam and then gets to add credentials to his or her name. The most important general certifying body is called CompTIA.

Who Is CompTIA?

The Computer Technology Industry Association (CompTIA) is a nonprofit industry trade association based in Oakbrook Terrace, Illinois. It consists of over 20,000 members in 102 countries. You'll find CompTIA offices in such diverse locales as Amsterdam, Dubai, Johannesburg, Tokyo, and Sãu Paulo.

Virtually every company of consequence in the information technology (IT) industry is a member of CompTIA. Here are a few of the biggies:

Adobe Systems	AMD	Best Buy	Brother International
Canon	Cisco Systems	CompUSA	Fujitsu
Gateway	Hewlett-Packard	IBM	Intel
Kyocera	McAfee	Microsoft	NCR
Novell	Panasonic	Sharp Electronics	Siemens
Symantec	Toshiba	Total Seminars, LLC (that's my company)	Plus many thousands more

CompTIA provides a forum for people in these industries to network (as in meeting people), represents the interests of its members to the government, and provides certifications for many aspects of the computer industry. CompTIA watches the IT industry closely and provides new and updated certifications to meet the ongoing demand from its membership.

CompTIA Certifications

CompTIA certifications enable techs to offer proof of competency in a variety of technology fields. Attaining the CompTIA A+ certification, for example, proves that you're a PC technician of some skill. You know how to build and fix PCs; you know the basics of networking, because modern PCs almost always connect to some network. The CompTIA Network+ certification, in contrast, goes pretty deep into networking. It's designed for network technicians.

To attain CompTIA A+ or CompTIA Network+ certifications takes time and commitment. Most commonly, the successful candidate is a working tech already and wants to prove his or her merit to an employer. But what about people who might want to become a tech but aren't there already?

CompTIA Strata

The CompTIA Strata Certificate Program is a collection of three U.S. exams and two UK exams that cover entry-level IT subjects. The U.S. exams include:

- CompTIA Strata IT Fundamentals, which covers technology and computer hardware basics
- CompTIA Strata IT for Sales, which covers knowledge of technology useful for those entering a sales position
- CompTIA Strata Green IT, which covers the emerging technologies that make up the green IT industry

For the UK, the CompTIA Strata IT Fundamentals exam is split into two exams, though they both cover the same set of competencies:

- CompTIA Strata—Fundamentals of PC Functionality, which covers basic PC components and vocabulary
- CompTIA Strata—Fundamentals of PC Technology, which covers PC characteristics and operational problems

This book is primarily concerned with the CompTIA Strata IT Fundamentals exam, which creates an entry point for people who think they might want to become a tech. To take the exam successfully, you'll need to understand the concepts and terminology that go with PCs and networks. You'll need a working knowledge of computer components and operating systems.

Because success on the exam requires a solid knowledge of computer and networking terminology, the CompTIA Strata certificate serves *another* audience as well: those who need to interface with techs. Techs often speak in their own technical jargon, using words and concepts unfamiliar to most office workers, even skilled computer users. You might be a master of Microsoft Word, for example, but not understand when a tech says that your computer is running slowly because it only has one gigabyte of RAM.

The CompTIA Strata certificate, therefore, applies to two different groups:

- Those thinking about becoming a tech
- People who need to communicate with techs knowledgably

About the Book

I designed the *CompTIA Strata™ IT Fundamentals All-in-One Exam Guide* to address the needs of both sets of people who need to get the CompTIA Strata certificate. The book approaches topics in plain language, gradually introducing you to terminology and technology.

The book is split into five sections:

   I. The Simple PC

  II. Maintaining and Upgrading the Simple PC

 III. The Complex PC

 IV. Networks of PCs

  V. Securing PCs

"The Simple PC" covers what you might expect: the basic components and workings of the personal computer. Chapters 1–5 teach you how computers work. I cover important jargon, tools, and concepts. You'll learn about the basic hardware and software and how everything works together.

"Maintaining and Upgrading the Simple PC" covers topics as diverse as cleaning supplies that work best to teaching you how to upgrade the programs on the computer. Chapters 6–8 describe important topics that every user, not just techs, should understand.

"The Complex PC" adds more pieces to the basic computer described in the first two sections of the book. *Complex*, in this context, does not mean *difficult*. Chapters 9–12 introduce components like wireless keyboards and mice. You'll learn about printers, including how to set them up and keep them working. These chapters enable me to talk about portable computers, from the standard clamshell-style laptop to the latest iPad slate.

"Networks of PCs" teaches you the terminology of networks. You'll learn how networks work, both wired and wireless. Chapters 13–16 take you the whole way, from a simple network to the Internet. You'll also learn how companies and individuals work to reduce the amount of electricity and other resources used in computing.

"Securing PCs" covers the process of making sure your machines and data are safe. The safety comes from avoiding mistakes, accidents, and so on. Plus, Chapters 17–18 tell the tales of viruses, hackers, and thieves, and what you need to do to protect yourself and others.

Getting the CompTIA Strata Certificate

To get a CompTIA Strata certificate, you need to take and pass one 100-question exam. That's it. Whether you are in Boston or Los Angeles, you can sign up for the exam online, where you will schedule a time and place to take it. The two Web sites you can use are those for VUE and Prometric, the two test-administering bodies.

www.vue.com

www.prometric.com

VUE and Prometric have testing sites all over the world, in cities large and small. You should be able to find one that's convenient to you.

As of this writing, the CompTIA Strata exam costs US$102 for non-CompTIA members, although you can purchase discount vouchers from several companies, including my own. Do a Google search for "CompTIA Strata discount voucher" or go to my company's site:

www.totalsem.com/vouchers

Once you succeed on the exam, you'll have a CompTIA Strata certificate. You can make decisions on pursuing a career in IT. If so, your next step should be pursuing the CompTIA A+ certification. That's the industry standard entry point for techs.

If you've studied Strata for knowledge and language and want more user-oriented training, then a lot of other options emerge. Certiport offers an excellent Computer Literacy certification, for example, called IC[3]. Microsoft has certifications for each of its Office products, such as Word, Excel, and PowerPoint. You can find many other application-specific certifications as well.

Here's a good starting point with explanations about tech certifications and some of the suggested pathways to take:

www.totalsem.com/certifications

Studying for the Exam

I wrote the *CompTIA Strata™ IT Fundamentals All-in-One Exam Guide* thematically, grouping topics together that made the most sense to me for learning. I didn't write a guide that followed the CompTIA Strata competencies in order. (It would have made for a very strange and repetitious book.)

With that in mind, I suggest you read the book twice. The first time, just read it through like a novel. Enjoy the new terms and Ford's fun illustrations. Don't try to memorize things yet. The second read through, make sure you have a copy of the CompTIA Strata competencies printed out or on screen. Read carefully, and check off topics as you cover them.

 NOTE There's a map in Appendix B so you know where I cover each competency in the book.

If you have questions or comments, good or bad, feel free to contact me. Here's my e-mail address:

scottj@totalsem.com

Good luck with your studies and with the CompTIA Strata exam!

—Scott

PART I

The Simple PC

How Computers Work

In this chapter, you will learn how to
- Describe different types of computers
- Explain ways to use computers
- Describe how computers work

Charles Babbage didn't set out to change the world. He just wanted to do math without worrying about human error, something all too common in his day. Babbage was a mathematician in the nineteenth century, a time well before anyone thought to create electronic calculators or computers (Figure 1-1). When he worked on complex math, the best "computers" were people who computed by hand. They solved equations using pen and paper.

Babbage thought of making machines that would do calculations mechanically, so the numbers would always be right. Although his ideas were ahead of his time, inventors in the mid-twentieth century picked up the concepts and created huge calculating machines that they called *computers*.

Figure 1-1
Charles Babbage,
father of the
computer

C. BABBAGE (MATHEMATICIAN)
Died Oct. 20, 1871, aged 79

NOTE   Charles Babbage (1791–1871) played with numbers and came up with amazing inventions during a very creative period in Western civilization, the Industrial Revolution. He taught math at Trinity College, Cambridge, England, but his interests and creations went well beyond just math. Babbage is considered to be the father of the computer.

This chapter explores the machines originally invented to help do math. We'll first examine the different devices that are called computers. Then we'll explore ways that these computers can help us do things. The chapter finishes with a section on the internal workings of a computer. The last section is an extremely important part in this book, so pay attention!

Now, let's have some fun and explore computers.

Types of Computers

In modern terms, a computer is an electronic device that can perform calculations. The most common types use special programming languages that people, known as computer programmers, have written and compiled to accomplish specific tasks.

When most people hear the word "computer," they picture *general* computing devices, machines that can do all sorts of things. The typical *personal computer (PC)* runs the operating system *Microsoft Windows* and is used for various tasks (Figure 1-2). You can use it to manage your money and play games, for example, without doing anything special to it, such as add new hardware.

Here are some other general-purpose computing devices:

- Apple Mac
- Apple iPad
- Smartphone
- Portable computer (Figure 1-3)

Figure 1-2
A typical PC

Figure 1-3
A portable computer

Plenty of other devices do *specific* computing jobs, focusing on a single task or set of similar tasks. You probably encounter them all the time. Here's a list of common specific-purpose computers:

- Apple iPod
- Pocket calculator
- Digital watch
- Digital clock
- Wi-Fi picture frame
- Typical mobile phone
- Xbox 360
- PlayStation 3
- GPS (Global Positioning System, the device that helps drivers figure out how to get where they need to go)
- TiVo
- Point of sale system (Figure 1-4)
- Digital camera
- Camcorder

Figure 1-4
A point of sale computer in a gasoline pump

This list isn't even close to complete! Plus, there are computers *inside* a zillion other devices. Here are some:

- Modern refrigerators
- Every automobile built since 1995
- Airplanes
- Boats
- Mall lighting systems
- Zambonis
- Home security alarms

You get the idea. Computers help the modern world function.

NOTE I picked 1995 as an arbitrary date for "all cars have computers." Computers have been used with cars for a long time. Simple computers helped make car factories work better starting in the 1970s, for example. The earliest mass-production car that I found that had a central processor chip that made performance happen was the BMW 3-series. The 1985–86 BMW 325, for example, can gain a few extra horsepower just from a ~$200 chip upgrade.

Uses for Computers

Computers are tools. General- and single-purpose computing devices enable life as we know it. That sounds like a crazy statement, but the following examples will show you just how important computers are to your life every day. Let's look at music, visual art, and games.

Music

My parents grew up in the 1940s and 1950s. When they wanted to listen to music, they had four choices. First, they could go to a live performance. They could also learn to play an instrument and thus create their own live performance. They could find a rich person who had a phonograph and copies of various albums. Each album could hold eight to ten songs—nice! Or they could tune in to the radio and listen to one of the few available stations (Figure 1-5).

By the time my generation got rolling, we had lots of radio stations, televisions, and portable cassette tape players, among many other choices for listening to music. Each cassette tape could hold up to two hours of music! Plus, we could always fall back on live music, too.

What do you use today? Most people I know have an Apple iPod of some generation. iPods and other similar music players are tiny devices that can hold thousands of songs and are small enough to slip into a shirt pocket or clip onto a collar (Figure 1-6).

Figure 1-5
A 1950s radio
(photo courtesy
of Masaki Ikeda)

Figure 1-6
An Apple iPod Nano

Visual Art

Computers have revolutionized many of the visual arts, though most obviously in animated movies and photography. People still paint with oil and canvas. Artists work with charcoal, paper, and ink. But compare the process used to create Walt Disney's classic tale *Bambi* with a modern Pixar film like *Finding Nemo*.

Disney's animators created their movies by drawing, by hand, each frame of the movie. A full motion picture displays 24 frames per second. Characters that moved from one moment to the next required more than 20 drawings showing slight movement, for each second of screen time! Master animators would create the first and last frames of a motion, and then other animators would create the individual steps in between. To produce an animated movie took hundreds of artists drawing a dizzying number of pictures.

Modern animated movies use three-dimensional models created on computers (Figure 1-7). When the artist wants to move a character, he or she puts the model in the beginning position and the end position. Then he or she tells the computer to fill in the movement in the middle automatically. One person with a computer can do a job that used to take hundreds of people.

NOTE I'm simplifying here. The "computer" used to create a Pixar-level movie isn't the standard beige box you might find in your house. Modern animation studios use extremely powerful computers called *supercomputers* to make the animation happen. Supercomputers make the math happen quickly and thus make a movie affordable to create.

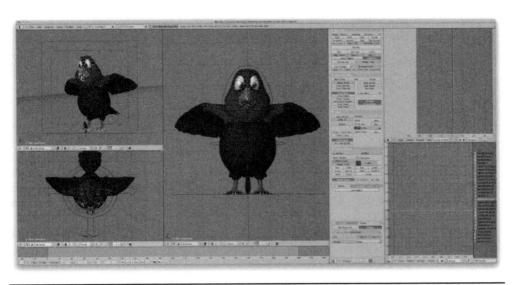

Figure 1-7 A 3-D modeling program on a personal computer

Photography has changed dramatically through computers as well. When I first learned photography, for example, the process of creating a finished print was very involved. We used rolls of film and spent hours in a darkroom with lots of smelly, toxic chemicals to develop it into photographs (Figure 1-8). Once those were developed, we would pick the best shots and print those using special photographic papers and machines.

It was not uncommon to shoot an entire roll of film (24–36 shots), spend the time and money to develop it, and get only one or two good pictures out of the roll. Even worse, you didn't know if you got the shot until after you finished shooting and spent hours in the darkroom!

Figure 1-8
Ancient
photographic
process, circa 1992

Modern digital photography is completely different. You have five components that make this work. Some are mechanical, but most are computing devices.

- Digital camera
- Digital storage card
- Personal computer
- Image-editing software
- Printer

With digital cameras, you take photographs and the camera's computer processes them immediately. The camera stores the images on its digital storage card, where you can quickly review them to see if you got the shot you wanted. If you didn't, you can delete it and try again (Figure 1-9).

The next step is to edit the images. You copy the pictures onto a personal computer and run a program that enables you to make small and large changes to each image.

Look at the accompanying before and after pictures (Figures 1-10 and 1-11). All the changes were made using a computer program called Adobe Photoshop. You simply couldn't do these kinds of things with pre-computer cameras and photography.

Figure 1-9
Reviewing an image
with a digital camera

Figure 1-10
Before

Figure 1-11
After

Figure 1-12
A printed image

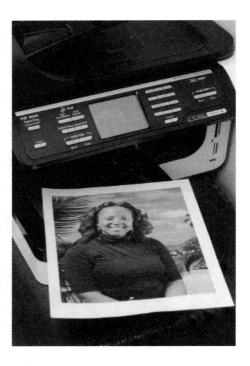

Once you finish editing the pictures, print them out on a modern inkjet printer to create beautiful prints to send to your friends and family (Figure 1-12).

Games

What's the first game you remember playing? Chances are good that you or one of your friends remember a game played on a computer or video game console. This too shows the enormous impact computers make on society.

Several years ago, few people played games on computers at all. Some arcades had pinball machines and early video games, such as Pac-Man, Galaga, and Asteroids. But the idea of a personal computer–based game in your living room was unknown.

A quick survey of my office mates, ranging in age from 50 to 21, reveals the shift in only one generation. They remember these as the first games they played.

- Marbles
- Checkers
- Chess
- Cards (solitaire, specifically)

- Tiddlywinks
- Candy Land
- Chutes and Ladders
- Trouble
- Operation
- Mario Brothers on the Nintendo
- Sonic the Hedgehog on the Sega Genesis

Take a wild guess about who played the computer games as their first games. If you said the people in their early 20s, you would be correct!

Today, many of us regularly play computer games on the Internet that enable us to talk, run, and explore with people all over the world at the same time. Members of my World of Warcraft guild, for example, stretch from Arkansas to California, from England to Canada, and on over to Australia and New Zealand. I'm often adventuring with people from Japan and Korea.

Figure 1-13 shows characters run by people from all over the world, together in one virtual environment. This sort of game, with global interaction, is normal today, not an exception.

Examples of how computers and computing devices have transformed modern life can go on and on. What other fields can you or your family discuss that have changed?

Figure 1-13
Tsarion's player lives in Texas. The others? All over the world.

Discovering the Past

Here's something you can try in the classroom. Ask teachers, parents, or grand-parents about the world 10, 20, 30, or 40 years ago. The answers you get might shock you.

1. When you want to know about what's happening in another part of the world, what do you do? Do computers play a part? How did it work before computers? How long ago was that? What did it mean to "check the news" a couple decades ago?

2. I want to compare the players and statistics on two of my favorite sports teams. (Pick your sport: Manchester United vs. Real Madrid, for example, or the Dallas Cowboys vs. the Pittsburgh Steelers.) How do you do this today? What about before computers?

How Computers Work

At this point, you know that all computers are machines. Machines are made up of different parts, of course, so computers have parts too. A modern computer consists of three major components:

- Hardware
- Operating system
- Applications

The *hardware* is the physical stuff that you can touch or hold in your hand. With a smartphone, for example, you hold the phone. On a typical PC, you touch the keyboard or view images on the monitor (Figure 1-14).

The *operating system* controls the hardware and enables you to tell the computer what to do. The operating system often appears as a collection of windows and little icons you can click (see Figure 1-15). These are called the *interface*, which means the software parts with which you can interact.

Figure 1-14
A typical computer

Figure 1-15   The Microsoft Windows 7 operating system

Applications (or programs) enable you to do specialized tasks on a computer, such as

- Type a letter
- Send a message from your desk to your friend's computer in Paris
- Wander through imaginary worlds with people all over the Earth

Very simple computing devices might have only an operating system with a few features that give you choices. A digital camera, for example, has a menu system that enables you to control things like the quality of the picture taken (Figure 1-16).

Figure 1-16
Changing settings on
a digital camera

Figure 1-17
Talking Carl talks
back to you—
perhaps not the
most *useful* app
on the planet, but
amusing.

More complicated devices offer more choices. An Apple iPhone smartphone, for example, can do some cool things right out of the box, including make a phone call. But you can visit the Apple online store and download applications (known as apps) to do all sorts of things that Apple never thought to include (Figure 1-17).

Finally, complicated multipurpose computers like the typical Windows PC offer applications to help you do everything from write a book on IT fundamentals to talk with someone on the other side of the world, with full audio and video (Figure 1-18).

Figure 1-18
Skype
communication

NOTE Most computer users lump operating systems and applications together under the term *software*. The terms software, programs, and applications all generally mean the same thing.

Stages

Computers work through three stages:

- Input
- Processing
- Output

You start the action by doing something—clicking the mouse, typing on the keyboard, or touching the touch screen. This is *input*. The parts inside the device or case take over at that point as the operating system tells the hardware to do what you've requested. This is *processing*.

In fact, at the heart of every computer is a *central processing unit (CPU)*, usually a single, thin wafer of silicon and tiny transistors (Figure 1-19). The CPU handles the majority of the processing tasks and is, in a way, the "brain" of the computer.

NOTE Chapter 2 gives a lot more information on CPUs and other processing components.

Figure 1-19
An Intel Pentium
i7 CPU in a
motherboard

Once the computer has processed your request, it shows you the result by changing what you see on the monitor or playing a sound through the speakers. This is *output*. A computer wouldn't be worth much if it couldn't demonstrate that it fulfilled your commands! Figure 1-20 shows the computing process.

 TIP An important part of the computing process is *data storage*. Data storage means saving a permanent copy of your work so that you can come back to it later. It works like this. First, you tell the computer to save something. Second, the CPU processes that command and stores the data. Third, the computer shows you something, such as a message saying that the data is stored. Any work that you *don't* save is lost when you turn the computer off or exit the application.

At this point, students often ask me a fundamental question: "Why should I care about the computing process?" The answer to this question defines what makes a good computer technician. Here's my response.

Why the Process Matters to Techs

Because the computing process applies to every computing device, it provides the basis for how every tech builds, upgrades, and repairs such devices. By understanding both the components involved and how they talk to each other, you can work with *any* computing device. It might take a couple minutes to figure out how to do input, for example, but you can get it because you know how all computing devices work.

Figure 1-20
The computing
process

Breaking It Down

The whole computer process from start to finish has a lot of steps and pieces that interact. The more you understand about this interaction and these pieces, the better you can troubleshoot when something goes wrong. *This is the core rule to being a great tech.*

Here are nine steps that apply to most computers and computing devices when you want to get something done.

1. Power up.
2. Processing parts prepare for action.
3. You provide input.
4. Processing parts process your command.
5. Processing parts send output information to your output devices.
6. Output devices show you the results.
7. Repeat steps 3–6 until you're satisfied with the outcome.
8. Save your work.
9. Power down the computer.

Let's put pictures and actions to each step. In the process, we'll create a scenario that fits the typical use of a computer.

Step 1: Power Up

The computer has a piece of hardware called a power supply that plugs into some kind of power source, like an AC outlet on a wall (Figure 1-21). The computer has a power button that tells the power supply to wake up. The power supply directly connects to a lot of pieces inside the case (Figure 1-22). These components wake up.

Figure 1-21
A typical computer power supply

Figure 1-22
The power supply
connecting to
devices

This might seem obvious, but put yourself in a tech's shoes for a moment. What would you suspect is the problem if you pushed the power button on a computer that worked yesterday but now appears to be dead? Could it be that something inside the case blew up and is dead, dead, dead? Sure, but isn't it more likely that somebody jiggled the plug or disconnected it when vacuuming? Of course. Check the easy stuff first!

Step 2: Processing Parts Prepare for Action

There are five main parts that handle processing: CPU, motherboard, RAM, hard drive, and operating system. Here's how they prepare for action.

First, the hard drive is a storage device. The operating system and programs live there. But the CPU can't work with the software directly from the hard drive because the hard drive is too slow (Figure 1-23).

Therefore, the CPU needs to load the operating system into special memory called random access memory (RAM) to be able to work with the OS. This is true for any software used by the computer, by the way. Everything has to load into RAM before it can be used (Figure 1-24).

Step 3: You Provide Input

At this point, the computer is ready to work. You need to tell it what to do next.

Most people load some sort of application to do specific tasks. For this example, we're going to write a letter to the editor of a local newspaper, complaining about the lack of cool bike paths in the city. I illustrate steps 3–8 using that project.

Figure 1-23 Processing parts

Figure 1-24 The system ready to work

Figure 1-25
Accessing Microsoft
Word

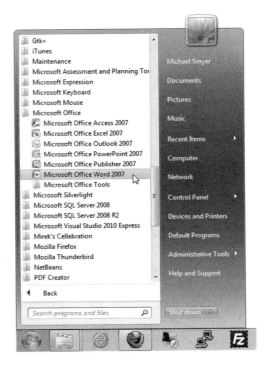

First, move the mouse cursor to Start | All Programs | Microsoft Office | Microsoft Word and click **Microsoft Word** (Figure 1-25). This is the initial input to the computer.

Step 4: Processing Parts Process Your Command

The operating system and CPU interpret the mouse movement and the clicking. "The user wants to load Microsoft Word!" Microsoft Word lives on the hard drive, but it needs to be copied to RAM to work, right?

The CPU tells the hard drive to copy Word to RAM, and the operating system guides the process (Figure 1-26).

Figure 1-26   Copying the application to RAM

Step 5: Processing Parts Send Output Information to Your Output Devices

Once the program is in RAM, the CPU sends the update to the video card and monitor so that the operating system that you see—the interface—will change to show Word as the active program (Figure 1-27).

Figure 1-27 The processing parts send changes to output devices.

Step 6: Output Devices Show You the Results

Sure enough, the monitor changes from the Windows Desktop to an open, blank document in Microsoft Word (Figure 1-28). Now you're ready to do more input!

Step 7: Repeat Steps 3 to 6 Until You're Satisfied with the Outcome

The standard process for creating a word-processing document is to start typing. Each thing you type is input. Likewise, each time you format those words (adding bold, italics, and so on) you input information. The processing components of the computer interpret what you type or click and process it. Then, the processing components update the output devices so that you see changes (in this case) on the screen (Figure 1-29).

Figure 1-28   Word is ready for action.

Figure 1-29
We'll get our bike
paths soon!

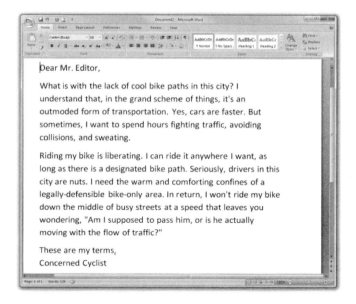

Step 8: Save Your Work

At some point in this process, especially when creating an original item, you'll want to save your changes. You can do this at the end, when you're satisfied with your work, or when you need to stop for a while and want to pick up later where you left off.

Or, and this is important, you can save every time you've reached a point where you don't want to have to re-create all the stuff you've already done just in case the electricity goes out. This is a bit of a lead in to Chapter 2. RAM is *volatile*, meaning RAM must have electricity to hold data. If the power goes out, all the data in RAM (like that letter to the editor you've been working on) just vaporizes. Gone. Save your work!

Most programs have some save function. In Microsoft Word, for example, you go to the Office button (top left) and select Save (Figure 1-30).

Step 9: Power Down the Computer

Once you've finished working or playing for the day, shut down your computer to save on electricity. The typical shutdown process for a Windows computer is to go to the Start button (lower left) and select **Shut Down** from the options.

NOTE Almost every modern computing device has some kind of sleep mode, a way for the device to shut almost everything down automatically. In Windows 7, for example, go to the Start button and hover over the arrow next to Shut Down and select Sleep. This means you don't have to turn off the computer or device every time you walk away for a few minutes.

The usual practice with personal computers is to turn them on at the beginning of your workday, and then shut them off at the end of the day. Let the sleep function do its job saving electricity in the time between.

Figure 1-30
Saving your document

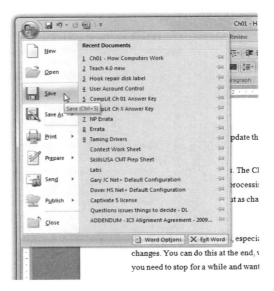

Chapter Review

We can do amazing things with computers of all types. Multifunction computers give us tools to accomplish tasks such as writing books, creating presentations, surfing the Web, writing e-mail, and playing games.

Specific or single-task computing devices have revolutionized the personal space. Jogging with music was a crazy affair just a few years ago. Now, you can run with thousands of your favorite songs, all with a device no bigger than your littlest finger.

Knowing the computing process helps techs handle everything from building computers to making sure they work as intended. Once you know how computers *should* work, you can figure out just about any computing device.

Questions

1. Which of the following is considered a general-purpose computing device?
   - A. Apple iPod
   - B. Digital watch
   - C. PlayStation 3
   - D. Windows PC

2. John wants to take people from two photographs and put them into one photo, as if all the people had been in the same room at the same time. How could he do this *before* computer photo-editing programs, like Adobe Photoshop?
   - A. In a photo-editing darkroom, he could mix the chemicals used for the two photos. That would cause the photos to blend.
   - B. In a photo-editing darkroom, he could mix the paper used for the two photos. That would cause the photos to blend.
   - C. During the development process, he could use a special mixing machine to make the two photos appear as one photo.
   - D. He probably could not do it.

3. Which of the following parts of the computer are considered touchable?
   - A. Applications
   - B. Hardware
   - C. Programs
   - D. Software

4. During which stage of the computing process does the computer show you what you have asked it to do?
   - A. Input
   - B. Output
   - C. Processing
   - D. Storage

5. How can understanding the computing process help you as a tech? (Select the best answer.)

    A. You can pick out the best part to buy.

    B. You can select the appropriate software application to solve a problem.

    C. You can troubleshoot any computing device.

    D. You can sound more important.

6. What is the first step required for working with computers?

    A. Power

    B. Installing an operating system

    C. Running an application

    D. Building the CPU

7. Where are the operating system and programs stored when not in use?

    A. CPU

    B. RAM

    C. Hard drive

    D. Monitor

8. How do you tell the computer what to do?

    A. Input

    B. Output

    C. Processing

    D. Storage

9. When you want to work on a document later, what should you do?

    A. Input information.

    B. Process the document.

    C. Power down the computer.

    D. Save the document.

10. What should you do with the computer once you're done working for the day?

    A. Process your document.

    B. Store your document.

    C. Open a Web browser.

    D. Power down the computer.

Answers

1. **D.** A Windows PC is a general-purpose computing device. Other such devices are Apple Macs and smartphones.

2. **D.** Although it was possible to do some crazy mixing among photos in the pre-computer days, it was very, very hard. Most likely, John would have been out of luck. Photoshop and other image-editing programs make such efforts relatively easy.

3. **B.** Hardware is the part of the computer that you can touch or hold.

4. **B.** The computer shows you the result of processed commands during the output stage. Note that when you save a file—the storage phase—the computer will usually tell you that a file has been successfully stored. The "telling you" part is output.

5. **C.** Understanding both the components involved and how they talk to each other, you can work with *any* computing device. This understanding enables you to troubleshoot when something goes wrong.

6. **A.** Nothing works without power, so that's definitely the first thing needed.

7. **C.** The operating system and programs are stored on the hard drive. When the computer needs to use them, the OS and programs are copied to RAM.

8. **A.** Input tells the computer what to do. Typical input is typing on the keyboard or clicking with the mouse.

9. **D.** Save your document so that you can work on it later.

10. **D.** Power down the computer at the end of your working day to save electricity.

Processing Components

In this chapter, you will learn how to
- Describe different types of CPUs
- Explain RAM types and technologies
- Identify motherboards
- Describe power supplies and cases

Computer processing happens inside the case, though a quick glance inside won't give you many clues about how everything works. Computer techs understand the processing, though, and the pieces that work together to make everything happen.

This chapter examines the processing components and the power that makes them function. The chapter first tackles the processor at the heart of the whole thing and then dives into memory and motherboards. The chapter finishes up with a look at power supplies and cases.

CPUs

Processing, as you'll recall from Chapter 1, is the magic part in the middle of the computing experience. You provide input with the mouse or keyboard to tell the computer what to do. The processing components process. Then the monitor or speakers provide output that you see or hear (Figure 2-1).

But processing isn't magic at all. It's actually something much darker and more terrifying: math. A *microprocessor*, or *central processing unit (CPU)*, handles most of the math processing in any kind of computing device. A CPU beats at the heart of every Windows PC, for example, but is also found in single-purpose computing devices, such as iPods and Xboxes.

Two companies make most of the CPUs found in today's devices: *Intel* and *Advanced Micro Devices (AMD)*. Intel has a much larger market share; AMD is the scrappy underdog.

All CPUs plug into motherboards designed specifically for those CPUs. (A motherboard, in case you're wondering, is the part inside of a computer that everything else plugs into. Think of it like a car's chassis.) If you have an AMD CPU, in other words, you can only use it with a motherboard designed for AMD CPUs. An Intel CPU won't work with that motherboard at all.

Figure 2-1
The computing
process illustrated

All processor manufacturers work hard to make each new generation of CPUs *better* than the one before. But what does "better" mean?

The CPU's job is to process information as quickly as possible. A better processor therefore performs tasks more quickly than a lesser processor. To accomplish this goal, processor makers have optimized CPUs in three areas: speed, sophistication, and reduced heat output and electricity usage, or "greenness."

Speed

The basic measurement of a CPU is its speed, or how many things it can do in one second under perfect conditions. Each thing is a cycle. Completing one cycle per second is known as 1 *hertz (Hz)*. CPUs of yesterday measured speed in millions of cycles per second, or *megahertz (MHz)*. Today's CPUs run at billions of cycles per second, or *gigahertz (GHz)*. Figure 2-2 shows the comparison.

The key to understanding how CPUs work is to know that they do math really, really fast. Add 2 + 3. How long did it take you? What about 323 + 718? How long did it take you to add those two numbers?

A typical CPU, like the one you might use to go to www.google.com, can add or subtract more than three *billion* such equations . . . in less than one second!

Such amazing speed translates into what seems like magic: that a math-calculating machine can make full motion pictures appear; that you can play fabulous games; that you can do astonishing feats. All this is a function of math. (And here you were bored during math class in grade school!)

Figure 2-2 Comparing CPUs

Motherboard Bus Speed and CPU Clock Multiplier

A CPU works directly with the motherboard to achieve the proper speed. Motherboards run at a specific clock speed, measured in MHz. This is called the *bus speed*. CPUs run at some multiple of that bus speed, such as 10× or 25×. If the motherboard runs at 100 MHz and the CPU has a 25× multiplier, the CPU runs at 2500 MHz (or 2.5 GHz).

EXAM TIP Motherboards run at a specific bus speed, measured in MHz. CPUs run at some multiple of that bus speed. If the motherboard runs at 100 MHz and the CPU has a 20× multiplier, for example, the CPU runs at 2000 MHz (or 2 GHz).

Speed and Marketing

Intel traditionally has produced CPUs with more raw speed than any of its competitors, so Intel's marketing folks have long trumpeted that "Speed is King" and the most important aspect of the CPU. On the other hand, AMD and other CPU makers have argued that efficiency is more important than pure speed.

EXAM TIP Other companies besides Intel and AMD make CPUs, such as Motorola and IBM. For many years, Motorola made the CPU used in Apple Macintosh computers. IBM and partners produce a CPU called the *Cell* that's used in an assortment of devices, including the PlayStation 3 (PS3).

A few years ago, Intel reached the maximum speed that the materials inside CPUs could handle, which was just less than 4 GHz. They were forced to change not only their marketing tune, but also the entire focus of their processor development (Figure 2-3).

 NOTE The lingering effects of Intel's earlier marketing campaign have left the public with the misconception that speed is the most important factor in selecting a CPU.

Sophistication

When CPU clock speeds hit the limit of roughly 4 GHz, the CPU makers needed to find new ways to get more processing power for CPUs. Many of these improvements go beyond an IT fundamentals discussion, but four are relevant here. First is the move from 32-bit to 64-bit computing. Second, chipmakers added multiple cores to a single CPU chip. Third, CPU manufacturers refined how CPUs work with programs. Finally, Intel, AMD, and others optimized the basic operation of the CPU through special RAM called *cache*.

Figure 2-3 Well, speed *used* to be king . . .

64-Bit Computing

For more than a decade, all CPUs had a *32-bit architecture*. This meant that the CPU could handle data that was 32 bits in complexity. If you know your binary math (and who doesn't?), the 32-bit CPU could work with numbers up to ~4 billion. Plus, it could handle an operating system or application with an equal number of lines of code. The details are not that important from a tech's standpoint. What's important to note is that 32-bit processing is very complex and powerful.

Today's 64-bit processors take a huge stride forward compared to their 32-bit brethren. From a binary math standpoint, doubling the complexity of an operating system, application, or processor requires just one more bit. Each bit added, therefore, doubles the complexity. That means that 32 bits doubled is only 33 bits. Double that again and it's 34 bits. You get the idea.

So, how complex is 64-bit computing? A 64-bit CPU can easily handle numbers up to 18,446,744,073,709,551,615. Yeah, I don't know what that number is either, but the CPU can handle an operating system or application with that many lines of code as well.

The bottom line is that 64-bit CPUs are far more powerful than 32-bit CPUs, even when working with 32-bit operating systems and applications (Figure 2-4).

 NOTE   Today, all new CPUs work with both the older 32-bit operating systems and applications and the current 64-bit versions. Microsoft sells both 32-bit and 64-bit versions of Windows Vista and Windows 7. The 32-bit versions of these OSes run on any CPU. The 64-bit versions need a modern 64-bit processor.

Figure 2-4   Comparing 64-bit and 32-bit CPUs

Multicore CPUs

Both Intel and AMD decided at virtually the same time to combine two CPUs into a single chip, creating a *dual-core architecture*. This architecture increases both processing capability and efficiency because each core can pick up the slack when the other core gets too busy. Prior to dual-core CPUs, all CPUs were *single core*.

Today, CPU makers offer CPUs with two (dual-core), four (quad-core), six (hexa-core), even eight cores (octa-core) on a single chip. These are known collectively as *multicore* processors (Figure 2-5).

Handling Programs

CPUs have a preset list of commands they understand called the *codebook* or *instruction set*. Programmers write applications in different computer languages that are translated into code understood by the CPU's instruction set (Figure 2-6). The processor then works through the code and outputs commands to various parts of the computer.

Figure 2-5 That's a lot of cores on one chip!

Figure 2-6 The CPU and its codebook

Every CPU works with incoming commands and data differently. Two CPUs with the same clock speed won't necessarily process the same image in a complex application like Adobe Photoshop in the same amount of time. Those same two CPUs might even reverse who wins when doing something simpler, like copying a huge file from one drive to another. Further, a processor from a generation ago with a fast clock speed will stagger in like a jalopy compared to a CPU of today with a much slower clock speed. It's all about the efficiency of processing (along with other features).

Obviously, both Intel and AMD CPUs can handle Windows and Windows applications. But if you think both brands of CPUs handle them in the same way, you'd be mistaken. In the past, AMD processors held the edge over Intel processors in simple efficiency, while Intel held the edge in speed. Now Intel has joined the efficiency race in a big way and holds both the speed and efficiency crowns, though at a very steep price. For a lot less money you can get an AMD processor that's nearly as good as a high-end Intel processor.

 NOTE Good techs do research all the time to stay current and to know which processor will give their customers the best bang for the buck.

A quick example should make this clear. At the time of this writing, a quad-core Intel Core i7 processor running at 3.06 GHz costs about $600 at retail. A quad-core AMD Phenom II X4 CPU running at 3.4 GHz costs about $200 retail. The Core i7 is a better CPU for overall processing power, but how much oomph do you need for what you or your customer want to accomplish (or spend)?

Cache

You'll recall from Chapter 1 that all running programs have to be in RAM; it's the only way the CPU can retrieve data fast enough to function properly. Some years ago, CPU makers discovered that adding a little bit of super-fast RAM directly onto the CPU could greatly speed up the whole computing process. That super-fast RAM is called *cache*.

Today's CPUs have several levels of cache, called level 1 (L1), level 2 (L2), and, on the highest-end processors, level 3 (L3). L1 is the smallest and fastest, L2 is bigger but slower, and L3 is the biggest and slowest type of cache. Note that all cache is so fast that it can run circles around regular system RAM.

CPU makers offer different amounts of cache on each CPU model, so you need to look at cache size when comparing two similar CPUs (Figure 2-7). The cache size of today's processors is often tied to the number of cores, so if you see one processor with a much larger cache, it probably has more cores, too.

Here's the general rule on cache. A bigger cache makes for a more efficient (and more expensive) CPU.

EXAM TIP   CPU cache is measured in kilobytes (KB) and megabytes (MB). A typical L1 cache might be 512 KB, for example. An L2 cache on the same CPU might be as big as 2 MB.

Greener CPUs

When trying to produce better processors, CPU makers need to overcome the fact that faster CPUs require more electricity and thus generate more heat. And heat kills electronics! How do you increase speed without increasing power consumption?

Figure 2-7
CPUs vary a lot in cache amounts and overall performance.

I can run at 2.66 GHz.

So can I, but my extra L1 and L2 cache means I can totally own you in game performance.

CPU makers discovered while working on processors for portable computers that if you make the components of the CPU very tiny, you can get the same performance with less electricity. Further, if you refine the way the CPU processes its codebook, the CPU can perform better with even less electricity.

NOTE Portable computers can run on batteries. Given a choice of two portables of equal power, consumers will almost always go for the one with the longer battery life. The less electricity each part uses, the more the battery life will be maximized.

Taking design cues from those portable processors, CPU makers have transformed current CPUs into leaner, greener processors. Today's CPUs might have slower clock speeds than yesterday's high-end CPUs, but they use less electricity *and* produce less heat. Plus, they outperform those earlier CPUs in a big way.

RAM

The CPU uses *random access memory (RAM)* to work with active programs. An active program is simply a program that has been copied from *mass storage* (a fancy term for a hard drive or optical disc) into RAM (Figure 2-8).

RAM is measured primarily in terms of capacity, or the amount of data that can be held at one time. The more RAM your system has, the more tasks it can perform at once. A typical stick of RAM, for example, might be able to hold 1 GB of data or programming. Many hard drives, which are also measured in terms of capacity, can hold more than 500 GB.

Figure 2-8 RAM doing its job

The big difference between RAM and hard drives is *volatility*. RAM is *volatile memory*, which means that if the power goes out, all the data in RAM disappears. It needs electricity to hold information. Hard drives are nonvolatile, so the data on the hard drive stays there even without power.

 EXAM TIP Computers come with other types of memory, including *read-only memory (ROM)*. The ROM stores important pieces of information for how the computer works. ROM is not volatile, so it retains information when the power goes off.

RAM comes in several sizes, types, and speeds, and a good tech can tell one RAM stick from another. Each motherboard accepts only one size or type of RAM but can handle different speeds.

 NOTE As a general rule, make all RAM in a computer match.

RAM Sticks

Modern RAM comes on small circuit boards called *RAM sticks*. There are several different types of RAM sticks, but the two most common are called DIMMs and SODIMMs. Typical desktop computers use DIMMs. Portable computers and some desktops use the smaller SODIMMs.

DIMMs

Dual inline memory modules (DIMMs) have two rows of connectors at the bottom of the stick, one row on one side, the other row on the reverse. You'll find individual RAM chips on one or both sides of the stick (Figure 2-9). Different technologies (see the next section, "RAM Technologies and Speeds") use slight variations in the number of pins or contacts, but the main form factor is the same ~4-inch-wide circuit board.

SODIMMs

Small outline DIMMs (SODIMMs) are about half the physical size of DIMMs, but they have similar capacities and perform just as well. Figure 2-10 shows an SODIMM and a

Figure 2-9
A typical DIMM with RAM chips visible on one side

PART I

Figure 2-10
SODIMM (top) and
DIMM (bottom)

DIMM for comparison. You'll find SODIMMs in most portable computers and in many all-in-one computers, like the Apple iMac (Figure 2-11).

 EXAM TIP Ancient RAM came on *single inline memory modules (SIMMs)* rather than DIMMs. You'll probably never see these old sticks in the field, but you might see them on the exam.

RAM Technologies and Speeds

In addition to capacity, RAM also has a speed rating that describes how fast it can transfer data. There are three different speed technologies: DDR, DDR2, and DDR3. Each is twice as fast as the technology that preceded it.

Double data rate (DDR) RAM can send or receive data twice for each clock tick on the motherboard. A motherboard that runs at 100 MHz will need DDR RAM that runs at (at least) 200 MHz.

DDR2 and DDR3 RAM run at 4× or 8× the motherboard speed, respectively. A motherboard that runs at 100 MHz would need DDR2-400, for example. A DDR3

Figure 2-11
An Apple iMac with
the RAM panel open
for adding SODIMMs

Table 2-1 RAM Technologies and Speeds	Motherboard Speed	Speed Rating
	100 MHz	DDR2-400
	133 MHz	DDR2-533
	166 MHz	DDR2-667
	200 MHz	DDR2-800
	100 MHz	DDR3-800
	133 MHz	DDR3-1066
	166 MHz	DDR3-1333
	200 MHz	DDR3-1600

motherboard at the same speed would need DDR3-800. Table 2-1 shows the speeds and names of common DDR2 and DDR3 RAM modules.

Here are the two key things every tech should know about RAM.

1. You can't mix RAM stick types or technologies. RAM sticks are keyed so that they only fit in the motherboard designed for that technology. Figure 2-12 shows the different notches or *keying* for DDR2 and DDR3 RAM sticks.

2. You can't install RAM that is too slow for the motherboard. It might fit, but you'll get a "dead" PC. RAM that's faster than the motherboard will simply slow down for the motherboard and work just fine.

DDR2
DDR3

Figure 2-12   DDR2 and DDR3. You *can't* mix and match!

Here's an example to make these two points very clearly.

John has a motherboard designed to use DDR3 sticks. The motherboard bus speed runs at 100 MHz. His friend hands him four sticks of RAM. Which will work?

1. DDR2-533

2. DDR2-667

3. DDR3-667

4. DDR3-1333

Because John has completed his Strata certificate, he knows that neither DDR2 stick will work. They simply won't plug into the motherboard, regardless of what speed they run. (It's a DDR3 motherboard!) The 667 MHz DDR3 stick won't work because the motherboard needs a stick that can run at least 800 MHz. The 1333 MHz stick will work because it is capable of a faster speed and will work at the slower one with no problem (Figure 2-13).

Figure 2-13
Only the DDR3-1333 stick will work.

Motherboards

Everything in a computer plugs directly or indirectly into the motherboard (Figure 2-14). The motherboard, therefore, is an essential component in the computing process.

Aside from connecting devices such as the CPU to RAM, the motherboard has a lot of circuits and processing chips that have their own distinct jobs. Older motherboards, for example, had a chip called a northbridge that took care of the data going from RAM to CPU and back again (Figure 2-15). Motherboards have chips that control various components, such as keyboards, mice, monitors, and so on.

Manufacturers create motherboards in many shapes and sizes. Motherboards can have a few components built in or a lot of them. The more components they have, the more the motherboard can do right out of the box. Most motherboards today offer built-in networking, sound, and more. Some even have built-in video connections.

Figure 2-16 shows three motherboards. All do excellent computing, but they vary a lot in size and capability.

TIP The *form factor* determines the size or shape of a motherboard. You don't need to know the form factors for the CompTIA Strata exam, but good techs can talk the talk. Plus, you need to put a motherboard into a case that matches the form factor; otherwise, it won't fit.

Figure 2-14
The motherboard provides connectivity among all the pieces.

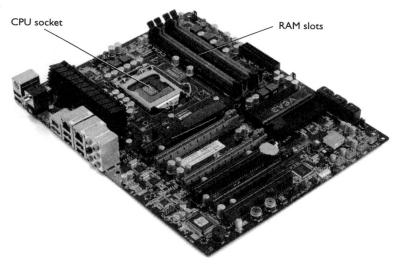

CPU socket

RAM slots

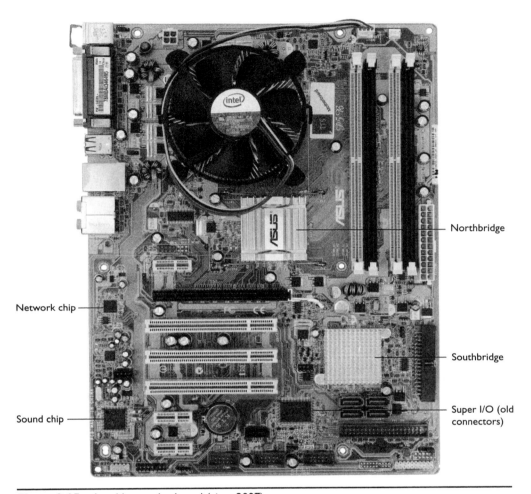

Figure 2-15 An older motherboard (circa 2007)

Figure 2-16 Three motherboards: ATX, microATX, and Mini-ITX (left to right)

Figure 2-17
Inside-out case

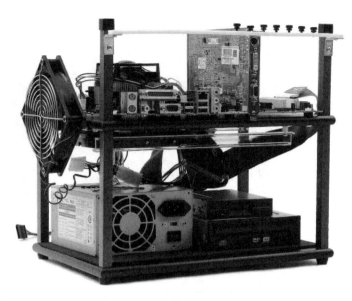

Power and Cases

Unless you're using some kind of crazy inside-out box (Figure 2-17), all the processing pieces hide inside the system unit or computer case. The power supply, the component that provides electricity so that all the other pieces can run, also lives inside the case.

Power supplies use multiple cables to power the motherboard. The motherboard then provides electricity for the CPU and RAM, among other things. Certain components, such as video cards and fans, use a separate connection to the motherboard or directly connect to the power supply. Figure 2-18 shows a power supply and connections.

Figure 2-18
A power supply connected to a motherboard

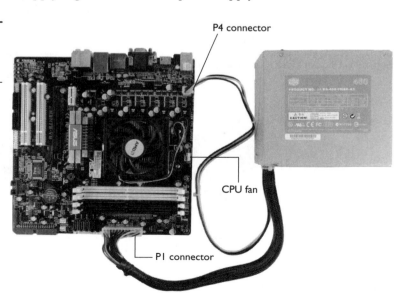

Almost all motherboards use a 24-pin connector called *P1* or *ATX* for primary power. Plus they use a 4-pin *P4* connector to help run more stably. (I don't know why they don't use a single 28-pin connector instead.)

 EXAM TIP You'll see the term *ATX* used to label the 24-pin main power connector for the motherboard on the exam.

Case manufacturers create all sorts of cases. You'll find beige, black, silver, and pink cases, for example. A trip to a computer store will show big cases and little cases and everything in between (Figure 2-19).

Different cases offer solutions for different rooms and purposes. A large office, for example, could easily handle a full-size case with lots of room inside for adding more things later. A small, all-in-one computer like a Dell Zino HD might work much better for a dorm room with limited space (Figure 2-20).

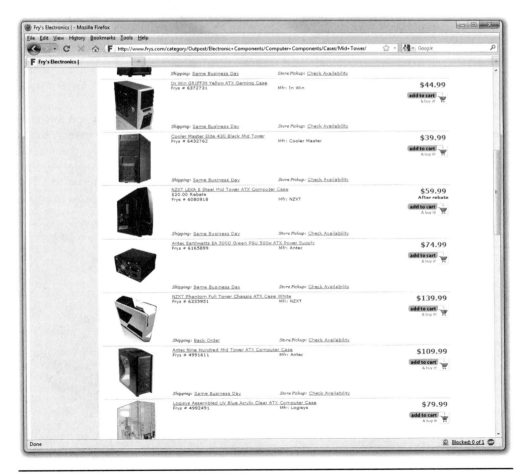

Figure 2-19 That's a crazy number of cases!

Figure 2-20
Dell Zino HD vs.
mid-tower PC
(Courtesy of
Dell, Inc.)

The key thing to keep in mind when choosing a case is to match the form factor of the motherboard. A large motherboard, for example, won't fit in a tiny case. A lot of bigger cases provide mounting connections for smaller motherboards, so the reverse isn't necessarily true.

Most power supplies come in a standard shape and size and work in every case. The few exceptions are the power supplies in the super tiny cases. A standard power supply, for example, is bigger than a Mac Mini (Figure 2-21)!

Figure 2-21
A standard power
supply and an Apple
Mac Mini computer

Chapter Review

Techs understand how computers process information. Knowing the parts and how they work together helps you fix any problems that crop up.

The CPU handles the math, the bulk of the processing duties, but it does this work with other pieces, too. Every CPU plugs into a motherboard. That motherboard has to be compatible with the specific type of CPU. An AMD CPU, for example, requires an AMD-focused motherboard. A 64-bit Intel CPU requires a motherboard that can handle a 64-bit Intel CPU.

CPUs use RAM to store working copies of data, such as programs and the operating system. Just like the CPU, the RAM needs to match the motherboard too. Each motherboard can support only DDR or DDR2 or DDR3 RAM. Plus, the RAM needs to work at the speeds set by the motherboard clock.

Motherboards vary in size and shape. The form factor determines the type of case you can use with a specific motherboard. The most common form factor is microATX.

Finally, the power supply connects to the motherboard using two connectors, a 24-pin ATX connector and a 4-pin P4 connector. These connectors power all the devices built into the motherboard, plus the core processing components, the CPU and RAM.

Questions

1. Which part of the processing components does the math?
    A. CPU
    B. Motherboard
    C. RAM
    D. Power supply
2. A typical modern CPU runs at which of the following speeds?
    A. 1 Hz
    B. 2 MHz
    C. 2 GHz
    D. 2 GB
3. Which of the following is *not* a processor type?
    A. AMD
    B. Cell
    C. Intel
    D. Windows

4. Modern CPUs have one or more small, very fast pieces of RAM built in. What's that RAM called?

   A. Cache

   B. DIMM

   C. SODIMM

   D. System RAM

5. Which of the following will most likely improve CPU performance? (Select two.)

   A. Lower speed

   B. Going from single core to multicore

   C. Adding more cache

   D. Lowering gigabytes

6. Which feature did desktop CPU makers borrow from portable versions of processors to make newer CPUs better?

   A. Multiple cores

   B. Extra cache

   C. Lower power consumption

   D. Bigger sockets

7. What type of RAM would you most likely find in a portable computer?

   A. DIMM

   B. PIMM

   C. SIMM

   D. SODIMM

8. Which of the following RAM sticks would work with a DDR2-533 MHz motherboard?

   A. DDR2-266

   B. DDR2-400

   C. DDR2-533

   D. DDR3-533

9. What's the basic rule on RAM?

   A. Make the RAM sticks match.

   B. Use only DDR2 or better RAM.

   C. Use only DDR3 or better RAM.

   D. Use only SODIMMs if possible.

10. When shopping for a computer case, what must you consider?

    A. The case needs to be able to handle the speed of the processor.

    B. The case should be black or at least black and silver.

    C. The case should be compatible with the motherboard form factor.

    D. It doesn't matter. Pick the case that looks the best.

Answers

1. **A.** The central processing unit (CPU) does the math.

2. **C.** Most modern CPUs run at some speed measured in gigahertz (GHz).

3. **D.** Windows is an operating system, not a processor type.

4. **A.** The cache is one or more small pieces of very fast RAM built into the CPU.

5. **B, C.** Among other improvements, CPU makers have gone from single core to multicore and added more cache to modern CPUs. These improvements lead to better performance.

6. **C.** Portable CPU engineers have long pushed for lower-power CPUs. Desktop engineers picked up that option and found that lower power meant also less heat. They could push the CPU even more and thus get better performance.

7. **D.** Most portable computers use SODIMM RAM sticks.

8. **C.** Of the four choices, only the DDR2-533 would work. The other two DDR2 sticks are too slow. The DDR3 stick won't fit in a DDR2 motherboard.

9. **A.** The basic rule with RAM is to use identical RAM sticks.

10. **C.** A computer case and a motherboard must be the same form factor. Otherwise, the motherboard won't fit.

Common Input/Output Devices

In this chapter, you will learn how to
- Describe the workings of keyboards
- Explain how to connect and use mice and other pointing devices
- Describe how to work with monitors

The standard computer uses two types of input devices and one output device. A keyboard and a mouse enable you to give commands to the computer. A monitor enables the computer to show you the results of those commands. Figure 3-1 shows the parts of a simple PC.

These three devices have been the mainstay of input/output (I/O) since the very early days of personal computers. Because they offer users amazing versatility in working with the PC, they don't look to go away any time soon.

NOTE   Creative folk have invented and manufactured many devices for I/O. Some of the more common devices are printers, speakers, touch-screen monitors, microphones, and more. Later chapters cover these and other devices in detail. For now, though, we will explore the basics.

Figure 3-1
The simple PC

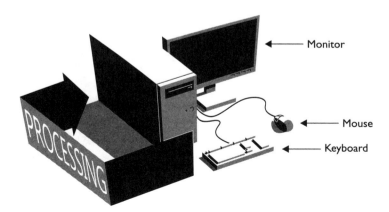

Monitor

Mouse

Keyboard

Keyboards

The keyboard enables you to communicate with the processing parts of the computer. You can type in commands, for example, that the computer understands even if you don't have an operating system (OS). Plus, each application installed on the computer, including the OS, supports specific keyboard commands. The keyboard is the primary input device for all personal computers and many computing devices.

How you use a keyboard changes with each specific application type. In a word-processing program such as Microsoft Word, you can use the keyboard to type letters, just as if you sat in front of an old typewriter (Figure 3-2).

Different applications require different keystrokes. A typical game, for example, uses the WASD keys to move your character forward, left, back, and right, respectively. That same game might have menus and screens that pop up depending on the key you press. In World of Warcraft, for example, pressing the J key brings up a list of fellow guild members (friends) that are currently online. You can select one and send a message to him or her or type a message that all can see (Figure 3-3).

Over the years, manufacturers have added extra keys to the standard keyboard, but most still have the same basic keys (Figure 3-4).

Standard keyboards in English-speaking countries all have the same layout, called *QWERTY*. That name refers to the first six letters on the top row of the keyboard. Above the QWERTY letters you'll find the number keys. Above them are the function keys. *Function keys* can change a lot depending on the program, but F1 is almost always Help.

NOTE Not every language uses the same alphabet. There are keyboard layouts available for most of the languages in the world. This is called *regionalization*. A Spanish keyboard, for example, would add accented characters such as é and Spanish-only characters such as ñ.

Figure 3-2
A classic typewriter

Figure 3-3   Viewing friends online in World of Warcraft

Other keys you'll find on a Windows-based keyboard are ESC, TAB, CAPS LOCK, SHIFT, CTRL, ALT, and WINDOWS. On every keyboard, you'll find keys such as HOME, END, BACK-SPACE, DELETE, and so on.

Figure 3-4
A QWERTY
keyboard

At the right side of all full-sized keyboards is the *numeric keypad*, or *number pad*. The number pad lays out the numbers 0–9 along with various math symbols (plus, minus, and so on) like a calculator. With the right application, such as Microsoft Excel, you can make the computer function as a calculator. That way the CPU can do simple math every once in a while! (Doesn't your computer deserve a break?)

EXAM TIP   The CompTIA Strata exam calls the number pad the *numeric* keypad.

Some keyboards, such as those with portable computers, leave off the number pad. You can buy a standalone number pad to plug into the computer if you want to add that feature later (Figure 3-5).

Keyboards use one of two connectors to plug into a computer. The old style is called *a mini-DIN* or *PS/2* connector. It is round, with six pins and a small tab so that you can only insert it one way (Figure 3-6). PS/2 connectors are still very common. Most motherboards color the keyboard PS/2 socket purple.

Many keyboards use a rectangular USB connector (Figure 3-7). Like the PS/2 connector, USB connectors are keyed so that you can't plug them in incorrectly. Sadly, they don't come in purple.

NOTE   Keyboards for Apple Mac computers have a few key differences from keyboards for Windows. Most notably, Macs have CONTROL, OPTION, and COMMAND keys rather than CTRL, WINDOWS, and ALT keys.

Figure 3-5
A standalone
number pad

Figure 3-6
A PS/2 or mini-DIN connector for a keyboard

You can make some adjustments to how keyboards work using utilities that come with the operating system. Windows 7 has a small configuration program—called an applet—in its toolbox specifically for keyboards. As you might guess, it's the Keyboard applet (Figure 3-8).

Figure 3-7
A USB connector for a keyboard

Figure 3-8
The Keyboard applet
in Windows 7

 NOTE All versions of Windows and Mac have a keyboard configuration tool.

There's not a whole lot you can do here, mainly because the keyboard is a fairly simple device. You can control how quickly a key repeats while held down, for example. This is good for new typists or people with slower fingers.

Mice and Other Pointing Devices

Mice and other pointing devices enable you to move a cursor around the screen and click things. Mice designed for Windows computers traditionally have two buttons (Figure 3-9). You can left-click to select something on the screen. Right-clicking gets you

Figure 3-9
A two-button mouse

Figure 3-10
A mouse with
a scroll wheel

information about whatever you click. In computer-speak, right-clicking brings up a *context menu*. You can also double-left click—this is a *double-click*—to tell Windows to do something with whatever you click.

Many current mice have a scroll wheel in the center that enables you to move up and down in a window (Figure 3-10). When you're on a Web page, for example, you can scroll up and down by clicking the arrows on the right side of the page or by moving the wheel (Figure 3-11).

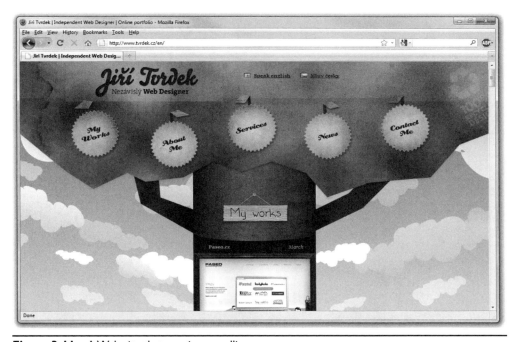

Figure 3-11   A Web site that requires scrolling

Mice use one of two connectors to plug into a computer, just like the keyboard. Older mice use a mini-DIN or PS/2 connector. Unlike the keyboard PS/2 connector, the mouse port is green. Most mice today connect via USB.

NOTE Mice for Apple Mac computers traditionally had only one button, not two. Modern Mac mice have two buttons and a scroll area in the middle, just like Windows mice.

Mouse Technologies

Mice originally came with a ceramic ball on the bottom (Figure 3-12). When you rolled the mouse around, sensors inside the body of the mouse tracked the movement and translated that to the computer. *Ball mice*, as they were called, collected dust and grime on the sensors and had to be cleaned periodically.

Current mice use a red light to keep track of their movement (Figure 3-13). These are called *optical mice*. You don't have to clean an optical mouse, so most folks prefer the newer technology.

Figure 3-12
A ball mouse

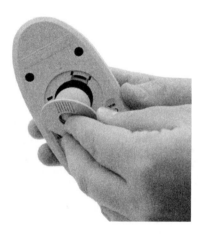

Figure 3-13
An optical mouse

Other Pointing Devices

Mice are the most common device used to make a cursor move across the screen, but two other devices find use in certain instances. A *trackball* reverses the ball mouse setup, placing the ball along the top of the device (Figure 3-14). You use your thumb or a finger to move the ball and thus move the cursor. Trackballs have buttons and wheels, just like mice. Trackballs are great when you don't have a normal table on which to work or when you have wrist difficulties.

Figure 3-14
A trackball

Figure 3-15
A touchpad

A lot of people use touchpads for moving cursors (Figure 3-15). More common than trackballs, a touchpad has no moving parts. Drag your finger across the pad and the cursor moves accordingly. Touchpads are used extensively with portable computers. You can get one for a regular desktop computer as well.

Most trackballs and touchpads connect to computers via USB. Some very old trackballs might connect to a PS/2 port.

NOTE Wired keyboards and mice do not need a separate connection for power. The power they need is provided by the PS/2 or USB port. Wireless versions are powered by batteries.

Computers come with a utility for adjusting the mouse or other pointing device (Figure 3-16). The Mouse applet in Windows 7, for example, enables you to change the speed of the cursor or the quickness of the double-click. You can adjust the function of the wheel and even reverse the left and right clicks, among other options.

Figure 3-16
The Mouse applet
in Windows

Monitors

The *monitor* is the primary output device for the computer. It displays the results of input and the computer's processing. This could be anything from moving through a level of an intense action game to moving your cursor across the desktop. When most people think about their interactions with a computer, they are probably thinking about what happens on the monitor.

NOTE Many folks call the monitor the *display*.

Monitors have advanced over the years, just like computers. Movies from the eighties and nineties loved using monochrome (or one-color) monitors with green text on a black background. You knew something important was about to happen when there was a lot of typing and they zoomed in close on the monitor. Then they would cut to someone dramatically pressing the ENTER key (while entirely ignoring the mouse).

Modern monitors display more than just green text, of course. Most can show millions of colors in high-definition videos and games.

Every monitor, while distinct, has the same basic components (Figure 3-17). The most important part is, of course, the display itself.

You can power the display on and off and adjust other settings using a set of buttons usually found on an edge of the monitor. Pressing the Menu button opens an on-screen

Figure 3-17
Front of monitor

Screen

Menu buttons

menu that enables you to adjust the brightness, contrast, color balance, size, and position of the display (Figure 3-18). Most monitors also have a button that will automatically choose the best settings for you.

The back of the monitor has connections for receiving a video signal from the computer and power from a wall outlet (Figure 3-19).

There are two varieties of monitors: CRT and LCD. *Cathode ray tube (CRT)* monitors use the same technology as old televisions. CRTs are the big beige boxes you saw on every office desk from the time people first had computers up until several years ago (Figure 3-20). They are large, heavy, and power-hungry. They are so power-hungry that you should never try to open one up. With 30,000 volts swimming around inside even hours after a monitor has been unplugged, opening one can kill you. Don't do it!

 EXAM TIP CRTs contain an assortment of hazardous materials, including lead, phosphorus, and mercury, so don't throw them out with the trash! Instead, contact a computer recycling company near you. They will dispose of old computer components for you.

Liquid crystal display (LCD) monitors are much thinner than their CRT siblings, saving big on desk space (Figure 3-21). They are also lighter and use less power. Most LCDs today also have a widescreen aspect ratio. Instead of being almost square, like old televisions, these monitors are much wider than they are tall—great for looking at two documents side by side (or watching movies).

 NOTE The *aspect ratio* is the measure of the width over the height of a screen. Non-widescreen monitors have an aspect ratio of 4:3, or four inches across for every three inches down. Most widescreen monitors have an aspect ratio of 16:9 or 16:10, just like a lot of movies.

Figure 3-18
On-screen
menu options

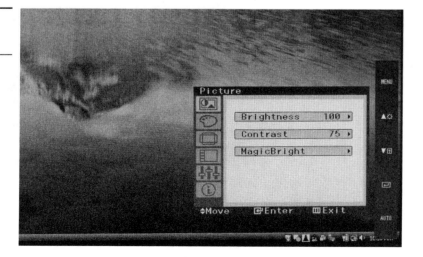

Power connector   Video connectors

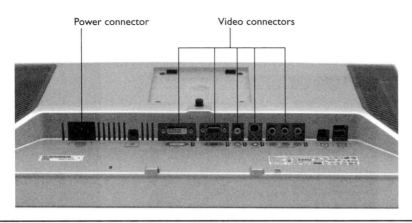

Figure 3-19   Back of monitor

Figure 3-20
A CRT monitor

Figure 3-21
An LCD monitor

Connecting to the Computer

Monitors connect to the computer's video card. The *video card* (or *GPU*, short for graphics processing unit) helps the CPU and operating system change the image on the display (Figure 3-22).

Monitors connect to the video card using a cable with one of three connectors. Depending on their age and sophistication, different video cards will have different combinations of connectors to use. Some will only have a single connector, while others may have two (or more) of each.

Figure 3-22   The video card controls the monitor.

Figure 3-23
A VGA connector

The oldest connector type is the blue *Video Graphics Array (VGA)* connector (Figure 3-23). It has 15 pins, laid out in three rows of five. The VGA connector is used primarily by CRT monitors, but can still be found on many LCD monitors, too.

Today's most commonly used connector is the *Digital Visual Interface (DVI)* connector (Figure 3-24). Depending on the monitor, the connector can have up to 29 pins.

The *High-Definition Multimedia Interface (HDMI)* connector is unique because it is used for both video and audio signals, whereas VGA and DVI only carry video signals (Figure 3-25). HDMI is found on more HD televisions than monitors, but it is becoming more popular with computers. It uses a connector that looks somewhat like USB but only fits in HDMI ports.

Figure 3-24
A DVI connector

Figure 3-25
An HDMI connector

The Display Applet

In addition to the physical buttons on your monitor, the Display applet in Windows also controls the appearance of your display (Figure 3-26). You don't use it to change basic things like brightness and contrast. Instead, the Display applet enables you to customize the more technical details of how your monitor functions.

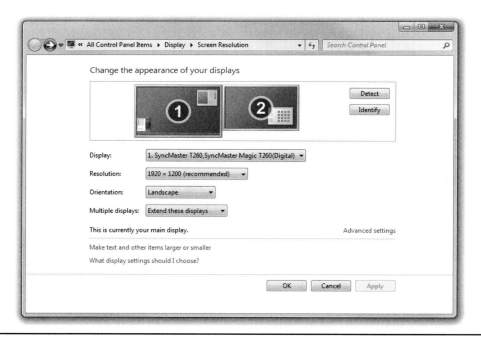

Figure 3-26   The Display applet

The primary feature of the Display applet is the resolution menu. The resolution determines the number of pixels used to create the image on the monitor. Resolution is measured as the number of pixels across by the number of pixels down (Figure 3-27). For instance, my monitor uses 1920 pixels by 1080 pixels, which would be written as 1920 × 1080. When you multiply those numbers, you get the total number of pixels used by the monitor: 2,073,600 pixels!

 NOTE A pixel (or picture element) is a single dot or small square that changes colors to create a picture on your display.

With the Display applet, you can adjust the resolution of your monitor from 800 × 600 all the way up to the maximum (or native) resolution of your monitor. Keep in mind that as you adjust the resolution, the size of windows and icons will change, too. With an LCD, things will appear very large but very blurry at low resolutions. At very high resolutions, things will be as sharp as a knife, but it can be tough to read what anything says.

To change the resolution in Windows Vista/7, go to Start | Control Panel | *Adjust screen resolution*. In Windows XP, go to Start | Control Panel, double-click on the Display applet, then select the Settings tab. Click the Resolution drop-down menu (in Windows Vista/7) and use the slider to make your choice.

Other options found on the Display applet include selecting the orientation. This enables you to switch between landscape view (wider than it is taller; the default setting for most monitors) and portrait view (taller than it is wider). Some people switch to portrait view when viewing long documents or Web pages, since you can see more at the same time (Figure 3-28).

Figure 3-27
Pixels and resolution

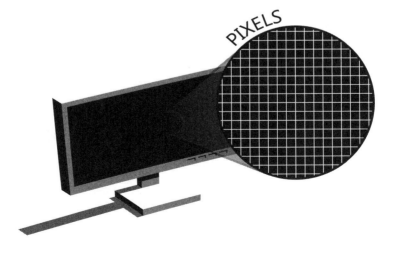

Figure 3-28
Using portrait view

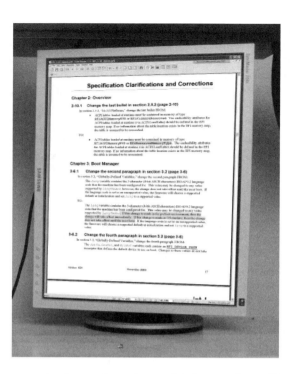

The Display applet also controls the settings for multiple monitors. If you have more than one monitor attached to your computer, you can either *mirror* the display on your first monitor onto a second (useful in presentation settings) or you can *extend* your display, in effect doubling the size of your display. Figure 3-29 shows my desktop sporting two monitors.

Figure 3-29
Two monitors in use

Chapter Review

In this chapter, you covered common input/output devices, from mice, to keyboards, to monitors. Keyboards enable you to input text; the keyboard is the primary input device for all personal computers and many computing devices. Most keyboards today connect to a computer using a USB connector, but you will still find some with the older PS/2 connector.

Mice enable you to move a cursor around the screen, greatly simplifying the ease with which you navigate your operating system. There are two types of mice: ball and optical. Ball mice use a ball to track movement. Optical mice use either a laser or a red LED.

Like keyboards, mice connect using either a USB port (most common) or a PS/2 port (older and less common). You will also find a few other pointing devices out in the wild, such as trackballs and touchpads, but no matter what kind of pointing device you use, you can adjust it using the Mouse applet.

Monitors are the primary output devices for computers of all kinds. Most modern monitors use LCD technology, but you will still see some older CRT monitors out there as well. Most monitors connect to a computer using either a VGA (older) or a DVI (newer) connector. The Display applet enables you to change a monitor's resolution and adjust other settings.

Questions

1. What are the two types of keyboard connectors? (Select two.)

    A. DVI

    B. HDMI

    C. PS/2

    D. USB

2. What term describes the standard English keyboard?

    A. DESWEDS

    B. QWERTY

    C. SUAVE

    D. 123456

3. What part of a standard keyboard is designed to work with a calculator program?

    A. Function keys

    B. Numeric keypad

    C. QWERTY

    D. Trackball

4. How do you open a context menu?

   A. Double-click

   B. Left-click

   C. Right-click

   D. Scroll

5. Which type of mouse do you need to clean regularly?

   A. Ball mouse

   B. Optical mouse

   C. Trackball

   D. Wheel mouse

6. Which applet enables you to control mice and other pointing devices in Windows?

   A. Keyboard

   B. Mouse

   C. Pointer

   D. Touch

7. Which type of display connects to a VGA port?

   A. Only CRTs

   B. Only LCDs

   C. All CRTs and some LCDs

   D. All LCDs and some CRTs

8. Which connector type carries both video and audio signals?

   A. CRT

   B. DVI

   C. HDMI

   D. VGA

9. Which connector type has 15 pins arranged in three rows?

   A. CRT

   B. DVI

   C. HDMI

   D. VGA

10. Which applet enables you to make some adjustments to the monitor?

   A. Display

   B. Keyboard

   C. Mouse

   D. Touch

Answers

1. **C, D.** Keyboards use one of two connectors, PS/2 (also called mini-DIN) or USB.

2. **B.** A standard keyboard is called a QWERTY keyboard to reflect the top keys.

3. **B.** The numeric keypad enables a computer to input numbers and symbols like a calculator.

4. **C.** Right-clicking an icon or menu usually brings up the context menu.

5. **A.** You should clean ball mice regularly. Trackballs should be cleaned as well but don't seem to get nearly as dirty.

6. **B.** The Mouse applet enables you to control mice and other pointing devices in Windows.

7. **C.** All CRTs and some LCDs use a VGA connector.

8. **C.** An HDMI connector carries both video and audio signals.

9. **D.** VGA connectors have 15 pins arranged in three rows.

10. **A.** The Display applet enables you to control some aspects of the display in Windows.

CHAPTER 4

Common Storage Devices

In this chapter, you will learn how to
- Describe floppy drives
- Explain how hard drives work
- Describe current optical disc technologies

Mass storage devices enable you to save programs and data for later use. All personal computers offer some sort of storage. The earliest PCs used floppy disk drives. Later PCs added hard drives. Just about every PC has some kind of optical drive, such as a DVD drive. This chapter explores all three technologies.

Floppy Drives

Floppy disk drives (FDDs) are mechanical devices used to read and write data from and to a magnetic disk called a floppy diskette. Figure 4-1 shows a standard 3.5" drive. The 3.5" drive has been available for personal computers since the mid-1980s.

Figure 4-1
A floppy disk drive

NOTE Floppy disk drive = floppy drive in common computer-person speak.

Floppy disk drives have been around the block a few times and don't really deserve to be discussed in a modern book. Seriously. The technology is ancient. The diskettes store only 1.44 MB of data (Figure 4-2). That's nothing with today's data storage needs. And did I mention that the whoppingly high-density 1.44 MB diskettes debuted in 1987?

What was going on in 1987?

- Ronald Reagan was President of the United States.
- Margaret Thatcher was Prime Minister of the United Kingdom.
- The stars of the *Harry Potter* films hadn't been born yet, the books hadn't been written yet, and the author hadn't even thought of the idea yet.
- The USSR, Czechoslovakia, East Germany, and Yugoslavia all still existed.
- The fastest way to connect to the World Wide Web was to—oh wait, it hadn't been invented yet.

But floppy drives show up on the CompTIA Strata exam, so you need to know them.

Figure 4-2
A floppy diskette

Figure 4-3
A mini power
connector

You need two cables to connect a floppy drive to a computer. The four-pin *mini* power connector provides electricity for the drive and the little light on the front (Figure 4-3).

Floppy drives transfer data through a *ribbon cable*—a flat cable composed of a series of wires. Floppy drive ribbon cables connect to 34-pin ports on the drive and the motherboard (Figure 4-4).

EXAM TIP In common computer speak, a floppy drive uses a *34-pin ribbon cable.*

Modern floppy drive data cables are keyed so that you can't install them incorrectly. Note the small notch on the connector in Figure 4-5.

NOTE Try finding a floppy disk, a floppy disk drive, and a computer capable of connecting to a floppy disk drive. If you find all three, don't do anything else. You've already wasted enough time.

Figure 4-4
A floppy drive port
on a motherboard
(bottom)

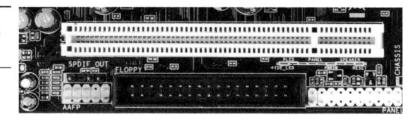

Figure 4-5
Floppy drive cable
connection close up

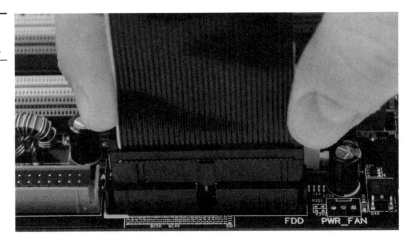

Hard Drives

Hard drives store data and programs. Hard drives are the primary data storage device in almost every computer. Like floppy drives, most hard drives are mechanical. Unlike floppy *diskettes*, though, hard drive disks—called *platters*—are encased in metal. Figure 4-6 shows the inside of a hard drive.

NOTE There are some non-mechanical hard drives based on flash technology—like you'd see in a thumb drive—but we'll look at those in Chapter 10.

Figure 4-6
Inside a standard
hard drive

Hard Drive Features

A couple of features set one hard drive apart from another. The platter rotation speed makes a big difference in overall data transfer rates. The size of the cache helps overall performance.

Once they spin up, the platters inside a hard drive spin at a constant speed, called the *rotation speed*. The common speeds, in revolutions per minute (rpm), are 3600, 5400, and 7200. The standard for almost every computer is 7200 rpm. The slower drives are either older or used for portable computers where slower speed translates to "needs less electricity to operate."

 NOTE   Some hard drive makers have released 10,000-rpm drives. The drives cost a lot and are much louder than standard drives, but they're fast!

Modern drives have a small amount of RAM to help get data to and from the drive faster. This RAM is called the *cache*. Standard cache sizes are 8, 16, and 32 MB (Figure 4-7).

 EXAM TIP   You'll see the abbreviation HDD on the CompTIA Strata exam. That stands for *hard disk drive*.

Figure 4-7
Hard drive packaging showing rotation speed and amount of cache (photo courtesy of Western Digital)

7200 RPM

16 MB caches

Figure 4-8
An 80-wire
ribbon cable

Connecting Hard Drives

There are two types of hard drive connections. The old style, called *parallel ATA (PATA)*, used a 40- or 80-wire ribbon cable for data. (Ancient drives used the 40-wire cable; later ones used the 80-wire cable.) Figure 4-8 shows an 80-wire ribbon cable.

 EXAM TIP Many techs call the 80-wire PATA cable an 80-*pin* ribbon cable. That's how you'll see it on the CompTIA Strata exam too.

All PATA drives use a four-wire *Molex* connector for power (Figure 4-9).

 EXAM TIP The CompTIA Strata exam uses the term *integrated drive electronics (IDE)* synonymously with PATA. Although this is technically incorrect, that's the way you'll see it on the exam as of this writing.

Modern hard drives connect with *serial ATA (SATA)* connections. Some SATA drives use a Molex connector for power, just like PATA drives. Most use a five-wire SATA power connection (Figure 4-10).

The SATA data cable is tiny compared with the PATA cables, using only seven wires (Figure 4-11). Both SATA power and data cables are keyed so that they only insert one way. You can't plug them in incorrectly.

Figure 4-9
A Molex connector

Figure 4-10
A SATA power cable

Hard drive manufacturers continue to push the limits of mechanical technology. Early drives were tiny, with only a 5-MB capacity. Current drives can hold more than 1 terabyte (TB) of data. For comparison, here is how the numbers break down.

1 bit = the smallest unit of measurement in computer data storage = a 1 or a 0

1 byte = 8 bits

1 kilobyte = 1024 bytes

1 megabyte = 1024 kilobytes, or 1,048,576 bytes

1 gigabyte = 1024 megabytes, or 1,073,741,824 bytes

1 terabyte = 1024 gigabytes, or some huge number that won't fit on this line

 NOTE Hard drive manufacturers traditionally label hard drives in a misleading fashion. When you install a shiny new "1 TB" drive, you'll notice that it doesn't have a whole terabyte of capacity. This is because the manufacturer measures the sizes differently—to them, 1 TB equals 1000 gigabytes, not 1024 gigabytes. You're missing out on 24 gigs!

Figure 4-11
A SATA data cable

Optical Drives

An optical disc is a 120-mm storage device that you read in a corresponding optical drive (Figure 4-12). Audio-only compact discs (CDs) were released in 1982. CDs were first used with computers with the CD-ROM format, released in 1985. Most computers had CD-ROM drives by the early 1990s to go along with their 3.5" floppy drives.

Unlike floppy drive technology, optical drive manufacturers and developers have continued to develop the standards for storing data on shiny plastic discs.

 NOTE To be fair, several companies invented replacements for the floppy drive. Some, like Iomega Zip drives, had commercial success for a time but flamed out eventually.

Currently, you can find about a dozen different formats of optical discs and optical drives. Here's an incomplete list:

- CD-ROM
- CD-R
- CD-RW
- DVD-ROM
- DVD-R
- DVD+R
- DVD-RW
- DVD+RW
- BD-ROM
- BD-R
- BD-RE

Plus, you can find variations within the optical formats listed here, making optical disc discussions difficult at best. Let's look at the three families of optical disc technology and then examine some features.

Figure 4-12
An optical disc

Optical Disc Families

You can divide optical disc technologies into three families:

- Compact Disc (CD)
- Digital Versatile Disc (DVD)
- Blu-ray Disc (BD)

Each family has read-only formats, writable formats, and rewritable formats. Aside from very faint markings on the discs, they all look alike (Figure 4-13).

CD-ROM discs are read-only. You can write once to a CD-R disc as long as you have a drive capable of writing to a disc. You can write and rewrite to a CD-RW disc. Again, you need a drive that can do this, in this case a CD-RW drive.

 EXAM TIP   A small-sized CD-R called a *MiniDisc* made a brief appearance in the tech world a few years ago. Designed for portable music players, MiniDiscs died a swift death when the Apple iPod rewrote the books on portable music.

Similarly, DVD-ROM discs are read-only. DVD makers went crazy with the writable and rewritable versions, releasing more than four distinct standards. Most DVD drives today are called *multi* drives, which can read from and write to all forms of DVD or CD. Multi drives are marketed as DVD±RW drives.

Blu-ray Disc makers took pity on IT writers and students by releasing only three types of discs and drives: BD-ROM discs are read-only, BD-R discs can be written to once, and BD-RE can be written to many times.

All drives of a later family can read all the discs of an earlier family. Any kind of BD drive, for example, can read any DVD or CD.

Capacity

The biggest difference among the families of optical disc technology is in how much data each disc can store. A standard CD can hold up to 700 MB of data. DVDs and BDs can hold a lot more.

Figure 4-13
Collection of optical discs

Table 4-1	Family	Layers	Capacity
Optical Disc Capacities	CD	Single	700 MB
	DVD	Single	4.7 GB
	DVD	Dual	8.5 GB
	BD	Single	25 GB
	BD	Dual	50 GB

Both DVDs and BDs come in single-layer and dual-layer formats. As you might suspect, a dual-layer disc holds twice as much data as a single-layer disc. Table 4-1 has the capacities for optical discs.

Movies on Optical Discs

DVD and BD technologies were originally released for movies rather than computer data storage. As such, the most common DVDs and BDs out there are movie discs (Figure 4-14).

In the early days of DVD movies, most television sets used an aspect ratio of 4:3, meaning four parts wide by three parts high. Accordingly, most movie studios released versions of movies altered to fit that ratio, just as they always had for television.

As widescreen televisions became more common, movie studios started releasing widescreen versions of their movies.

Figure 4-14
Gratuitous shot of movie packaging and disc

To help consumers during the transition, a lot of studios released *double-sided DVDs*. On one side they placed a 4:3 ratio version of the movie, and on the other side was the widescreen version. Sweet!

 EXAM TIP Dual-layer, double-sided DVDs are rare. You'll probably never see one. If you do, know that the capacity of such a disc is just over 17 GB, which is a lot smaller than even a single-layer Blu-ray Disc.

Connecting Optical Drives

Optical drives come in two formats: PATA and SATA. They connect to the motherboard just like a PATA or SATA hard drive, with a ribbon or data cable (Figure 4-15). They use the same power connectors as PATA or SATA hard drives, too, so you know those as well: Molex or SATA.

(Isn't it great when you get to the last section of a chapter and you already know the answers?)

Figure 4-15
The business end of a SATA optical drive

Chapter Review

Floppy drives use magnetic discs to store a very small amount of data (1.4 MB). They have been made obsolete by flash drives and optical media, so while you might see them on the test, you won't see them a lot out in the real world.

Hard drives cover a computer's long-term storage needs. Hard drives connect to a motherboard using one of two connectors: parallel ATA (PATA) and serial ATA (SATA). PATA—the older, slower connection—uses a wide ribbon cable for data and a smaller connector (called a Molex connector) for power. SATA—the newer, faster connection—uses narrow cables to connect to the motherboard, making installation much easier.

Most hard drives store data on magnetic platters, which are basically metal disks that spin at thousands of rotations per minute. Modern hard drives are measured in gigabytes or terabytes.

Optical drives have taken over from floppy drives as the removable media of choice in the computer world. Optical discs come in three varieties that you should know about: CD, DVD, and Blu-ray Disc (BD).

CDs store up to 700 MB of data and are the oldest type of optical media on the test. DVDs store up to 4.7 GB per layer and can have up to two layers per side of the disc. BDs are the newest optical technology on the block. They hold 25 GB per layer, up to a maximum of 50 GB. Each optical disc type also comes in readable/writable and readable/rewritable versions, such as CD-R or DVD-RW. Just like hard drives, optical drives use either PATA or SATA connectors.

Questions

1. What is the size of a standard floppy disk?

    A. 2.5"

    B. 3"

    C. 3.5"

    D. 4"

2. Which two cables do you need to connect a floppy drive to a computer? (Select two.)

    A. 4-pin mini power connector

    B. 40-wire PATA cable

    C. 34-pin ribbon cable

    D. 80-wire PATA cable

3. The RAM used in hard drives is called the _____.

    A. platter

    B. serial

C. key

D. cache

4. Which of the following makes the biggest difference in overall data transfer speeds for hard drives?

   A. Platter size

   B. Platter position

   C. Platter rotation speed

   D. Platter power

5. What are two hard drive connection types? (Select two.)

   A. Serial ATA

   B. Platter ATA

   C. Super ATA

   D. Parallel ATA

6. How many wires are in the SATA data cable?

   A. Four

   B. Five

   C. Six

   D. Seven

7. Sam installs an IDE hard drive into a computer. He connected the data cable, but the drive doesn't seem to work at all. What might he have forgotten?

   A. Sam needs to connect the seven-wire SATA cable.

   B. Sam needs to connect the SATA power connector to the drive.

   C. Sam needs to connect the Molex power connector to the drive.

   D. Sam needs to connect the mini power connector to the drive.

8. Of the following optical standards, which holds the most data?

   A. CD-ROM

   B. CD-R

   C. CD-RW

   D. DVD-ROM

9. John wants to back up his 500 GB hard drive. Which optical technology would give him a good backup and use the fewest discs?

   A. DVD-R

   B. DVD+R

   C. BD-ROM

   D. BD-R

10. Most DVDs and BDs out there are used for what purpose?

   A. To store movies

   B. To store music

   C. To store data

   D. To store pictures

Answers

1. **C.** A standard floppy disk is 3.5" in size.

2. **A, C.** To connect a floppy drive, you use a 4-pin mini power connector and a 34-pin ribbon cable.

3. **D.** Hard drives use a small piece of internal RAM called cache.

4. **C.** The faster the platter rotation speed a hard drive has, the faster its overall data transfer speeds will be.

5. **A, D.** Most hard drives connect to PATA or SATA connectors. Note that PATA is the same as IDE in CompTIA Strata speak.

6. **D.** A SATA data cable has seven wires.

7. **C.** All IDE or PATA drives use a Molex power connector. Drives need electricity!

8. **D.** Any DVD disc holds more data than CD-ROM, CD-R, or CD-RW discs.

9. **D.** John should use BD-R discs. Each will store 25 or 50 GB of data, depending on whether he uses single- or dual-layer discs.

10. **A.** Most DVDs and BDs are used for playing movies.

Configuring the Operating System

5

In this chapter, you will learn how to
- Adjust basic Windows settings
- Explain user accounts in detail
- Describe how to store, retrieve, rename, and delete files and folders in Windows

A new Windows PC has a lot of things set up by default to help you jump in and get work done. And by *work*, I mean creating new things, playing excellent games, surfing cool Web sites, and so forth. This chapter examines the essential ways you can customize Windows to work best for you.

The chapter starts by showing you how to adjust basic Windows settings, such as making changes to both the look and feel of the interface and the background stuff that matters. The second section discusses user accounts in some detail. The chapter finishes with a discussion about working with files and folders.

Adjusting Windows Settings

Windows gives you many options for configuring the interface. Microsoft works very hard to create an intuitive, easy-to-master user interface for each version of Windows. Microsoft makes Windows customizable as well, though, to cater to the quirks of the millions of Windows users around the world.

Customizing the Start Menu

The Start menu offers a great place to start customizing Windows. It enables you to open frequently used programs quickly, plus access almost everything you need in Windows.

To start, if you'll pardon the pun, right-click the Start button and select Properties from the context menu. This opens the Taskbar and Start Menu Properties dialog box with the Start Menu tab selected (Figure 5-1).

Figure 5-1
The Taskbar
and Start Menu
Properties dialog box

The initial screen on the dialog box offers a few customization options, but clicking the Customize button opens the configuration flood gates (Figure 5-2).

From the Customize Start Menu dialog box, you can display various options as links, as menus, or not at all. How you customize the Start menu should depend on how you use Windows. I access my Games frequently, for example. By default, the Start menu shows the Games folder as a link. By changing it to display as a menu, I can save myself a click or two by going directly to the game I want to play at that moment. Figure 5-3 shows Games as a menu on my system.

If you want to simplify the Start menu on a computer, you can turn off infrequently used options by selecting the appropriate *Don't display this item* radio button. Some users with limited computing experience might not need the Control Panel, for example. If you get a little too happy displaying or not displaying options, you can always click the Use Default Settings button to return the Start menu to its original form. This way you can experiment and not have to worry about making mistakes.

Figure 5-2
The Customize Start
Menu dialog box

Figure 5-3
Game options on
the Start menu

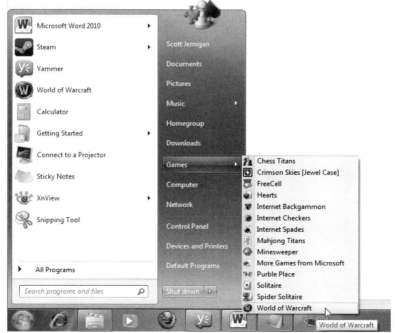

Essential Control Panel Applets

The Control Panel contains numerous areas for customizing the operating system. The default Category view in Windows 7, for example, offers eight areas to make adjustments (Figure 5-4). This section of the chapter discusses three of them:

- Appearance and Personalization
- Clock, Language, and Region
- Ease of Access

 EXAM TIP To open the Control Panel, go to Start | Control Panel in Windows Vista and Windows 7.

Appearance and Personalization

The Appearance and Personalization category is full of great customization features that enable you to set up Windows to look and feel precisely how you like it. Figure 5-5 shows the many options.

Figure 5-4
Category view of the Windows 7 Control Panel

Figure 5-5
Appearance and
Personalization
options

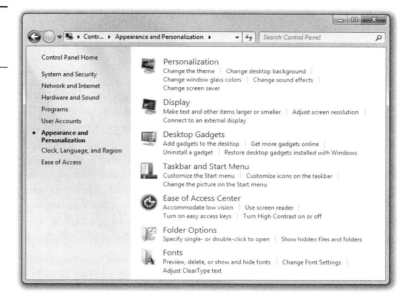

You can change individual colors of screen elements, for example. You can make radical changes by altering the entire theme. Figure 5-6 shows two screen shots of a single desktop. Only the theme has changed, but the change is remarkable.

 EXAM TIP To change your computer's volume, click the speaker icon on the far right corner of the taskbar and move the slider up or down.

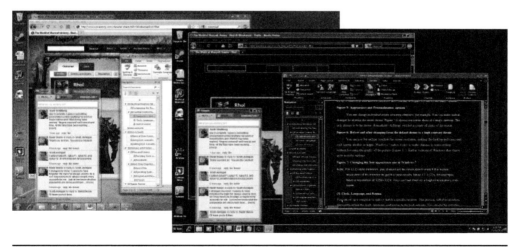

Figure 5-6 Before and after changing from the default theme to a high-contrast theme

You can use Appearance and Personalization to adjust the screen resolution, but increasing the resolution makes the desktop font and icons and such appear smaller. To counteract this, you can make your fonts and icons larger (Figure 5-7). Versions of Windows before 7 don't have quite as many options.

NOTE For best results, you should set the resolution of LCD-style monitors to match the native resolution of the monitor. Most 17" LCDs, for example, have a resolution of 1280 × 1024. You can't set them to a higher resolution, only lower.

Clock, Language, and Region

You can set up a computer for a specific location. This process, called *localization*, is easily accomplished in Control Panel with the Clock, Language, and Region applet (Figure 5-8). You can change the region setting, which can change the default language used in Windows. You can change the time or time zone here too.

EXAM TIP You can also use the Clock, Language, and Region applet to change the time zone.

Aside from simply changing the time to match the local time, you can also add a clock gadget to your desktop in Windows 7. (You add gadgets to the Sidebar in Windows Vista rather than to the desktop.) Other gadgets include a Calendar, a CPU Meter, and so on as you can see in Figure 5-9.

Figure 5-7
Changing the font appearance size in Windows 7

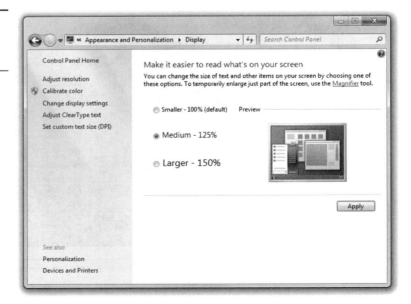

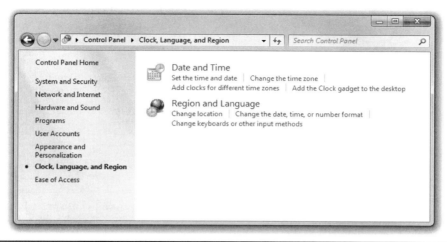

Figure 5-8   Clock, Language, and Region applet

Ease of Access

The Ease of Access category enables you to set up a computer to help people work with the computer more easily. You can change things such as how the mouse and keyboard work. *Sticky Keys*, for example, enables you to press key combinations using only one key at a time (Figure 5-10). This is a perfect option for someone learning how to use a keyboard or someone who needs to do input with one hand or finger.

Figure 5-9
Adding gadgets

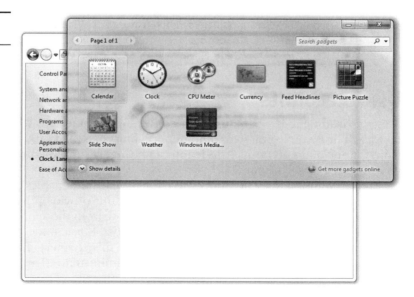

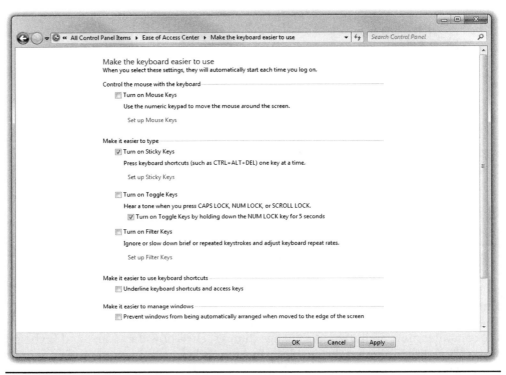

Figure 5-10 Sticky Keys and other options

EXAM TIP Although Ease of Access is not specifically mentioned in the CompTIA Strata objectives, such features of Windows often appear in CompTIA exam questions. You should be familiar with Mouse Keys, Sticky Keys, Toggle Keys, and Filter Keys.

User Accounts

A *user account* defines what a user can do on the machine, and what actions they can take. Each time you log on to a computer, you must present a valid user name and password for one of the accounts. This logon can be highly simplified, or even invisible, but you still need a user account.

Having multiple user accounts on a single machine enables people to share the computer and retain some privacy. Multiple accounts provide private folders in which each user can keep his or her personal files separate from those of other users.

Each user gets his or her own Documents folder, Music folder, Pictures folder, and so on (which you will learn more about later in this chapter). These folders can't be accessed by another user, unless he or she is an administrator. This adds a level of organization and security to the files kept on your computer.

Different user accounts also have different privileges. Some users may not be knowledgeable enough about computers to know how to install files properly or adjust Windows settings. Assigning each user the proper account type protects the system from unfortunate accidents.

Types of User Accounts

Windows offers several types of user accounts, such as administrator, standard user, and guest. The professional versions of Windows have a lot more than that, but let's stick with the big three for now.

A user with an *administrator* account type can install new software, change any setting in Control Panel, add new users, and do pretty much anything else that can be done on a computer. This makes the administrator account the most powerful account type.

As you might expect, this level of power carries with it a similar level of responsibility. Make sure that users with administrative privileges know what they're doing on a computer. The number of administrator accounts on a single machine should be as limited as possible: both Windows 7 and Vista require only one administrator account, while Windows XP requires two.

The next rung down the ladder is the *standard user* account type (Windows XP refers to this as a *limited* account). Standard users can use most programs and access personal files but cannot install programs or change any settings that could affect other users. If you try to do anything that only an administrator can do, a dialog box will pop up and ask for an administrator's user name and password (Figure 5-11). Windows calls this

Figure 5-11
Show me your
permissions!

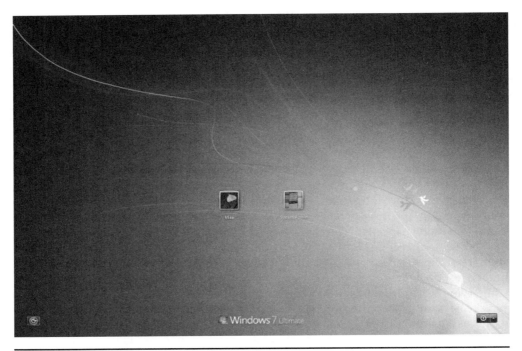

Figure 5-12 The Windows 7 Welcome screen

User Account Control (UAC). User Account Control acts as a gatekeeper between users and sensitive Windows settings. This ensures that an administrator always knows what happens on the computer. The majority of users on a machine should have standard user account types.

The *guest* account type is for temporary users who don't normally use that particular machine. Access is extremely limited. Guest users can run most programs but can't change any settings, access any personal files, or install software. The guest account is turned off by default to keep random strangers from being able to log on to your computer.

Using User Accounts

Each time you boot your computer, Windows greets you with the *Welcome screen* (Figure 5-12). The Welcome screen serves as the gateway to the rest of Windows and your usual computing experience. The OS lists each user account with its user name and icon. Click the icon for your user account to log on to Windows. If your account is password protected, you will be prompted to enter your password.

Once you log on, you can log off easily (though you might want to use the computer first). From the Start menu, click the arrow next to Shut down and select Log off from the menu (Figure 5-13). Windows logs you out of your account and returns you to the Welcome screen.

Figure 5-13
The Shut down
pop-up menu

Adding User Accounts

While Windows requires only two or three user accounts, you can always add more. If
you have kids or coworkers who share a single machine, giving everyone his or her own
account is a great way to keep everyone's stuff separate and secure. To add a user account, you need to use the User Accounts Control Panel applet (Figure 5-14) and be
logged in as an administrator.

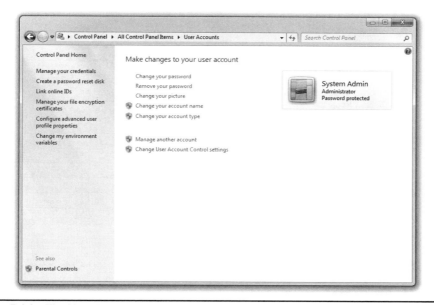

Figure 5-14 The User Accounts applet

Here are the steps to add an account in Windows 7 Home Preview.

1. In Windows 7, open the Start menu and click Control Panel.
2. Click the User Accounts and Family Safety category.
3. Then click the User Accounts applet.
4. From the list of options, select *Manage another account*.
5. Find the *Create a new account* link beneath the list of existing accounts and click it.
6. Put in a user name for the account. This can be whatever you want. Most people use their real name as their user name.
7. Next, select whether this user account will be a standard user account or an administrator account. Unless the user really knows what he or she is doing, stick to creating standard user accounts.
8. Once you have decided which type to use, click Create Account.

Maybe you noticed that you didn't need to create a password for that user account. By default, Windows user accounts are *not* password protected.

To add a password to the account you just created, click the user account's icon on the Manage Accounts window (Figure 5-15). From the list of options, select *Create a password*. Type in a password (and then type it in again to confirm it). You'll also need a password hint that Windows will use to remind you if you forget your password.

Figure 5-15 The Manage Accounts window

EXAM TIP Passwords are the ultimate key to protecting your computer. Make sure you use strong passwords: at least eight characters in length, including letters, numbers, and punctuation symbols.

Working with Files and Folders

Windows organizes data well. To understand how data organization works, imagine your computer is nothing more than a giant filing cabinet. The actual data in your computer is stored as individual *files* on your hard drive. Think of files as the pieces of paper that you'd actually put inside a filing cabinet. These include things like your documents, movies, music, and even important system data that you'll never actually open or look at yourself.

Just like a filing cabinet may contain some files with financial information and other files with photographs, there are many different types of computer files, separated by different *file extensions*. File extensions are the three or four letters (though they can be longer) that you see after a period in a filename. For example, birthday.jpg's file extension is JPG, and budget.xlsx is an XLSX file. The file extension tells the computer which program opens the file. Because of file extensions, your computer knows to open the birthday.jpg file with an image program, and the budget.xlsx file with Microsoft Excel (Figure 5-16).

Your computer is filled with hundreds of thousands (maybe even millions) of files, and it would take forever to find the file you needed if they were just stored in one big clump. Windows organizes these files by putting them into different folders. A *folder* in

Figure 5-16
Different programs
open different file
types.

your computer works just like a folder in a filing cabinet—you put files into them to organize them. Windows creates many different folders when it's installed (more on these folders in a bit), and you can also create your own (more on this in a bit, too) to organize your data.

Understanding what files and folders are will only get you so far, of course. You need to familiarize yourself with the program that enables you to navigate these folders, Windows Explorer.

The Many Faces of Explorer

Windows handles file and folder management through the *Windows Explorer* utility program. Windows Explorer has many faces, however, and most of them don't say "Explorer" in Windows 7. So here's the scoop.

- When you click on Start | Documents, or Start | Pictures (or Start | Music, or Start | Your Username for that matter), you open Windows Explorer.
- You can open the same utility by right-clicking the Start button and selecting Open Windows Explorer (or Explore in Windows XP).
- There's also a shortcut at Start | All Programs | Accessories | Windows Explorer.
- Finally, go to Start | Computer to open Explorer focused on your drives (hard drive, CD-media, and so on).

Let's look at Documents first, and then go to the classic Explorer interface. This section wraps up with a look at Computer.

Documents

Microsoft first introduced *My Documents* and other "My" folders in Windows 2000 to give users a simple and clear place to store their documents. Users of old versions of Windows tended to store things willy-nilly all over their hard drives and, as a result, had trouble finding files they wanted. The "My" was dropped in Windows Vista, but the folders still exist and serve the same purpose.

If you follow the path of least resistance and use the Microsoft folder structure, you'll save music files in Music, pictures in Pictures, and so on (Figure 5-17).

When you go to Start | Documents, you open Windows Explorer focused on that folder. On top is a toolbar with options like Organize, Open, and Burn. (The options change depending on what is selected.) You can perform common tasks on the folders and files in the Documents folder, such as rename, move, copy, and delete, by clicking on the folder or file, then clicking Organize. You can also perform any of these functions by right-clicking a folder or file and selecting the appropriate option from the context menu.

NOTE Windows 7 uses *libraries* to group similar files in one location, regardless of which folder they're in. If you have documents spread out over three or four locations, for example, you can add those locations to your Documents library and have a single point of access to the documents.

Figure 5-17
Libraries

Working with the Navigation Pane

Windows gives each storage device a letter and organizes its contents using folders and subfolders. The *Navigation pane*—open on the left side of a Windows Explorer window—is extremely useful for working with files and folders, because it gives you a graphical, hierarchical view of the window's contents. Notice that only folders and drives appear in the Navigation pane, while both folders and files appear in the Contents pane (on the right). See Figure 5-18.

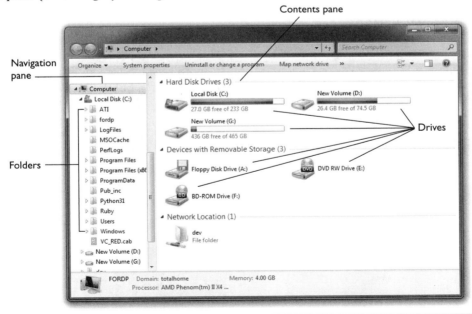

Figure 5-18 Windows Explorer

Clicking the white drop-down arrow in front of a folder in the Navigation pane expands the folder so that you can see its subfolders. When a folder displays its subfolders, a black arrow pointing downward replaces the white arrow. Clicking the black arrow hides the subfolders.

Changing Views

Windows Explorer gives you multiple options for how you view the contents of a folder. Clicking the Views button in Windows Vista or the Change your view button in Windows 7 (Figure 5-19) enables you to choose how Windows displays the folder contents:

- Extra Large, Large, Medium, and Small Icons
- List, which displays a list of filenames
- Details, which displays the same list with details
- Tiles, which are icons with details
- Content, which is similar to Tiles

The currently chosen view is marked with an arrow.

Details view is particularly useful for quickly finding a particular file within a folder. The folder in Figure 5-20 is displayed in Details view, showing the name, size, file type, and modified date of each file. You can sort the files using the headers for the details being displayed. In Figure 5-20, the Date modified header has been clicked, sorting the files by the date they were last changed.

Standard Actions

The classic Windows Explorer with the Navigation view enables you to accomplish standard actions—create, move, copy, cut, and delete—on folders and files between folders and drives. Each action works the same with Desktop folders as it does in Computer (because they're all just faces of Windows Explorer!), but drag and drop becomes even more powerful.

Figure 5-19
Selecting a folder
view in Windows
Explorer

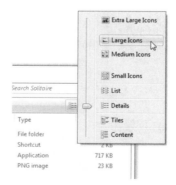

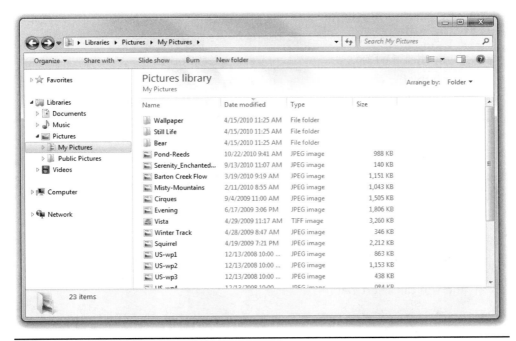

Figure 5-20   A folder sorted by file details

To create a folder or file, right-click a blank spot on the screen and select New. This will give you a fly-out menu of the folder and file types Windows recognizes (Figure 5-21). When you select a type, Windows will create it.

To move or copy a folder from one location to another, for example, simply left-click the folder, hold down the mouse button, and drag the folder. If you want to copy something rather than move it, press the CTRL button. When it shows a + sign, you're about to copy; when it shows an arrow sign, you're about to move that folder. Try it, you'll see!

Figure 5-21
Creating a new file

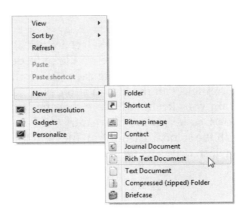

You can also copy files or folders using a number of other techniques. For example, you can

- Right-click the file you want to copy and select Copy.
- Select the file you want to copy and press CTRL-C.
- Right-click the file you want to copy and drag it to where you want it to go. When you release the right mouse button, the context menu will come up and you can select Copy.

You can cut files using very similar techniques. When you copy a file, it stays in its original location, but a copy is created somewhere else. When you cut a file, the file gets removed from its original location and pasted somewhere else. To cut a file or folder,

- Right-click the file you want to copy and select Cut.
- Select the file you want to copy and press CTRL-X.
- Right-click the file you want to copy and drag it to where you want it to go. When you release the right mouse button, the context menu will come up and you can select Cut.

To complete the copy/cut process, you have to paste your file or folder somewhere, copying (or moving) it to that location. To paste a file that you've copied or cut,

- Right-click inside the folder you want to paste into and select Paste.
- Select the folder you want to copy into and press CTRL-V.

To delete a file or folder, select it and press the DELETE key on the keyboard. Pressing CTRL-X will do the trick as well.

Selecting Multiple Targets

Windows Explorer enables you to perform standard tasks on multiple files and folders at the same time. Select two or more files or folders by clicking the first one and then pressing the SHIFT key while clicking the last one in the list, as shown in Figure 5-22. This is called a *shift-click*.

If the files or folders you want to select are not all next to each other, then you can use the *control-click* method to select each file or folder. Figure 5-23 shows files selected by holding the CTRL key while clicking each file for the selection.

Finally, you can select all the files in a folder by selecting Organize | Select All, or by pressing CTRL-A on your keyboard. Note that the latter technique works in many programs in Windows, so it's always worth a try.

You can do all the standard actions on files and folders in Computer. You can quickly transfer files between drives using this view of Windows Explorer.

Figure 5-22 Click the first file, and then SHIFT-click the last file to select a group of files that are listed contiguously.

Figure 5-23 CTRL-click each file to select files that are not listed together.

Renaming Files

As with people and corporations, files sometimes need new names. To rename a file or folder in Windows, right-click it and select Rename. Type in the new name and press ENTER. You can also do a slow double-click on an item to change its name, but if you click too fast, you might open the file.

Sometimes you'll come across files or folders that you can't rename, either because they're important Windows files or because they're being used by an open program. In the latter case, close the program that's using the file and try again.

 NOTE You can also rename files by selecting the file and pressing the F2 key on your keyboard.

Hard Drive Organization

A typical Windows PC organizes folders and files on the hard drive in standard locations. User files go into folders based on user account names. Operating system files go into the OS folder. Program files tend to go into program folders. How organized is that?

This section examines how a typical Windows hard drive organizes data. You know how to access programs and personal data from previous chapters and earlier in this chapter. This last bit goes under the hood to see how Windows stores those programs and data.

User Folders

Windows organizes the user folders, such as Pictures in Windows 7 and My Documents in Windows XP, on the primary hard drive by default. Windows Vista/7 arranges these folders differently than Windows XP. Let's look at both.

User Files in Windows Vista/7   Windows Vista/7 store user folders on the C: drive in a subfolder called Users. Within Users you'll find subfolders for each user on the computer. Figure 5-24 shows a typical system with two users, Mabel and Puck.

By default, neither Mabel nor Puck can see the contents of the Users folder for each other's account. If one or the other is an administrator, she or he can gain access pretty easily. Not so with standard users.

You can access your user folder in a few ways.

1. You can click Start and select your user name. This shows all the folders, such as Contacts, Desktop, Downloads, and so forth (Figure 5-25).

2. Or you can do it the long way:

   - Click Start | Computer
   - Double-click Local Disk (C:)
   - Double-click Users
   - Double-click your user name

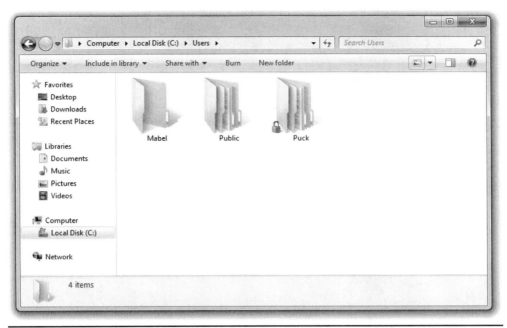

Figure 5-24 User folders

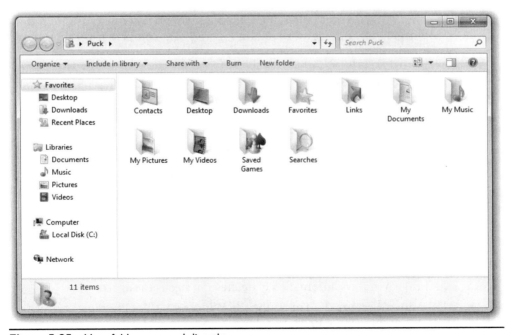

Figure 5-25 User folder accessed directly

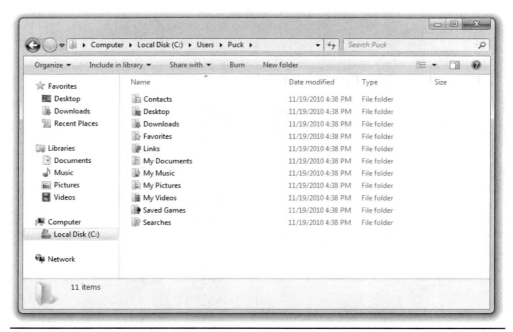

Figure 5-26 User folder accessed through the full path

3. The long way gets you to the same folders but shows you the location on the hard drive. Look at the location bar in Figure 5-25. Compare it with the long-way location bar in Figure 5-26.

Operating System Folders

The modern versions of Windows organize essential files and folders in a relatively similar fashion. All have a primary system folder for storing most Windows internal tools and files.

SystemRoot is the tech name given to the folder in which Windows has been installed. Most versions of Windows use C:\WINDOWS.

The system folder contains many subfolders, too numerous to mention here, but let's run through a few subfolders you should know about (these folders are in all versions of Windows):

- **C:\Windows\Fonts**   All of the fonts installed in Windows live here.

- **C:\Windows\Offline Web Pages**   When you tell your Web browser to save Web pages for offline viewing, they are stored in this folder. This is another folder that Windows automatically deletes if it needs the space.

- **C:\Windows\System32**   This is the *real* Windows! All of the most critical programs and files that make Windows run are stored here.

- **C:\Windows\Temp** Anytime Windows or an application running on Windows needs to create temporary files, they are placed here. Windows deletes these files automatically as needed, so never place an important file in this folder.

Program Folders

Windows has one or two folders that help organize your programs. They sit in the root directory at the same level as the system folder, and of course they have variations in name depending on the version of Windows. We'll assume that your computer is using the C: drive—a pretty safe assumption.

C:\Program Files (All Versions) By default, most programs install some or all of their essential files into a subfolder of the Program Files folder. If you installed a program, it should have its own folder in here. Individual companies decide how to label their subfolders.

Installing Photoshop, which is made by Adobe, for example, creates the Adobe folder and then an Adobe Photoshop subfolder within it. Installing Silverlight from Microsoft, on the other hand, only creates a Microsoft Silverlight folder with the program files within it.

 NOTE Some programmers choose to create a folder at the root of the C: drive, bypassing Program Files altogether, but that's becoming increasingly rare.

C:\Program Files (x86) The 64-bit versions of Windows Vista and Windows 7 create two directory structures for program files. The 64-bit applications go into the C:\ Program Files folder. The 32-bit applications, in contrast, go into the C:\Program Files (x86) folder. The separation makes it easy to find the proper version of whatever application you seek.

Chapter Review

Windows has a great interface by default, but you can change it to your heart's content. To modify the Start menu, you need to right-click it and select Properties. The Customize button offers even more customization options.

The Control Panel enables you to make Windows into a tool that works the way you need it to work. Control Panel applets offer many options:

- Appearance and Personalization
- Clock, Language, and Region
- Ease of Access

The various categories and applets give you control over the color and size of screen elements. You can change date and time settings. You can even select a specific language to complete the localization of the OS.

Ease of Access enables you to make changes to essential input devices, such as keyboards and mice, to help everyone connect to the computer. You can use Ease of Access to enable Sticky Keys, Mouse Keys, and more.

Most versions of Windows offer three user account types: administrator, standard or limited user, and guest. The accounts have different levels of permissions. Administrators can do pretty much anything. Standard users (Windows Vista/7) can work with programs and files easily. Limited users (Windows XP) have more limitations on what they can and cannot do. Finally, guests can do very little aside from surfing the Web and running default programs.

Windows organizes files into folders and saves those files and folders on the hard drive. The primary user tool for accessing this data is Windows Explorer, though it has many names and faces, such as

- My Documents
- Pictures
- Computer

Using various keyboard shortcuts enables you to accomplish standard actions—create, move, copy, rename, cut, and delete—on folders and files between folders and drives. Select a file and press CTRL-C, for example, to copy the file. Click in another folder and press CTRL-V to paste a copy of the file into that folder.

By default, Windows places essential folders and files in regular places on the hard drive. The user data goes into C:\Users in Windows Vista/7, for example, and C:\Documents and Settings in Windows XP. Windows OS files reside in C:\Windows for the most part.

Programs are usually stored in one of two places. In 32-bit versions of Windows, most programs install into a subfolder in the C:\Program Files folder. In 64-bit versions of Windows, all 64-bit program files go there. The 32-bit programs go into a special place reserved for lesser programs called C:\Program Files (x86).

Questions

1. How can you change the size of icons and print in Windows 7?

   A. Right-click the Start menu and select Properties. Set the display options on the Customize tab.

   B. In the Control Panel, select Appearance and Personalization, and adjust the display options.

   C. In the Control Panel, select Desktop, and adjust the display options.

   D. You can't. Monitors have a fixed resolution.

2. What option enables you to press key combinations using only one key at a time?

   A. Filter Keys

   B. Single Keys

    C. Sticky Keys

    D. Toggle Keys

3. Bill wants to create a new user account on a Windows 7 computer. What kind of user account must he have to succeed?

    A. Administrator

    B. Limited

    C. Guest

    D. Standard

4. Which of the following is the best password for a user account named Jane?

    A. Jane88

    B. Fluffy

    C. Password

    D. Ja#e1988

5. How does Windows know what program to open when you double-click a file?

    A. Every file has a data fork that carries the file type along with the data.

    B. The file extension tells Windows what program is associated with a file.

    C. Windows keeps track of all files created on the computer and simply knows the file association.

    D. The first three letters of the filename tell Windows what program is associated with a file.

6. Which part of a Windows Explorer window gives you a graphical, hierarchical view of the window's content?

    A. Contents pane

    B. Folder pane

    C. Hierarchy pane

    D. Navigation pane

7. What keyboard combination enables you to cut a file or folder?

    A. CTRL-C

    B. CTRL-D

    C. CTRL-V

    D. CTRL-X

8. What keyboard combination enables you to select all files in a folder?

    A. ALT-A

    B. ALT-C

    C. CTRL-A

    D. CTRL-C

9. Where can you find private files for the user named John on a Windows XP computer?

   A. C:\Documents and Settings\John

   B. C:\Documents and Settings\Users\John

   C. C:\Users\John

   D. C:\John

10. Diana needs to access a critical operating system file. The technician tells her to go to SystemRoot and then double-click the System32 folder. She doesn't see any folder called SystemRoot on her C: drive, so she can't find System32. What should she do?

   A. In Computer, double-click the Windows folder. She'll find System32 in there.

   B. In Computer, double-click the Program Files folder. She'll find System32 in there.

   C. In Computer, double-click the Program Files (x86) folder. She'll find System32 in there.

   D. She must have the wrong version of Windows.

Review Answers

1. **B.** You can make all sorts of crazy changes to the look and feel of Windows in the Appearance and Personalization area of the Control Panel.

2. **C.** Sticky Keys, found in the Ease of Access area of the Control Panel, enables you to input key combinations using only one key at a time.

3. **A.** Administrators can create user accounts.

4. **D.** Although Jane88 isn't bad, it's too short. Ja#e1988 offers much better security.

5. **B.** The file extension in Windows tells the associated program.

6. **D.** The Navigation pane offers a fine view of the contents of a window.

7. **D.** CTRL-X enables you to cut a file or folder.

8. **C.** CTRL-A enables you to select all files in a folder.

9. **A.** On a Windows XP computer, you'll find all user files by default in subfolders of the C:\Documents and Settings folder.

10. **A.** SystemRoot is the techie term for "where to find the critical operating system files." By default, most versions of Windows put the SystemRoot in C:\Windows.

PART II

Maintaining and Upgrading the Simple PC

Maintaining Computers

In this chapter, you will learn how to
- Care for the external parts of the computer
- Describe methods for keeping the inside of the case problem-free
- Explain how to keep data inside the hard drive safe

Maintaining a computer requires you to focus on three distinct areas: external cleaning and maintenance, internal physical maintenance, and data maintenance. This chapter tackles all three areas.

Outside the Case

A properly maintained computer starts with a properly maintained and ordered space. You should also keep external components clean and free of dust and hair. Take care to use proper cleaning solutions and methods, especially for sensitive components such as monitors. Finally, once a solution or component has reached the end of its usefulness, you should dispose of it properly.

Placement of Wires and Devices

Nothing turns a happy day sad faster than accidentally dumping a soda onto a poorly placed surge suppressor and watching the lights go out as all the circuits trip. You must maintain the physical space. In my house, for example, we don't eat or drink at the computer. It just leads to crumbs in the keyboard or accidents that can be dangerous.

Secure the electrical connections. The power supply inside the case takes electricity from the wall socket and transforms it into electricity the computer uses. Although power supplies can connect directly into a wall socket, most people use a *surge suppressor* to make sure the computer is protected from electrical surges.

 EXAM TIP   You might see a surge suppressor called a *surge protector* on the CompTIA Strata exam.

Most surge suppressors have five or six outlets (Figure 6-1). Those outlets provide a great surface area for spills and accidental electrical connections. Keep them out of the path of any potential spills.

Figure 6-1
A surge suppressor

EXAM TIP Surge suppressors ensure only proper power makes it to the computer. In CompTIA Strata language, surge suppressors *mitigate*—make not as bad—*electrical issues.*

It's also important to place electrical and network cables where you won't kick, stand on, or trip over them. Catching a cable by accident and dropping a monitor off a desk doesn't do good things to the monitor.

Proper Cleaning Materials

Aside from dust, the exterior parts of a computer don't get very dirty in a typical environment. Use a vacuum cleaner or soft cloth to clean the case, mouse, and keyboard.

In a non-typical environment, the game changes and more aggressive cleaning is required. For a PC in an automotive shop or other high-grime environment, use a *mild soap and water* solution. Be very careful when cleaning keyboards to unplug them from the PC first and allow them to dry out completely before reattaching. If you plug in a keyboard with any moisture inside, it'll short out and become more landfill fodder.

EXAM TIP Use mild soap and water with a soft cloth to clean any dirty external parts of the computer.

Cleaning Monitors and Removable Media

Cleaning monitors and removable media requires a little caution, especially with the substances used to clean them. Glass cleaners on a typical LCD monitor (Figure 6-2), for example, will melt the screen. A tiny bit of moisture under the screen panel on any monitor can take out the electronics as soon as you plug in the monitor.

To clean a monitor, use a damp cloth or a mild soap and water solution. Make sure the cloth itself is super-soft, like a chamois or microfiber towel.

Figure 6-2
An LCD monitor

With removable media, such as CD-R and DVD discs, you need to take care not to scratch, crack, or warp the media when cleaning. Use a soft cloth, possibly damp, and wipe from the inside edge to the outside edge with a straight movement. Don't clean by wiping in a circular motion (Figure 6-3). Do not put optical discs into the dishwasher! The water is usually too hot and will warp the disc, making it unreadable.

 NOTE If you find that a lot of your discs seem difficult for the computer to read, it might not be the fault of the discs. Try cleaning the inside of the drive. Use long cotton swabs and a little denatured or isopropyl alcohol. Definitely disconnect the computer from the electrical outlet before going inside the drive chamber.

Safe Disposal

When you finish cleaning, pour your mildly soapy water down the sink and throw your cleaning cloths into the wash. When you finish with a computer *part*, on the other hand, you need to take care how you dispose of it.

Figure 6-3
Cleaning an
optical disc

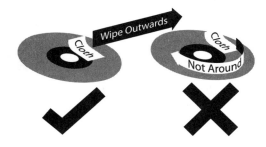

Most computer part makers have adopted the *Restriction of Hazardous Substances (RoHS)* Directive to make their products more environmentally friendly and thus easier to discard safely (Figure 6-4). The RoHS guidelines are a European Union (EU) standard that regulates toxic substances, such as lead, mercury, and cadmium.

The biggest change for most computer part makers has been shifting from lead-based solder to tin-based solder. This helps reduce the risk of lead exposure to the people who work in electronics recycling around the world.

 NOTE   If you don't make your own electronics, here's the scoop. Solder is used to make a connection point between wires. Solder points look like little globs of solid silver on a circuit board.

To be on the safe side, always follow proper recycling guidelines when getting rid of old electronics. Many major cities offer convenient recycling centers specifically for hazardous materials. Monitors are the most difficult to get rid of, especially the older CRTs. Check for a monitor recycling program near you. Because of the toxic levels of lead and mercury in old monitors, don't dump them in a landfill. Replace worn-out CRTs with newer, more efficient LCD monitors.

 EXAM TIP   The CompTIA Strata exam refers to the environmentally friendly disposal of computers, monitors, and other consumables as Green IT or Green computing.

Inside the Case

Most computers are not a single piece, but a collection of parts inside a box. The box or case has vents into and out from it and can become home to gobs of dust and hair. If too much debris builds up, the computer could overheat and break down. It is important to open up the case and clean the inside every once in a while.

Opening the side of a typical case generally requires you to remove only two screws (Figure 6-5). Getting in is the first step to cleaning the inside.

You need to understand three things to accomplish this task correctly. First, opening a case exposes the internal components to danger from you. You need to know the risks

Figure 6-4
RoHS-compliance
labeling

Figure 6-5
Remove these two
screws and the side
will come off.

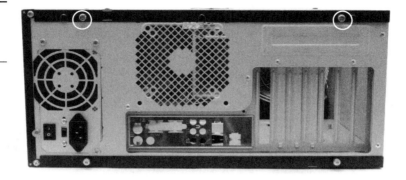

and ways to mitigate those risks. Second, cleaning various internal components requires special tools. And third, you should take steps to ensure proper ventilation and
moisture levels.

Proceed with Caution (Avoiding ESD)

Electrostatic discharge (ESD) can permanently damage or destroy computer components
inside the case. ESD is the transfer of static electricity from you to something you touch.
If you've ever been shocked when touching a door knob in the winter time, you know
exactly what ESD feels like.

Unlike you, though, a computer component can't say "Ouch!" and flinch from the
contact. It just dies a little, inside, where it counts.

You can do several things to avoid damaging computer parts with ESD. First, as
soon as you open the case, touch the metal of the power supply (Figure 6-6). This will
discharge any static electricity you have without harming anything.

Figure 6-6
Touching the
power supply

Figure 6-7
An antistatic wrist
strap connected
to a PC

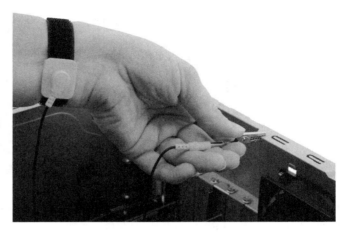

Second, if you plan to be inside the computer case for a while, purchase an *anti-static wrist strap*. Connect one side to your wrist and the other to the power supply or case (Figure 6-7). This keeps everything safe from ESD.

Finally, if you take any computer component out of the case or its packaging, place it inside an *antistatic bag* (Figure 6-8). You can get both antistatic wrist straps and anti-static bags at any electronics store, such as Radio Shack or Tandy's.

 EXAM TIP   Connecting to the power supply or metal frame of a case with an antistatic wrist strap is the best way to avoid ESD when working inside a computer.

Figure 6-8
A component inside
an antistatic bag

Figure 6-9
Compressed air

Cleaning Inside

Once inside the case, you have three basic options for cleaning: You can blow the dust out, you can pull it out, or you can scrub it out.

You use a product called *compressed air* to blow out dust, cat hair, and anything else out of the case. Compressed air comes in small cans like spray paint, usually with a little tube for directional blowing (Figure 6-9). You can purchase compressed air at any electronics or computer retail store. Just make sure to do the blowing outdoors, not inside! Otherwise, you'll make a huge mess.

You can use a special vacuum cleaner designed for electronics to vacuum out the inside of the case (Figure 6-10). Normal vacuum cleaners create a static electricity charge as the dust flows through the plastic nozzle, so you shouldn't use them inside a computer. You can find electronics or *antistatic vacuums* at computer and electronics stores.

 EXAM TIP   CompTIA calls electronics vacuums *antistatic vacuums*.

Figure 6-10
Antistatic vacuum

Ventilation, Dust, and Moisture Control

A well-maintained computer ensures proper ventilation and limits the amount of dust that comes into the case. Further, the case protects the inside from any unwanted moisture. The key issue from a maintenance standpoint is to make sure the case covers are properly in place.

The front of the PC usually has extra covers for drives you might want to add later. Figure 6-11 shows a typical PC with one of the covers off. That's bad, because case manufacturers design the cases for air to flow across the drives and motherboard. Missing covers can disrupt the flow. Plus, they let in even more airborne debris.

More important than the front covers are the slot covers on the back of the computer. Figure 6-12 shows the back of a PC with a missing slot cover. That can disrupt the airflow even more and cause the PC to overheat. Keep these covers in place!

Inside the Drive

The final steps in maintaining a computer have to do with digital cleanliness rather than physical cleanliness. Windows includes several tools that help keep your data neat and tidy, enabling you to quickly remove unused files, compress files to save disk space, and make backups for safekeeping. You need to keep your hard drives clean, and keep the data organized and safe.

Figure 6-11
The front of a PC

Missing drive cover

Figure 6-12
The back of a PC

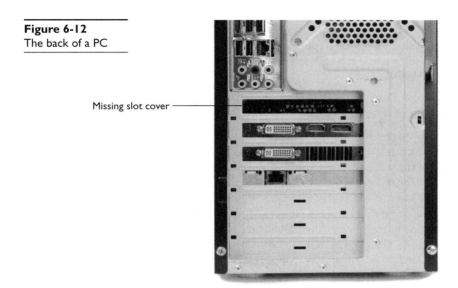

Missing slot cover ————

PART II

Disk Cleanup

Running *Disk Cleanup* regularly helps keep your hard drive clear of clutter. The program comes with all modern versions of Windows, so it's easy enough to find. Go to Start | All Programs | Accessories | System Tools | Disk Cleanup to run it. You can select things to delete, such as Downloaded Program Files or Temporary files (Figure 6-13). You can empty the Recycle Bin or get rid of setup files. Take your pick to clean up unnecessary files.

Figure 6-13
Disk Cleanup

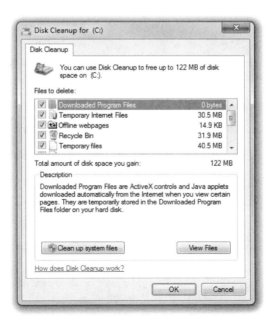

EXAM TIP On a more complex computer with multiple hard drives, you can run Disk Cleanup on a specific drive. Go to My Computer or Computer, right-click a drive, and select Properties. On the General tab, click Disk Cleanup to run the program.

Disk Compression

If you have a computer with a small hard drive, you can maximize the available space on the drive by compressing it. This process, usually called *disk compression*, can make data on a drive occupy less space, though it comes at a price. Compressed data has to be uncompressed for the computer to use it. In practice, a compressed drive can hold more data but the overall computing process is slower.

To compress a drive in Windows, open Computer or My Computer. Right-click a drive and select Properties. Select the check box next to "Compress this drive to save disk space" and click OK (Figure 6-14). Windows will crunch for a while, and you'll have more available hard drive space.

You can also compress individual files and folders. This saves a smaller amount of hard drive space but enables you to pick and choose what you want to compress. To

Figure 6-14
Local Disk (C:)
Properties

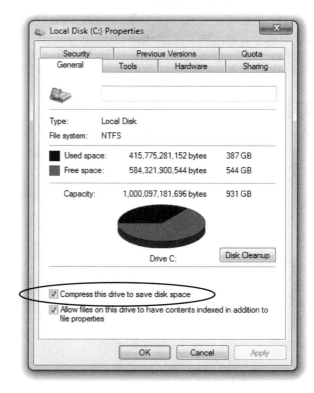

compress a file or folder, right-click it and select Properties. Click Advanced; then click the check box next to "Compress contents to save disk space."

Backup

The old tech joke goes, "There are only two kinds of computer users: Those who have lost data and those who *will* lose data." What that means is that you should always prepare for that loss by backing up any important data. Different versions of Windows offer different tools to accomplish backups. Let's look at the tools and then turn to the backup process.

Tools

Current versions of Windows use the Windows Backup program for making full copies of hard drives. You can run the program by going to the Control Panel and clicking the *Backup your computer* link in the Category view. If you're in Icon view, click *Backup and Restore*. Either path opens the Backup and Restore applet (Figure 6-15).

Click *Set up backup* to start Windows Backup (Figure 6-16). You can select to back up your hard drive to any other connected mass storage device.

Earlier versions of Windows came with a program called Windows Backup as well, though it was more complicated than the current tool. The easiest way to get to the program is by going to Start | Run, typing ntbackup, and pressing ENTER. Follow the wizard to back up your files (Figure 6-17).

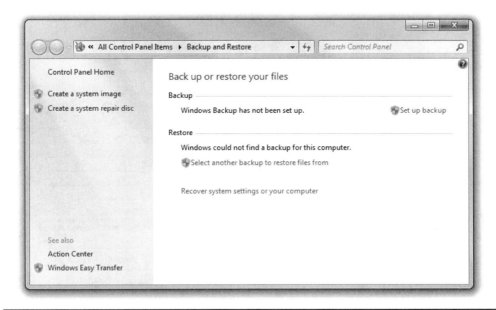

Figure 6-15 Backup and Restore

Figure 6-16
Deciding where to
back up the drive

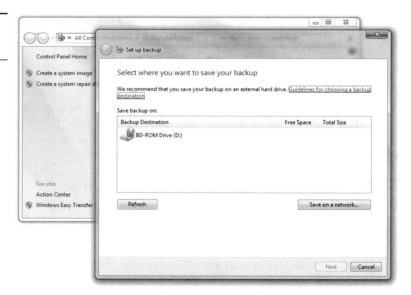

Guidelines

Microsoft recommends backing up your drive to an external hard drive. This offers a couple of benefits. First, you can connect the drive without opening the case. Second, you can store the backed-up drive in a different location than the computer. If the location of the computer experiences a catastrophic event (fire, flood, and so on), the backup is safely elsewhere (assuming you took it there).

Figure 6-17
NTBackup in
Windows XP

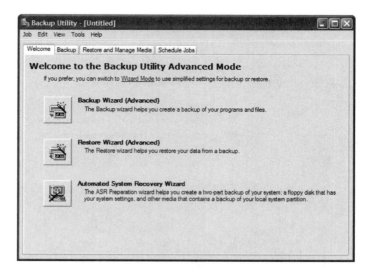

External hard drives come in a variety of packages. Technically, the hard drive part of an external drive is the same as an internal drive. The difference is that external drives are in an *enclosure* that plugs into an AC electrical outlet and into a port on the back of the computer (Figure 6-18). The most common external drives plug into USB ports. Better ones plug into eSATA ports.

NOTE See Chapter 8 for more details on USB, eSATA, and other connectors.

You should back up your files regularly. The answer to the key question, "How often?" depends on how you use the computer. If you're creating (writing, doing art) or importing pictures or music a lot, then back up frequently, like every week. If the computer is primarily used as an Internet browsing and e-mail-checking device, then backing up once a month is probably sufficient. You should have a backup that can help you recover from a catastrophic crash.

If you have a work computer, follow the company policy for backing up your drive. If you don't know it, ask!

Procedures

Windows makes backing up and restoring drives fairly simple. You follow the wizard. With the older version of Windows Backup, you needed to select what folders to back up. Current versions enable you to back up the full hard drive, so they're even easier to use. Select the destination drive and then schedule how often to back things up. Windows will do the rest.

Figure 6-18
An external hard
drive enclosure

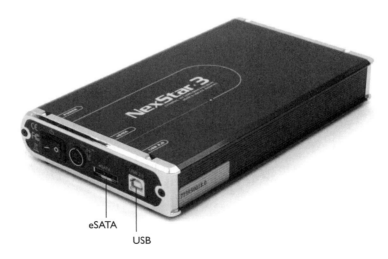

eSATA

USB

Chapter Review

Maintaining a computer involves three different levels. First, you should keep the area around the computer clear, clean, and safe. Make certain all power cords are away from accident-prone feet.

Second, you should use compressed air or an electronics vacuum cleaner to clean the inside of the case. Touch the power supply or use an antistatic wrist strap to avoid damaging components with ESD. Keep slot covers in place to make sure the computer cools things properly and the dust stays outside.

Finally, run regular disk cleanups to remove unneeded files. Run Windows Backup routinely to ensure the safety of your precious data.

Questions

1. What device helps a PC avoid electrical problems?

   A. AC outlet

   B. DC outlet

   C. Cable splitter

   D. Surge suppressor

2. How should you clean removable media, such as a DVD?

   A. Use a soft cloth and wipe with a circular movement.

   B. Use a soft cloth and wipe inside to outside with a straight movement.

   C. Use a soft scrub brush and wipe left to right.

   D. Put the disc in the dishwashing machine.

3. Rich has inherited a computer that used to live in his uncle's machine shop. What should he use to clean up parts such as the case, keyboard, and mouse?

   A. A dry, soft cloth

   B. A soft cloth with distilled water

   C. A soft cloth with mild soap and water

   D. A soft cloth with a commercial cleaning solution

   E. A cat

4. What standard offers computer part makers guidelines for making environmentally friendly parts?

   A. FTC

   B. RIAA

   C. RoHS

   D. VHS

5. What can you use to prevent ESD from damaging components when cleaning inside a computer?

   A. Antistatic wrist strap

   B. Antistatic bag

   C. Antistatic wipe

   D. ESD presents no danger to components, so nothing special is needed.

6. What should you use to remove dust and animal hair from inside a computer case?

   A. Blow dryer

   B. Compressed air

   C. Household vacuum cleaner

   D. Mild soap and water

7. What problem can missing slot covers on the case cause?

   A. Electromagnetic interference from other electronics nearby

   B. Electrostatic discharge from dust and animal hair

   C. Disruption of airflow inside the computer leading to overheating

   D. Disruption of airflow outside the computer leading to overheating

8. Which software tool will remove unnecessary files from the hard drive?

   A. Disk Cleanup

   B. Drive Erase

   C. File Format

   D. Magic Erase

9. What should you do to keep your data safe?

   A. Clean your computer regularly.

   B. Compress the hard drive.

   C. Run Windows Backup regularly.

   D. Uncompress the hard drive.

10. Where is the best place to back up data?

    A. Into a folder on the same hard drive so that you have access to it immediately

    B. Onto a set of optical discs, such as CD-Rs, so that you can store the data in a safe place

    C. Onto an external hard drive so that you can store the data in a safe place

    D. Any of these options is as good as the others

PART II

Answers

1. **D.** Surge suppressors/protectors prevent electrical problems such as electrical spikes and surges from damaging computers.

2. **B.** To clean removable media discs, use a soft cloth, possibly damp, and wipe from the inside edge to the outside edge with a straight movement.

3. **C.** Mild soap and water is about as fierce a solution as may be needed for cleaning external parts of the computer.

4. **C.** The Restriction of Hazardous Substances (RoHS) Directive has guidelines for making products more environmentally friendly.

5. **A.** Connect to the power supply with an antistatic wrist strap to protect the PC from ESD.

6. **B.** Use compressed air outdoors to blow out dust and hair. An electronics or antistatic vacuum will also work.

7. **C.** Missing slot covers can disrupt airflow inside the case and can lead to overheating. They can also lead to excessive dust and animal hair inside the case. This can cause overheating too.

8. **A.** Run Disk Cleanup regularly to get rid of unnecessary files.

9. **C.** Back up your data regularly to keep it safe.

10. **C.** Use an external hard drive for backup if possible.

Upgrading Software

In this chapter, you will learn how to
- Describe the risks involved with upgrading and not upgrading
- Discuss the process of upgrading software
- Explain steps to take once you've upgraded

Most software comes out of the box ready to install and use. The operating system (OS) provides both the interface for you to work with the hardware and a structure to install applications and store files. Applications enable you to accomplish specific tasks.

When they release an OS or application, the software developers essentially proclaim that the software is complete and ready for use. It's as good as they know how to make it and now they're ready to show it off (Figure 7-1).

Once the software hits the real world, though, something happens. Users get their grubby mitts on the software and start putting it through its paces. Perhaps they use the program in a fashion not imagined by the software developers (Figure 7-2). Perhaps the program conflicts with some other software or hardware on users' machines.

Figure 7-1
New application,
ready for prime time

Figure 7-2
You want me to
do what?

The real-world use of an OS or application provides *feedback*—responses both good and bad—so that software developers can make better products. Once the programmers know what works and what doesn't, or what features customers would like added or changed, they go back to work (Figure 7-3).

 NOTE "Programmer" is just another name for a software developer.

Figure 7-3
Getting updated!

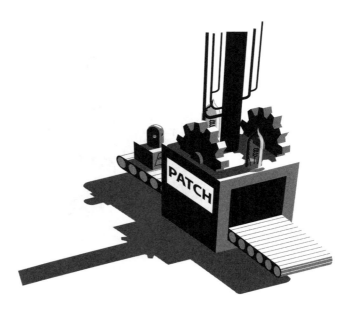

Depending on the number and scope of changes made, the developers will release the new and sparkly software as a patch, a service pack, or an upgrade. A *patch* fixes a problem and usually happens pretty fast. Smaller programs might get one or two big patches over the course of the program's life. Once patched, programs work better and often can do things that they previously couldn't do (Figure 7-4).

With big, complicated programs or operating systems, like Windows, the developers just keep patching for the lifespan of that piece of software. Microsoft periodically bundles patches together into *service packs* and releases those to customers.

An *upgrade* is generally a new program you need to purchase. The honor of upgrading from Windows Vista to Windows 7, for example, means shelling out another ~$150 (Figure 7-5).

 NOTE The price of applications and operating systems frequently changes. Depending on when you are reading this, the upgrade version of Windows 7 may cost anywhere from $100 to $200.

The benefits you get from upgrading your software vary from program to program, but some general considerations apply.

1. Patches designed to fix flaws in security should always be applied.

2. Application patches fix problems in the original program and should be applied.

Figure 7-4
No problem now!

PART II

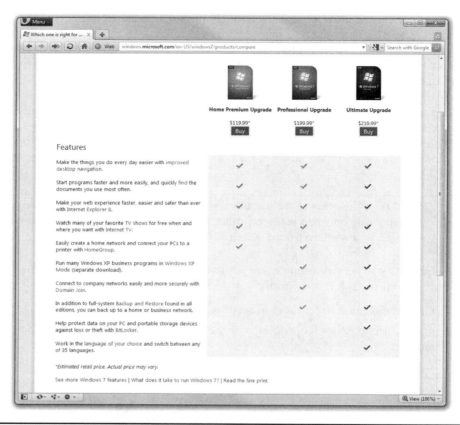

Figure 7-5 Windows 7 upgrade pricing

3. Service packs fix a lot of things and often add new features. They're generally a great upgrade for users.

4. Full program upgrades, like from Version *x* to Version *y*, add new features, improve operation, and generally provide a better experience. This applies to both applications and operating systems.

With full upgrades, you should address two questions:

1. Do you need those new features and improvements to use that application or OS efficiently?

2. Does the improved software offer value for the money for how you use the computer?

The upgrade from Windows XP to Windows Vista provides the classic example of point number two. Unfortunately for Microsoft, a very high percentage of users found

Figure 7-6   Windows XP and Windows 7

nothing compelling about Windows Vista and stayed with Windows XP. They just never upgraded at all until Microsoft forced the issue by ending most support for Windows XP nearly 10 years after they released the OS. A decade of life for a software program is like a human living happily and healthily for 150 years (Figure 7-6). Unbelievable!

The benefits to upgrading software are clear, so the rest of this chapter examines the process of upgrading. We'll first look at risks associated with upgrading, both if you do and if you don't upgrade. Second, the chapter goes through the nuts and bolts of upgrading and how you accomplish these tasks effectively. The chapter wraps with a look at post-upgrade tasks, such as software licensing and removal.

Risks

While some updates are free and others are not, all carry a hidden cost—the chance that your shiny new patch or upgrade will completely destroy your computer. It's an extreme example, of course, but you need to know what can happen when you deal with updating software on your computer. Operating system upgrades and application upgrades present different risks, so we'll address the two separately.

TIP   Different OSes use different methods for patching and upgrading software. Windows does things one way, while Mac OS and Linux do things differently. The risks and issues associated with the process, however, are the same for each OS.

Operating Systems

Microsoft and other OS makers continuously release patches, trying to make the OSes better, by which I mean more stable and safe from malicious software writers. Plus, every few years, the OS makers release a new version of their operating system. Patches and new versions bring very different risks to the table, so let's take a look.

Automatic Updates

Microsoft's programmers work tirelessly to make Windows more stable and safe. In earlier versions of Windows, Microsoft released patches and service packs with the assumption that people would voluntarily download and install them. When that *surprisingly* didn't happen and people got hit with viruses and security exploits that Microsoft had already fixed, Microsoft changed the game.

Current versions of Windows use *Windows Update* to update automatically any computer connected to the Internet. Allowing automatic updates adds one major risk to your computer. What if Microsoft gets it wrong and applies a buggy patch to your computer?

You might wake up on Wednesday (patches are released on Tuesdays by tradition) to find your computer not as happy as the night before. Figure 7-7 shows the potential result of a bad patch. That's not love!

 NOTE Figure 7-7 shows what the industry calls a *Blue Screen of Death (BSoD)*, a critical error where Windows shuts itself down to avoid damaging anything. Microsoft officially calls a BSoD a *Windows stop error*.

You can control how Windows Update handles patching from the Control Panel applet of the same name (Figure 7-8).

```
A problem has been detected and windows has been shut down to prevent damage
to your computer.

NO_MORE_IRP_STACK_LOCATIONS

If this is the first time you've seen this stop error screen,
restart your computer. If this screen appears again, follow
these steps:

Check to make sure that any new hardware or software is properly installed.
If this is a new installation, ask your hardware or software manufacturer
for any windows updates you might need.

If problems continue, disable or remove any newly installed hardware
or software. Disable BIOS memory options such as caching or shadowing.
If you need to use Safe Mode to remove or disable components, restart
your computer, press F8 to select Advanced Startup Options, and then
select Safe Mode.

Technical information:

*** STOP: 0x00000035 (0x00000000,0xF7E562B2,0x00000008,0xC00000000)


***     wdmaud.sys - Address F7E562B2 base at F7E56000, DateStamp 36B047A5
```

Figure 7-7   A Blue Screen of Death is never fun.

Figure 7-8
The Windows
Update options
screen

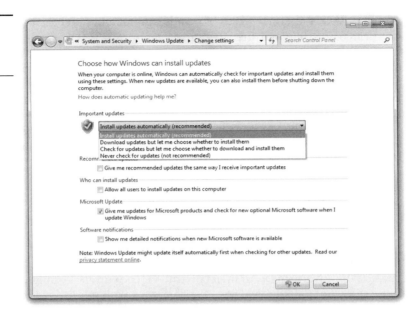

You have four options on how Windows downloads and patches your OS:

1. Install updates automatically (recommended).

2. Download updates but let me choose whether to install them.

3. Check for updates but let me choose whether to download and install them.

4. Never check for updates (not recommended).

The obvious risk in not allowing Windows to patch automatically is that you'll miss an important security patch and leave your computer vulnerable to attack. That's not a good thing. If you're disciplined about going to Windows Update regularly, that might not be as big a problem. But if you're like most users and don't think about manually patching the computer, you put your computer at risk.

 EXAM TIP   You risk exposing your computer to malicious software if you turn off automatic updates.

Version Update

Updating to a new version of Windows or any other operating system opens up a host of risks to your computer. The risks fall in three categories:

1. Compatibility issues

2. Upgrade issues

3. Potential data loss

Compatibility Issues A lot of people ran out and purchased copies of Windows 7 when Microsoft released the operating system. But if you recall from earlier in the chapter, a lot of those people were running Windows XP, not Windows Vista. The difference between hardware capable of running Windows XP and computers capable of running Windows 7 is pretty extreme. A lot of these users found that they simply couldn't install Windows 7 at all or that various parts of the computer didn't work with the new OS (Figure 7-9).

In some cases, the PC didn't meet the minimum hardware requirements necessary to install Windows 7. The PC owners had the option to upgrade the hardware or not install Windows 7.

NOTE The hardware requirements for various versions of Windows are listed in the later section "How to Upgrade."

Upgrade Issues When a new version of an operating system debuts, users tend to compare the advertising with their current PC. The current PC might be a little buggy or a little slow. An upgrade to a new OS promises a path to renewed computer happiness. But there's a catch.

Figure 7-9 Not so fast, mister!

To upgrade your PC to a new operating system, you should do a clean installation rather than upgrading from an existing version of the OS, sometimes known as an in-place upgrade. This means you have to install everything from scratch, including all of your applications. People don't want to spend that time, so they think they can cut corners by upgrading.

With an upgrade, though, the problems with the current OS usually both persist with the new OS and magnify. You get a computer that's slower and *more* buggy than the one you had before! Worse, if the installation doesn't go well, you'll need to install from scratch both the OS and your applications anyway. You might as well save yourself some pain and avoid problems: install from scratch.

NOTE To ensure a successful upgrade, you can use the Windows 7 Upgrade Advisor, available for free from Microsoft's Web site. It scans your hardware and software to determine what you need to do to upgrade your operating system.

Potential Data Loss During the upgrade process you have the option to format the hard drive. This essentially erases all data from your drive and creates a shiny renewed home for the new OS. It's like buying an old house. You wouldn't want to keep all the former owner's stuff, right? Get rid of it and have the house clean and ready for your stuff.

The problem from a computer standpoint is that the old stuff is *your stuff, too.* You wouldn't want to lose data. You need to make sure you have a good backup *before* you do any kind of upgrade. Without a good backup, you could lose precious and irreplaceable data.

EXAM TIP Always back up your data before you upgrade the operating system.

Applications

Upgrading applications involves a few risks, though nothing as dire as upgrading an operating system. You can get patches from various sites, not just the manufacturer's Web site. What's the risk? Doing a version upgrade offers some risks, though mainly to your wallet, not your data.

Patching

You can find software updates from several sources, such as big sites like CNET's Download.com, as well as from manufacturers' Web sites (Figure 7-10). It's tempting to go with the big sites, especially if the manufacturer's site has a much slower connection and the patch is big.

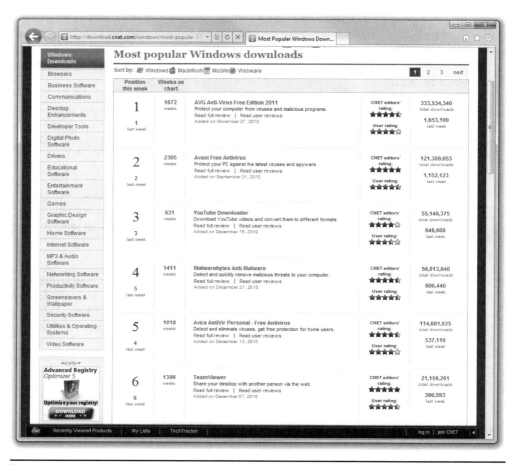

Figure 7-10   Software downloads from Download.com

The downside to using a Web site other than the manufacturer's Web site for patches is that you might not get the latest patch. You might download what seems like a good security patch, for example, but still not protect your computer from malicious software because you didn't apply the latest fix from the manufacturer.

 EXAM TIP   Manufacturers regularly release patches for applications that fix security issues. This is especially true of Internet-aware applications, such as Web browsers and office productivity software.

A further risk from using a Web site other than the manufacturer's for getting a patch is that you can't know that the patch has not been modified in some malicious way. (This worry does not apply to CNET or SourceForge, both reputable sites.) Be very careful if you have to use a third-party Web site for software.

TIP SourceForge.net enables you to download a lot of great applications. You'll find some Windows programs, plus an extensive collection of applications for Linux.

Version Update

Upgrading to a new version of an application brings a set of risks, such as compatibility problems and meeting the minimum requirements. A new program version might not work with an older hardware tool, for example. Or you might find that the new software interferes with other old software and causes problems. If you're not careful, you could get new software and find that your computer can't run it (Figure 7-11).

The problem with software incompatibilities is that you don't usually discover the problem until after you've purchased and attempted to install the program. Most stores won't take back any opened software. You're stuck with the option to purchase improved or compatible hardware or have a program that sits around collecting virtual dust, unused (Figure 7-12).

Figure 7-11 I'm so not installing on that PC.

Figure 7-12
I could have been
so great!

How to Upgrade

The process of upgrading software follows fairly predictable steps.

1. Make sure the computer can handle the upgrade.
2. Be certain that you have the necessary rights to install the upgrade.
3. Download or acquire the software on disc.
4. Make sure you have the proper license to install the software.
5. Go through the installation process.

Minimum Requirements

Computer software won't function—or even install—without the proper hardware or operating system in place. Programmers write applications to work with specific operating systems. Adobe Photoshop CS5, for example, has versions that run on OS X and Windows 7, but the versions are totally different from each other (Figure 7-13).

To a lesser extent, programs might work only in some versions of each OS. Applications written to take advantage of unique aspects of Windows 7, for example, won't necessarily work on Windows XP.

NOTE Some applications rely on minimum hardware requirements, but these are pretty obvious. A sound recording application requires a functional sound card, for example.

Figure 7-13   Different versions of Photoshop

Operating systems require a certain level of hardware, notably a fast enough CPU, enough RAM, and enough free hard drive space. With Apple computers, you don't need to worry much because Apple controls the hardware that runs Mac OS X. Apple writes the OS to work with specific hardware. Windows computers, in contrast, have a lot of variety in hardware. Table 7-1 lists the minimum hardware requirements for recent versions of Windows.

Windows Vista and Windows 7 add additional video card requirements if you want them to look good. The card needs at least 128 MB of RAM and must be compatible with DirectX version 9 or later. Lesser video cards can't handle the Windows Aero interface, the capability to have transparent windows and other graphical flourishes (Figure 7-14).

 EXAM TIP The CompTIA Strata exam will probably ask about minimum RAM requirements or 32-bit vs. 64-bit CPU support. You might get something on the Windows Aero interface and the video card, though that's more a CompTIA A+ question.

Rights

You need *administrative rights* to install software in every modern operating system (Figure 7-15). This applies to both commercial and open-source OSes.

You get administrator rights by logging in as the Administrator account in Windows or as Root in OS X or any Linux OS. Alternatively, you can log in with an account that's a member of the Administrators group, such as the primary account in a Windows 7 machine. Finally, if you're logged in as a standard user, the OS will prompt you to type in the account name and password for an account that has administrator rights.

Operating System	Bit Complexity	CPU	RAM	Free Hard Drive Space
Windows XP	32-bit	233 MHz	64 MB	1.5 GB
Windows Vista	32-bit	800 MHz x86	512 MB	15 GB
Windows Vista	64-bit	1 GHz x64	1 GB	15 GB
Windows 7	32-bit	1 GHz x86	1 GB	16 GB
Windows 7	64-bit	1 GHz x64	2 GB	20 GB

Table 7-1 Windows Minimum System Requirements

PART II

Figure 7-14 Windows 7 with Aero (top) and without Aero (bottom)

Figure 7-15
You need
administrative rights
to install software.

If you're not an administrator, you aren't installing any software, buddy.

EXAM TIP Although the OS will prompt for credentials when you try to install a program as a standard user, the CompTIA Strata exam interprets that as a *failure to install*.

Media

You have a couple of options for getting software upgrades. You can purchase them from a store—online or brick and mortar—or download them from the Internet. Either way works fine, though most bigger programs require purchasing a boxed installation disc.

If you opt for physical media, be careful not to scratch the disc. If you download the program, I advise getting it from the software developer directly rather than from a third-party Web site.

Licensing

Software developers release programs under three types of licenses:

- Commercial
- Shareware
- Freeware

Depending on the program you want to install, you need to make sure you have the proper license to install the software. If you don't, you violate the law in just about every country on the planet. Here's the scoop.

A *commercial license* gives you permission to install a program on *one* computer. Sometimes you can install on two machines, such as on a desktop computer and a portable, but those licenses are rare. Your payment for the program gives you a commercial license.

Most commercial licenses allow you to install the software on a second machine, but only if you remove it from the first machine. Some are more draconian, however, and state that the license is limited to a single machine. Read the fine print!

EXAM TIP   If you need to install a program on more than one computer, such as in a classroom, you can purchase a *multiuser license* or a *site license*. Either one will give you more flexibility on installation. Not all companies offer these sorts of licenses, though, so you might need to purchase additional copies of the application.

A *shareware license* enables you to install the program on any number of computers, but usually imposes some limit on the software. You might have 30 days of free use, for example, to evaluate the program, but after 30 days, you'd need to pay for it or it would stop working (Figure 7-16).

Other companies release shareware without a time limit, but disable many important features. A shareware picture-editing program, for example, might enable you to explore all the cool features, but not allow you to save an edited image.

Figure 7-16
Evaluation timing

Freeware is just what it sounds like: free. You can install it on any number of computers and enjoy the fruits of some programmer's labor. Most freeware is distributed under the *GNU Public License (GPL)*, which says you can use the freeware and even customize it, but you can't charge other people money for the changed version. Plus, you must make the altered software available as a free download. The many Linux operating systems available follow this pattern, as do many of the applications written for those OSes.

Upgrade Process

Once you have the media present, you can install the program. The steps differ between applications and operating systems.

With applications, put the physical media into the optical drive. The computer should recognize the disc and begin the installation. You will get prompted in Windows by User Account Control (UAC), a mechanism designed by Microsoft to help stop malicious code from installing itself on your computer. When the UAC prompt appears, click OK and the installation will begin (Figure 7-17).

Operating system installations generally require you to boot to the CD or DVD that holds the OS. You enable the boot process by changing the boot order in the System Setup utility. You might need a tech to help you with this, or you can take a stab at it yourself. Here are the steps.

1. Reboot your computer and watch the screen. In the text mode, before Windows loads, look for some key to press to access the System Setup

Figure 7-17
UAC

Figure 7-18
Read the screen.

American Megatrends
www.ami.com

```
AMIBIOS(C)2009 American Megatrends, Inc.
ASUS M3N78-VM ACPI BIOS Revision 1390
CPU : AMD Athlon(tm) II X2 245 Processor
 Speed : 2.90 Ghz     Count : 2
UnGanged Mode, DRAM Clocking = 667 MHz

Press DEL to run Setup
Press F8 for BBS POPUP
Press ALT+F2 to execute ASUS EZ Flash 2
1 AMD North Bridge, Rev C2
Initializing USB Controllers .. Done.
2048MB OK



(C) American Megatrends, Inc.
64-1309-000001-00101111-091109-MCP78S-A1041000-Y2KC
```

utility (Figure 7-18). It's sometimes called the CMOS Setup utility. For most computers you press the DELETE key, but some brands differ, so you need to look.

2. Press the key or key combination to have the setup program load.

3. Look through the text screens to find the option that says Boot Sequence or something similar and select it (Figure 7-19).

Figure 7-19
The Boot options

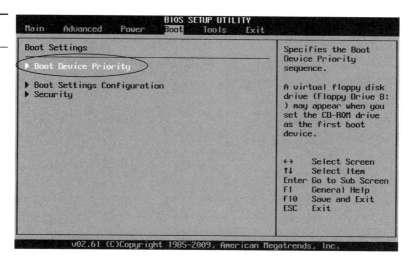

Figure 7-20
Boot order changed
to show optical
drive first

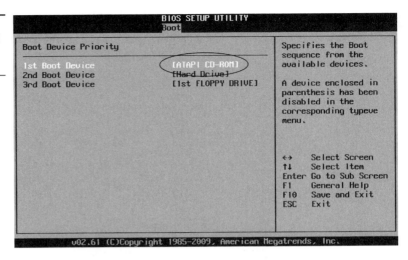

```
                            BIOS SETUP UTILITY
                            Boot

  Boot Device Priority                          Specifies the Boot
                                                sequence from the
  1st Boot Device        [ATAPI CD-ROM]         available devices.
  2nd Boot Device        [Hard Drive]
  3rd Boot Device        [1st FLOPPY DRIVE]     A device enclosed in
                                                parenthesis has been
                                                disabled in the
                                                corresponding typeve
                                                menu.


                                                ↔     Select Screen
                                                ↑↓    Select Item
                                                Enter Go to Sub Screen
                                                F1    General Help
                                                F10   Save and Exit
                                                ESC   Exit

            v02.61 (C)Copyright 1985-2009, American Megatrends, Inc.
```

4. Change the boot order so that the optical drive is above the hard drive in the boot order (Figure 7-20).

5. Insert the optical disc with the new operating system.

6. Save the changes to the System Setup program and exit. The computer will reboot.

7. Keep watching the screen.

8. When you see the prompt to "Press any key to boot to the optical disc," press a key (Figure 7-21).

9. Follow the installation prompts through the OS installation.

Figure 7-21
Booting to the DVD

```
Press any key to boot from CD or DVD._
```

TIP   Going through the preceding steps does *not* prepare you adequately to install an operating system by yourself the first time. Ask an experienced tech or advanced user to help you with the process.

After the Upgrade

Tasks after an upgrade involve dealing with legal issues and reading documentation. You might need to make adjustments to your firewall settings if the application is Internet-aware. If you need to move the software to another computer, reinstall it, or remove it altogether, you should understand the rights you have under current law. If you have problems with your computer after you install a new application, you may need to check your hard drive for errors. Let's look at all these issues.

Registration, Activation, and DRM

Most software enables you to register with the company that created it. Some programs also require activation as well. Finally, some programs require an Internet connection just to work.

Registration connects you with the company that produced the software. In exchange for personal data about you, you get access to technical support for a duration of time.

Activation ties your computer directly to the software and puts that information into the hands of the company that produced the software. Activation is an antipiracy measure popularized by Microsoft.

The process of registration and activation these days happens quickly through Internet connections. You add a few bits of information into a standardized form and press Send (or Create, in this case) and you're done (Figure 7-22).

Figure 7-22
Registering an
application

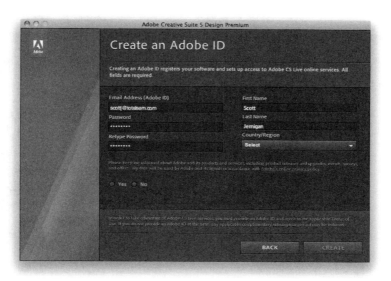

Some companies use a form of *digital rights management (DRM)* when you want to run their applications. One classic use of DRM for managing programs is Steam, the brainchild of Valve Software, the company that produces the game Half-Life. To run one of the Valve games, you need to log on to a valid Steam account (Figure 7-23).

There was a lot of outcry about the use of DRM with Steam when it first came out, but the implementation is now wildly popular. Steam remembers which games you've purchased and enables you to download and play them on any computer. If I'm stuck somewhere with nothing but a borrowed laptop and an Internet connection, I can always connect to Steam, download one of my games, and be playing in just a few minutes.

Read Documentation

In the early years of personal computers, software came bundled with thick manuals—the documentation—that described each aspect of the program. You could and should read the manual to learn how to do things efficiently with the program. These days, you'll find the manual in electronic format such as an Adobe Acrobat document, also known as a *PDF* file (Figure 7-24).

NOTE You need a third-party program to read Adobe Acrobat documents. Adobe offers Acrobat Reader as a free download. Alternatively, you can download the free Foxit Reader from www.foxitsoftware.com. That's the program I prefer because it's small and fast.

Figure 7-23
Some of my games
on Steam

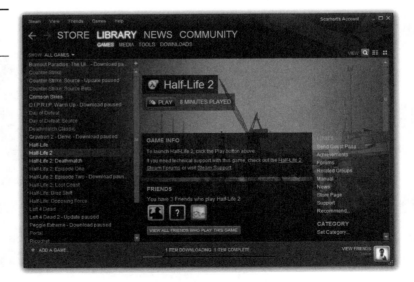

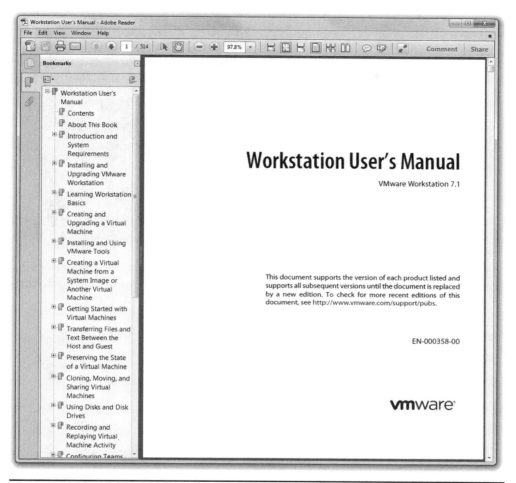

Figure 7-24   Documentation for a program

Adjust Firewall Access

Some programs require Internet access to work properly. One of my favorite programs, TrackMania, for example, enables you to race a variety of cars on a crazy number of tracks (Figure 7-25). The game also enables you to compete with other players around the world, which is pretty slick.

When you install the game on an Internet-ready computer, the installer will make changes to settings in your firewall, the part of the operating system that protects your computer from evil programs on the Internet. Usually this happens automatically. With some other programs, though, you'll be prompted before such changes are made. Figure 7-26 shows the firewall settings for my computer. Note the exceptions made for TrackMania and other Internet-aware games.

Figure 7-25
TrackMania

I will go into detail on Internet access and Internet-aware programs in Part IV of this book. For now, just know that some applications make adjustments to network settings so that they can function properly.

Figure 7-26
My firewall settings

Figure 7-27
Program uninstall feature in the Start menu

Software Removal

If you find a need to remove software from your computer, you can do so readily through the Control Panel in Windows or the Finder in OS X. Many programs have an uninstall option as well (Figure 7-27). Either method will perform a clean uninstallation, where all the pieces of a program are removed.

Figure 7-28 shows the Programs and Features applet in Windows. To uninstall a program, select it and click the Uninstall button on the screen. To uninstall a program from a Mac, select the program in the Applications folder in Finder and drag it to the Trash icon. Simple!

Reinstallation

Once you own a program, you can install it as many times as you like. That's the beauty of digital media. Even if you deleted a program, you can reinstall it fresh, creating a *clean installation*, if you so desire. Follow the same procedures you did when first installing it.

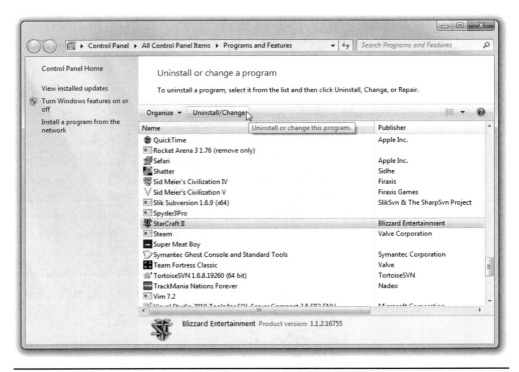

Figure 7-28   Uninstalling from Programs and Features

Checking for Errors

If, after installing new software, you find that your once perfect PC is now crashing to Blue Screens of Death like they are going out of style, you may have what is known as a drive error. These errors affect the file system that tells the hard drive how to store files and can cause freezes, crashes, or worse. To scan for these errors in Windows, use the Check Disk utility (Figure 7-29). Open Computer and right-click on the hard drive you wish to scan. Select Properties, then click on the Tools tab. Click on Check now (you will need administrator privileges). The Check Disk dialog box opens. Click Start to begin the scan.

Figure 7-29
The Check Disk
utility

Chapter Review

Most software comes out of the box ready to go. The real-world use of an OS or application provides *feedback*—good and bad—so that software developers can make better products. Depending on the number and scope of changes made, the developers will release the new and sparkly software as a patch, which fixes a few problems, a service pack, which is a collection of patches, or an upgrade, which is an entirely new edition of the product.

Operating system upgrades and application upgrades present different risks. Current versions of Windows use *Windows Update* to update automatically any computer connected to the Internet, though it is possible (if unlikely) that one of these patches may inadvertently harm your computer. You can choose to disable Windows Update, but you would need to remember to manually download and install all patches released by Microsoft.

Updating to a new version of Windows opens up a host of risks to your computer, including compatibility, upgrade, and data loss issues. Make sure your hardware is compatible with the new OS and is capable of running it. Perform a clean installation of the upgraded OS to ensure no old bugs come along for the ride. Back up your data before performing an OS installation to protect yourself from data loss.

Upgrading applications involves a few risks. You can find software updates from several sources, such as big sites like CNET's Download.com, as well as from manufacturers' Web sites. Using the manufacturer's Web site ensures you get the latest version of the patch. Make sure the computer can handle the upgrade. Be certain that you have the necessary rights to install the upgrade. Download or acquire the software on disc. Make sure you have the proper license to install the software. Go through the installation process. If necessary, read the documentation, activate and register your product, and adjust any applicable firewall settings.

If you ever get tired of the application or no longer need it, you can uninstall it from your system.

Questions

1. What is the recommended setting for Windows Update?

    A. Install updates automatically.

    B. Download updates but let me choose whether to install them.

    C. Check for updates but let me choose whether to download and install them.

    D. Never check for updates.

2. How do users using an application or OS help software developers make a better product?

    A. The more an application or OS is used, the more smoothly it runs.

    B. More users provide more feedback for software developers to use.

    C. If an application sells well enough, developers can spend the money on making something entirely different.

    D. Software developers need a lot of users before they are willing to spend the time and effort on fixing something.

3. Which form of update is a collection of patches all released at the same time?

   A. Patch pack

   B. Upgrade patch

   C. Service pack

   D. Service patch

4. What is the unofficial name for a Windows stop error?

   A. Blue Screen of Death

   B. Green Screen of Death

   C. Blue Screen of Doom

   D. Mondays with Windows Me

5. What is the most important issue when upgrading to a new version of an OS?

   A. Aero Desktop

   B. Compatibility

   C. Ease of use

   D. Available hard drive space

6. Why should you perform a clean installation of an upgraded OS?

   A. To save hard drive space

   B. For faster installation time

   C. To remove any bugs from the current OS

   D. For less chance of data loss

7. What limitations are placed on freeware?

   A. Most functions are disabled.

   B. The application will stop working after a week.

   C. The application must be run by an administrator.

   D. None. Freeware is free.

8. What does it mean to activate software?

   A. Installing an application

   B. Tying an application to a specific computer

   C. Running an application

   D. Updating an application

PART II

9. How many licenses are usually included when you purchase applications or OSes?

 A. None

 B. Unlimited

 C. One

 D. Two

10. What is the best way to remove applications in Windows?

 A. Right-click the .EXE file and select Delete.

 B. Right-click the folder containing the application and select Delete.

 C. Use the Programs and Features applet.

 D. Delete the shortcut on the desktop.

Answers

1. **A.** The recommended option is to have Windows automatically download and install updates.

2. **B.** Users provide feedback—good and bad—for the developers to use when trying to improve their product.

3. **C.** A collection of patches is known as a service pack and is commonly used by Microsoft for big Windows updates.

4. **A.** A Windows stop error is more commonly known as a Blue Screen of Death, or BSoD.

5. **B.** While making sure you have enough space on your hard drive is important, making sure that your hardware and software will work with the new OS is more important.

6. **C.** Performing a clean install will remove all traces of the existing OS, along with any bugs or problems that OS might have been experiencing.

7. **D.** They call it freeware for a reason—freeware has none of the restrictions of shareware.

8. **B.** Activation is an antipiracy measure popularized by Microsoft Windows that ties your computer to the specific copy of an application you own.

9. **C.** Traditionally, one license is included with each copy of an application you purchase.

10. **C.** The best and cleanest way to remove applications in Windows is to use the Programs and Features applet.

Upgrading Hardware

8

In this chapter, you will learn how to
- Determine when a computer needs hardware upgrades
- Explain optimal upgrades to peripherals
- Discuss the process of upgrading internal hardware

A personal computer offers all sorts of upgrade opportunities. You can add new features, for example, such as a video recorder or special sound device. You can upgrade existing parts as well, making the PC faster, stronger, and firmed up in all the right places.

This chapter examines the process of upgrading the computer's hardware. The first section describes symptoms that show that a computer needs an upgrade. The second section explores the typical PC, teaching you how to know which port type to use for external peripheral upgrades. The final section covers the internal upgrade process. You'll learn how to upgrade with minimal risk, plug in new components, test them, and deal with the unwanted, older parts.

Recognizing the Need for an Upgrade

Competent techs and advanced users recognize when a PC needs an upgrade. The symptoms calling for an upgrade include:

- The computer lacks a specific capability that you know other PCs can perform.
- The PC works poorly. A formerly wonderful computer starts to fail in some way. This can be a mundane failure, or something particularly spectacular.
- The computer looks a little shabby or perhaps could use a better component. Perhaps it runs a little sluggishly after upgrading all that software in Chapter 7.

Several examples illustrate the need to upgrade a computer's hardware.

1. Poor performance
2. Out of space
3. Application fails to load
4. Critical errors

Poor Performance

Peripherals with moving parts, such as keyboards, mice, trackballs, and other pointing devices, get dirty and wear out. Even with regular cleaning, you'll need to replace them at some point.

You know you need to replace them when they malfunction in some way. The keys on a keyboard might stick, for example. The mouse or trackball might move the cursor across the screen in a jerky fashion, rather than smoothly.

You have several upgrade options available for input/output devices. You can trade up for an optical mouse, for example, that doesn't have a ball to get gunked up. While considering that upgrade, perhaps the time has come to leave the wires behind and choose a wireless keyboard and mouse (Figure 8-1).

Out of Space

Every OS needs free space to function properly. When you open some types of programs, for example, Windows will take part of the hard drive free space and use it for automatically saving your files (known as autosave). If the computer crashes and you've forgotten to save your term paper, for example, Windows can recover at least some of it for you. The OS will get cranky and slow without enough free space (Figure 8-2).

To add more hard drive space, you can exchange your old hard drive for a drive with more capacity. Or you can add a second drive and move some things to the new drive. Both options require you to open the case and go into the computer.

Figure 8-1
A wireless keyboard and mouse

Figure 8-2
Windows Low Disk
Space warning

Alternatively, you can add an external hard drive that plugs into a port on the back of the computer (Figure 8-3). An external hard drive adds another dimension to the computer. Not only can you free up space on the internal drive, but you can also use it for backing up your data. With an external drive, you can back up your data and then take the backup to another location for an added layer of protection.

You saw hard drives in Chapter 4, and you might note that Figure 8-3 doesn't look like the pictures from the earlier chapter. That's because external hard drives come inside an *enclosure*, a case that can plug directly into a wall outlet for electricity.

Hard drive enclosures connect to one of several types of ports on the back of a computer. You learned about USB way back in Chapter 2. It's the most commonly used connector, but there are several varieties. There are other options, too, with outlandish names such as FireWire and eSATA.

Figure 8-3
An external hard
drive enclosure

Application Fails to Load

Not enough physical RAM in a computer can cause an application to fail to load. This usually happens when you have a ton of stuff open at once and the OS says, "No!" when you try to open one more application (Figure 8-4). A stick of RAM rarely goes bad without warning, but if something that used to work now doesn't, that might just be the case.

Increasing the amount of RAM in the computer is the first, best hardware upgrade you can make. Every tech should know how to do this task.

Critical Errors

Nothing says Monday morning like walking into your office and seeing a Blue Screen of Death (BSoD). A BSoD is a catastrophic error that stops the computer and puts a message on the screen that says what went wrong (Figure 8-5).

Critical or catastrophic errors can cause the computer to lock up, blue-screen, dramatically slow down, crash, or spontaneously reboot. The hardware-related errors can be caused by faulty drivers or hardware failure.

Some failures are spectacular. You might load a graphically intense game, for example, and suddenly all the colors go haywire and the machine slows to a crawl.

Other failures are simple. You might have been able to connect to the Internet yesterday, for example, but find you have no network connection at all today. The culprit? A nice electrical storm during the night fried the network card.

You can fix some hardware-related critical errors by updating or changing *drivers*. That's the software that helps the OS communicate properly with the hardware. Other times, though, the only fix is to replace the faulty hardware.

 EXAM TIP To see how well your PC is performing, type *perfmon* into the Start search bar and press ENTER. The Performance Monitor utility will open. this utility provides details on the processor, RAM, hard drive, and network connection. If you sense something is wrong, this tool should help you confirm it.

Figure 8-4
Insufficient memory
error

Figure 8-5
BSoD

```
A problem has been detected and Windows has been shut down to prevent damage
to your computer.

NO_MORE_IRP_STACK_LOCATIONS

If this is the first time you've seen this stop error screen,
restart your computer. If this screen appears again, follow
these steps:

Check to make sure that any new hardware or software is properly installed.
If this is a new installation, ask your hardware or software manufacturer
for any Windows updates you might need.

If problems continue, disable or remove any newly installed hardware
or software. Disable BIOS memory options such as caching or shadowing.
If you need to use Safe Mode to remove or disable components, restart
your computer, press F8 to select Advanced Startup options, and then
select Safe Mode.

Technical Information:

*** STOP: 0x00000035 (0x00000000,0xF7E56282,0x00000008,0xC0000000)

***    wdmaud.sys - Address F7E56282 base at F7E56000, DateStamp 36B047A5
```

Upgrading External Components

Once you know that a computer needs or should have a hardware upgrade, you need to examine the computer to see what upgrades it can handle. Adding external components, such as an external hard drive, mouse, keyboard, or monitor, means examining the ports on the back of the computer.

 NOTE The terms port, socket, and connector are sometimes used interchangeably.

Modern computers come with many sockets for adding or replacing external devices. Figure 8-6 shows the back side of a PC with nothing connected so that you can see all the sockets.

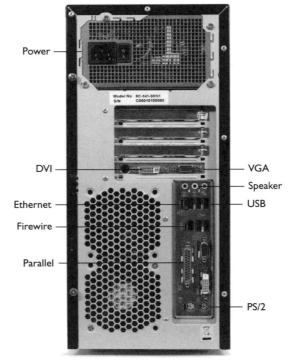

Figure 8-6 The back of a typical PC

Here's a list of the common socket types and what devices can plug into them (Table 8-1). Plus, the table offers a bonus column with some details about the sockets.

 NOTE If a socket is "hot-swappable," it means devices can be connected and disconnected without turning off the computer.

 EXAM TIP Table 8-1 is one big exam tip.

You learned about some of these ports way back in Chapter 2, so I won't go into them again here. Those are the PS/2 and video ports. Audio ports and RJ-45 ports are also single-purpose ports and don't require much explanation.

Socket	Used by ...	Details
PS/2 or mini-DIN (purple)	Keyboard	Not hot-swappable
PS/2 or mini-DIN (green)	Mouse	Not hot-swappable
DVI	Monitor	Only LCD; replaces VGA
VGA	Monitor	CRT and LCD; phasing out
HDMI	Monitor	Used for connecting to an HD television, mostly
Parallel	Printer	Legacy
Serial	Various	Legacy; still used for some network devices
USB	Various; common for keyboard, mouse, printer, flash-memory drives, digital cameras, smartphones, and external drives	Hot-swappable; multiple varieties within the standard. See the later section "USB" for details.
FireWire	Various; common for camcorders and external drives	Apple-developed, hot-swappable port. See the later section "FireWire" for details.
eSATA	External drives	Faster by far than USB or FireWire; hot-swappable
Mini-audio	Speakers, microphone, line-in	Common on every modern computer
RJ-45	Network	Common on every modern computer

Table 8-1 Standard External Ports

Let's look at multiple-use port types so that you can compare. We'll start with the serial and parallel ports, which are often called legacy ports. The modern ports—USB, FireWire, and eSATA—get their own sections. We'll finish up with connecting wireless peripherals and then a comparison section.

Legacy Ports

Serial ports and parallel ports enable you to attach some devices to the PC. The standards have been around since the beginning of the PC era, so it's surprising to find them still in use on some computers. Serial and parallel ports do not offer anywhere near the flexibility of USB or FireWire. Neither standard is hot-swappable, for example.

Serial ports are male, *D*-shaped, and have nine pins (Figure 8-7). Techs refer to serial ports by their pins, calling the connection a *DB-9*. They're used today mainly for connecting to a few network devices. On early personal computers, mice plugged into serial ports.

 EXAM TIP   Serial ports are called DB-9 ports.

Parallel ports are female, *D*-shaped, and have 25-pin sockets (Figure 8-8). Manufacturers color-code parallel ports fuchsia, a dark pink color. Parallel ports are sometimes called *DB-25* ports. About the only things that use a parallel port today are receipt printers and old laser printers.

 EXAM TIP   Parallel ports are called DB-25 ports.

Figure 8-7
A DB-9 (serial) port

Figure 8-8
A DB-25
(parallel) port

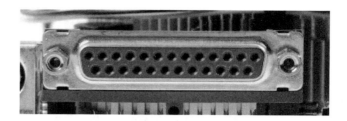

USB

The Universal Serial Bus (USB) enables you to add a remarkable variety of peripherals to a computer. Every major OS supports USB, and you find the ports on all but the most ancient computers.

All USB devices are hot-swappable, meaning you can plug them in without turning the power off. Most devices prefer to be turned off before you remove them, though. In Windows, click the Safely Remove Hardware icon in the notification area (the far right side of the task bar). See Figure 8-9. Use this option to avoid any potential data loss.

 EXAM TIP   Use the Safely Remove Hardware tool before you disconnect a USB device from the computer. This helps avoid data loss.

USB comes in two flavors: USB 2.0 and USB 3.0. USB 2.0 has two standards: USB and Hi-Speed USB. USB 3.0 is called SuperSpeed USB.

USB 2.0

Regular USB—often mistakenly called *USB 1.1*—devices transfer data at speeds of 1.5 or 12 megabits per second (Mbps). *Hi-Speed USB* is faster still, capable of bursts up to 480 Mbps.

Figure 8-9
Safely Remove
Hardware and Eject
Media in Windows 7

EXAM TIP   The CompTIA Strata exam refers to regular USB as *USB 1.1* and Hi-Speed USB as *USB 2.0.*

Note that despite the huge difference in speeds, Hi-Speed USB technology is fully backward-compatible with regular USB devices. You can plug a regular USB device into a Hi-Speed port, in other words, and it will work.

When you plug a Hi-Speed USB device into a regular USB port, the computer will tell you:

"This device can perform faster if you connect it to a Hi-Speed port."

You have two options at this point. You can leave the device where it is and it will run at 12 Mbps rather than 480 Mbps. Or you can plug the device into a different USB port and hope it's a Hi-Speed port.

USB 2.0 ports come in three varieties: A, B, and mini. All are female and rectangular-shaped. The connectors are keyed so that you can't insert the USB cable improperly.

You plug the flat USB A connector into the corresponding port on a PC or *USB hub*—a generic term for a device with multiple USB ports (Figure 8-10).

Most larger peripherals, such as printers and scanners, have a B port into which you'd plug a B connector (Figure 8-11).

Figure 8-10
USB A-type ports
on a hub

Figure 8-11
A USB B-type port
and connector

Small USB devices, such as digital cameras and music players, use the mini port. Figure 8-12 shows a mini USB port and connector.

USB 3.0

SuperSpeed USB runs at up to 5 Gbps. How very exciting for it! SuperSpeed connectors differ from USB 2.0 connectors, though the devices are backward-compatible.

 NOTE USB 3.0 looks almost exactly like USB 2.0 except that it is blue. I'd show you a picture of it, but this book is printed in black and white, so that wouldn't be very helpful.

As of this writing (early 2011), only a few SuperSpeed devices have hit the market. I've seen expansion cards that add USB 3.0 ports to a PC and a couple of external hard drives. By the time you read this, manufacturers will have released many more Super-Speed devices.

Figure 8-12
A mini USB port
and connector

PART II

FireWire

The IEEE 1394 standard—called *FireWire* by most techs and manufacturers—enables you to add a variety of peripherals to the computer. All OSes support FireWire. Like USB devices, FireWire devices are hot-swappable. FireWire connectors and ports are keyed so that you can't plug them in incorrectly (Figure 8-13).

The original specification for FireWire—*1394a*—can transfer data at up to 400 Mbps. The current generation of FireWire—*1394b*—is capable of speeds up to a blinding 800 Mbps. What's even more impressive is that the design specification for FireWire states that speeds of up to 1600 Mbps are possible. FireWire technology is a very good match for video, external hard drives, backup storage devices, and other hardware that needs real-time data access.

 EXAM TIP   The CompTIA Strata exam uses both terms, FireWire and IEEE 1394, to describe the technology.

eSATA

Most drives inside the computer connect to a serial ATA (SATA) port. But the connection—called a *bus*—is not just for internal devices.

Figure 8-13
A FireWire port
and connector

External SATA (eSATA) extends the SATA bus to external devices, as the name implies. Figure 8-14 shows eSATA connectors on the back of a motherboard. eSATA cables can be up to 2 meters (about 6 feet) long. Like USB and FireWire, eSATA devices are hot-swappable.

eSATA runs as fast as internal SATA, either 150 megabytes per second (MBps) or 300 MBps. eSATA is much faster than both USB and FireWire, so it makes a great connection for external hard drives and optical drives, such as Blu-ray Disc drives.

Wireless

Connecting peripherals to a computer using radio waves frees your desk of cord clutter and can make the computing experience better. Several technologies compete for wireless market share.

The most common technology is used for mice and keyboards and is simply branded *wireless*. The standard device has a small receiver that plugs into a USB port on the computer. The keyboard or mouse has a small transmitter that connects to the receiver, usually at a standard 2.4 MHz frequency. (That's the same wireless signal type used by a lot of cordless telephones.) Figure 8-15 shows a wireless keyboard and receiver.

Figure 8-14
eSATA connectors

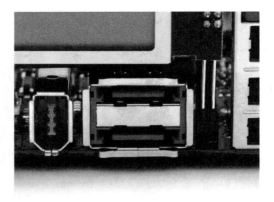

Figure 8-15
A wireless keyboard
and receiver

Pick a wireless device when you want to place the device near the computer, usually less than six feet away. Device signal strength varies a lot among manufacturers and devices, so check the specifications before you buy.

Bluetooth extends the range for wireless devices a long way, up to 30' from the receiver. Bluetooth requires a Bluetooth receiver as well as the device. Some portable computers have Bluetooth receivers built in. Other Bluetooth receivers will plug into a USB port on the computer. Bluetooth devices look like any other wireless device (Figure 8-16).

 NOTE Bluetooth is named after the ninth-century Danish King Harald Bluetooth. Because that has so much to do with wireless connectivity.

Figure 8-16
A Bluetooth mouse

You can connect multiple Bluetooth devices to a single receiver, creating a *personal area network (PAN)*. Plus you can find a wide variety of Bluetooth devices. Here are some examples:

- Keyboard
- Mouse
- Headset (for telephones)
- Headphones (for personal media players or computers)

How to Choose the Right Connection for the Job

Now that you understand and can recognize the external connections, you can advise someone on how to optimize an upgrade. With the single-function ports, such as PS/2 or DVI, you don't have to do much. If someone wants to upgrade an old monitor with a new one, for example, you need to check his computer. If it only has VGA ports, you'll want to get a monitor with a VGA connection. If you get one with DVI only, you'll need a converter to make the connection.

 EXAM TIP One of the risks associated with upgrading hardware is incompatibility. The exam might ask something about connectors such as PS/2, VGA, or DVI and the devices that use them.

Recommendations change depending on the device desired. Let's look at simple peripherals and then more complex ones.

Simple Peripherals

What if a client wants to upgrade a keyboard? Assuming the computer has been built within a few years, it will have both PS/2 and USB ports. You would have these options:

- PS/2
- USB
- Wireless (receiver into a USB port)
- Bluetooth (receiver into a USB port)

Your recommendation should change depending on the type of computing environment desired. Someone who wanted to do fast-action gaming might not do so well with a wireless keyboard, for example, because of the brief time lag between pressing a key and the computer responding. That same person might adore a Bluetooth keyboard for his media room, though, so he could surf the Web from his couch.

Complex Peripherals

With something more complex or throughput-hungry, like a hard drive, you have to understand a lot more about the connections than just if the device will fit. You need to weigh cost against speed.

NOTE *Throughput* measures the amount of data being moved. A higher throughput means more data can be moved faster.

External hard drives come in several varieties:

- USB 2.0 (Hi-Speed) only
- USB 2.0 (Hi-Speed) and FireWire
- USB 2.0 (Hi-Speed), FireWire, and eSATA
- USB 2.0 (Hi-Speed) and eSATA
- USB 3.0 (SuperSpeed)

Here are the speeds of the connection types, slowest to fastest (Table 8-2). I've listed them all in bits per second for easy comparison.

TIP The *listed* speeds for the various technologies don't tell the true performance story. In reality, you'll almost always get much better performance from FireWire 400 than Hi-Speed USB. And, as of this writing, eSATA outstrips every other interface, even SuperSpeed USB. If you have a choice, go with eSATA or FireWire over any USB option.

Table 8-2
Connection Speeds

Technology	Maximum Throughput
FireWire 400 (IEEE 1394a)	400 Mbps
USB 2.0 (Hi-Speed)	480 Mbps
FireWire 800 (IEEE 1394b)	800 Mbps
eSATA	3 Gbps
USB 3.0 (SuperSpeed)	5 Gbps

Upgrading Internal Devices

To upgrade some hardware, you need to go inside the case. The typical first upgrades inside are RAM, hard drives, and video cards. Going inside adds an element of danger to the computer, so you need to understand the risks and how to avoid them.

To accomplish upgrading any internal component, you need to be able to recognize the type of slots or connections for each. Plus, you must know what the computer can handle. For that latter knowledge, you'll need a book that describes the capabilities of the motherboard called the *motherboard manual*.

Avoiding ESD

As you'll recall from Chapter 6, the biggest danger of going inside the case is shocking a computer component with electrostatic discharge (ESD). Use an antistatic wrist strap or touch the bare metal of the power supply when you go in to put you safely at the same electrical potential of the components (Figure 8-17).

You also need to be careful when handling the component you want to put into the case. RAM, hard drives, and video cards are susceptible to ESD damage.

Unfortunately, you might unknowingly damage a component you're putting into a computer and have it fail later once it's in use. To avoid this kind of damage, always keep a component inside an antistatic bag when not in use.

 EXAM TIP A computer component is most likely to fail within 30 days of installation. This is called *burn-in failure*.

Figure 8-17
Using an antistatic
wrist strap keeps
internal components
safe from ESD

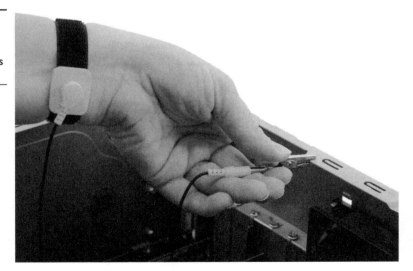

RAM

Motherboards differ both in the number of RAM slots available and in the specific type of RAM used. You need to see what slots the motherboard has available, plus read the manual to determine specific details.

A typical motherboard might have four RAM slots, for example, which means it can handle four RAM sticks (Figure 8-18).

There's a lot of variation in motherboards, though, so you have to look. You'll find one to eight RAM slots on today's systems. Plus, you need to see how many are already populated with RAM sticks.

Once you know the physical options for a RAM upgrade, you need to know the specifics for that motherboard. The motherboard manual will tell you the following details:

- What technology of memory the motherboard uses, such as DDR, DDR2, or DDR3

- What maximum capacity of stick each slot can handle

- What total amount of RAM the motherboard can handle

- What configuration (placement) of sticks optimizes the motherboard configuration

Figure 8-19 shows the RAM specifications found in a typical motherboard manual. A lot of systems come with digital rather than paper manuals. Check the discs that came with your computer.

 EXAM TIP The first place I go to when upgrading RAM is the motherboard manual. That tells me how much RAM the computer can handle.

Figure 8-18
RAM slots on a
typical motherboard

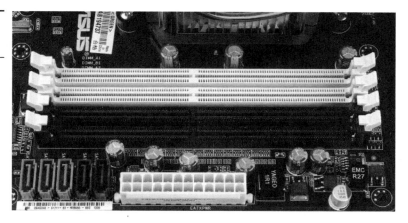

Figure 8-19
The RAM specs in a
motherboard manual

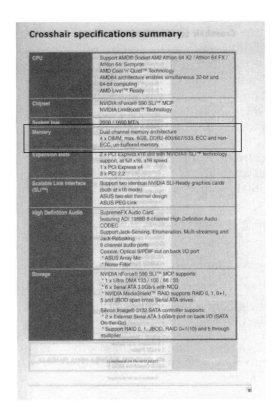

Need More RAM

As people make the jump from Windows XP to Windows 7, the first thing they might notice is that the new OS runs more slowly than the old one if they didn't upgrade the hardware too. At a minimum, Windows 7 requires 1 GB of RAM, as you'll recall from Chapter 7. The difference in speed between Windows XP with a gigabyte of RAM and Windows 7 with the same hardware is pretty astonishing.

The upgrade path for any two machines can differ a lot. Here are two quick examples.

- One customer's computer has 1 GB of RAM and she wants at least 2 GB. You open it up to discover that it has four 128-MB sticks in its four slots. To upgrade, you'll have to replace existing RAM. Plus, you'll need to check if the motherboard can handle 1 GB sticks or whether it tops out at 512 MB sticks.

- A second customer's computer has 1 GB of RAM and he wants at least 2 GB. Same scenario, right? Except when you open up the second customer's case, you find a single 1 GB stick of RAM and two empty RAM slots. Easy upgrade: just add an identical 1 GB stick and he's good to go.

Note also that the operating system makes a big difference on upgradeability. My fancy system at the office has six RAM slots and supports 12 GB of RAM. Running a 32-bit version of Windows, however, limits my usable RAM to only 4 GB. That's all that a 32-bit OS can see. To unlock the full 12 GB glory of the motherboard requires a 64-bit version of Windows.

Installing RAM   This next section falls into the "not on the test but still important" category. Here are the steps to install RAM.

1. Open your computer case (after taking the aforementioned ESD precautions). This can be the most difficult step, as many computer cases are tricky to open. If removing the screws on the back of the case doesn't do the trick, there might be a handle or lever underneath the front of the case. Keep experimenting until you get it open.

2. Find the RAM slots. These are about four inches long and have clips on either end of them. Also, at least one slot will already have RAM installed in it, which should be a big giveaway.

3. If you have to uninstall the old RAM sticks to install new ones, unclip the clips on the ends of the RAM slots and gently pull upward on the RAM stick to remove it.

4. To install the new RAM, make sure that the notch at the bottom of the RAM stick lines up with the raised portion of the slot, then push the RAM stick into the slot until the clips click shut.

Hard Drive

Motherboards can have two types of connectors for hard drives, parallel ATA (PATA) or serial ATA (SATA). Some will have both. You saw the hard drive connections in Chapter 4, so Figure 8-20 shows what they look like on a motherboard.

To add a SATA hard drive to a computer, you simply need a free SATA port. Each drive connects directly to the motherboard. PATA is a little more complex.

Figure 8-20
PATA and SATA
connections on
a motherboard

SATA

PATA

Figure 8-21
A PATA cable with
one connection free

Each PATA connection can handle up to two drives. If you have a free spot on an existing PATA cable, you can add a PATA drive to that connection (Figure 8-21).

To help the hard drive controller distinguish between the two drives, you need to move a small piece of plastic and metal, called a shunt, to change jumper settings. Figure 8-22 shows a shunt.

Although this goes beyond the CompTIA Strata exam, here's the scoop on jumper settings with PATA. You can make a drive master, slave, or cable select. Each PATA connection can have only these options:

- Master (or standalone)—one drive
- Master and slave—two drives
- Cable select—one drive
- Cable select and cable select—two drives

Figure 8-22
The business end
of a PATA drive

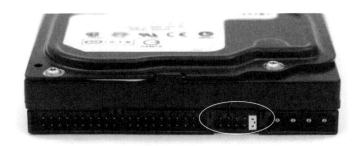

You can't have two masters or two slaves. You shouldn't mix cable select with master and slave (though sometimes it works).

 EXAM TIP One of the biggest dangers with changing out hard drives is data loss. Always back up your computer fully before messing around with your drives. Follow the process outlined in Chapter 6.

Video

Computers use dedicated video processors to translate math into pictures to put on the monitor screen. You'll recall this from Chapter 2. These video processors have various names:

- Graphics processing unit (GPU)
- Video processing unit (VPU)

Most computers have a card that holds the video processor and a set of RAM also dedicated to video. Some have the video processor built into the motherboard. This is called *integrated video*. Figure 8-23 shows a video card.

Almost all motherboards have an expansion slot dedicated to video. This is true even of motherboards with integrated video. Two slot types dominate the market:

- Accelerated Graphics Port (AGP)—the older standard
- PCI Express (PCIe)—the current standard

Although both slots support video, you can't mistake one for the other. AGP slots are smaller and usually brown (Figure 8-24). PCIe slots are longer, slimmer, and all sorts of colors (Figure 8-25).

Figure 8-23
A typical video card

Figure 8-24
AGP

Most AGP cards can move data multiple times during each click of the motherboard clock speed. This greatly increases the overall data transfer rate. An AGP 4× card, for example, can move data four times faster than an AGP 1× card. An AGP 1× card has a maximum data throughput of 266 MBps. The standard stopped at AGP 8×, so the top transfer rate is 2.1 GBps.

PCIe cards work differently from AGP, but the multiplying effect is similar. PCIe cards can use multiple *lanes*—essentially extra wires—to increase data transfers. A PCIe ×1 card transfers data up to 250 MBps; a PCIe ×16 card, therefore, goes up to a whopping 4000 MBps. (That translates to 3.9 GBps, almost double AGP 8×.)

 EXAM TIP Two other slots used for video were PCI and PCI-X. These standards topped out at 133 MBps and 1 GBps, respectively, in data transfer rates. Both were slower than AGP 8× or PCIe ×16.

When upgrading video, you need to examine the motherboard or read the motherboard manual, and then get a video card that matches the available slot. If you have the option, always go for PCIe as it's the fastest standard. If the motherboard only has AGP, then go for AGP 8× over slower AGP or PCI.

Figure 8-25
PCIe

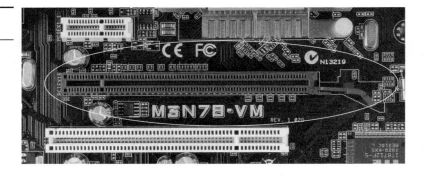

Installing a Video Card

Once again, this information isn't specifically on the CompTIA Strata exam, but you should know it anyway. Here are the steps to install a video card (or any other PCI/PCIe card).

1. Open the computer case. Remember to follow ESD-avoidance procedures.

2. If the slot is empty, remove the slot cover off the back of the case. If there is a card installed in the slot, remove the screw (or screws) holding it in place. Undo the clip at the end of the PCIe slot and gently lift the old card free.

3. Push the new card down into the PCIe slot until the PCIe clip secures it.

4. Screw the card to the case.

5. For a more powerful video card, you may have to attach it to your power supply for it to work, so be sure to check for extra power connections on the card.

Finishing the Internal Upgrade

Once you've finished the physical act of upgrading hardware, you have three tasks left to do.

1. Install drivers.

2. Test the hardware.

3. Recycle the old or dead equipment.

Drivers

The operating system needs programming to communicate properly with any hardware. With some devices, like RAM and hard drives, the motherboard has the drivers built into the System ROM chip, so you don't have to install anything. Other devices need software drivers that you install. You can find the drivers on the installation disc that came with the device, or you can download them from the manufacturer's Web site. Figure 8-26 shows a typical driver disc.

Figure 8-26
A driver disc

I recommend downloading drivers directly from the manufacturer with any new device. This ensures that you get the latest drivers. The ones that come on the disc might not be the latest version. Manufacturers regularly update drivers for hardware, especially video cards (Figure 8-27).

Testing

Excellent techs care about the people who use computers the techs repair. When you upgrade hardware, spend time after the installation to make sure the device works well.

- Access the new hard drive. Does it need partitioning and formatting? (See Chapter 10 for those topics.)
- Run a graphically intensive game that the customer wants to play. Does it work with the new video card? Do you need to configure the application settings to optimize the experience (Figure 8-28)?

Spending a few extra minutes testing makes a huge difference in customer satisfaction. You know the device works, and so does the user. It also helps you avoid return trips to the job site.

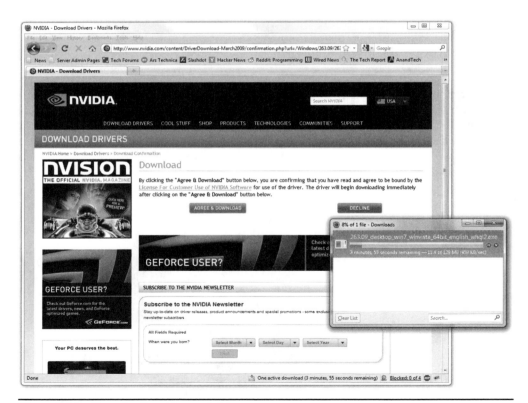

Figure 8-27   Downloading video card drivers

Figure 8-28
The default settings for Counter-Strike: Source with a new video card leave a lot to be desired!

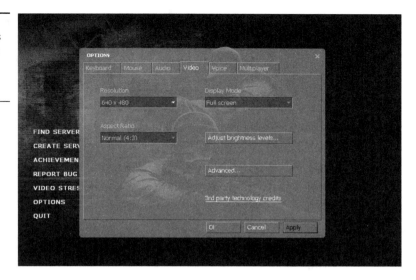

Recycling

Upgrading hardware invariably leaves spare parts scattered in the wake. It's tempting to toss a dead part into a trash can and walk away, but don't do it!

Computer gear (and any electronics) should be recycled or reused. Most major cities have some method of dealing with or place to take dead electronics gear. You can also contact computer part retailers. They often take recycled materials.

The greenest method for dealing with the old parts is to reuse them. This is especially true if the device still works fine for some purposes. An old 17" LCD monitor, for example, is a great upgrade for someone using a 15" CRT monitor.

Donate old, working gear to a charity. The device won't end up in a landfill. Someone gets a new-to-them upgrade. You get a tax write-off. Everybody wins!

Chapter Review

Upgrading hardware presents unique issues for techs. You need first to recognize when a computer needs an upgrade.

The computer might not have a specific capability that a user wants, for example. The computer might be running poorly. A sudden rash of BSoDs might point to failing hardware as well.

Once you've determined that a computer needs an upgrade, you have similar tasks for external and internal components. Look at the computer to see the available connections.

On the exterior of the computer, check for USB, DVI, FireWire, eSATA, and so on. What free sockets are there? Check the motherboard manual if necessary to determine what standard the specific connection uses. Is the USB port the slow USB 1.1 version or the faster Hi-Speed USB 2.0?

When you go inside the computer, take steps to avoid ESD. You don't want to risk damaging anything! Once inside, check the free slots or sockets, depending on what upgrade you want to make. Check the motherboard book for specifics about things like RAM capacity for the motherboard.

Once you've completed the upgrade, test it and recycle the old gear. The best way to recycle is to donate so that the item doesn't end its useful life.

Questions

1. The cursor on Bill's screen doesn't seem to track well and jerks across the screen. What should he do?

   A. Replace the monitor.

   B. Replace the mouse.

   C. Replace the keyboard.

   D. Upgrade Windows.

2. Which of the following might cause a program to fail to load?

   A. Insufficient RAM

   B. Low free hard drive space

   C. AGP video installed

   D. PCIe video installed

3. Which of the following ports enables you to hot-swap a keyboard?

   A. PCI

   B. PS/2

   C. Serial

   D. USB

4. What type of socket uses a DB-9 connector?

   A. PCI

   B. PS/2

   C. Serial

   D. USB

5. Which port offers the highest rate of data transfers?

   A. eSATA

   B. IEEE 1394a

   C. USB 1.1

   D. USB 2.0

6. Amy wants to use a wireless keyboard to control her media center PC. The PC sits next to the television, and her couch and coffee table are approximately nine feet away. What technology offers her the best option for an upgrade?

   A. Bluetooth keyboard

   B. eSATA keyboard

   C. RJ-45 keyboard

   D. Standard wireless keyboard (running at 2.4 GHz)

7. How can you determine the amount of RAM you can install in a computer?

   A. Open the case and look.

   B. Check the motherboard manual.

   C. Open the Memory Control Panel applet.

   D. Put in sticks until the extra memory stops being recognized.

8. What can you do to minimize risk when upgrading a hard drive? (Select two.)

   A. Back up the drive contents.

   B. Use an antistatic wrist strap.

   C. Wear soft gloves.

   D. Use the Safely Remove Hardware option.

9. Ron wants to upgrade his video card. When he opens the case, he discovers that the motherboard has two slot types for expansion: PCI and AGP. What's his best option for upgrading?

   A. Buy a PCI video card.

   B. Buy an AGP video card.

   C. Buy an AGP 8× video card.

   D. Buy a PCIe video card and get a converter to use the AGP slot.

10. Mary has replaced her keyboard and mouse with wireless versions of the same thing. What's her best option to deal with the functional but older wired versions of the keyboard and mouse?

   A. Toss them in the trash. No one wants used computer gear.

   B. Tuck them in a closet for later, just in case the wireless versions stop working.

   C. Take them to an electronics recycling center.

   D. Donate them to charity.

Answers

1. **B.** A jerky cursor is usually the fault of a dirty ball mouse or trackball. Replacing it with an optical-based mouse provides a significant upgrade.

2. **A.** Not enough RAM can stop a program from loading. Low free hard drive space generally lowers performance.

3. **D.** Of the four connections mentioned, only USB enables you to hot-swap devices such as a keyboard.

4. **C.** A serial port uses a DB-9—a two-row, nine-pin connector.

5. **A.** Of the four ports listed, eSATA offers the highest rate of data transfers.

6. **A.** Both Bluetooth and standard wireless potentially would work, but the range of the latter standard might be too short. Bluetooth can easily handle the nine-foot distance.

7. **B.** Opening up the case enables you to see how many RAM slots are populated or free. But only the motherboard manual will tell you the maximum a motherboard can handle.

8. **A, B.** Back up the data before going inside the case and use an antistatic wrist strap to control ESD.

9. **C.** Ron's best option is to go with the AGP 8× video card. PCI is very slow in comparison. PCI Express cards can't use an AGP slot, so that option is out.

10. **D.** You could make arguments for B and C, but reusing functional equipment is the greenest way to dispose of them.

PART III

The Complex PC

Advanced Input/Output Devices

In this chapter, you will learn how to
- Explain visual capture devices
- Describe audio devices, both input and output
- Explore game controllers
- Explain television tuners

The people who make devices that plug into computers come up with very inventive ones. They range from visual capture devices that put still or moving pictures in the computer to audio devices for playing or capturing sound.

Games come with their own set of specialized controllers. You can even install a device that enables you to watch broadcast television right from the comfort of your computer chair. This chapter examines all these more advanced input/output devices.

Visual Capture Devices

Scanners, digital cameras, camcorders, and Web-based cameras enable you to take a visual image and import it into the computer. Each device functions similarly, though they operate very differently and for different purposes.

Scanners

You can use a scanner to make digital copies of existing paper photos, documents, drawings, and more. Better scanners give you the option of copying directly from a photographic negative or slide, providing images of stunning visual quality—assuming the original photo was halfway decent, of course! In this section, you'll look at how scanners work and then turn to what you need to know to select the correct scanner for you or your clients.

How Scanners Work

All consumer-level scanners—called *flatbed scanners*—work the same way. You place a photo or other object face down on the glass, close the lid, and then use software to initiate the scan. The scanner runs a bright light along the length of the glass tray once or more to capture the image.

Along with the bright light, the moving scanning arm contains sensors, fine glass and mirrors, and electronics. These work together to translate the light into electrons that the computer can read. Figure 9-1 shows an open scanner.

The scanning software that controls the hardware can vary a lot, depending on the manufacturer. Nearly every manufacturer has some sort of drivers and other software to create an interface between your computer and the scanner. When you push the front button on the Epson Perfection scanner, for example, the Windows Fax and Scan tool opens, enabling you to scan the image and save it to your computer (Figure 9-2).

Figure 9-1
Scanner open with photograph face down

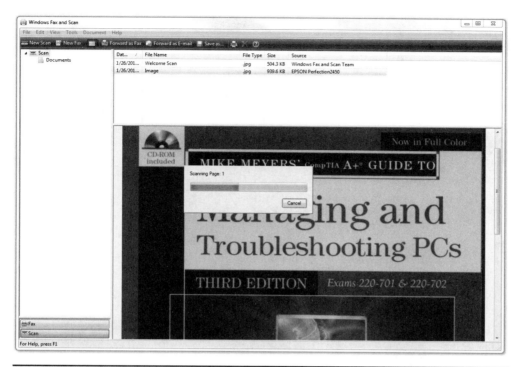

Figure 9-2 Windows Fax and Scan

You can also open your favorite image-editing software first and choose to acquire a file from a scanner. Figure 9-3 shows the process of acquiring an image from a scanner in the popular image-editing application, Adobe Photoshop. As in most such software, you choose File | Import and then select a source. In this case, the scanner uses the traditional TWAIN drivers. *TWAIN* stands for *Technology Without an Interesting Name*—I'm not making this up!—and has been the default driver type for scanners for a long time.

At this point, the drivers and other software controlling the scanner pop up, providing an interface with the scanner (as shown in Figure 9-3). Here you can set the resolution of the image as well as many other options.

 NOTE In addition to loading pictures into your computer, many scanners offer a feature called *optical character recognition (OCR)*, a way to scan a document and have the computer turn the picture into text that you can manipulate by using a word processing program.

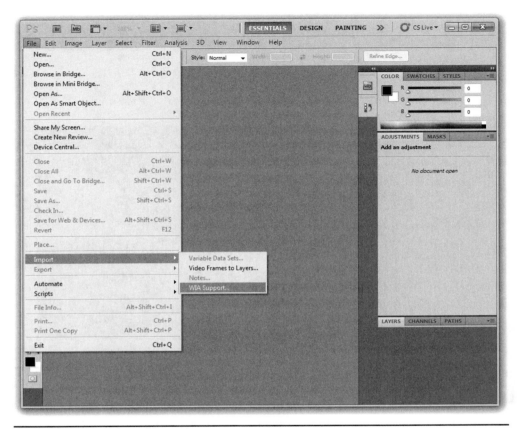

Figure 9-3 Acquiring an image in Photoshop

How to Choose a Scanner

These days, it's hard to find an inadequate scanner. Even inexpensive ones will scan a photograph at high resolution and enable you to bring that photo into your computer. All modern scanners can do 48-bit scans for capturing a lot of color information. Most plug into a Hi-Speed USB 2.0 port, though a few of the better ones come with a FireWire port as well.

NOTE The 48-bit number is a little misleading. It represents three 16-bit sensors, one for each color: red, green, and blue (referred to as RGB). The number of bits reflects how many variations of color can be captured from one spot. An 8-bit scan, for example, can capture 512 variations. Each bit you add doubles the complexity, so a 16-bit scan can capture 65,536 variations from the same capture spot. It's a huge difference!

Judging one scanner from another, therefore, boils down to three factors.

- Quality of the optics, sensors, and electronics
- Capability of scanning transparent objects
- Auto-feeding capability

The quality of the optics, sensors, and electronics makes a big difference when you scan negatives and slides at high resolution. (Scanned photos look fine on almost all scanners.) As a general rule, you get what you pay for with scanners. The more expensive ones have better optics, sensors, and electronics than the cheaper ones.

Scanning transparent objects such as slides or negatives requires special hardware. Figure 9-4 shows my Epson scanner converted to scan negatives. A flatbed scanner without the extra feature cannot scan a negative or slide.

Some scanners offer the option of an autofeed tray (Figure 9-5). This enables you to grab images of documents more swiftly than if you had to do them by hand, one after the other.

Figure 9-4
Scanner with
negative tray

Figure 9-5
MFD (multifunction
device) with
autofeed tray

Autofeed tray

TIP Scanners differ a lot in *grayscale depth*, a number that defines how many shades of gray the scanner can save per dot. This matters if you work with black-and-white images in any significant way, because grayscale depth is usually a much lower number than color depth. Current consumer-level scanners come in 8-bit, 12-bit, and 16-bit grayscale varieties. I recommend 16-bit if you're trying to scan old black-and-white photos.

Installation and Scanning Tips

Most USB and FireWire devices require you to install the software drivers before you plug in the device for the first time. I have run into exceptions, though, so I strongly suggest you read the scanner's documentation before you install.

As a general rule, you should obtain the highest-quality scan you can manage, and then play with the size and image quality when it's time to include it in a Web site or an e-mail. The amount of RAM in your system—and to a lesser extent, the processor speed—dictates how big a file you can handle.

NOTE The "quality" settings for a scan include the color depth and the resolution. Essentially, that means how much information you're telling the device to capture on the image. Color depth is usually 16-bit, though some scanners go beyond that. Resolution is defined by dots per inch (dpi). That translates into how many samples the scanner will take for each inch. A bigger number means higher quality.

The basic rule is to scan at 300 dpi (or 600 dpi if you're scanning negatives). That gives you a lot of room to play when you bring the image into an image-editing program. You can always reduce the quality of the image later.

If you travel a lot, you'll want to make sure to use the locking mechanism for the scanner light assembly. Just be sure to unlock it before you try to use it, or you'll get a light that's stuck in one position. That won't make for very good scans!

 EXAM TIP The CompTIA Strata exam tests you lightly on troubleshooting scanner problems and preventive maintenance issues. Look for questions on using the locking mechanism, keeping the scanner surface clean, and avoiding scanning sharp objects that could damage the scanner.

Digital Cameras and Camcorders

Digital cameras and *camcorders* electronically simulate older film technology and provide a wonderful tool for capturing a moment or moments and then sending that capture to friends and relatives.

Digital cameras excel at capturing still images. They're usually small and boxy (Figure 9-6), though better ones get bigger.

Camcorders record moving pictures well. They're usually shaped round rather than square, though there's a lot of variation out there (Figure 9-7).

Modern digital cameras and camcorders don't just stay in the still/motion roles but can do both. You can record a movie on a small camera, for example, or still images on a camcorder. For exam purposes, though, think of both types of devices as *digital cameras*.

 EXAM TIP The CompTIA Strata exam uses the term *digital camera* to refer to both cameras and camcorders.

Digital cameras include a dizzying array of features and quality, so you need to do your homework to pick the right one for your budget or for a recommendation.

Figure 9-6
Typical small camera

Figure 9-7
Typical small
camcorder

Storage Media—Digital Film for Your Camera

Every consumer-grade still camera saves the pictures it takes onto some type of flash-based *removable storage media*. Think of it as your digital film. Probably the most common removable storage media used in modern digital cameras (and probably your best choice) is the Secure Digital (SD) card (Figure 9-8). You'll learn more about various types of flash-memory cards in Chapter 10.

Most camcorders use SD cards too, though some use high-speed tape or tiny hard drives called Microdrives. The most common tape is called MiniDV (Figure 9-9).

Figure 9-8
Secure Digital card

Figure 9-9
MiniDV tape for
a camcorder

Connection

These days, almost all digital cameras plug directly into a Hi-Speed USB port (Figure 9-10). Another common option, though, is to connect only the camera's storage media to the computer using one of the many digital media readers available.

You can find readers designed specifically for SD cards, as well as other types. Plenty of readers can handle multiple media formats. Many computers come with a decent built-in digital media reader (Figure 9-11).

Camcorders plug into Hi-Speed USB, FireWire, or HDMI ports. FireWire was the connection of choice until late 2010/early 2011 when HDMI started appearing on more camcorders.

Figure 9-10
Camera connecting
to USB port

Figure 9-11
Digital media reader built into computer

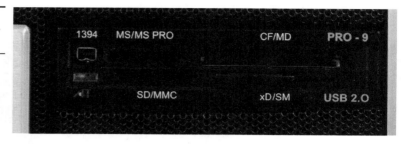

 EXAM TIP Digital cameras plug into Hi-Speed USB, FireWire, or HDMI ports.

Quality

You should consider the amount of information a particular model of camera can capture when comparing camera features. That is expressed as some number of *megapixels*. Instead of light-sensitive film, digital cameras have one or more CCD (charge-coupled device) or CMOS (complementary metal-oxide semiconductor) sensors covered with photosensitive pixels (called *photosites*) to capture the image. The more pixels on the sensor, the higher the resolution of the images it captures.

Not so long ago, a one-megapixel digital camera was the bleeding edge of digital photographic technology, but now you can find cameras with ten times that resolution for a few hundred dollars. As a basis of reference, a two-megapixel camera produces snapshot-sized (4 × 6–inch) pictures with print photograph quality, whereas a five-megapixel unit can produce a high-quality 8 × 10–inch print.

Another feature of most digital cameras is the capability to zoom in on your subject. The way you ideally want to do this is the way film cameras do it, by using the camera's optics—that's the lens. Most cameras above the basic level have some *optical zoom*—meaning the zoom is built into the lens of the camera—but almost all models include multiple levels of *digital zoom*, accomplished by some very clever software in the camera. Choose your camera based on optical zoom: 3× at a minimum or better if you can afford it. Digital zoom is useless.

Form Factor

As was the case with film cameras, size matters on digital cameras. Digital cameras come in several form factors. They range from tiny, ultra-compact models that readily fit in a shirt pocket to monster cameras with huge lenses. Although it's not universally true, the bigger the camera, the more features and sensors it can have. Bigger is usually better in terms of quality. Cameras come in one of two general shapes: a rectangular package into which a lens retracts, or an SLR-type with a lens that sticks out of the body. Figure 9-12 shows both styles.

Figure 9-12
Typical digital
cameras

HD vs. SD

Camcorders capture video in one of two formats, *High Definition (HD)* or *Standard Definition (SD)*. The two formats mean a couple of things. HD captures will be widescreen to match HD televisions. SD captures stay within the 4:3 aspect ratio to match older-style televisions and monitors. HD captures higher-resolution images for the most part, though a high-end SD camera will outperform a lower-end HD camera any day.

Web Cameras

PC cameras, often called *webcams* because their most common use is for Internet video communication, are fairly new to the world of advanced I/O devices. Too many people run out and buy the cheapest one, not appreciating the vast difference between a discount webcam and more expensive models; nor do they take the time to configure the webcam properly. Let's consider some of the features you should look for when buying webcams and some of the problems you can run into when using them.

The biggest issue with webcams is the image quality. Webcams measure their resolution in pixels. You can find webcams with resolutions of as few as 100,000 pixels and webcams with millions of pixels. Most people who use webcams agree that 1.3 million pixels (megapixels) is pretty much the highest resolution you can use before your video becomes so large it will bog down even a broadband connection.

The next issue with webcams is the frame rate, that is, the number of times the camera "takes your picture" each second. Higher frame rates make for smoother video; 30 frames per second is considered the best. A good camera with a high megapixel resolution and fast frame rate will provide you with excellent video conferencing capabilities. Figure 9-13 shows Mike Meyers using a headset to chat via webcam using Skype software.

Most people who use online video also want a microphone. Many cameras come with microphones, or you can use your own. Those who do a lot of video chatting may prefer to get a camera without a microphone and then buy a good-quality headset with which to speak and listen.

Figure 9-13
Video chatting by
webcam with Skype

Many cameras now can track you when you move, a handy feature for fidgety folks using video conferencing! This interesting technology recognizes a human face with little or no "training" and rotates its position to keep your face in the picture. Some companies even add funny extras, which, although not very productive, are good for a laugh (Figure 9-14).

Figure 9-14
This webcam
program's animated
character mirrors
your movements as
you conference with
friends or coworkers.

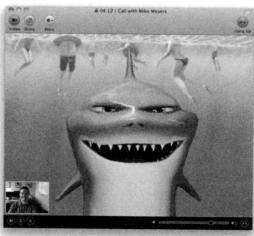

Almost all webcams use USB connections, though many are built into monitors and laptops. Windows comes with a limited set of webcam drivers, so always make sure to install the drivers supplied with the camera before you plug it in. Most webcams use Hi-Speed USB, so make sure you're plugging your webcam into a Hi-Speed USB port.

Once the camera's plugged in, you'll need to test it. All cameras come with some type of program, but finding the program can be a challenge. Some brands put the program in the system tray (also called the notification area), some place it in Computer (or My Computer), others put it in the Control Panel, and some do all three! Figure 9-15 shows the Control Panel applet that appeared when I installed the webcam driver.

The biggest challenge to using webcams is getting your applications to recognize that your webcam is available and configured for use. Every program does this differently, but the steps are basically the same (with plenty of exceptions):

1. Tell the program you want to use a camera.

2. Tell the program whether you want the camera to turn on automatically when you chat.

3. Configure the image quality.

4. Test the camera.

If you're having problems with a camera, always go through these general I/O configuration steps first, as this will clear up most problems. If you're still having trouble getting the camera to work in a program, be sure to turn off all other programs that may be using the camera. Windows allows only one program at a time to use a webcam.

Figure 9-15
Camera Settings
applet

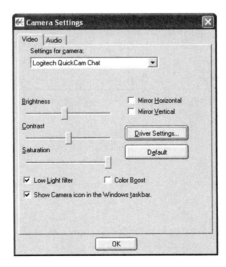

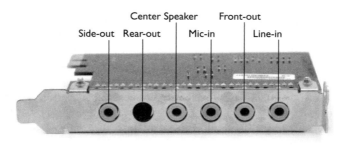

Figure 9-16   Mini-audio jacks

Audio Devices

Sound controllers enable the computer to play sound and to record sound. All modern computers come with sound controllers built into the motherboard. (Older computers that didn't have built-in sound came with an add-on sound card.)

The simplest sound controllers have three 3.5 mm audio ports, called jacks. More complex sound controllers have five or six jacks (Figure 9-16).

Each jack has a specific purpose, such as audio out for connecting to speakers or headphones. Most sound controllers have color-coded jacks for the specific connections. Table 9-1 displays the name, color, and purpose of typical mini-audio jacks.

Connector	Color	Purpose
Line out	Green	Main speakers or headphones
Microphone	Pink	Recording sounds
Line in	Blue	Sound input from an audio device
Subwoofer	Orange	Thumping bass with a subwoofer attached
Rear surround sound	Black	Rear speakers
Middle surround sound	Gray	Extra speakers in a 7.1 sound setup

Table 9-1   Names and Color Codes for 3.5 mm Audio Jacks

Sound Output

The computer uses the sound processor and audio software to play music and sounds through speakers or headphones. Better motherboards offer high-definition audio processors. One HD standard licensed by Intel, the CPU maker, is called Azalea. Typical audio software includes the Windows Media Player, which comes with Windows, and Apple iTunes, which you can download from apple.com (Figure 9-17).

Do yourself a favor if you can afford it and replace an inexpensive pair of speakers with a high-quality 2.1 rig from Klipsch (my favorite) or Logitech (Figure 9-18). The 2 refers to the pair of stereo speakers or satellites. The 1 refers to the subwoofer that provides the bass. The difference in the sound experience between a pair of sub-$50 speakers and a ~$100–150 2.1 set is simply stunning. Your ears will love you for it.

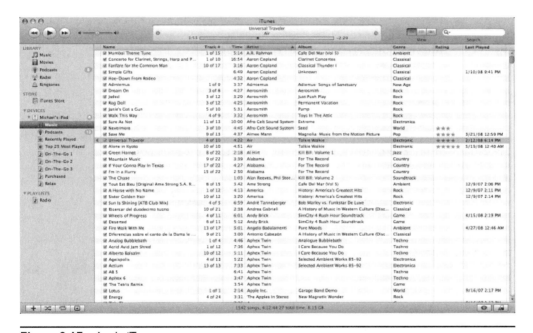

Figure 9-17   Apple iTunes

Figure 9-18
Klipsch ProMedia 2.1
speakers

NOTE For creating a surround-sound experience in a media room, try a 5.1 or 7.1 speaker set. These have a single subwoofer and multiple satellites for placing in the rear and center of the room.

Sound Input

The computer uses the sound processor, audio software, and a microphone or other audio device to record sound. All OSes come with some recording capability, although it is usually limited. Windows includes the simplistic Sound Recorder (Figure 9-19).

To record your favorite garage band requires more robust programs and microphones. Adobe Audition is a great choice, but there are many excellent audio programs available. Some are even freeware, such as Audacity (Figure 9-20).

Figure 9-19
Not much to it!

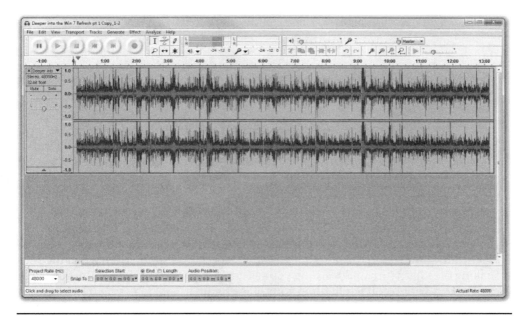

Figure 9-20 Audacity in action

Game Controllers

Video games come with a host of crazy controllers for controlling aspects of the game. You can get a *joystick* for controlling flight simulation games (flight sims), for example (Figure 9-21). A *game pad* offers versatile input for games ranging from racing games to fighting games (Figure 9-22).

Figure 9-21
A joystick

Figure 9-22
A game pad

Force feedback game controllers are output devices as well as input devices. It can be quite thrilling and add to the realism of a game, especially a simulation, when the stick is shaking on a hard turn and resisting your efforts. Likewise, it's pure gaming joy when the stick kicks with recoil while firing your plane's guns.

All modern game controllers plug into a USB port. Decent to good force feedback controllers will also have a power adapter to plug into a wall socket.

Ancient game controllers had a dedicated port, usually as part of the sound card, called a MIDI/joystick port. The port had 15 pin sockets in two rows (Figure 9-23).

 EXAM TIP A DB-15 connection with fifteen pins or sockets in two rows is for MIDI/joystick connections. You won't find this on a modern system, but you might see it on the CompTIA Strata exam.

Figure 9-23
A MIDI/joystick port

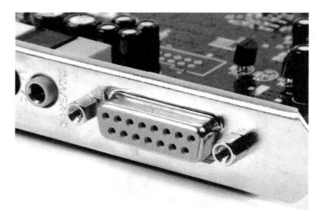

TV Tuners

With a *TV tuner*, you can have it all in one package: a computer and the latest TV shows as well. Most local stations (in the United States, at least) broadcast high-definition signals, so with the proper TV tuner, you can watch HDTV without any of the artifacting you see with both cable and satellite feeds. Plus you can make use of typical cable or satellite feeds to watch television as you would with a regular TV. To make it all happen requires four components: a tuner device, an antenna or cable connection, a tuning application, and some sort of program guide. We'll look at troubleshooting at the end.

Tuner Hardware

TV tuners come in just about every expansion option available for computers: expansion cards that plug into PCI or PCIe slots on the motherboard; PC Card or ExpressCard for portable computers; or Hi-Speed USB for desktop and laptop computers. Figure 9-24 shows a PCIe version of an ATI tuner card.

To install a TV tuner, follow the PCIe card installation procedures outlined in Chapter 8.

 NOTE TV tuners often include components for video capture, so you can get both devices on one card or expansion device.

To pick up a signal on the TV tuner, just as with a standalone television, you need some source. Most can handle a cable TV connection, for example, or an over-the-air

---

Figure 9-24
ATI TV tuner card

PART III

antenna. Figure 9-25 shows a USB Hauppauge HDTV tuner card with retractable antenna. For such a small device, it picks up HDTV signals quite well. You'll get the best results for uncompressed HD signals by using a serious, mounted-on-the-rooftop metal antenna.

Tuner hardware comes with a standard coaxial connection. You can plug in a cable or satellite source just as you would any regular television.

Tuner Software

Once you've installed the hardware, you need to load the specific application or applications that make the tuner work as a tuner. If you have Windows Media Center (through either that version of Windows XP, Windows Vista Ultimate, or Windows 7), that will often be the tool of choice. Tuner card distributors bundle third-party applications with their cards. Figure 9-26 shows the EyeTV software enabling the computer to show television shows.

Tuner Troubleshooting

The two biggest issues with TV tuner devices are operating system compatibility and poor reception. Some cards simply don't work with Windows Vista, due to driver incompatibility or some other issue. The only fix for this problem is to use one that does work.

The antenna that comes with your tuner should enable you to pick up TV broadcasts in most places, certainly around cities. But a small sliver of metal can only do so well, so you'll experience stuttering, lost frames that may or may not make the program you're viewing watchable. So an antenna used primarily for portable computing, such as the telescoping model pictured in Figure 9-25, is great, but if you install a tuner in a stationary computer, consider investing in a proper outdoor antenna.

Figure 9-25
Hauppauge TV tuner
with retractable
antenna

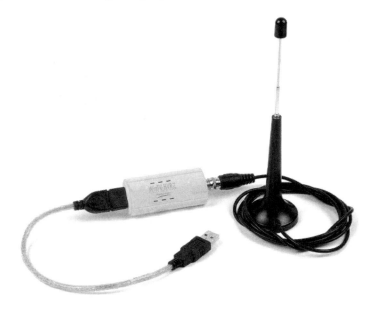

Figure 9-26
EyeTV tuner
application

Chapter Review

Creative manufacturers have invented many ways to interact with the computer. Earlier chapters looked at the standard devices, such as mice, trackballs, keyboards, and monitors. This chapter looked at more advanced I/O devices.

Visual capture devices enable you to bring a static or moving picture from life into the computer. We discussed four variations:

- Scanners
- Digital still cameras
- Camcorders
- Webcams

Scanners capture images from other images, so you can scan an old and treasured photograph to bring it into the computer for editing. Digital cameras, both still cameras and camcorders, capture images or movies of what you can see. There are many styles and feature sets. Webcams are essentially just simple camcorders designed to work with the computer for doing things like teleconferencing.

Sound controllers enable the computer to play sound and to record sound. All modern computers come with sound controllers built into the motherboard. The standard sound connection for devices is the 3.5 mm mini-audio jack. You'll find connections for speakers, microphones, and more.

Game controllers enable you to interact with games in ways that are more intuitive than just a keyboard or a mouse. A flight sim works better with a joystick than a mouse, for example. A game pad helps bring those fighting games alive. All modern game controllers plug into USB ports.

TV tuners turn your computer into a television set. The reception of broadcast TV signals can be picked up by an antenna and displayed on your monitor.

Questions

1. What device is associated with TWAIN drivers?

    A. Camcorder

    B. Scanner

    C. TV tuner

    D. Webcam

2. Paula wants to scan in old photographs and share them with her friends online. She places a photo onto the scanner bed and uses the included utility to start scanning. She notices, however, that the scanner's light isn't moving, and when it is finished, the imported image does not look right. What most likely happened?

    A. The scanner was not plugged in.

    B. The scanner was not using the correct drivers.

    C. The scanner's light assembly was locked.

    D. The original photo was bad.

3. Which is the most common memory card format used with digital cameras?

    A. Secure Digital

    B. CompactFlash

    C. Memory Stick

    D. xD Picture Card

4. Digital camera quality is measured by several different factors, but how is the maximum resolution image a digital camera can take expressed?

    A. Zoom range

    B. Number of colors

    C. Number of bits

    D. Number of megapixels

5. In terms of digital camcorder quality, which of the following is true?

    A. Always HD over SD

    B. Always SD over HD

    C. A low-end SD camera over a high-end HD camera

    D. A high-end SD camera over a low-end HD camera

6. In Windows, how many programs can use a webcam at the same time?

    A. One

    B. Two

    C. Three

    D. Four

7. What does a sound controller do?

   A. It enables the playback of sound.

   B. It enables a user to adjust the volume level of the speakers.

   C. It enables the playback and recording of sound.

   D. It enables the recording of sound.

8. Which speaker configuration ensures the best surround-sound experience?

   A. Internal PC speaker

   B. 2.1 system

   C. 5.1 system

   D. 7.1 system

9. How does force feedback change a standard game controller?

   A. It increases the sensitivity of the controls.

   B. It shakes the controller and increases resistances in response to what is happening on-screen.

   C. It shakes the user's chair in response to what is happening on-screen.

   D. It changes nothing. All game controllers have force feedback.

10. What are the two biggest concerns when installing a TV tuner card that will be used with an antenna? (Select two.)

    A. Compatibility

    B. Reception

    C. Number of channels

    D. Weight

Answers

1. **B.** TWAIN drivers enable a computer and a scanner to communicate.

2. **C.** Scanners include a locking mechanism to keep the light assembly in place while the scanner is being transported.

3. **A.** Secure Digital cards are commonly used in digital cameras and camcorders.

4. **D.** The number of megapixels determines the maximum resolution of a digital camera.

5. **D.** A higher-end SD camera will outperform a lower-end HD camera any day.

6. **A.** In Windows, only one program at a time can use the webcam.

7. **C.** The sound controller enables the playback and recording of sound on a computer.

8. **D.** A 7.1 sound system includes seven satellites (enabling rear and center channel sounds) and a subwoofer for the best surround-sound experience.

9. **B.** Force feedback turns a normal game controller into an input and output device that shakes the controller and increases its resistance in response to what is happening on-screen.

10. **A, B.** The two most important factors to consider when installing a TV tuner card are whether it will be compatible with your OS and whether or not you will get good reception using your antenna.

CHAPTER 10

Advanced Storage Topics

In this chapter, you will learn how to
- Explain how hard drives store data
- Describe the differences between traditional hard drives and flash-based storage
- Explain how SCSI technology works

In Chapter 4, you learned about floppy drives, hard drives, and optical drives, but these drives are more than just their physical components. An OS can only read to and write from a properly configured hard drive. Flash-based storage, including solid-state hard drives, removes the mechanical components of traditional hard drives, increases speeds, and saves energy. Before eSATA and USB emerged as dominant external storage connectors, the SCSI interface was the only high-performance connection available. This chapter discusses all of these topics, so let's dive in!

Using Hard Drives

A freshly installed hard drive isn't useful to anyone until it knows what to do with itself. It needs a bit of programming to understand what it will do with the data it stores. How this data is stored is determined by two things: partitions and formatting.

Imagine a farmer's field with crops laid out in every direction. If the farmer is growing corn and potatoes, he or she doesn't mix them together. The field would be divided into sections: one area for corn, another for potatoes. In hard drive terms, this is called partitioning.

Partitioning creates distinct sections on a hard drive. Hard drives can have a single partition or multiple partitions, and each partition appears in Windows as a separate drive (Figure 10-1). For instance, when you see your C: drive in Computer in Windows Vista/7 (or My Computer in Windows XP), that is a partition.

But a partitioned hard drive is still one step short of a functioning hard drive. *Formatting* creates a file system for the drive—essentially a big spreadsheet that tracks what piece of data is stored in which location (Figure 10-2). Without a file system, the OS wouldn't know where anything is. Windows supports three different file systems: FAT, FAT32, and NTFS.

Figure 10-1
A hard drive with
two partitions

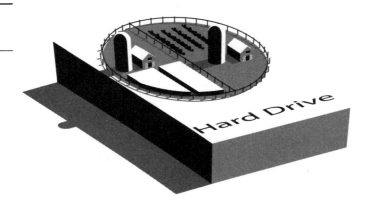

All OSes support the *File Allocation Table (FAT)* format, the oldest format of the three. FAT does not support partitions larger than 2.1 GB and includes no security, so it's not incredibly useful today.

FAT32 is the 32-bit version of FAT and can handle partitions as large as 2 TB. It is more efficient than FAT but, again, has no security. You'll find FAT and FAT32 used in flash media storage (see the next section), but not so much on modern hard drives.

NTFS is the best formatting solution for today's hard drives. It can handle partitions up to 16 TB and includes built-in compression and encryption capabilities. And in case you're curious, NTFS stands for *New Technology File System*. Considering Microsoft released it in 1983, the name has a certain ironic twist that just gets better each year.

NOTE Compressing a hard drive creates more space for storing more data. Encrypting data on a hard drive prevents anyone from accessing the data without logging in with the user account that encrypted the data.

Figure 10-2
A file system

Once you (or the computer's manufacturer) partitions and formats a hard drive, it's open for business. You learned a lot about how traditional hard drives work in Chapter 4, so let's explore some alternative technologies and see how they compare.

 EXAM TIP FAT stands for File Allocation Table. NTFS stands for New Technology File System.

Flash-Based Storage

The traditional hard disk drive (HDD) found in most computers operates like a highly advanced record player. A record player (if you haven't seen one in a while, or *ever*) uses a swiveling arm with a needle on it to pick up vibrations in a spiral groove (Figure 10-3). The vibrations are amplified and played back as sound.

Similarly, multiple platters spin at high speed in an HDD, while tiny parts at the end of a swiveling arm read and write data to the drive. An HDD stores a lot of data cheaply but is relatively fragile and slow. In contrast, *flash-based storage* uses no moving parts, making it faster and tougher.

PART III

Figure 10-3
A record player

Flash-based storage uses small memory chips instead of platters to store data, similar to how RAM works. Unlike RAM, however, these chips are *nonvolatile*, meaning they retain the stored data even without power. You can write to them, read from them, and delete data just as you would on an HDD.

Many implementations of flash-based storage are portable, so they are somewhat similar to rewritable optical discs, but much easier and faster to use.

In addition, flash-based storage can be found in many portable devices, including phones, MP3 players, GPS navigation systems, e-book readers, and more (Figure 10-4). Every time you pop a memory card into your digital camera, that's flash-based storage. Some devices also use built-in flash-based storage that cannot be removed.

Invented in the 1980s, flash-based storage took off in a big way in the late 1990s with the rise in digital camera use. At first, these memory cards were expensive and only stored a few megabytes. As prices dropped, memory card use became more widespread. Nowadays, you can find affordable 16 GB cards (or incredibly expensive 64 GB cards) that hold thousands of photos, music albums, or videos.

Popular memory card formats include:

- CompactFlash
- Secure Digital (SD) (Figure 10-5), as well as SDHC, SDXC, miniSD, and microSD
- xD-Picture Card
- Memory Stick

Figure 10-4
Devices using flash-based storage

Figure 10-5
An SD memory card

The formats are not interchangeable—a camera designed to handle CompactFlash cards, for example, can't read from or write to Memory Sticks. Some professional-level devices have two memory card slots, enabling you to double your storage capacity.

When you finish using the memory card and want to download the data back to your computer, you have two options: plug in the device directly using a USB cable or use a memory card reader and writer. There are as many types of memory card readers as there are memory cards, but there are also *multi-card readers and writers* (Figure 10-6). These devices have slots for multiple memory card formats. Some can read from and write to as many as 56 different formats.

NOTE Memory card readers and writers can be internal or external. Many laptops include slots for reading from and writing to at least one memory card format, but you can also purchase external memory card readers and writers that plug into a USB port.

Figure 10-6
Multi-card reader
and writer

Many people use USB flash drives (also known as jump drives or thumb drives) to easily move files from one computer to another (Figure 10-7). These devices use chips similar to those found in memory cards but have a built-in USB connector. That means you can plug one into any computer and the OS can read from it and write to it immediately. With capacities reaching 256 GB or more, USB flash drives can out-store optical discs by a wide margin.

In recent years, the cost of flash-based storage has fallen far enough for it to be used in place of traditional hard drives. A *solid-state drive (SSD)* uses the same chips found in memory cards but packages many of them together inside a standard hard drive enclosure (Figure 10-8). These drives use the same connectors as traditional drives (primarily SATA) and work the same in Windows and other OSes.

 EXAM TIP HDD refers to traditional, magnetic disk hard drives. SSD refers to flash-based, solid-state drives.

Traditional Storage vs. Flash-Based Storage

A comparison of an SSD to an HDD shows that both have strengths and weaknesses. The decision to buy one or the other is primarily based on storage needs versus cost.

SSDs have four advantages over HDDs:

1. Speed
2. Physical durability
3. Energy use
4. Storage efficiency

Figure 10-7
USB flash drives

Figure 10-8
A solid-state drive

HDDs have three advantages over SSDs:

1. Price

2. Capacity

3. Electronic longevity

Let's examine both sets of advantages.

Why SSDs Rule

Most of the advantages to using flash-based storage over traditional hard drives stem from the fact that traditional hard drives contain several moving pieces. There are arms twitching and platters spinning at 7200 RPM. All of those tiny pieces can malfunction or break.

The fact that there needs to be movement at all makes traditional hard drives very slow devices, compared to the rest of a computer. Traditional hard drives also use more energy to drive all the moving parts.

With flash-based storage, the memory chips just sit there, motionless, and work. There are no moving parts to break or power, so flash-based devices are tougher and use less energy. Many of them are also faster, since there is no need to spin up platters. It also makes them quieter.

NOTE Do you remember in Chapter 4 when I said that hard drive manufacturers label their devices using misleading math, saying that 1 TB is 1000 gigabytes instead of 1024 gigabytes? Flash-based drives don't do that. There's a complicated reason for it, but just know that when a flash-based drive lists its capacity as 1 TB, it means 1 terabyte. That's 1024 gigabytes.

PART III

SSDs retrieve data more efficiently than HDDs. This enables them to ignore one of the primary causes for slowness with HDDs, what's called fragmentation.

Remember the farmer's field? When data is deleted and replaced on traditional hard drives, the old "corn" and new "corn" aren't separated. New data will be written into the gaps between old data, which is not very efficient (Figure 10-9). This is *fragmentation*. Fragmentation can be a source of slowdowns for your system, since it takes longer to read the data if it is spread out in many places on the platters.

A specific utility in Windows (and other OSes) called Disk Defragmenter can fix this fragmentation. Windows Vista and Windows 7 run it automatically. With Windows XP, you need to run the utility manually.

Because SSDs don't have a read/write arm to move to retrieve data, fragmentation doesn't matter. Data is just retrieved.

NOTE SSDs are great for laptops because of their small size and low power consumption.

Why HDDs Rule

Platter-based hard drives have been around since nearly the beginning of the PC. Manufacturers have mastered the art of creating HDDs.

Initially they cost a lot and had very low capacity. The first HDD for the PC, for example, cost $2,000 and held a whopping 5 MB.

Figure 10-9
Data fragmentation

Today, HDDs offer the best capacity at the lowest price of any fast storage device. You can buy a two-terabyte (TB) drive for under $100, as of this writing. That's 2000 gigabytes of storage. A 1-TB SSD is the biggest you can get right now, and they cost over $3000.

Perhaps the biggest knock on SSDs is that repeatedly deleting and rewriting of data will, over time, make the drives slower in writing data. (They stay fast on read speeds.) The early SSDs suffered badly from this problem. Newer ones aren't so bad and will undoubtedly improve.

Until SSDs improve the rewrite-degrade problem, you need to avoid any use of a disk defragmenting program. If you are using Windows Vista or Windows 7 with a solid-state drive, you should disable the automatic defragmentation schedule to avoid damaging them.

To disable automatic defragmenting, go to Start | Control Panel and select System and Maintenance in Windows Vista or System and Security in Windows 7. Under Administrative Tools, click Defragment your hard drive (don't worry, you won't). In Windows Vista, uncheck the Run on a schedule (recommended) option (Figure 10-10). In Windows 7, click Configure schedule and uncheck Run on a schedule (recommended).

NOTE You will need administrative privileges to change the Disk Defragmenter schedule.

EXAM TIP For the CompTIA Strata exam, make sure you know the key differences between SSDs and HDDs.

Figure 10-10
Uncheck or deselect
this option

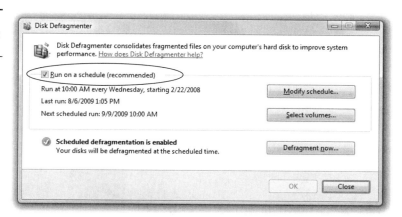

SCSI

The *Small Computer System Interface (SCSI)* is an old technology dating from the late 1970s (Figure 10-11). Many peripherals, including scanners and printers, used SCSI because it was faster than the other connectors available at that time.

With the introduction of USB, FireWire, and eSATA connectors, SCSI ports have all but disappeared from most computers. Unlike the ancient floppy disk drive, however, SCSI still clings to life as a high-performance interface option for hard drives and optical drives. In fact, the newest versions of SCSI are still faster than the most advanced SATA devices.

SCSI Chains

One of the key features of SCSI is the *SCSI chain*. Most interfaces work on the principle of one connector, one device. A SATA port, for example, enables a single hard drive to connect to the motherboard. Some connectors, like PATA, string together two hard drives on a single ribbon cable. SCSI takes this concept one step further with the idea of the chain.

The chain begins inside the computer. Few motherboards include built-in SCSI connectors, so a separate device known as a *SCSI host adapter* must be installed (Figure 10-12). This typically adds two SCSI connectors to a system—one inside the case for internal SCSI devices, and one on the back of the computer for external SCSI devices.

There are many types of SCSI connectors, each with a different number of pins. Typical internal SCSI devices, for example, connect to a 68-pin ribbon cable with multiple connectors that looks and functions just like a PATA cable (Figure 10-13).

External devices can use 50-, 68-, or 80-pin connectors, depending on the SCSI style being used. These external connectors are *D*-shaped so you can't plug them in backward (Figure 10-14).

Figure 10-11
The SCSI connector and port

Figure 10-12
A SCSI host adapter

Figure 10-13
A SCSI cable with
multiple connectors

Figure 10-14
An external SCSI
connector

Figure 10-15   A daisy chain of SCSI devices

Each device connected to a host adapter is a part of the SCSI chain. Chains can be internal, external, or both. While internal chains are achieved using ribbon cables with multiple connectors, external chains are accomplished by connecting one device to another in what is known as a *daisy chain* (Figure 10-15). For example, you could have a SCSI scanner connected to a SCSI optical drive connected to a SCSI hard drive connected to the host adapter. This daisy chain can extend to up to 15 devices. You could, of course, use only a single device with the SCSI port, but the capability is handy if you have a lot of SCSI devices.

If you connect more than one device to the same SCSI chain, you need to provide a way for the host adapter to differentiate them. The *SCSI ID* is a number ranging from 0 to 15 that is assigned to each device on the SCSI chain. Each device receives a unique number. The method used to set the SCSI ID changes from device to device.

Chapter Review

A newly installed hard drive can't do anything until it is programmed to hold data. This process includes partitions, which divide the space on the hard drive, and formatting, which creates the file system that dictates how files are stored. Windows PCs have traditionally used one of three file systems: FAT, FAT32, and NTFS. NTFS is the best choice because it can handle the largest capacity and includes compression and encryption capabilities.

Flash-based storage uses memory chips to store data. Varieties of flash-based storage include built-in storage in devices like iPhones, e-Book readers, and more; removable memory cards used with cameras, camcorders, and MP3 players; USB thumb drives; and solid-state drives used to replace traditional primary hard drives.

Flash-based storage improves upon traditional hard drives by being faster and more physically durable. SSDs use less electricity than HDDs, and they store and retrieve data more efficiently. HDDs hold their own by being much less expensive than SSDs and with more capacity. HDDs don't degrade over time like SSDs.

SCSI is an older interface technology used for many devices, including hard drives, optical drives, scanners, printers, and more. SCSI is used for internal and external devices. Multiple SCSI devices can be linked together into a SCSI chain. Each device in the chain has a unique SCSI ID.

Questions

1. Which process creates the spaces on a hard drive that can be formatted?

   A. Defragmenting

   B. Partitioning

   C. Deleting

   D. Installing

2. What does a hard drive's file system do?

   A. Reorganizes pieces of data so that the hard drive is more efficient

   B. Encrypts data so that other users cannot access it

   C. Organizes the drive so that it can store and retrieve data

   D. Compresses the data so that more information can be stored

3. Which file system is the best?

   A. FAT

   B. FAT32

   C. NTFS

   D. SCSI

4. How many moving parts does flash-based storage use?

   A. One

   B. Two

   C. Three

   D. None

5. Which of the following is *not* a memory card format?

   A. Memory Stick

   B. CompactFlash

   C. xD Picture Card

   D. Picture Stick

6. Which device is designed to read multiple memory card formats?

   A. iPhone

   B. Multi-card reader and writer

   C. Scanner

   D. USB thumb drive

PART III

7. Which advantage does flash-based storage *not* have over traditional hard drives?

   A. Flash-based storage is compatible with multiple operating systems.

   B. Flash-based storage is more efficient.

   C. Flash-based storage is faster.

   D. Flash-based storage is tougher.

8. What action should you take after installing a solid-state primary hard drive?

   A. Disable the firewall.

   B. Enable disk compression.

   C. Disable antivirus software.

   D. Disable automatic disk defragmenting.

9. What is the maximum number of devices that can be connected to a SCSI chain?

   A. Two

   B. Five

   C. Nine

   D. Fifteen

10. What does the SCSI ID do?

   A. Uniquely identifies a SCSI device on a SCSI chain

   B. Determines the number of devices that can be connected to a SCSI chain

   C. Enables access to the contents of the SCSI device

   D. Determines which device drivers to install

Answers

1. **B.** The usable spaces on a hard drive are created by partitioning the hard drive.

2. **C.** The file system enables the hard drive to store and retrieve data.

3. **C.** NTFS is the best file system because it has a high maximum capacity and includes compression and encryption capabilities.

4. **D.** Flash-based storage uses no moving parts.

5. **D.** Picture Stick is not a memory card format.

6. **B.** A multi-card reader and writer is designed to read from and write to multiple memory card formats.

7. **A.** Both traditional and solid-state hard drives can be used with multiple operating systems.

8. **D.** After installing a solid-state drive as your primary hard drive, you should disable automatic disk defragmenting to prevent damaging the drive.

9. **D.** Up to fifteen devices can be connected to a single SCSI chain.

10. **A.** A SCSI ID uniquely identifies a SCSI device on a SCSI chain.

CHAPTER 11

Printers

In this chapter, you will learn how to
- Explain the characteristics and functions of printers
- Demonstrate the ability to set up a printer
- Demonstrate green printing practices

If you stop and think about it, you might realize how incredible printers are. You're taking something that only exists as 1s and 0s inside a computer and turning it into a physical object that exists in the real world. Printers basically create something out of nothing—a hundred years ago, they would have called that magic.

Besides that, the world needs printing. Businesses couldn't operate if they didn't have a way of creating physical copies of documents, and governments across the world would crumble if they didn't have a way of printing out arbitrary forms for people to fill out. Because printers are so necessary, you'll find them everywhere—schools, hospitals, offices, homes, and even grocery stores. If you're interested in dealing with technology at all, you'll find it necessary to know a thing or two about printers.

Common Printers

Printers, as you probably know, output data from a computer onto paper. Printers can print text as well as pictures, and there are even 3-D printers out there capable of printing out three-dimensional objects. The printers that the Strata exam focuses on are the more mundane two-dimensional kind.

There are lots of different types of printers out there, with names like dye-sublimation, thermal, or dot-matrix, and they all work very differently. Fortunately for you, there are really only two types of printers as far as most of the world (and the Strata exam) is concerned—inkjet and laser.

Inkjet Printers

Inkjet printers create printouts by squirting ink out of special inkjet cartridges. They use both black and colored ink cartridges, and they can combine ink colors to create a wide range of hues. Because of this, people use inkjet printers for both text and images. Inkjet printers use either liquid ink cartridges or solid, wax-based ink cartridges. Figure 11-1 shows a typical inkjet printer.

Figure 11-1
A typical inkjet
printer

An inkjet printer is a *nonimpact* printer because its print mechanism never actually touches the paper. Because an inkjet printer processes an entire page at a time before it starts to print it, it is referred to as a *page* printer. The inkjet printer uses a *friction feed* mechanism to feed paper through the printer. Sheets of paper are stacked in the paper tray, where small rollers press down to create friction and pull a sheet of paper through the printer.

Most liquid inkjet printers and all solid inkjet printers use a thermal process to eject ink onto the paper. The printing element heats up, boiling the ink in the case of liquid inkjet printers, and melting it in the case of solid inkjet printers. A tiny bubble of ink forms on the end of the print nozzle. Once the bubble gets big enough, it pops, at which point electrically charged plates deflect the ink onto the paper. Sounds kind of messy, but it's actually precise.

An inkjet print head contains between 300 and 600 nozzles, each about the diameter of a human hair. Figure 11-2 illustrates a typical inkjet print head. When the inkjet cartridge is not in use, pump pressure keeps the ink from leaking out the nozzle.

Epson printers use a different, proprietary inkjet technology featuring a special crystal at the back of the ink reservoir that flexes when an electric current is applied to it. When the crystal flexes, it forces a drop of ink out of the nozzle. The way it flexes determines the size and placement of the resulting drop.

A common problem with inkjet printers is the tendency for the ink inside the jets to dry out when the printer is not used, even for a relatively short time. To counter this problem, all inkjet printers move the print head to a special park position that keeps the ink from drying.

Except for replacing the inkjet cartridges and print heads, you don't need to do much maintenance. In some cases, you may need to replace the rubber paper rollers or tracking belts, but most serious repairs are simply not cost-effective. The low cost of new liquid ink inkjet printers makes them candidates for replacement rather than repair. The solid ink printers, on the other hand, are very expensive and should be repaired rather than replaced.

PART III

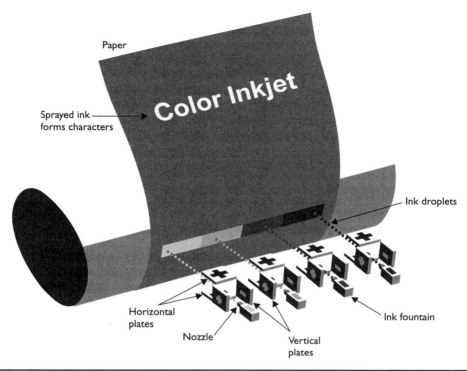

Figure 11-2 Detail of an inkjet print head

Laser Printers

Laser printers rely on the photoconductive properties of certain organic compounds. *Photoconductive* means that particles of these compounds, when exposed to light (that's the photo part), will conduct electricity.

NOTE Laser printers use lasers as a light source because of their precision. LED or light-emitting diode printers work exactly the same as laser printers, except that they use tiny LEDs as a light source instead of lasers. Both types of printer are usually called *laser printers*.

Unlike inkjet printers, the relatively high initial cost of laser printers makes their repair a practical and popular option. Figure 11-3 shows a typical laser printer.

Like inkjet printers, laser printers are nonimpact page printers—the print mechanism never touches the paper, and the entire page is imaged before being transferred to paper. Some laser printers support *duplex* printing, which enables printing on both sides of the paper, either through a built-in mechanism or an add-on duplexing tray device. (We'll talk more about duplexing in the section "Green Printing.") Modern laser printers are capable of resolutions as high as 2400 × 2400 dots per inch (dpi).

Figure 11-3
A typical laser
printer

 EXAM TIP Know that printer resolution is measured in dots per inch (dpi) and printer speed is typically measured by the number of printed pages per minute (ppm).

It used to be that color wasn't available in laser printers—at least, not without spending prohibitively big bucks! The price of laser printing in color has dropped dramatically, however, so you can expect to see full-color laser printers deployed in the workplace, though they're still not as common as black-and-white laser printers.

Installing Printers

You need to take a moment to understand how Windows handles printing, and then you'll see how to install and configure printers.

To Windows, a "printer" is not a physical device; it is a *program* that controls one or more physical printers. The *physical* printer is called a "print device" in Windows (although I continue to use the term "printer" for most purposes, just like almost every tech on the planet). Printer drivers and a spooler are present, but in Windows they are integrated into the printer itself (Figure 11-4). This arrangement gives Windows amazing flexibility. For example, one printer can support multiple print devices, enabling a system to act as a print server. If one print device goes down, the printer software automatically redirects the output to a working print device.

 NOTE The print *spooler* is software used by the OS for channeling print jobs from the PC to the printer. You can see the spooler status either by double-clicking the printer's icon in the Printers applet or by clicking the tiny printer icon in the system tray if it's present. (If you're having a problem, the icon is almost always there.)

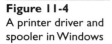

Figure 11-4
A printer driver and
spooler in Windows

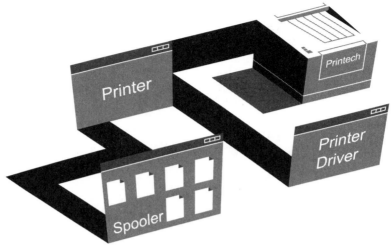

Physical Connection

Print devices connect through a multipurpose port, such as USB, FireWire, or parallel; or wirelessly through Bluetooth, Wi-Fi, or infrared. USB and parallel ports are the most common connections for printers, but for some reason most printers don't come with the appropriate cable when you buy them. Make sure to buy a cable when you purchase a printer. Getting that fancy new printer home is going to be a disappointment if you can't use it!

You might encounter a dedicated serial printer or a SCSI (Small Computer Systems Interface) printer, but these are so rare as to be almost not worth mentioning. Some printers have a slot for an add-on network card, so you can connect them directly to a network switch, just like a PC. Finally, you can connect to a print server on a network and install a networked printer rather than a local printer.

Setting Up Printers

Most of the time, a printer will come with a driver disc of some sort, which you insert into your computer's optical drive. The on-screen instructions usually tell you what to do, right down to when you should plug the printer in. Installing a printer is the art of inserting a disc and clicking the Next button over and over again until it works.

If the system does not detect the printer, open up the Control Panel and find the Printers menu item in Windows Vista, or the Devices and Printers item in Windows 7—it is either by itself or, in the categorized view, under Hardware.

As you might guess, you install a new printer by clicking the Add a printer button. This starts the Add Printer wizard. After a pleasant intro screen, you must choose to install either a printer plugged directly into your system (also called a local printer) or a network printer (Figure 11-5).

Figure 11-5
Choosing a local or
network printer in
Windows 7

If you choose a local printer, the applet next asks you to select a port (Figure 11-6); select the port in which you installed the new printer. Once you select the port, Windows asks you to specify the type of printer, either by selecting the type from the list or using the Have Disk option, just as you would for any other device. When you click Next on this screen, Windows installs the printer.

Figure 11-6
Selecting a port in
Windows 7

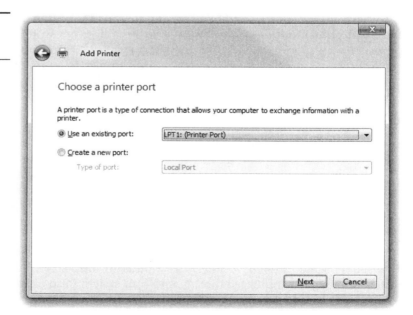

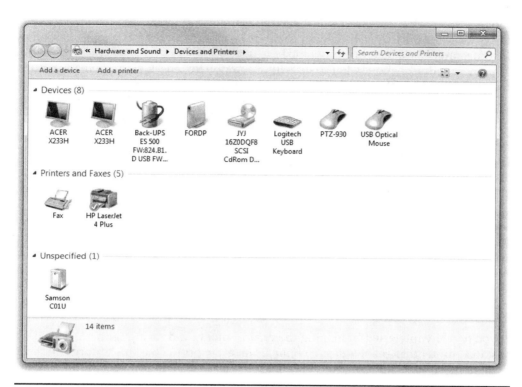

Figure 11-7   An installed default printer in the Devices and Printers applet

Figure 11-7 shows a typical Windows 7 Devices and Printers screen on a system with one printer installed. Note the small check mark in the icon's corner; this shows that the device is the default printer. If you have multiple printers, you can change the default printer by right-clicking a printer and selecting Set as default printer.

Green Printing

For all the good that printers do, they're also incredibly wasteful. There isn't any other part of your computer that requires you to throw stuff away, after all. Toner and ink cartridges, paper, and even sometimes printers themselves all eventually make their way to the trash heap. Fortunately, while you can't really get around having to buy new ink, you can lessen the impact your printer waste has on the environment.

Dealing with Consumables

All printers tend to generate a lot of trash in the form of consumables. Inkjet printers use paper and ink cartridges, and laser printers use paper and toner cartridges. In today's environmentally sensitive world, many laws regulate the proper disposal of most printer components. Be sure to check with the local sanitation department or disposal services company before throwing away any component. Of course, you should never throw away toner cartridges—certain companies will pay for used cartridges, and many manufacturers have recycling programs!

When in doubt about what to do with a component, check with the manufacturer for a *material safety data sheet (MSDS)*. These standardized forms provide detailed information about the potential environmental hazards associated with different components and proper disposal methods. Surf here, for example, to find the latest MSDS for all Hewlett-Packard products:

www.hp.com/hpinfo/globalcitizenship/environment/productdata/index.html

This isn't just a printer issue—you can find an MSDS for most PC components. When in doubt about how to get rid of any PC component, check with the manufacturer for an MSDS.

When cheaper printers break, they're usually more expensive to repair than to replace, effectively making them consumables themselves. Always take old printers to a local electronics recycling place rather than throwing it away. Also, when upgrading to a newer, fancier printer, why not do the right thing and give your printer to someone else who can use it? You might even be able to sell it.

Duplex Printing

If you're really interested in helping the environment (and saving money!), you'll invest in a printer that enables *duplex printing*. Not every printer has this feature, but those that do are able to print on both sides of a sheet of paper automatically, halving the amount of paper you need for a print job. Once a duplex printer has printed on one side of a page, it runs the page back through to print on the other side.

In printer terms, duplex printing reduces the *cost per page (CPP)* for a print job. The toner use is the same, but paper use drops by nearly half.

If you don't want to spend the extra money getting a duplex printer, don't worry. Windows has a feature that turns any printer into a duplex printer—called *manual duplexing*. With manual duplexing, you have to put the paper back in the print tray by hand once one side has been printed on, which can be a pain if your printer is on the other side of the office. To enable manual duplexing, check the appropriate box in the Print dialog box.

Chapter Review

The two most common printers are inkjet and laser printers. Inkjet printers use tiny dots of ink to make images on paper and are good for printing both text and images. Laser printers use lasers (or sometimes LEDs) to attach toner to paper, and are usually used for text, though color laser printers are available.

Most printers attach to computers using either USB or parallel ports. Installing a printer usually just involves inserting a driver disc and following the onscreen instructions until the printer works. Installing older printers, however, often involves using the Add Printer wizard.

Consumables like ink and toner cartridges should always be recycled—check online to see if the manufacturer or a third-party company offers a recycling program. Old printers should be either recycled or donated to someone else. Duplex printing enables printing on both sides of a piece of paper, halving the paper required for a print job. This saves your wallet and the environment.

Questions

1. Which of the following port types commonly support printers? (Select two.)
   A. Parallel
   B. USB
   C. Infrared
   D. RJ-11

2. What do laser printers use to create images?
   A. Ink
   B. Graphite
   C. Photons
   D. Toner

3. What should you do when you upgrade to a newer printer?
   A. Throw the old printer in the trash.
   B. Make sure that it's shared on the Internet so that other people can use your printer.
   C. Donate or sell your old printer to someone else who can use it.
   D. Throw out all your old printer paper, since it probably won't work with the new printer.

4. What can inkjet printers print that many laser printers can't?
   A. Text
   B. Color images
   C. Black-and-white images
   D. Three-dimensional objects

5. Why is duplex printing a good thing?
   A. It halves the amount of paper required for a print job.
   B. It enables multiple people to use one printer.
   C. It halves the amount of ink or toner required for a print job.
   D. It isn't—it's just a waste of money.

6. What should you always remember to do when buying a printer (not doing this means you can't use your printer)?
   A. Haggle.
   B. Get extra ink or toner cartridges.
   C. Buy a cable to connect the printer to your PC.
   D. Ask about recycling programs.

7. What can you use to manually install a printer in Windows?

   A. Networked drivers

   B. The Windows install disc

   C. The Recovery Console

   D. The Add Printer wizard

8. What feature enables you to use duplex printing on a printer that doesn't have a built-in duplexing feature?

   A. There is no such feature.

   B. Auto duplexing

   C. Manual duplexing

   D. Dual duplexing

9. What do some laser printers use instead of lasers?

   A. LEDs

   B. UV lights

   C. Heat guns

   D. Ink jets

10. What should you do if you don't know how to dispose of a consumable?

    A. Just throw it away.

    B. Put it in a "plastics only" recycling bin.

    C. Check with the manufacturer about a recycling program or an MSDS.

    D. Incinerate it.

Answers

1. **A, B.** You'll find almost all printers connected to parallel or USB ports.

2. **D.** Laser printers use lasers or LEDs to attach toner to paper.

3. **C.** Donating your old printer means it won't end up in a landfill.

4. **B.** Most laser printers only print black and white.

5. **A.** Duplex printing means printing on both sides of a piece of paper—halving the paper required for a print job.

6. **C.** Most printers don't include the cable that you need to hook the printer up to your PC.

7. **D.** The Add Printer wizard enables you to install a printer in Windows manually.

8. **C.** Manual duplexing enables any printer to print on both sides of a page.

9. **A.** Some laser printers use LEDs. (They're still called laser printers, though.)

10. **C.** Always check with the manufacturer if you're uncertain about disposing of a consumable.

CHAPTER 12

Portable Computing Devices

In this chapter, you will learn how to
- Describe portable computing devices
- Describe the expansion slots available on portable computers
- Maintain and clean portable computers

The computing world today differs vastly from that of several years ago, and this is perhaps most evident in the world of portable computers. The term *portable* acts as an umbrella term describing a number of different devices. Generally speaking, *portable* refers to any of the three most common types of mobile computing devices: *laptop computers*, *handheld computers*, and *personal digital assistants (PDAs)*. Advances in display screen technology, battery life, CPU muscle, and networking capabilities have prompted many folks to opt for portables in addition to, or often instead of, desktop PCs.

Portable Computers

As the name implies, portable computers are made to be mobile, and are therefore smaller and lighter than desktop systems. Figure 12-1 shows a typical portable computer. Portables are usually called *laptop* computers or *notebook* computers. A *netbook* is a smaller, cheaper portable computer with limited capabilities designed specifically for browsing the Internet (Figure 12-2).

Laptops range in size from tiny *netbooks* with displays anywhere from 4 to 11 inches across and weighing only a few pounds, to gigantic *desktop replacement* systems with displays of 17 inches or more and tipping the scales at more than 15 pounds. You'll also hear some laptop computer models described as *notebook* or *subnotebook* computers, but these are marketing terms and not really cut-and-dried official definitions.

Figure 12-1
A laptop computer

Handheld Computing Devices

We humans are hand-oriented beings, so it was inevitable that we'd want to shrink computers down to something that we can hold in our hand like any other tool. Manufacturers produce multifunction and single-function handheld computing devices.

Figure 12-2
A netbook computer

The most popular example of a handheld device is the smart cellular telephone, or smartphone. Popular smartphones include

- Apple iPhone
- RIM BlackBerry
- Motorola Droid

Smartphones are not just mobile phones; they're tiny computers that help you stay connected by enabling you to access the Internet on the go. They also help you stay organized by giving you a way to copy and carry around data that you'd normally store on your PC, such as your address book, calendar, task lists, and so on—tasks that were once handled by the now obsolete personal *digital assistant (PDA)*.

Most smartphones have enough processing power to enable you to play games, edit text documents and spreadsheets, read books, listen to music, and do many other computing tasks on the go. There are several different smartphone operating systems, including

- Apple iPhone OS (Figure 12-3)
- Google Android
- Microsoft Windows Mobile
- RIM BlackBerry, Symbian
- Palm webOS

Handheld devices have a small built-in display screen that can also act as a data input device. Modern devices often have touchscreens with virtual keyboards, while some devices use handwriting recognition software that enables you to enter text by writing on the screen with a pen-like instrument called a *stylus*. Many also have small integrated hardware keyboards (Figure 12-4).

Figure 12-3
An Apple iPhone

Figure 12-4
A RIM BlackBerry

Specialized or single-purpose handheld computing devices enable you to perform tasks that used to require extensive or bulky equipment. With an *electronic book (e-book)* reader, for example, you can carry around and read the equivalent of a small library full of books in your jacket pocket (Figure 12-5). Click a button and you're "thumbing" through the latest best seller.

Portable digital music/media players (also called *MP3 players* after the most popular file type for digital music), such as the Apple iPod, put a full-blown stereo system and your collection of audio CDs into a stylish, palm-sized package (Figure 12-6).

Figure 12-5
An Amazon Kindle

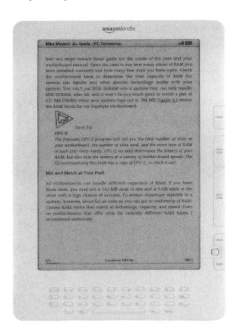

Figure 12-6
An Apple iPod

One Big Happy Family

A few years ago, a cell phone, a PDA, a camera, and a portable music player were all separate devices, each doing its own thing. A cell phone was used to call someone, a PDA was used as an organizer, and so on. But today, these devices are often combined into sophisticated hybrid versions of each handheld device:

- Cell phones with cameras
- Cell phones with built-in MP3 players
- Cell phones with pretty much *anything*

Keep in mind, though, that the digital camera in a cell phone pales in comparison to a dedicated digital camera.

Power Management

In early portable computers, every component drew power continuously, regardless of what component was being used. The hard drive would continue to spin whether or not it was being accessed, for example, and the screen would continue to display, even when nobody was actively using the system. Modern systems use specialized hardware, the BIOS, and the OS itself to enable *power management* functions.

You configure power through Windows. You'll find power management settings in the Windows Vista/7 Control Panel applet Power Options. Windows 7's built-in power schemes enable you to better control power use by customizing a Balanced, High performance, or Power saver power plan (Figure 12-7).

The different plans put the system into Standby or Suspend mode after different intervals in order to save power. You can also require the system to go into Standby mode after a set period of time or turn off the monitor or hard drive after a time, thus creating your own custom power scheme. This is technically called adjusting the sleep timers. You can customize a power saver plan for your laptop, for example, and configure it to turn off the display at a certain time interval while on battery and a different interval when plugged in.

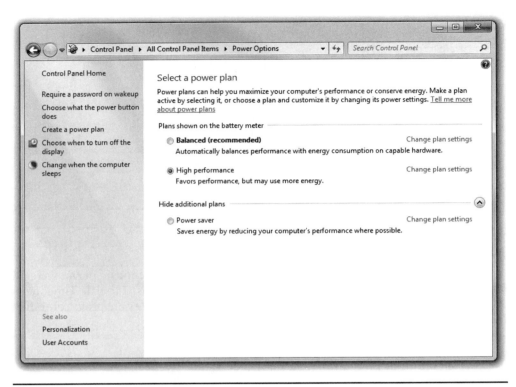

Figure 12-7   Power Options in Windows 7

NOTE   You can also access Power Options by typing **power options** into the search bar in the Start menu and pressing ENTER.

Another feature, Sleep mode, takes everything in active memory and stores it on the hard drive just before the system powers down. When the PC comes out of Sleep mode, Windows reloads all the files and applications into RAM. You can change when the computer goes to sleep by clicking Change Plan Settings in the Power Options applet (Figure 12-8). You don't want your computer going to sleep too soon, so you'll want to set this value somewhere around 15 minutes.

EXAM TIP   These days, power management features in laptops are so helpful that many companies have started replacing power-hungry desktop systems with low-power laptops.

Figure 12-8
You can change when
to put the computer
to sleep.

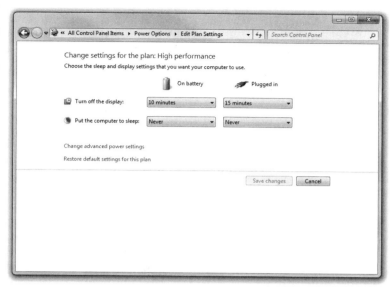

Upgrading Portable Computers

You might not know this, but if your laptop doesn't do all the stuff you want it to, you don't have to throw it out and buy a new one. *Expansion cards* provide you with a way to upgrade your laptop's capabilities without breaking the bank. There are two main types of expansion cards out there (not to mention on the Strata exam!), parallel and ExpressCard.

PC Cards

The *Personal Computer Memory Card International Association (PCMCIA)* establishes standards involving portable computers, especially when it comes to expansion cards, which are generically called PC Cards. PC Cards are credit-card-sized devices that enhance and extend the functions of a portable PC. PC Cards are as standard on today's mobile computers as the hard drive. PC Cards are easy to use, inexpensive, and convenient. Figure 12-9 shows a typical PC Card.

Figure 12-9
PC Card

EXAM TIP The Strata certification exam uses the older term *PCMCIA* cards to describe PC Cards. Don't be shocked if you see that as an option on your exam. You'll hear many techs use the phrase as well, even though the PCMCIA trade group has not used it for many years.

Almost every portable PC has one or two PC Card slots into which you insert a PC Card. Each card will have at least one function, but many have two, three, or more. You can buy a PC Card that offers connections for removable media, for example, such as combination Secure Digital (SD) and CompactFlash (CF) card readers. You can also find PC Cards that plug into multiple types of networks. All PC Cards are *hot-swappable*, meaning you can plug them in without powering down the PC.

 EXAM TIP Many manufacturers use the term *hot-pluggable* rather than hot-swappable to describe the ability to plug in and replace PC Cards on the fly. Look for either term on the exam.

The PCMCIA has established two versions of PC Cards, one using a parallel bus and the other using a serial bus. Each version, in turn, offers two technology variations as well as several physical varieties. This might sound complicated at first, but here's a map to help you sort it all out.

Parallel PC Cards

Parallel PC Cards come in two flavors, *16-bit* and *CardBus*, and each flavor comes in three different physical sizes, called Type I, Type II, and Type III. The 16-bit PC Cards, as the name suggests, are 16-bit cards that can have up to two distinct functions or devices, such as a modem/network card combination. CardBus PC Cards are 32-bit cards that can have up to eight different functions on a single card. A 16-bit PC Card will fit into and work in a CardBus slot, but the reverse is not true. CardBus totally dominates the current PC Card landscape, but you might still run into older 16-bit PC Cards.

Type I, II, and III cards differ only in the thickness of the card (Type I being the thinnest and Type III the thickest). All PC Cards share the same 68-pin interface, so any PC Card will work in any slot that's tall enough to accept that card type. Type II cards are by far the most common. Therefore, most laptops will have two Type II slots, one above the other, to enable the computer to accept two Type I or II cards or one Type III card (Figure 12-10).

Figure 12-10
PC Card slots

NOTE Most PC Cards normally come with a hard plastic storage case. Always be sure to use this case to store the cards when you're not using them. If dust, dirt, or grime gets into the array of contacts at the end of the card, the card won't work when you try to use it next.

Also, be careful when using PC Cards that extend out of the PC Card slot past the edge of your laptop. One dark night, I set my laptop on the floor with a PC Card NIC sticking out of it while I went to get a drink of water. On my way back, I accidentally stepped on the card sticking out of my laptop and nearly snapped it in half. Luckily, my laptop wasn't damaged, but the card was toast!

ExpressCard

ExpressCard, the high-performance serial version of the PC Card, has replaced PC Card slots on newer laptop PCs. Although ExpressCard offers significant performance benefits, it is completely incompatible with PC Card technology. You cannot use your PC Card in your new laptop's ExpressCard socket. The PC Card has had a remarkably long life in portable PCs, and you can still find it on some new laptops, but get ready to replace all your PC Card devices.

ExpressCard comes in two widths: 54 mm and 34 mm. Figure 12-11 shows a 34 mm and a 54 mm ExpressCard. Both cards are 75 mm long and 5 mm thick, which makes them shorter than all previous PC Cards and the same thickness as a Type II PC Card.

ExpressCards connect to either the Hi-Speed USB 2.0 bus or a PCI Express (PCIe) bus. These differ phenomenally in speed. The amazingly slow-in-comparison USB version has a maximum throughput of 480 Mbps. The PCIe version, in contrast, roars in at 2.5 Gbps.

Figure 12-11
34 mm and 54 mm
ExpressCards

EXAM TIP To power ExpressCards, the ExpressCard standard specifies voltages of either 1.5 V or 3.3 V; CardBus slots can use 3.3 V or 5.0 V.

Software Support for PC Cards

The PCMCIA standard defines two levels of software drivers to support PC Cards. The first, lower level is known as *socket services*. Socket services are device drivers that support the PC Card socket, enabling the system to detect when a PC Card has been inserted or removed and providing the necessary input/output to the device. The second, higher level is known as *card services*. The card services level recognizes the function of a particular PC Card and provides the specialized drivers necessary to make the card work.

In today's laptops, the socket services are standardized and are handled by the system BIOS. Windows itself handles all card services and has a large set of preinstalled PC Card device drivers, although most PC Cards come with their own drivers.

 NOTE ExpressCards don't require either socket or card services, at least not in the way PC Cards do. The ExpressCard modules automatically configure the software on your computer, which makes them truly Plug and Play.

Maintaining Portables

Most portable PCs come from the factory solidly built and configured. Manufacturers know that few techs outside their factories are technically savvy enough to work on them, so they don't cut corners. From a tech's standpoint, most maintenance involves taking care of the batteries and extending the battery life through proper power management, as discussed earlier. You also need to keep the machine clean, avoid excessive heat, and be careful about physical damage.

Everything you normally do to maintain a PC applies to portable PCs. You need to keep current on Windows patches and Service Packs, and use stable, recent drivers. Run an error-checking utility with some frequency, and definitely defragment the hard drive. Disk Cleanup is a must if the laptop runs Windows. That said, let's look at issues specifically involving portables.

For troubleshooting, portable PCs have distinctive issues regarding power and networking. You can run into issues with the screen and input devices, as well.

Cleaning

Most portable PCs take substantially more abuse than a corresponding desktop model, but constant handling, travel, food crumbled into the keyboard, and so on can radically shorten the life of a portable if you don't take action. One of the most important things you should do is clean the laptop regularly. Use an appropriate screen cleaner or damp, lint-free cloth (not a glass cleaner!) to remove fingerprints and dust from the fragile LCD panel.

If you've had the laptop in a smoky or dusty environment where the air quality alone causes problems, try cleaning it with compressed air. Compressed air works great for blowing out the dust and crumbs from the keyboard and for keeping PC Card sockets clear. Don't use water on your keyboard! Even a minor amount of moisture inside the portable can toast a component.

If your computer seems to run poorly on battery power, make sure you've cleaned the battery connectors with a microfiber cloth dipped in rubbing alcohol. You'll find the connectors on the underside of the battery—they look like little gold squares or fins (Figure 12-12).

 EXAM TIP   If you ever have to dispose of your laptop or other portable device, make sure you don't just throw the battery in the trash. They contain caustic chemicals that can be extremely damaging to the environment. Check in your local area for electronics recycling centers to help you get rid of those old batteries.

Protect the Machine

While prices continue to drop for basic laptops, a fully loaded system is still pricey. To protect your investment, you'll want to adhere to certain best practices. You've already read tips in this chapter to deal with cleaning and heat, so let's look at the "portable" part of portable computers.

Tripping

Pay attention to where you run the power cord when you plug in a laptop. One of the primary causes of laptop destruction is people tripping over the power cord and knocking the laptop off a desk. This is especially true if you plug it in at a public place such as a café or airport. Remember that the life you save could be your portable PC's!

Storage

If your laptop or PDA isn't going to be used for a while, storing it safely will go a long way toward keeping it operable when you do power it up again. It's worth the extra few dollars to invest in a quality case—preferably one with ample padding.

Figure 12-12
Contacts on a
laptop battery

Smaller devices such as PDAs are well protected inside small shock-resistant aluminum cases that clip on to your belt, while laptops do fine in well-padded cases or backpacks. Not only will this protect your system on a daily basis when transporting it from home to office, but it will keep dust and pet hair away as well. Lastly, remove the battery to protect your device from battery leakage if you'll be storing it for an extended period of time.

Chapter Review

Portable computing devices come in many shapes and sizes, such as laptops, netbooks, PDAs, and smartphones. Because battery life is so important when using portable computers, you should learn to take advantage of the power management settings offered on your device, such as the Power Options applet in Windows Vista/7.

You can expand your laptop's capabilities using PCMCIA cards, such as the older, parallel versions, or the newer ExpressCards.

You should always keep your portable devices clean and free of dust to prevent damage or overheating. Additionally, you should store your portable computers in places where they won't be damaged or stolen.

Questions

1. Which of the following is not true about PC Cards?
   A. They're larger than ExpressCards.
   B. They're faster than ExpressCards.
   C. They come in three sizes.
   D. PC Cards are hot-swappable.

2. How many Type III cards can typically fit into a laptop at one time?
   A. 1
   B. 2
   C. 3
   D. 4

3. What do you call a small, low-power laptop designed for maximum portability?
   A. Nettop
   B. Netmag
   C. Netbook
   D. Netscape

4. PDAs have been largely replaced by what devices?
   A. iPods
   B. Smartphones

   C. Tablet PCs

   D. E-book readers

5. If your laptop has three USB ports, but you want to attach five USB devices at one time, what can you do?

   A. Buy a new laptop with more USB ports.

   B. Deal with cycling through three devices at a time.

   C. Use two of the devices on a desktop computer.

   D. Buy an ExpressCard with additional USB ports.

6. How can you adjust your computer's power management settings?

   A. Using a different type of surge protector

   B. Using the Power Options applet in the Control Panel

   C. Adjusting settings on the power supply

   D. Using the Power Options selection in CMOS

7. How can ExpressCards interface with portable computers? (Select two.)

   A. PCI

   B. ISA

   C. PCIe

   D. USB 2.0

8. What should you do with an old, unneeded laptop battery?

   A. Throw it in the trash.

   B. Drain the chemicals inside it and then dispose of them.

   C. Take it to an electronics recycling center.

   D. Magnetize it before disposing of it.

9. If your laptop seems to be running poorly on battery power, what should you do first?

   A. Clean the battery connectors.

   B. Buy a new battery.

   C. Remove USB peripherals.

   D. Adjust settings in the Power Options applet.

10. What do you call a large, heavy laptop with a 17" monitor and powerful components?

   A. Netbook

   B. Ultrabook

   C. PDA

   D. Desktop replacement

Answers

1. **B.** ExpressCards are much faster than PC Cards.

2. **A.** Only one Type III PC Card can fit into a laptop at a time because of the thickness of these cards.

3. **C.** These tiny laptops are called netbooks.

4. **B.** These days, smartphones have almost entirely replaced PDAs.

5. **D.** ExpressCards enable you to add additional features to your laptop.

6. **B.** The Power Options applet enables you to adjust your computer's power usage.

7. **C, D.** ExpressCards use PCIe or USB 2.0 to interface with portable computers.

8. **C.** Always take old electronics (and especially batteries) to electronics recycling centers.

9. **A.** The battery connectors are the gold fins or squares on the bottom of your laptop.

10. **D.** These powerful laptops are known as desktop replacements.

PART IV

Networks of PCs

Wired Networks

In this chapter, you will learn how to
- Explain what a network does
- Describe the components of a wired network
- Use a network to share resources

Few PCs are islands unto themselves. To experience the full power of computers, you must connect them to other computers. Imagine you receive a new computer, but it's not on a network, so you can't send e-mail, download music, or interact across the Internet with your friends. How boring would that be? If, in today's world, you can't connect your computer to someone else's, you might as well not have a computer at all.

When you link computers together to share files and communicate and do all the things we like to do, you create a *network*. Networks range in size from the smallest and simplest network—two computers connected together—to the largest and most complex network of all—the Internet.

This chapter covers all the pieces that come together to make a computer network, including the hardware needed to make the physical connections. It also explains how you can use networks to share resources between multiple computers.

What is a Network?

Networks come in many sizes and vary widely in the number of computers attached to them. Some people connect two computers in their house so that they can share files and play games together—the smallest network you can have. Some companies have thousands of employees in dozens of countries, in contrast, and need to network their computers together to get work done. Network folks put most networks into one of two categories: LANs and WANs.

A *local area network (LAN)* covers a small area and contains a modest number of computers (Figure 13-1). LANs are usually in a single building or group of nearby buildings. Typical LANs include home and school networks.

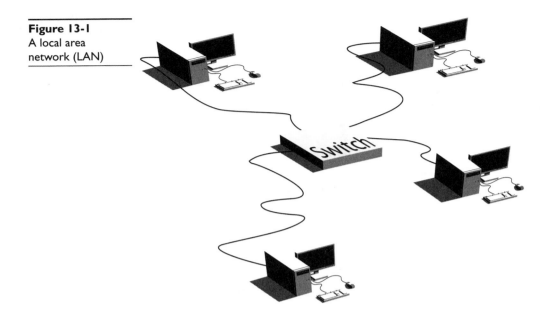

Figure 13-1
A local area
network (LAN)

A *wide area network (WAN)* covers a large area and can have a substantial number of computers (Figure 13-2). Usually, a WAN is composed of two or more LANs connected together. All of the LANs in all of the schools in your district, for example, link together to form a WAN. Computers in a WAN usually connect through some type of public network, such as a telephone system, leased lines, or satellites. The largest WAN in existence is the *Internet*, which is a worldwide network that connects millions of computers and networks.

An *intranet*, in contrast, is essentially a private network that is a scaled-down version of the Internet for a very specific group of users. Another similar term, *extranet*, is used to denote a private intranet that is also made accessible to a select group of outsiders using the Internet.

Servers and Clients

People use two types of computers in networks these days: servers and clients. In a nutshell, *servers* share things—such as files, folders, and printers—and *clients* enable you to access those shared things. Let's get one thing straight: Almost any personal computer can act as a server or a client or both! A lot of it has to do with how you set up the computer.

Computers running Windows, Macintosh, and the many varieties of Linux make up the vast majority of clients. You'll also find other devices that are clients, though, such as the following examples.

- Game consoles like the Xbox 360
- Smartphones and tablets
- DVRs like TiVo and other set-top boxes

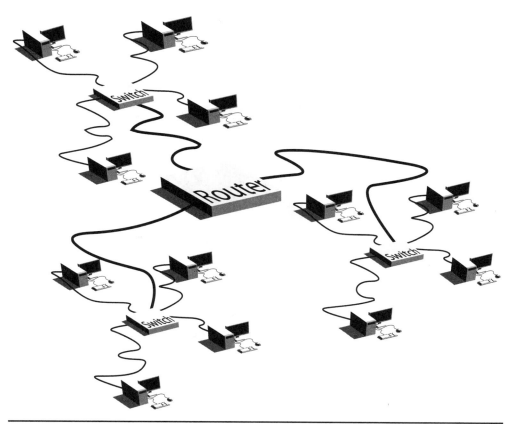

Figure 13-2 A wide area network (WAN)

Server computers come in all shapes and sizes, but they serve—if you'll pardon the pun—a similar purpose. Servers manage *network resources* (like printers, e-mail—all the stuff that makes a network valuable), provide central storage of files, and provide services for the users (like having the printer server tell the printer to print, or having the e-mail server send your e-mail) (Figure 13-3).

Client computers enable you to access the shared resources and services on server machines (Figure 13-4). Most users access servers via clients, although there's no law that says you can't access a server from another server machine. The latter machine, in that case, would be *acting* as a client regardless of the firepower of the box!

Networks are traditionally classified into *client/server* and *peer-to-peer*, depending on the role played by each computer in the network. In a client/server network, one computer system acts as a server while the remaining computers are clients that access resources from the server. On some home or small office networks, however, there may not be a separate server. Instead, every computer on the network acts as both a client and a server. Such networks are called peer-to-peer networks.

Figure 13-3
A server sharing
network resources

Advantages and Disadvantages of Networking

Networks can greatly enhance your computing experience, but they can also harm your data in ways that are unimaginable for a non-networked computer.

Figure 13-4
A client accessing
network resources

The Good Side of Networking

Networks offer many benefits over standalone computing in several somewhat-overlapping categories:

- Enhanced communication and collaboration
- Easier sharing of files and resources
- Increased personal productivity
- Lower costs because of the sharing
- Easier management of machines in the network

Communication is pretty straightforward. You can e-mail your friends, family, and co-workers while sipping café au lait from a bistro in Paris, even if they live and work back home in Kansas. Using Google Talk or another instant messaging program, your computer can alert you when your friends come online and you can send them a quick hello, any time of day or night.

Communication leads to collaboration and increased personal productivity by enabling you to work (and play) with others over a network. Rather than simply e-mailing to say hello, you could send your next best-selling manuscript to your agent in Los Angeles from your secret hideaway in Tahiti. You can work on a project with five other people, all of whom live in different cities. You can smack your best friend in an online game when he's 3000 miles away. Only your imagination limits the possibilities here!

Networks enable you to share resources, such as

- Files
- Folders
- Printers
- Scanners

Accessing resources shared by others can lead to lower costs of operation. If you have ten people in your class who need to print something, you could share a single printer among all ten computers. It sure beats buying one for every desk!

Finally, grouping computers into a network enables centralized control over certain aspects of those computers. One computer can be designated as a file server (shares files), for example, or a print server (shares a printer). You can create a workgroup for all the users and require proper user names and passwords, thus enhancing security. This might immediately make you wonder, why security? Let's look at the downside of network computing.

The Bad Side of Networking

Creating a computer network can make you lose control over your computer, add cost, and cause security problems. Also, due to security concerns, a network user will not usually have complete control over his computer settings and software. The additional costs for servers, cables, and network cards can add up.

PART IV

You've also got a human cost—someone's got to handle the administration of network resources, and other folks need to maintain the network and fix problems. Network hardware or software failure is also a hazard that must be considered. If there is a network-wide system failure, no one will be able to use the system.

Finally, opening up a folder full of your data onto a network of any size creates a gaping security hole. Only your vigilance and forethought will stop a hacker or thief from grabbing or deleting your files. Just being on the Internet can create huge problems too, with the many viruses and evildoers out there running rampant.

Weighing the downside versus the upside in networking tips the balance in favor of networking, but you have to implement and maintain security. The life you save might be your computer's!

Network Components

Whether you want to put together a LAN or connect a couple of LANs into a WAN, you need connectivity between the PCs and a way to handle communication. Computers connect to a network in one of two ways:

- Directly connected to a LAN via a cable from the computer to a LAN port
- Wirelessly to the LAN (as will be covered in Chapter 14)

A typical network client has a *network adapter* or *network interface card (NIC)* that connects to a cable that connects to a central network box, called a hub or switch. (I'll explain the difference between them in a moment.) Figure 13-5 shows a typical NIC.

Figure 13-5
A network
interface card

EXAM TIP   When connecting two computers to a network, you can skip the central box and directly connect both systems using a special cable called a *crossover cable.*

To make this into a nicely configured network, add another network client. Throw in a server. Don't add water, but turn on network sharing and voilà! You have a network. Each machine attaches to a network cable that then connects at the other end to the hub or switch. Any machine attached to a network—client, server, printer, or whatnot—is called a *node*.

Software

Of course it takes both hardware and software to make network communication work well. If Johan's computer requests an MP3 file from Michael's computer, Michael's operating system and other software take that MP3 file and break it into small, individually numbered units called *packets*. The NIC then takes the packets and, following the Ethernet standards, wraps up those packets into *network frames* that get sent out along the cable to the central network hub or switch (Figure 13-6).

Ethernet

You might be wondering how you can tell what sort of cable to use for this network and how to determine the type of hub or switch required for a network. Networking means communicating; the computers need to be able to speak the same language and follow the same technology.

The *Ethernet* standard defines everything about modern network hardware. Ethernet cables have standard connectors, for example, such as the *RJ-45 connector* shown in

Figure 13-6
Packets wrapped in frames sent along an Ethernet CAT 5 cable

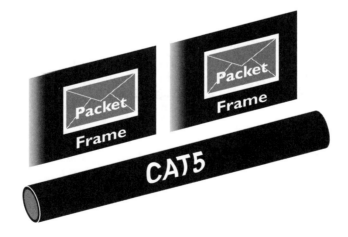

PART IV

Figure 13-7
An RJ-45 connector

Figure 13-7. Ethernet defines electrical signaling as well. That way the sending NIC will break data down into little pieces and the receiving NIC will know exactly how to put them back together.

 EXAM TIP Both ends of an Ethernet cable use an RJ-45 connector, which has eight pins arranged in four pairs of two.

If two machines do not have the same kind of networking technology—a common problem in the early days of computer networks—then they can't network together. I won't bore you with a list of all the networking technologies that have had a brief moment of glory and market share in the past. Suffice it to say that today, Ethernet is king.

Most modern Ethernet networks employ one of three technologies (and sometimes all three), *10BaseT*, *100BaseT*, or *1000BaseT*. As the numbers in the names suggest, 10BaseT networks run at 10 Mbps, 100BaseT networks run at 100 Mbps, and 1000BaseT networks—called Gigabit Ethernet—run at 1000 Mbps, or 1 Gbps.

Each Ethernet technology requires a specific kind of cabling that can handle its top speed. 100BaseT networks use Category 5 (CAT 5) Ethernet cables (Figure 13-8), while Gigabit Ethernet runs on Category 6 (CAT 6) Ethernet cables.

Figure 13-8
Category 5 (CAT 5)
cable

NOTE   The CompTIA Strata exam only covers the Ethernet connections and cables described above: RJ-45 and CAT 5 and CAT 6. This type of network uses electricity over copper wires to communicate between two computers.

You might have heard of the other kind of Ethernet, called *fiber-optic Ethernet*. It uses light pulses over glass cables to send data between computers. The cables and connectors differ a lot from the copper-based versions. You won't find fiber-optic Ethernet in the typical office or school. It's still really expensive.

Duplex and Half-Duplex

All modern NICs can run in *full-duplex* mode, meaning they can send and receive data at the same time. The vast majority of NICs and switches use a feature called *auto-negotiating* to accommodate very old devices that might attach to the network and need to run in half-duplex mode. *Half-duplex* means that the device can send and receive, but not at the same time.

EXAM TIP   Auto-negotiating senses both the duplex mode and the speed of the cables and connected devices so that your network transfers data as fast as possible.

HomePlug

Many people use computers and other networkable devices in multiple rooms of their home. Connecting these devices to a network can be tricky, time-consuming, or just plain messy. You could, for example, run the Ethernet cables down the hallway, but that's both ugly and a tripping hazard waiting to happen. You could also drill a lot of holes and run the cabling through your walls, floors, and ceilings, but that can be difficult to do yourself and expensive to hire someone else to do for you. There is, however, a third option.

HomePlug (also known as *Ethernet over Power*) technology enables you to run a network signal through the existing power outlets in your home (Figure 13-9). It is not a single product, but a set of industry standards. Here's how it works: plug your Ethernet cable into the HomePlug device, plug the device into an outlet, and then do it again in another room. The two rooms are now linked as if a long Ethernet cable ran between them. This system is not as fast as the fastest Ethernet cables, but it also doesn't require power tools, so it might just be worth it.

Hubs and Switches

Hubs and switches sit at the very center of networking, handling the tasks of receiving and sending packets of data to the connected computers. Each functions quite differently when they receive an Ethernet frame.

A *hub* repeats the frame down every network cable connected, hoping one of the computers connected is the recipient machine, such as Johan's laptop, for example (Figure 13-10).

PART IV

Figure 13-9
A HomePlug device plugged in (courtesy of Belkin)

A *switch*, in contrast, learns the network address of every machine connected to it, reads the recipient address on the frames, and sends them along only on the appropriate connection (Figure 13-11).

The radically more efficient switches now dominate the marketplace, although you'll still see lots of hubs in service throughout the world.

Figure 13-10
A hub repeating frames down every network cable

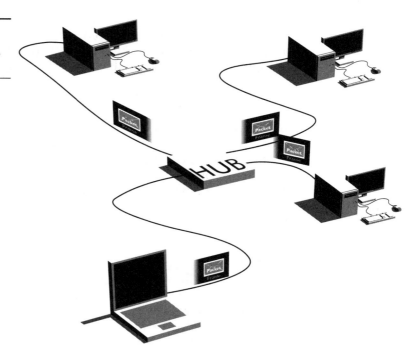

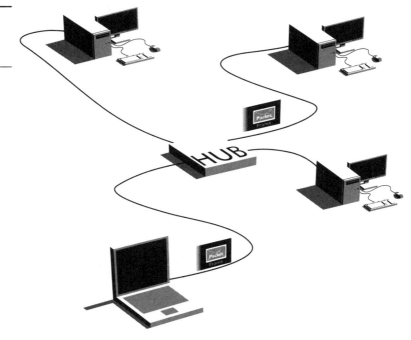

Figure 13-11
A switch sending
frames only to the
recipient

Using Networks

So you've got a server and a couple of clients, but what's next? I want to access the information on the server from one of the client computers. In short, I want a network! To create a network, you need to connect a client computer to a server in some way. That's where the Ethernet cables, hubs, and switches come into play.

NOTE   You can also share files with other users on the same computer. This is known as a *local share*. Sharing files with users on other computers is known as a *network share*.

Once you've assembled the pieces for a network, you can sit down at a client computer and access a file on a server. As cool as they may seem, networks aren't magic. A whole bunch of stuff happens in the background when you access network resources. Let's look at that process now.

Johan has a slick new Windows 7 laptop and wants to access an MP3 music file on his friend Michael's computer. Two things need to be in place before anything else happens. Both Johan and Michael's computers need to be connected to the same network, and Michael needs to share the folder that holds the MP3 file (Figure 13-12).

Figure 13-12
Johan and Michael's
network setup

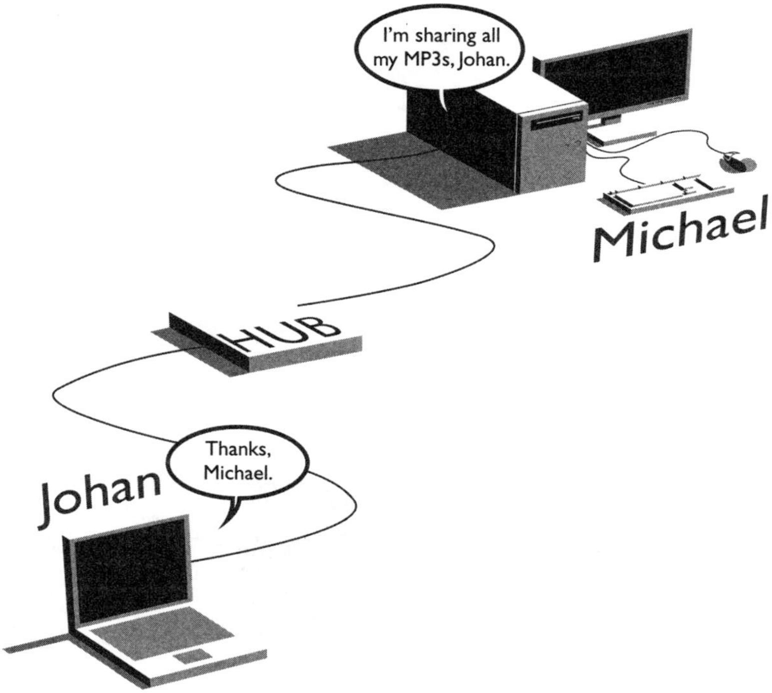

The connection part should be easily implemented. If both computers have Ethernet NICs, they can plug them into two ports on a switch or hub. Michael then needs to set up the shared folder with permissions that allow Johan to access it. Permissions define what a user can do with a particular shared file or folder, such as:

- Accessing the file
- Deleting the file
- Moving the file
- Copying the file
- And more

How you share and set permissions varies among different operating systems. In Windows 7, for example, Michael would open Computer, right-click the folder containing his MP3 file, and select Properties to open the folder's Properties dialog box (Figure 13-13).

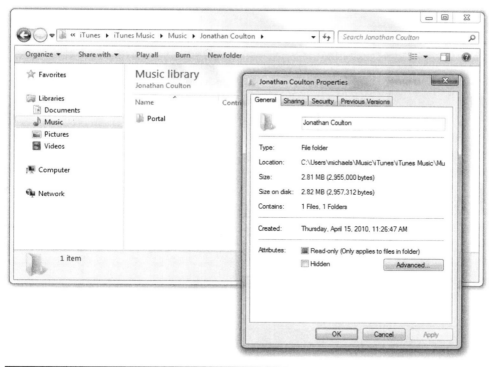

Figure 13-13 A folder's Properties dialog box

By default, nothing is shared, so Michael would need to:

1. Open the Sharing tab and click the Advanced Sharing button (Figure 13-14).

2. When asked for permission to continue the operation, click Continue to open the Advanced Sharing dialog box.

3. Check the Share This Folder check box. Michael can then give it a share name such as Music and specify the number of users who can access the folder simultaneously. (In Figure 13-14, Michael used the default share name. Windows picked up the folder name, Jonathan Coulton.)

The default permission on a new share in Windows 7 gives what's called "Read" access to everyone who has access to the share. To change permissions, click the Permissions button to open the Permissions dialog box. Michael can change the permission level by clicking in the desired check box. He can allow or deny read, change, and full control access for everyone or for individual users (Figure 13-15).

PART IV

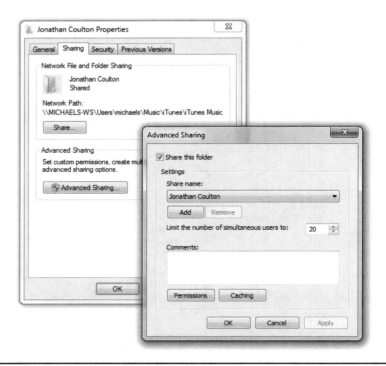

Figure 13-14 The Sharing tab in an Advanced Sharing dialog box

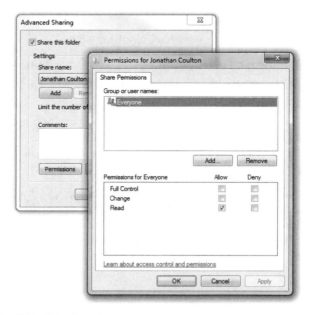

Figure 13-15 The Permissions dialog box

Windows 7 also has a Public folder that you can use to share a bunch of folders or files with other users. Drop any folders or files you wish to share into the Public folder. By default, share permissions are not enabled for the Public folder, so you have to enable them using the method you just learned.

Once connectivity, sharing, and permissions are taken care of, Johan can open up his Network folder, navigate to Michael's PC, and double-click Michael's shared Music folder to reveal the contents. Simply right-clicking and selecting Send to | Documents from the menu will get that MP3 file on its way to his hard drive.

Behind the scenes, as soon as Johan accesses the file on Michael's PC, a message shoots across the cable from his laptop to Michael's PC, saying, in effect, "Hey! Michael's computer! My user wants a copy of this specific MP3 file in the shared Music folder." Assuming all is well and Johan has permission to copy files from the shared folder, Michael's PC sends the file out through the NIC. The file goes down the cable, into the hub or switch, and then down the other cable to Johan's laptop.

Chapter Review

A network is formed whenever more than one computer are connected together for the purpose of communicating or sharing resources. This could be anything from sharing files and printers to playing multiplayer games. While this can save time and money, networking your computers also opens them up to more security risks, such as viruses. Any device connected to a network is known as a node.

Networks are divided into local area networks (LANs) and wide area networks (WANs). A LAN is a network contained in a single location, such as a home or office. A WAN is a collection of LANs that spread over a large area, such as the Internet.

Networks are made up of servers and clients. Servers provide the resources to be shared, and clients use those resources. Clients and servers are wired together using Ethernet cables. There are several varieties of cables, including CAT 5 and CAT 6, but all use the same RJ-45 connector. HomePlug is an industry standard that enables you to create an Ethernet connection between two existing power outlets. Additionally, a network requires a central device to which each node connects. This could be a hub or switch.

You must also configure your operating system to allow resources to be shared over a network. Access the Sharing tab from a file or folder's Properties dialog box to configure who can access what and with which permissions.

Questions

1. How many computers make up the smallest networks?

   A. One

   B. Two

   C. Three

   D. Four

2. What is the difference between a LAN and a WAN?

   A. A LAN is composed of only two computers, while a WAN is made up of three or more.

   B. A WAN is a single group of computers, while a LAN is a collection of WANs.

   C. A LAN is only ever in one building, while WANs cover multiple buildings.

   D. A LAN is a single group of computers, while a WAN is a collection of LANs.

3. Which of the following is not an advantage of networked computers over non-networked computers?

   A. Increased collaboration and communication

   B. Increased security

   C. Increased resource sharing

   D. Increased productivity

4. Which type of cable enables you to skip using a hub or switch and directly connect two computers?

   A. CAT 5 cable

   B. 10BaseT cable

   C. Ethernet cable

   D. Crossover cable

5. How fast can CAT 5 Ethernet cable transfer data?

   A. 10 Mbps

   B. 10 Kbps

   C. 100 Mbps

   D. 100 Kbps

6. What is the name of the set of industry standards for Ethernet over Power?

   A. EP

   B. HomePlug

   C. EtherPlug

   D. Gigabit Ethernet

7. Which device is being used if packets are repeated down every attached Ethernet cable?

   A. Modem

   B. Switch

   C. Frame

   D. Hub

8. What technology determines the speed and duplex mode of a network connection?

   A. Switch

   B. Auto-negotiation

   C. Plug and Play

   D. HomePlug

9. What is the default permission given to a newly shared folder in Windows 7?

   A. Read for everyone

   B. Read for a single user

   C. Co-owner for everyone

   D. Contributor for everyone

10. How many pairs of wires (or pins) are there on an RJ-45 connector?

    A. One

    B. Two

    C. Three

    D. Four

Answers

1. **B.** The smallest networks are made up of only two computers.

2. **D.** A LAN (local area network) is a small group of computers, while a WAN (wide area network) is a collection of LANs.

3. **B.** Networking your computers together does not increase security. In fact, it decreases it because there are new avenues for bad folks to get at your stuff!

4. **D.** A crossover cable can be used to connect two computers directly without the need for a hub or switch.

5. **C.** A CAT 5 Ethernet cable can transfer data at a rate of 100 Mbps.

6. **B.** HomePlug is the name of the set of industry standards for Ethernet over Power.

7. **D.** A hub repeats packets down every attached network cable.

8. **B.** Auto-negotiation is used to set the speed and duplex mode of the attached network devices to ensure the fastest connection possible.

9. **A.** By default, Windows 7 gives everyone on a network the Read permission for a newly shared file or folder.

10. **D.** RJ-45 connectors use four pairs of wires (or pins), meaning they have a total of eight wires.

Wireless Networks

In this chapter, you will learn how to
- Describe the basics of wireless networking
- Explain the differences between wireless networking standards
- Configure a wireless network

Some of the biggest hurdles to setting up a wired network are the wires. Most businesses frown on having CAT 5 cables running down every hall and along every wall, so wiring a building for networking means installing cabling up into ceiling crawl spaces and down behind walls and paneling. Any tech who's had to do this more than a few times can tell you that "pulling cable" is a tough job even under the best conditions.

Installing network cabling can be impractical or, in some cases, prohibited, such as in a building that's been designated a historical landmark. Thankfully, developments in wireless technology give you several alternatives to traditional wired networks.

Wireless Networking Basics

A wireless network eliminates the need for the network cabling that connects PCs to one another in a typical wired network. Instead of a physical set of wires running between networked PCs, servers, printers, or other nodes, wireless networks use radio waves to communicate with one another.

Various kinds of wireless networking solutions have come and gone. The types of wireless radio wave networks you'll be supporting these days are those based on the most common implementation of the IEEE 802.11 wireless Ethernet standard *(Wi-Fi)* and those based on *Bluetooth* technology.

 EXAM TIP   Wireless local area networks are called WLANs.

Wireless Networking Components

Wireless networking capabilities of one form or another are built into many modern computing devices. Wireless Ethernet and Bluetooth capabilities are practically everywhere as integrated components, or they can easily be added using PCI or PCIe cards.

275

Figure 14-1
A USB wireless NIC

You can also add wireless network capabilities using an external USB wireless NIC (Figure 14-1).

Wireless NICs aren't limited to PCs. Many smartphones have built-in wireless capabilities (Figure 14-2).

To extend the capabilities of a wireless Ethernet network, such as by connecting to a wired network or by sharing a high-speed Internet connection, you need a *wireless access point (WAP)*, as seen in Figure 14-3. A WAP centrally connects wireless network

Figure 14-2
A smartphone with a
built-in wireless NIC

Figure 14-3
A wireless
access point

nodes in the same way that a network hub or switch connects wired PCs. Many WAPs also act as high-speed switches and Internet routers (which will be covered in the next chapter).

Wireless Networking Software

In terms of configuring wireless networking software, you need to do very little. Wireless network adapters are Plug and Play, so any modern version of Windows will immediately recognize one when installed into a PCI or PCIe slot, or a USB port, prompting you to load any needed hardware drivers.

You will, however, need a utility to set your network name. Windows XP and Windows Vista/7 include built-in tools for configuring these settings (Figure 14-4).

Figure 14-4
Selecting a wireless
network in
Windows 7

Using this utility, you can determine your link state and signal strength, configure your wireless networking *mode* (discussed in the next section), set security encryption and power saving options, and perform other networking tasks.

Wireless Network Modes

The simplest wireless network consists of two or more PCs communicating directly with each other without cabling or any other intermediary hardware. More complicated wireless networks use a WAP to centralize wireless communication and bridge wireless network segments to wired network segments. These two different methods, or *modes*, are called *ad hoc* mode and *infrastructure* mode.

Ad Hoc Mode

In ad hoc mode, sometimes called peer-to-peer mode, each wireless node is in direct contact with every other node in a decentralized free-for-all (Figure 14-5). Ad hoc–mode networks are easier to configure than infrastructure-mode networks and are suited for small groups of computers (less than a dozen or so) that need to transfer files or share printers. Ad hoc networks are also good for temporary networks such as study groups or business meetings.

It's important to note that computers in ad hoc mode can only speak with others in their group. You can't use ad hoc mode and go beyond, like to connect to the Internet.

Figure 14-5
A network using
ad hoc mode

Infrastructure Mode

Wireless networks running in infrastructure mode use one or more WAPs to connect the wireless network nodes to a wired network segment (Figure 14-6). If you plan on setting up a wireless network for a large number of PCs or need to have centralized control over the wireless network, you need to use infrastructure mode. To connect wirelessly to another network, such as the Internet, you need to use infrastructure mode.

 EXAM TIP   Wireless networks in infrastructure mode use WAPs, while ad hoc wireless networks do not.

Wireless networks running in infrastructure mode require more planning and are more complicated to configure than ad hoc–mode networks, but they also give you finer control over how the network operates. Infrastructure mode is better suited to business networks or networks that need to share dedicated resources such as Internet connections and centralized databases.

Wireless Networking Security

One of the major complaints about wireless networking is that it offers weak security. In many cases, the only thing you need to do to access a wireless network is walk into an unsecured WAP's coverage area and turn on your wireless device! Further, data packets float through the air instead of traveling safely wrapped up inside network cabling.

PART IV

Figure 14-6
A network using
infrastructure mode

What's to stop an unscrupulous PC tech with the right equipment from grabbing those packets out of the air and reading that data?

Wireless networks use multiple methods to secure access to the network itself and secure the data that's being transferred. Changing the default *Service Set Identifier (SSID)* parameter—also called the *network name*—and administrator password is the first step. The SSID is a 32-bit identifier for your WAP that is meant to be unique, but many WAPs ship with the same SSID. Also, enabling wireless encryption through *Wired Equivalent Privacy (WEP)*, *Wi-Fi Protected Access (WPA)*, or *WPA2* ensures that the data packets themselves are secure while in transit.

SSID and Administrator Password

One of the main security weaknesses with wireless networks is that out of the box, *no* security is configured at all! Wireless devices *want* to be heard, and WAPs are usually configured to broadcast their presence to their maximum range, welcoming all other wireless devices that respond.

Always change the default SSID to something unique, and change the administrator password right away. Configuring a unique SSID name and password is the very least that you should do to secure a wireless network. The default SSID names and passwords are well known and widely available online. This is intended to make setting up a wireless network as easy as possible, but it can cause problems in places with a lot of overlapping wireless networks. Each wireless network node and access point needs to be configured with the same unique SSID name. This SSID name is then included in the header of every data packet broadcast in the wireless network's coverage area. Data packets that lack the correct SSID name in the header are rejected.

Change the default SSID and password or a potential hacker will pick up the wireless access point named "Linksys" that's broadcasting madly and try to access it using the default password.

NOTE You can also configure most WAPs to allow administrative access only through a wired connection rather than wirelessly. If you have secure access to the physical WAP, this adds another layer of security to the wireless network.

WEP

The next step up in wireless security is enabling encryption. Wired Equivalent Privacy (WEP) encryption was meant to secure data being wirelessly transmitted. WEP encryption uses a standard 40-bit encryption to scramble data packets. Many vendors also support 104-bit encryption.

WEP sounds secure, but when implemented, it contains some serious security flaws. Shortly after it was released, hackers demonstrated that WEP could be cracked in a matter of minutes using software readily available off the Internet. WEP is better than nothing, but only stops casual prying into a network. It will not deter any serious hacker. The industry quickly came out with a replacement for WEP called WPA.

WPA

Wireless Protected Access (WPA) encryption was designed to address the weaknesses of WEP, and it functions as a sort of security protocol upgrade to WEP-enabled devices. WPA offers security enhancements such as an encryption key integrity-checking feature and user authentication through the industry-standard *Extensible Authentication Protocol (EAP)*. The use of EAP is a huge security improvement over WEP. User names and passwords are encrypted and therefore much more secure.

WPA2

Recent versions of Mac OS X and Microsoft Windows support WPA2 for locking down wireless networks. WPA2 uses the Advanced Encryption Standard (AES), among other improvements, to provide a secure wireless environment. If you haven't upgraded to WPA2, you should.

 EXAM TIP   WEP is the least secure encryption option, while WPA2 is the most secure. Use WPA2 if at all possible.

Wireless Networking Speed

Wireless networking data throughput speeds depend on several factors. Speed is mostly dependent upon the standard used by the networked wireless devices. Wireless throughput speeds range from a measly 2 Mbps with one standard to a snappy 100+ Mbps on another.

Another factor affecting speed is the distance between wireless nodes (or between wireless nodes and centralized WAPs). Wireless devices dynamically negotiate the top speed at which they can communicate without dropping too many data packets. Speed decreases as distance increases, so the maximum throughput speed is achieved only at extremely close range (less than about 25 feet). At the outer reaches of a device's effective range, speed may decrease to around 1 Mbps before it drops out altogether.

Finally, throughput speed can be affected by interference from other wireless devices operating in the same frequency range, such as cordless phones and baby monitors, as well as by solid objects. So-called *dead spots* occur when something capable of blocking the radio signal comes between wireless network nodes. Large electrical appliances (and some smaller ones, such as microwaves) are very effective at blocking wireless network signals. Other culprits include electrical fuse boxes, metal plumbing, and air conditioning units.

Wireless Networking Range

Wireless networking range is hard to define, and you'll see most descriptions listed with qualifiers such as *"around* 150 feet" or *"about* 300 feet." This is simply because, like throughput speed, range is greatly affected by outside factors. Interference from other wireless devices affects range, as does interference from solid objects. The maximum ranges listed in the next section are presented by wireless manufacturers as the theoretical maximum ranges. In the real world, you'll see these ranges only under the most ideal circumstances. True effective range is probably about half what you see listed.

Range can be increased in a couple of ways. First, you can install multiple WAPs to permit "roaming" between one WAP's coverage area and another's. Second, you can install a higher-gain antenna on some models that increases a single WAP's range.

Wireless Networking Standards

To help you gain a better understanding of wireless network technology, here is a brief look at the standards that they use. We'll look at 802.11-based wireless networking and then talk about Bluetooth technology.

 EXAM TIP Early wireless networks used the Radio Frequency (RF) standard to connect multiple computers, but it never really caught on. Today, RF technology is often found in wireless mice and keyboards.

IEEE 802.11–Based Wireless Networking

The IEEE 802.11 wireless Ethernet standard defines methods by which devices can communicate using spread-spectrum radio waves. *Spread-spectrum* broadcasts data in small, discrete chunks over the different frequencies available within a certain frequency range. The 802.11-based wireless technologies broadcast and receive on one of two license-free industrial, scientific, and medical (ISM) radio bands: 2.4 GHz and 5.8 GHz. Even though the ISM band is 5.8 GHz, we just say "5 GHz" for some reason.

Wi-Fi Wireless Networking Standards

Currently, Wi-Fi is by far the most widely adopted type of wireless networking. Not only do thousands of private businesses and homes have wireless networks, but many public places such as coffee shops and libraries also offer Internet access through wireless networks.

Technically, only wireless devices that conform to the extended versions of the 802.11 standard—802.11a, 802.11b, 802.11g, and 802.11n—are Wi-Fi certified. Wi-Fi certification comes from the Wi-Fi Alliance, a nonprofit industry group made up of more than 175 member companies that design and manufacture wireless networking products.

Newer wireless devices can communicate with older wireless devices, so if you are using an 802.11n WAP, all of your 802.11g devices can use it. The exception to this is 802.11a, which requires that all the equipment directly support it. The following paragraphs describe the important specifications of each of the popular 802.11-based wireless networking standards.

802.11a Despite the "a" designation of this extension to the 802.11 standard, 802.11a was actually developed *after* 802.11b. 802.11a differs from the other 802.11-based standards in significant ways. It operates in a different frequency range, 5 GHz. This less-popular frequency range means that 802.11a devices are less prone to interference from other devices. 802.11a also offers considerably greater throughput than 802.11 and 802.11b, reaching speeds up to 54 Mbps. Range, however, suffers somewhat, topping out at about 150 feet. Despite the superior speed of 802.11a, it isn't widely adopted in the PC world.

802.11b 802.11b was the first standard to take off in wireless networking. The 802.11b standard supports data throughput of up to 11 Mbps (with actual throughput averaging 4 to 6 Mbps)—on par with older, wired 10BaseT networks—and a maximum range of 300 feet under ideal conditions. In a typical office environment, its maximum range is lower. The main downside to using 802.11b is, in fact, that it uses a very popular frequency. The 2.4 GHz band is already crowded with baby monitors, garage door openers, microwaves, and wireless phones, so you're likely to run into interference from other wireless devices.

802.11g 802.11g came out in 2003, taking the best of 802.11a and b and rolling them into a single standard. 802.11g offers data transfer speeds equivalent to 802.11a, up to 54 Mbps, with the wider 300-foot range of 802.11b. More importantly, 802.11g runs in the 2.4 GHz band, so it is backward-compatible with 802.11b, meaning that the same 802.11g WAP can service both 802.11b and 802.11g wireless nodes. The 802.11g standard is popular, but losing ground to the newest version, 802.11n.

802.11n The 802.11n standard brings several improvements to Wi-Fi networking, including faster speeds and new antenna technology implementations. The 802.11n specification requires all but handheld devices to use multiple antennae to implement a feature called *multiple in/multiple out (MIMO)*, which enables the devices to make multiple simultaneous connections. With up to four antennae, 802.11n devices can achieve amazing speeds. (The official standard supports throughput of up to 600 Mbps, although practical implementation drops that down substantially.)

Like 802.11g, 802.11n WAPs can run in the 2.4 GHz band, supporting earlier, slower 802.11b/g devices. The 802.11n standard also has a more powerful so-called *dual-band*. To use dual-band 802.11n, you need a more advanced (and more expensive) WAP that runs at both 5 GHz and 2.4 GHz simultaneously; some support 802.11a devices as well as 802.11b/g devices. Nice!

Table 14-1 compares the important differences between the versions of the 802.11 standards.

NOTE Most Wi-Fi devices you can buy right now support WPA2, but what about the millions of older Wi-Fi devices out there working for a living? You can update some devices to support WPA2 with a firmware upgrade or driver update. You'll also need to patch earlier versions of Mac OS X and Windows. Windows Vista/7 support WPA2 out of the box.

Standard	802.11a	802.11b	802.11g	802.11n
Max. throughput	54 Mbps	11 Mbps	54 Mbps	100+ Mbps
Max. range	150 feet	300 feet	300 feet	300+ feet
Frequency	5 GHz	2.4 GHz	2.4 GHz	2.4 and 5 GHz
Compatibility	802.11a	802.11b	802.11b, 802.11g	802.11b, 802.11g, 802.11n (802.11a in some cases)
Description	Products that adhere to this standard are considered Wi-Fi Certified. Eight available channels. Less prone to interference than 802.11b and 802.11g.	Products that adhere to this standard are considered Wi-Fi Certified. Fourteen channels available in the 2.4 GHz band (only 11 of which can be used in the U.S. due to FCC regulations). Three non-overlapping channels.	Products that adhere to this standard are considered Wi-Fi Certified. Improved security enhancements. Fourteen channels available in the 2.4 GHz band (only 11 of which can be used in the U.S. due to FCC regulations). Three non-overlapping channels.	Same as 802.11g but adds the 5 GHz band that 802.11a uses. 802.11n can also make use of multiple antennae (MIMO) to increase its range and speed.

Table 14-1 Comparison of 802.11 Standards

Bluetooth

You learned about Bluetooth back in Chapter 8, but let's review that material, then go into it more deeply. Bluetooth wireless technology, named for a ninth-century Danish king (a fact that is *still* of little use to you), is designed to create small wireless networks preconfigured to do very specific jobs. Some great examples are audio devices like headsets that connect to your smartphones, personal area networks (PANs) that link two PCs for a quick-and-dirty wireless network, and input devices such as keyboards and mice (Figure 14-7). Bluetooth is *not* designed to be a full-function networking solution, nor is it meant to compete with Wi-Fi.

Bluetooth, like any technology, has been upgraded over the years to make it faster and more secure. Two major versions of Bluetooth are widespread today. The first generation (versions 1.1 and 1.2) supports speeds around 1 Mbps. The second generation (2.0 and 2.1) is backward-compatible with its first-generation cousins and adds support for more speed by introducing Enhanced Data Rate (EDR), which pushes top speeds to around 3 Mbps.

Generally, the faster and further a device sends data, the more power it needs to do so, and the Bluetooth designers understood a long time ago that some devices (such as a Bluetooth headset) could save power by not sending data as quickly or as far as other Bluetooth devices may need. To address this, all Bluetooth devices are configured for

Figure 14-7
A Bluetooth
keyboard

one of three classes that define maximum power usage in milliwatts (mW) and maximum distance:

- **Class 1**   100 mW, 100 meters
- **Class 2**   2.5 mW, 10 meters
- **Class 3**   1 mW, 1 meter

Configuring Wireless Networking

The mechanics of setting up a wireless network don't differ much from those for a wired network. Physically installing a wireless network adapter is the same as installing a wired NIC, whether it's an internal PCI or PCIe card or an external USB device. Simply install the device and let Plug and Play handle detection and resource allocation. Install the device's supplied driver when prompted, and you're practically done.

EXAM TIP   The wireless configuration utility in Windows XP is called Wireless Zero Configuration (WZC). In Windows Vista/7 it is called WLAN AutoConfig.

As mentioned, wireless devices want to talk to each other, so communicating with an available wireless network is usually a no-brainer. The trick is to configure the wireless network so that specific wireless nodes can connect and to secure the data that's being sent through the air.

Wi-Fi networks support both ad hoc and infrastructure operation modes. Which mode you choose depends on the number of wireless nodes you need to support, the type of data sharing they'll perform, and your management requirements.

Ad Hoc Mode

The only requirements in an ad hoc–mode wireless network are that each wireless node be configured with the same SSID and that no two nodes use the same IP address. You may also have to select a common channel for all ad hoc nodes and ensure that the File and Printer Sharing service is running.

PART IV

Infrastructure Mode

Infrastructure-mode wireless networks require one or more WAPs and typically connect to a wired network segment, a corporate intranet or the Internet, or both. As with ad hoc–mode wireless networks, infrastructure-mode networks require that the same SSID be configured on all nodes and access points. You can set this using the WAP's configuration utility.

Access Point SSID Configuration

WAPs have an integrated Web server that you configure through a browser-based setup utility. Typically, you connect a PC to a WAP with an Ethernet cable and then fire up a Web browser. Enter the WAP's default IP address, such as 192.168.0.1 or 192.168.1.1, to bring up the configuration page. You may need to enter a username and password to log in. Setup screens vary from vendor to vendor and from model to model (Figure 14-8).

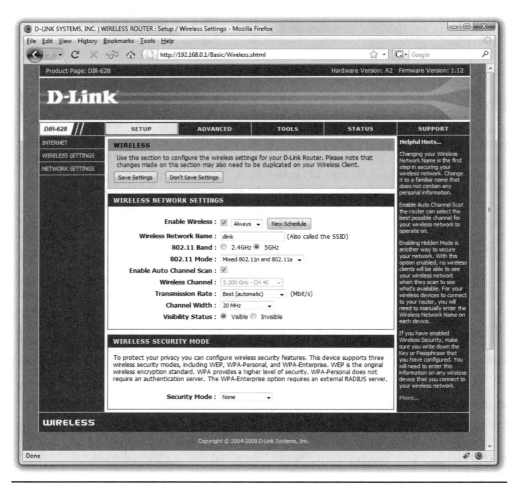

Figure 14-8 A WAP's configuration screen

Figure 14-9
A WAP's security
settings screen

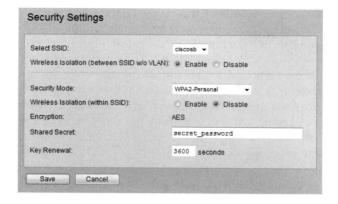

Configure the SSID option where indicated, and you're in business. Channel selection is usually automatic, but you can reconfigure this option if you have particular needs in your organization (such as if multiple wireless networks are operating in the same area). Remember that it's always more secure to configure a unique SSID and change the password than it is to accept the well-known default one.

Encryption

Set up encryption by turning it on at the WAP and then generating a unique security key (password), as seen in Figure 14-9. Then go to each of your wireless devices and type in the password when you attempt to connect to the wireless network.

Chapter Review

A wireless network eliminates the need for running cables between computers and hubs or switches. The two wireless technologies that are widely used today are IEEE 802.11, or Wi-Fi, and Bluetooth.

Many computers and portable devices include built-in wireless connectivity. In addition, you can add wireless capability to a computer that doesn't have it built in using an internal PCI or PCIe wireless NIC or an external USB wireless NIC.

Wireless networks can use two different modes. Ad hoc mode is used with smaller networks and involves wirelessly connecting each computer to every other computer. This makes them easy to set up but hard to manage. Infrastructure mode involves wirelessly connecting each computer to a central device known as a wireless access point (WAP). Infrastructure mode is harder to set up but provides a finer level of control over the network.

Securing your wireless network is important. Remember to change a new WAP's default SSID (or network name), administrator username, and password. WAPs are shipped with commonly known usernames and passwords; if you don't change them, someone can easily break into your network. Also, be sure to use the included encryption functionality with your WAP. The three common protocols are WEP, WPA, and WPA2, with WEP being the weakest and WPA2 being the strongest.

PART IV

Four Wi-Fi standards exist today. 802.11b was the first popular Wi-Fi flavor, using the 2.4 GHz range and supporting a throughput up to 11 Mbps. 802.11a was developed later, using the 5 GHz range, which was faster but had a shorter range. 802.11g has the best of both worlds: the range of 802.11b with the speed of 802.11a—54 Mbps. 802.11n uses both 2.4 GHz and 5 GHz and is capable of multiple simultaneous connections, dramatically increasing speeds. It also has a much wider range.

Bluetooth is designed to be used for very small networks that are preconfigured to perform a specific task, such as linking a cell phone to a wireless headset. The fastest version of Bluetooth tops out at 3 Mbps. Depending on the class of device, Bluetooth signals can reach up to 100 meters.

Utilities are included in your OS and WAP for configuring wireless networks. Be sure to change the SSID on the WAP. Then go to each connected device and select the WAP with that SSID to join it.

Questions

1. What is IEEE 802.11 more commonly known as?

    A. Bluetooth

    B. WAP

    C. Wi-Fi

    D. WPA

2. What are ad hoc–mode wireless networks best for? (Select two.)

    A. Small networks

    B. Large networks

    C. Temporary networks

    D. Permanent networks

3. What are infrastructure-mode wireless networks best for? (Select two.)

    A. Small networks

    B. Large networks

    C. Temporary networks

    D. Permanent networks

4. Which wireless encryption method is the strongest?

    A. WPA

    B. WPA2

    C. WAP

    D. WEP

5. Which Wi-Fi standard has the largest range?

    A. 802.11a

    B. 802.11b

C. 802.11g

D. 802.11n

6. What is the name of the feature that allows 802.11n to make multiple simultaneous connections using multiple antennae?

A. Bluetooth

B. SSID

C. Dual-band

D. MIMO

7. Which Wi-Fi standards use the 2.4 GHz frequency range? (Select three.)

A. 802.11a

B. 802.11b

C. 802.11g

D. 802.11n

8. What is the maximum range of a 2.5 mW Bluetooth device?

A. 1 meter

B. 5 meters

C. 10 meters

D. 100 meters

9. After configuring the SSID on your WAP, what utility in Windows 7 helps you connect to your wireless network?

A. WLAN AutoConfig

B. Wireless Zero Configuration

C. Wi-Fi Automatic Configuration

D. AutoWLAN

10. What are two common default addresses for a WAP's configuration utility? (Select two.)

A. 192.168.0.1

B. 192.169.1.1

C. 192.168.2.1

D. 192.168.1.1

Answers

1. C. IEEE 802.11 is more commonly known as Wi-Fi.

2. A, C. Ad hoc wireless networks are great for small, temporary networks, like a study group.

3. **B, D.** Infrastructure-mode wireless networks are better for larger, permanent networks. These work great in home and office settings.

4. **B.** WPA2 is the strongest wireless encryption technology and should be used on all WAPs if possible.

5. **D.** At 300+ feet, 802.11n has the largest range of the Wi-Fi standards.

6. **D.** Multiple-in/multiple-out (MIMO) enables 802.11n WAPs to make multiple simultaneous connections to a wireless device, providing greater throughput.

7. **B, C, D.** Every Wi-Fi standard except 802.11a uses the 2.4 GHz frequency range. (802.11n cheats—it uses both 2.4 GHz and 5 GHz.)

8. **C.** A 2.5 mW Bluetooth device has a range of up to 10 meters.

9. **A.** The name of the Windows 7 utility that helps you connect to a wireless network is WLAN AutoConfig.

10. **A, D.** Most WAPs use either 192.168.0.1 or 192.168.1.1 as the default address for their configuration utilities.

Connecting to the Internet

15

In this chapter, you will learn how to
- Describe the hardware used to connect to the Internet
- Explain protocols and software used with networking and the Internet
- Discuss Web content and Web-delivered services

How great would it be if you could connect your computer or LAN to other computers and other LANs? And not just to one other network, but to every other network in the country? Or the *world*? You could share data back and forth, spreading news and information, music, and pictures, across the planet almost instantaneously! An entirely new culture could form around it, bringing about new platforms for media and business, not to mention changing forever the term "multiplayer gaming"—it would probably be the greatest thing since the invention of the paper clip. I'm just glad I thought of it first. Wait, that idea's taken? Well of course it is—it's the Internet!

This chapter covers the various methods of connecting to the Internet, the protocols used to control those connections, as well as the software you'll use to interact with it, such as browsers and e-mail clients. It also discusses some of the content you can find on the Internet, including Web-delivered services and streaming audio and video.

The Physical Connection

Hundreds of thousands of smaller networks connected together form the Internet. People often think of the Internet as some monolithic, centralized *thing*, but that perception couldn't be farther from the truth. Like the worldwide telephone network, the Internet is a "supernetwork" of smaller networks.

The designers of the Internet wanted to make certain that nothing could stop the flow of communication, not even a nuclear attack, so they specified a highly *decentralized* network with multiple connections between the various computers (Figure 15-1). The central heart of the Internet—called the *backbone*—consists of many university, corporate, and government networks, connected together via thick bundles of glass filaments, called *fiber optic*.

Figure 15-1
The decentralized
Internet

Routers

Routers provide the connection points between the networks and determine the route for a data packet to take from the source network to the destination network (Figure 15-2).

Routers range from the high-end machines that direct huge amounts of Internet traffic to the little box attached to your cable modem at home. Home routers (or broadband routers) often offer multiple functions; most have built-in switches and wireless access points (and are often referred to as "wireless routers").

Routers know the destination of packets of data because routers use TCP/IP, the common tongue of the Internet. They read the network ID of each data packet and send the data packet by the shortest route they know about to its destination (Figure 15-3).

Figure 15-2
A router

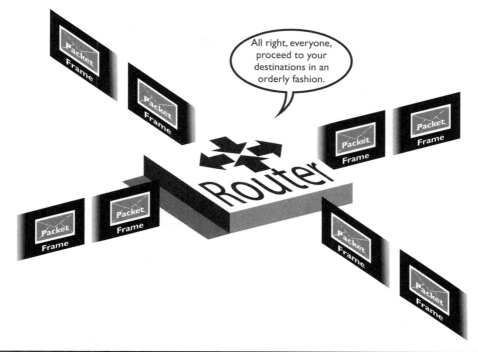

Figure 15-3 A router directing Internet traffic

 NOTE Keep both TCP/IP and network IDs in your back pocket for now. You'll learn more about both later in the chapter. The important thing to know now is that routers can direct traffic efficiently.

The multiple connections between the backbone networks offer great resilience for the Internet in times of crisis. If one route goes down, the routers update their maps of the Internet and re-route traffic another way (Figure 15-4).

 EXAM TIP A disruption to your Internet connection is also known as a *loss of service.*

All of this wonderful technology doesn't do much for you if you're not on—or connected to—one of those university, corporate, or government computer networks. Getting your computer connected to the Internet requires some sort of intermediary network with a router into which you can tap. This router, in turn, connects to the Internet. An *Internet service provider (ISP)* leases connections to the Internet from one of

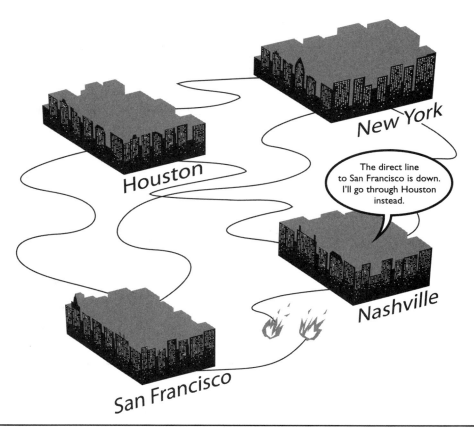

Figure 15-4   Router changing route due to problems

the backbone networks and, in turn, rents a portion of those connections to you. An ISP acts as your *gateway* to the Internet (Figure 15-5).

Establishing a link between your computer and the ISP requires three things:

- Some kind of network device on your computer, like a modem or network card
- A cable or radio transmitter that enables the network device to access the world outside your door
- Programs to make that hardware go, like the built-in network software in Windows and TCP/IP installed

Let's turn now to the common ways you can connect to an ISP. First, we'll look at dial-up, and then turn to broadband connections.

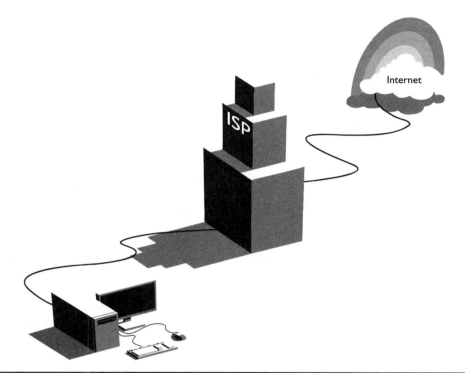

Figure 15-5 Your computer connects to an ISP; the ISP provides the connection to the Internet

Dial-Up Connections

The least expensive Internet connection is called *dial-up networking*. It consists of three pieces:

- A modem
- A working telephone line
- An ISP

The *modem* enables the computer to communicate via phone lines (Figure 15-6). The phone line provides the link between the modem and the computers at the ISP. The ISP computers connect to the Big Kahuna of all networks, the Internet. Properly installed and configured, the modem–telephone line–ISP connection enables you to surf, shop, and otherwise explore Web sites hosted by computers all over the world.

For this process to work, you must have a properly installed modem with the correct drivers loaded. You need properly set up software, such as Dial-up Networking (DUN) in Windows. Your ISP gives you the configuration information, such as a telephone number, user name, and password. Of course, the ISP computers need to be set

Figure 15-6
A dial-up modem

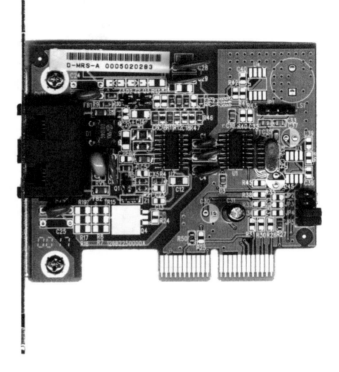

up properly to receive your modem's call. If the ISP computers don't recognize your name and password, for example, you can call all day long and not get a connection to the world at large.

Benefits, Reliability, and Disadvantages

Dial-up connections provide the least expensive method of getting your computer onto the Internet. Prices in the typical metropolitan area in the United States, for example, range from free to about $20 U.S. per month. The technology has been around for a decade or more and works smoothly and easily. So, what's the catch?

Dial-up connections provide the *slowest* type of connection to the Internet, a bottleneck that continues to get worse as more Web sites incorporate multimedia content such as movies, Flash animations, and other things. How slow is slow? Let's turn to the numbers so this makes sense.

Dial-Up Rates   Numbers without context mean very little, right? Here's the scoop about dial-up. First, the fastest dial-up download speed you'll ever get is around 56 Kbps. More commonly, especially outside the big cities in the U.S., you'll get closer to 40 Kbps consistently. It would take around 47 seconds at the fastest dial-up speed (at 56.6 Kbps, the theoretical maximum dial-up speed) and a whopping 90 seconds at 28.8 Kbps to open up the Microsoft home page (www.microsoft.com), and that's a fairly plain Web site.

ISDN, the Other Dial-Up

Early on, people realized that computer information traveled slowly over regular analog telephone lines. The concept of an *Integrated Service Digital Network (ISDN)* began in 1984 (Figure 15-7). It was supposed to evolve into a completely digital telephone system so that data would go faster through phone lines. ISDN never caught on at as massive a scale as was expected because other, faster technologies soon came along, such as DSL and cable (see the next sections). ISDN supports data transfer rates of 128 Kbps.

Although dial-up speeds served us well in the twentieth century when the Web offered relatively simple pages of text and graphics, people use the Internet today for a variety of much more complex things, such as:

- International phone calls
- Video conferencing
- Multiplayer gaming

To make convenient use of some of these higher-end features and the rich, multimedia sites on the Web, you need a dedicated, high-speed connection.

Figure 15-7
An ISDN modem

PART IV

Dedicated or Broadband Connections

A dedicated, or *broadband*, connection gives your computer or network access to the Internet through a single high-speed connection. It's always on, as opposed to, say, a dial-up connection, where you have to sit and wait for the connection to go through. It's also much faster. Two technologies dominate the broadband connection field:

- Cable
- DSL

Both technologies require the same sorts of equipment on your PC:

- An Ethernet network interface card (NIC)
- Installed drivers
- Software set up to make the connection between your computer and the ISP

Cable

Cable connections use regular cable TV cables to serve up lightning-fast speeds. Cable blows dial-up out the window, with upload speeds of up to 1.5 Mbps and download speeds from 2 to as high as 24 Mbps. Remember that Microsoft homepage that took upward of half a minute to download via dial-up? It's an almost instantaneous download on cable!

 NOTE The cable speeds listed here refer to the United States. Other countries, like Japan and South Korea, have prioritized Internet speed and get more than 100 Mbps from the same type of cable. The technology is proven and ready; the companies in control in the United States are not.

Cable connections use a *cable modem* that then connects to a NIC in your PC via an Ethernet cable (Figure 15-8). The cable TV companies take advantage of the fact that their cable TV signals occupy only a fraction of the capacity of the cables running into your home.

DSL

Digital Subscriber Line (DSL) uses your telephone line as its pipeline, but it does so in a very clever way. The details are quite technical, but basically DSL exploits the fact that standard copper telephone lines can handle a much greater range of frequencies, or *bandwidth*, than what is needed to transmit your voice during phone calls. DSL uses this extra bandwidth capacity to send data over the telephone wires without disturbing their ability to carry voice conversations.

DSL connections use a standard telephone line, like dial-up connections. The special DSL equipment on each end creates always-on Internet connections at blindingly fast speeds, especially when compared with dial-up connections (Figure 15-9). Service levels vary around the U.S., but the typical upload speed is ~512 Kbps, while download speed comes in at a decent ~1–6 Mbps.

Figure 15-8
A cable modem

DSL requires very little setup from a user standpoint.

1. A tech comes to the house to install a NIC in the Internet-bound PC and drop off a *DSL receiver* (often called a "DSL modem").

2. The receiver connects to the Ethernet NIC and to the telephone line; the telephone line goes to special hardware at the neighborhood telephone switch and from there to the Internet.

3. The tech (or the user, if knowledgeable) then configures the TCP/IP protocol options for the NIC to match the settings demanded by the DSL provider, and that's about it.

Figure 15-9
A DSL receiver

Within moments, you're surfing at blazing speeds. You don't need a second telephone line. You don't need to wear a special propeller hat or anything.

NOTE The only bad thing about DSL is that your house has to be within a fairly short distance from a main phone service switching center—the neighborhood switch—something like 18,000 feet. This pretty much stops everybody but inner-city dwellers from having access to DSL service.

Dial-up, Cable, or DSL?

At this point in the discussion, students often wonder which is better: cable or DSL? For that matter, why would you ever choose dial-up in an increasingly high-speed world? Three factors affect your choice.

First, cable and DSL generally cost a lot more than dial-up. Cable is the most expensive at ~$50 U.S., but offers the highest download speeds. DSL sits in a nice sweet spot between cable and dial-up in both cost and speed.

Second, you can get cable in every metropolitan area (in the United States, at least), but it's not available in many rural settings. DSL coverage is even more limited, with availability limited even within cities. You can get dial-up almost anywhere.

Third, cable and DSL offer extra inducements. If you have a TV tuner card in your PC, you can use the same cable connection (with a splitter) to watch TV on your PC. With DSL, on the other hand, you can use your existing phone lines and not worry about installing cable or any other equipment.

Both DSL and cable modem Internet connections, including those in a home, can be used by two or more computers if they are part of a LAN.

Protocols and Settings

Once you have a physical connection to the Internet, your computer (especially your NIC), switch, and router all need to start talking to one another, exchanging data. In order for them to know *how* to communicate, they need to use a predetermined language. Protocols fill that need.

TCP/IP

Computer networks have many pathways that send information back and forth. They can send it through the old-fashioned copper wires of telephone lines or through high-tech fiber optic lines that use tiny hairs of glass instead of copper. Computer networks can even send information to each other through radio waves and lasers.

The major issues for computer networks have never been which pathway you use to send information. Rather, they're concerned with how you send the information so that it goes to the right place. Plus, the receiving network must be able to read the data.

These issues became a big problem for the U.S. military. The Navy bought their computer stuff from one company, and the Army from somebody else. They couldn't send information back and forth, since these different systems had different ways of treating information. The United States Department of Defense (DoD) solved these problems by developing a set of commands and controls for the networks to use, what's called the *TCP/IP protocol suite*. That's quite a mouthful, no? Let's break the phrase down into its components.

In the mundane world of princes and presidents, *protocols* determine how the leaders and their staffs handle meetings. Who enters the room first, the prince or the president? Who stands up first and what sort of greeting should occur, a handshake or a hug? For that matter, what language should they speak? Following protocols ensures that both parties are comfortable, won't insult each other, and can focus on the important thing—communicating.

The *Transmission Control Protocol/Internet Protocol (TCP/IP)* protocol suite does the same thing for networks, providing a common set of rules and guidelines (or *standards* in network terminology) for electrical signals, packaging of information, and so on. The Internet uses TCP/IP, which makes the protocol suite the common tongue of the computer world.

NOTE Multiple smaller protocols, such as TCP, IP, UDP, and so on, form the TCP/IP protocol suite; hence the "suite."

As its name suggests, the Transmission Control Protocol (TCP) controls the sending and receiving of information. Two computers communicating use TCP to make a connection and handle the flow of data between them.

Computers use the Internet Protocol (IP) to determine packaging and labeling of data. When you send an e-mail to someone, it doesn't just go out in a big blob of information. Your e-mail is neatly cut up and packaged into bits of information that are all the same size. Your operating system uses IP to determine how to package the e-mail, and the operating system on the receiving computer knows how to unpack the information (and how to put it back together) so that it can be read like a normal e-mail because it too follows IP.

But how does your message know to go to the right place? Just as an old-fashioned letter will have the destination address and a return address on the envelope, your operating system uses IP to put a numerical destination and return address—called *IP addresses*—onto the packets of information that make up your e-mail (Figure 15-10).

IP addresses follow specific conventions. Most commonly, IP addresses have four sets of numbers ranging from 0 to 255, separated by periods, like this: 192.168.1.52. There are two different components to an IP address:

- The *network ID* defines your network.

- The *host ID* describes your *node*—the computer you use to access the Internet.

No two machines on a network can share the same IP address, just as you wouldn't want two houses in the same city to share a street name and number.

PART IV

Figure 15-10
A packet identified
by its IP address

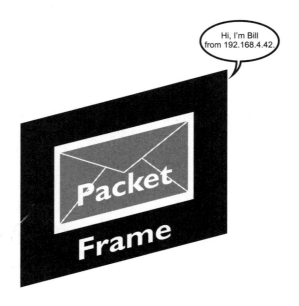

For example, Marco's school has 40 computers linked together into a network. His computer has the IP address of 192.168.7.23. All the other computers in the school have the same network ID—192.168.7—but have a different host ID, from 1 to 40. Marco's host ID is 23. Network IDs become very important when you connect two or more networks.

The IP addresses I'm showing you here are technically IP version 4, or IPv4, addresses, but this type of addressing has a bit of a problem—we're running out of possible IP addresses. Soon, there won't be any left.

IP version 6, the newest version of the Internet protocol, which will save us all from an Internetless world, uses a 128-bit address instead of IPv4's 32-bit address. What this means is that there are more possible addresses than with IPv4. *A lot more.* My favorite illustration is to think of all of the molecules that make up the Earth, and divide them by 7. That's how many possible IPv6 addresses there are.

The drawback is that IPv6 addresses are not quite as svelte and easy to remember as in IPv4. For example, an IPv6 address looks like this: 2001:0db8:85a3:0000:0000:8a2e: 0370:7334. Not quite as easy to work with as 192.168.1.1, eh? IPv6 also handles routing and various other things differently than IPv4, but the main things to know are that the IP addresses look remarkably different and there are enough of them to last for a while. There's no solid plan yet for when everyone is going to switch to IPv6, but it'll be a big change when it happens.

EXAM TIP   Know the differences between IPv4 and IPv6. IPv4 is older and uses four sets of numbers separated by periods, while IPv6 is newer and uses eight sets of letters and numbers separated by colons.

DNS

Knowing that users could not easily remember many IP addresses, early Internet pioneers came up with a way to correlate those numbers with more human-friendly computer designations.

Special computers, called *Domain Name Service (DNS)* servers, keep databases of IP addresses and their corresponding names. For example, a machine called www.totalsem .com will be listed in a DNS directory with a corresponding IP address, such as 209.34.45.163. So instead of typing 209.34.45.163 into a Web browser to get to my company's Web site, you can just type the name. Your system will then query the DNS server to get the IP address for www.totalsem.com and use that to find the right machine. Unless you want to type in IP addresses all of the time, a TCP/IP network will need at least one DNS server.

The Internet has regulated *domain names*. The Web site above, for example, has the domain name of www.totalsem.com. If you want a domain name that others can access on the Internet, you must register your domain name and pay a small yearly fee. In most cases, your ISP can handle this for you. Domain names end with one of several *top-level domains*, including .com, .edu, and .net. You'll learn more about these later in the chapter.

DHCP

Most TCP/IP networks support the *Dynamic Host Configuration Protocol (DHCP)*. DHCP enables you to create a pool of IP addresses that are given temporarily (thus the "dynamic") to machines. DHCP is especially handy for networks of several laptops that join and leave the network on a regular basis. Why give a machine that is on the network for only a few hours a day a static (or permanent) IP address? For that reason, DHCP is quite popular. If you add a NIC to a Windows system, the default TCP/IP settings are set to use DHCP. When you accept those automatic settings, you're really telling the machine to use DHCP.

TCP/IP Services

After you've established a connection between the PC and the ISP, you can do nothing on the Internet without applications designed to use one or more TCP/IP services, such as Web browsing and e-mail. TCP/IP has the following commonly used services:

- The World Wide Web
- E-mail
- FTP (File Transfer Protocol)
- VoIP (Voice over IP)

Each of these services (sometimes referred to by the overused term *TCP/IP protocols*) requires a special application, and each of those applications has special settings. Let's look at each service. As a quick reference, Table 15-1 shows some common port numbers the CompTIA Strata IT Fundamentals exam expects you to know.

PART IV

TCP/IP Service	Port Number
HTTP	80
HTTPS	443
FTP	20, 21
POP3	110
SMTP	25

Table 15-1
TCP/IP Service Port Numbers

NOTE Each TCP/IP service uses a port number (or two) to identify it. Port numbers are really just another way to refer to the specific service. These are important to know, especially when setting up firewalls, which you'll read more about in Chapter 18.

The World Wide Web

The Web provides a graphical face for the Internet. *Web servers* (servers running specialized software) provide Web sites that you access by using HTTP on port 80 and thus get more or less useful information.

Using Web-browser software, such as Internet Explorer or Mozilla Firefox, you can click a link on a Web page and be instantly transported not just to some Web server in your home town, but to anywhere in the world (Figure 15-11). Where is the server located? Does it matter? It could be in a closet in my office or in a massive data center in Houston. The great part about the Web is that you can get from here to there and access the information you need with a click or two of the mouse.

NOTE The full domain name plus the protocol is called the *Uniform Resource Locator*, or *URL*. The URL for my company's Web site, therefore, is http://www.totalsem.com.

One thing that HTTP lacks, however, is security. When you want to buy something from an online retailer like Amazon, for example, you don't want someone else covertly sniffing out your credit card information.

The most famous of all encryptions is the *Secure Sockets Layer (SSL)* security protocol, which is used to create a secure connection to Web sites. SSL was subsequently incorporated into the more far-reaching HTTPS (HTTP over SSL) protocol. These protocols make it possible to create the secure connections people use to make purchases over the Internet.

Although HTTPS looks a lot like HTTP from the point of view of a Web browser, HTTPS uses port 443. It's easy to tell if a Web site is using HTTPS because the Web address starts with HTTPS instead of just HTTP. The Web browser also displays a lock symbol to remind you that you're using an encrypted connection.

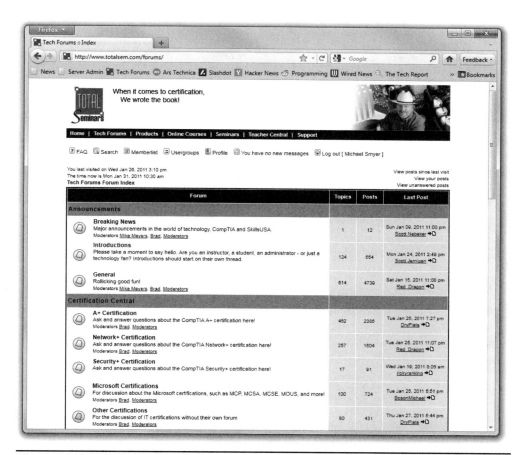

Figure 15-11 Mozilla Firefox

FTP

The *File Transfer Protocol (FTP)*, using ports 20 and 21, is a protocol used to share files between systems. Visually, it works similarly to HTTP. Instead of typing in a Web address and seeing a Web page, typing an FTP address like ftp://ftp.example.com brings you to a file and folder directory structure like the one on your computer. Here, you can upload and download files (if you have permission to do so).

FTP server software exists for most operating systems, so you can use FTP to transfer data between any two systems regardless of the OS. To access an FTP site, you must use FTP client software such as FileZilla, although older versions of most Web browsers provide at least download support for FTP (Figure 15-12).

PART IV

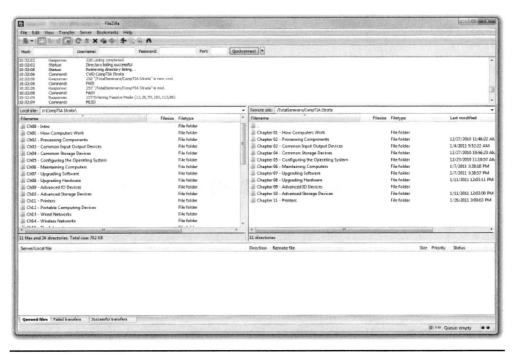

Figure 15-12 FileZilla

All FTP sites require you to log on. Most FTP clients will assume that you want to log on as "anonymous." If you want to log on as a specific user, you have to add your user name to the URL. Instead of typing **ftp://ftp.totalsem.com**, for example, you would type **ftp://scottj@ftp.totalsem.com**. The FTP server then would prompt for a password.

An anonymous logon works fine for most public FTP sites. Many techs prefer to use third-party programs such as FileZilla for FTP access because these third-party applications can store user name and password settings. This enables you to access the FTP site more easily later.

E-Mail Protocols

E-mail clients, such as Microsoft Outlook or Mozilla Thunderbird, need to be configured before you can use them to access your e-mail (Figure 15-13). First, you must provide your e-mail address and password. All e-mail addresses come in the now-famous *accountname@Internet domain* format.

The second thing you must add are the names of the Post Office Protocol version 3 (POP3) or Internet Message Access Protocol (IMAP) server and the Simple Mail Transfer Protocol (SMTP) server. The POP3 or IMAP server is the computer that handles incoming (to you) e-mail.

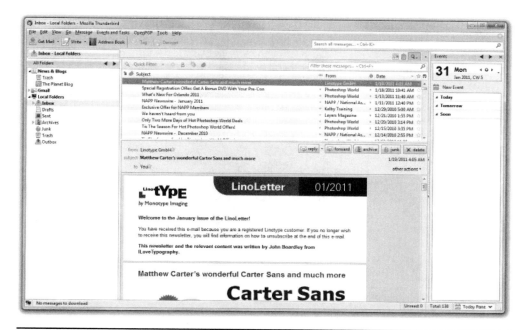

Figure 15-13 Mozilla Thunderbird

POP3 is by far the most widely-used standard, although the latest version of IMAP, *IMAP4*, supports some features POP3 doesn't. IMAP4 enables you to search through messages on the mail server to find specific keywords, for example, and select the messages you want to download onto your machine. Even with the advantages of IMAP4 over POP3, the vast majority of incoming mail servers use POP3.

The SMTP server handles your outgoing e-mail. This server may have the same name, or close to the same name, as your POP3 server. All these settings should be provided to you by your ISP. If they are not, you should be comfortable knowing what to ask for. If one of these names is incorrect, either you will not get your e-mail or you will not be able to send e-mail. If an e-mail setup that has been working well for a while suddenly encounters errors, it is likely that either the POP3 or SMTP server is down, or the DNS server has quit working.

 EXAM TIP Make sure you know about TCP/IP and its associated services and ports, including HTTP, HTTPS, FTP, POP3, and SMTP.

VoIP

You can use *Voice over IP (VoIP)* to make voice calls over your computer network. Why have two sets of wires, one for voice and one for data, going to every desk? Why not just use the extra capacity on the data network for your phone calls? That's exactly what VoIP does for you. VoIP works with every type of high-speed Internet connection, such as DSL and cable.

Figure 15-14   A Skype conversation

VoIP doesn't refer to a single protocol but rather to a collection of protocols that make phone calls over the data network possible. Vendors such as Skype and Vonage offer popular VoIP solutions, and many corporations use VoIP for their internal phone networks (Figure 15-14).

A key to remember when installing or upgrading VoIP is that low network latency is more important than high network speed. *Latency* is the amount of time a packet takes to get to its destination and is measured in milliseconds. A higher latency means more problems, such as noticeable delays during a VoIP call.

Internet Content

Once you connect to the Internet, you can enjoy all the amazing capabilities of the Internet. Web sites use more than just text these days; the Internet has grown more dynamic and interactive, with "streaming content" and "social networking" being the big buzzwords. Entire software suites can now be used online without the need to download anything. With the endless amount of available content, it's a good idea to sort out where you should go looking for things online.

Web Sites

Web site domains, just like e-mail address domains, have two portions:

- The network name
- The top-level domain (also called the domain code or *extension*—the two- or three-letter code at the end)

Just glancing at a Web site address can tell you a lot about a Web site before you even visit it. You can tell the *type* of Web site you check out by looking at the top-level domain.

.com	General business	**.org**	Nonprofit organizations
.edu	Educational organizations	**.gov**	Government organizations
.mil	Military organizations	**.net**	Internet organizations
.uk, .jp, .de	International		

Commercial (.com)

The .com Web extension was designed for commercial use, but all sorts of sites, commercial or otherwise, use it. The Web site for Alien Scooters in Austin, Texas, provides a good example of a .com site, at www.alienscooters.com (Figure 15-15). The Web site gives you information about electric bikes and scooters and tells you about the company. You can purchase electric bikes and scooters directly from the Web site as well, which makes the site an *e-commerce site*.

Figure 15-15   The Alien Scooters Web site

Academic (.edu)

Educational facilities—primarily universities and some two-year colleges in the United States—use the .edu extension. The Rice University site provides a good example (Figure 15-16). You can find information about programs, degrees, departments, faculty, research, admissions, and much more.

Organizational (.org)

Nonprofit and political organizations use the .org extension. An example of a .org site is www.aclu.org for the American Civil Liberties Union (Figure 15-17). You can learn about the organization in great detail here, including ongoing programs and fund-raising. You can donate money, but you can't purchase anything at this site, so it's not an e-commerce site at all.

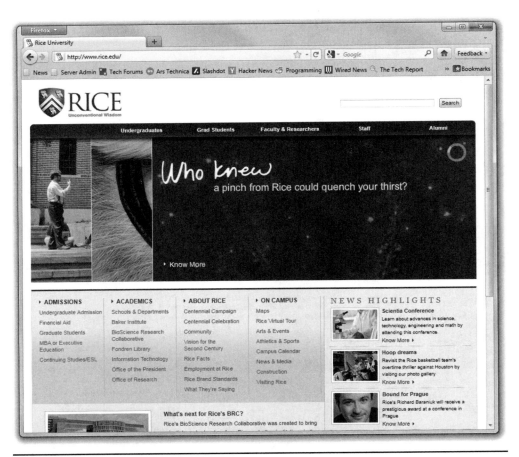

Figure 15-16   The Rice University Web site

Figure 15-17 The ACLU Web site

Governmental (.gov)

Governmental agencies of the United States, including sites hosted by local, state/regional, and national governments, use the .gov extension. The National Aeronautics and Space Administration (NASA), the fine folks who put a man on the moon, has a site that is chock-full of information about space, the planets, the NASA missions, and more (Figure 15-18).

Figure 15-18   The NASA Web site

International (.uk, .jp, .de)

Many non-U.S. Web sites use the international extension for their home country. Web sites from the United Kingdom end in .uk, for example, while Web sites from Spain will end in .es (for España, which is how you say Spain in Spanish). Typing in www.steam-car.co.uk will take you to the Web site of the British Steam Car Challenge, a group dedicated to making a steam-powered car that can go very fast (Figure 15-19).

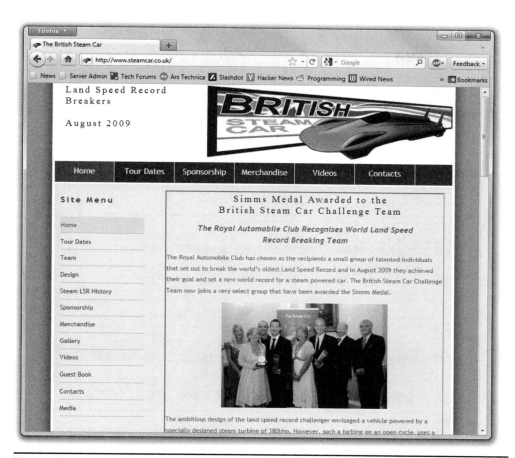

Figure 15-19 Go steam!

Newsgroups/Forums

Getting e-mail from a group that's into the same topics you're into can get overwhelming. When you get busy with other things or when some news hits that sets the list on fire, the simple volume of e-mail in your Inbox can become too much. An alternative way to post and access the same information is to use a public *newsgroup* or *forum* (sometimes called a *message board*), such as the one shown in Figure 15-20. That way, you can access the newsgroup when you have time and pass it by when you don't.

The *USENET* is a collection of literally thousands of newsgroups that contain posts from individuals on every topic you can imagine, and probably quite a few that you didn't need to know about. You access USENET over the Internet using special news-reader software.

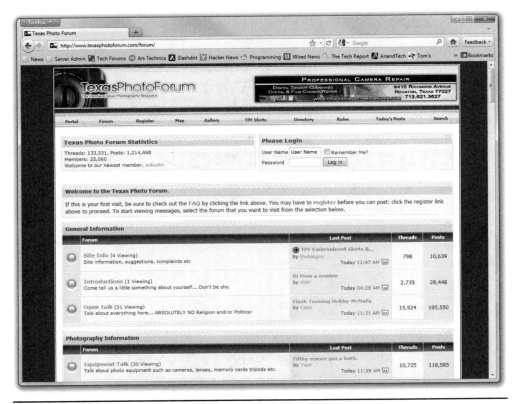

Figure 15-20   A message board on TexasPhotoForum.com

Chat Rooms

The Internet offers real-time communication with multiple people at the same time through various chat programs, the most famous of which is Internet Relay Chat (IRC). IRC servers can host *chat rooms*, places that act like mailing lists on steroids, where everyone can talk to everyone else (Figure 15-21). As you might suspect, you use an IRC client to connect to an IRC server, just as you use a newsreader to connect to a newsgroup server or an e-mail client to connect to an e-mail server. Chat rooms usually have a common theme or interest among their users, just like newsgroups.

Blog Posts

More and more people are putting their thoughts and ideas on the Web these days by posting *Weblogs*, or *blogs*. Blogs are unedited articles and commentaries published online, usually by individuals. Figure 15-22, for example, shows the Clean Break blog written by Toronto Star columnist Tyler Hamilton. He blogs here on topics that don't necessarily make sense to put in his print column.

Figure 15-21
A chat room

Figure 15-22 The Clean Break blog

Anyone, even you, can publish writing online through a blog post. Blogs are generally public and can be read by anyone on the Internet. The best part is that you can blog about anything, from thoughts about somebody's prom or vacation to in-depth technical essays. Several Web sites, such as www.blogspot.com and www.wordpress.com, enable you to create blogs for free and get published in no time.

Blogs make great sources of online information, since they cover pretty much every topic under the sun. Be wary of using a blog as your only source of information, however, especially when you are unsure about the credibility and expertise of the author.

Social Networking

Social networking refers in general to the process of connecting and interacting online with friends, colleagues, acquaintances, and people with similar interests. Today, social networking Web sites are a key source of online information, both personal and global.

There are several social networking Web sites that enable personal as well as professional networking. Facebook currently holds the #1 slot among social networking sites and, as of this writing, has about 400 million active users (Figure 15-23). Facebook enables you to:

- Stay connected with friends and family across the world
- Share files such as your latest pictures, interesting articles, and videos from other Web sites
- Post messages on your profile as well as on your friends' pages
- E-mail and chat with friends
- Blog
- Play games
- Get invited to events
- Tend a virtual farm
- Keep virtual pets
- Do a whole bunch of stuff that you would never have imagined you could do online

Businesses and organizations have Facebook pages, too, and you can "like" any organization about which you want to stay informed.

Other well-known social networking Web sites include LinkedIn, which is more of a professional network, and MySpace, which was the most popular social networking site until it was overtaken by Facebook.

You should always pay close attention to the information you share on social networking sites and keep a tab on who you allow access to your information. As your online presence expands, other people get access to more and more information about you, making you vulnerable to identity theft, spammers, and other forms of malicious attacks.

Learn the privacy settings that each service offers and remember that the default settings are never those that give you the most privacy. Make sure to change the settings to suit your comfort level. Always use common sense while sharing personal information on such Web sites.

Figure 15-23 Facebook

Web-Delivered Services

While you can find several Web sites that enable you to download software and run it on your computer, there are also entire software solutions that are usable directly from the Web. These *Web-delivered services* often re-create software that runs on your desktop, but they run it inside your browser instead. This allows you to use the application anywhere and access any files you may store with the service.

One of the best examples of Web-delivered services is the suite of applications offered by Google, known as Google Apps (Figure 15-24). This collection of services includes Web-based e-mail and calendars, as well as a full set of office applications (alternatives to Microsoft's Word, PowerPoint, and Excel) and Web site-building tools. With Google Docs, Google's office suite, you can type up documents, make spreadsheets, and design slide shows just as you would using a desktop application. As an added bonus, Google Docs enables you to collaborate on your documents with other Google users.

Web-delivered services usually require creating an account with the service provider. Once you do, you can log on to the service from anywhere, work with your information, save it, and then access it again later from another computer.

PART IV

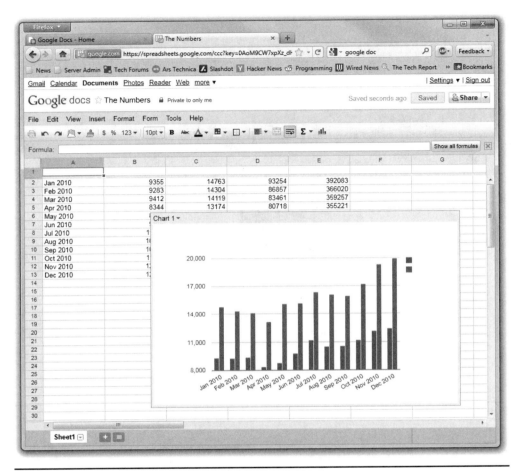

Figure 15-24 Google Docs, a part of Google Apps

 NOTE Web-delivered services are a form of *cloud computing*. You'll learn more about cloud computing in Chapter 16.

Streaming Content

Perhaps the most amazing (and productivity-killing) recent development in Internet technology has been the rise of streaming audio and video content. *Streaming* content means that you don't have to download an entire video before you view it. In fact, you don't really download anything in the traditional sense, since the video doesn't stay on your computer after you finish watching it.

When you click the Play button on a site like YouTube or Vimeo, your computer begins to download pieces of video from their servers (Figure 15-25). Once enough data has been downloaded to play the beginning of the video, it starts playing.

Figure 15-25 A streaming video on YouTube

While you watch the first part of the video, your PC continues downloading the rest, hopefully at a fast enough pace that you don't catch up and run out of downloaded video. If that happens, you'll probably see a message like "Buffering," which means it needs a head start downloading more data. You'll need to wait until it starts playing again to continue watching the video.

 EXAM TIP Make sure you know about Web-delivered services and different types of streaming content.

Chapter Review

The Internet is a decentralized collection of smaller networks connected together by multiple pathways. Routers both connect these networks and direct traffic between clients. Routers come in many shapes and sizes, from large, powerful routers that direct high volumes of traffic across the Internet, to small home routers with built-in switches and wireless access points.

To access the Internet, you need a connection to an Internet service provider (ISP). The ISP is your gateway to the Internet. Different connection methods include dial-up,

ISDN, cable, and DSL. Each method uses different hardware devices to connect your computer or network to the Internet through an ISP.

Computer networks communicate using protocols, a common language that each piece of network hardware speaks. The Internet uses the Transmission Control Protocol/Internet Protocol (TCP/IP). The Internet Protocol packages and labels data with an IP address so that it is sent to the proper destination on the network.

A Domain Name Service (DNS) is a large database of IP addresses and the corresponding names of various hosts and domains on the Internet. The Internet uses regulated domain names, with top-level domains including .com, .edu, and .net.

The Dynamic Host Configuration Protocol enables you to create a pool of temporary IP addresses that are handed out when a computer joins a network.

TCP/IP services include HTTP for the Web; FTP for file sharing; and POP3, IMAP, and SMTP for e-mail clients. Voice over IP is a collection of protocols for using your computer to make phone calls.

There are several different kinds of Web sites and content on the Internet, including commercial and academic Web sites, social networks, and blogs. Web-delivered services are applications that run in your browser; the Google Apps suite is a good example of this. Audio and video can be streamed to your desktop by simultaneously downloading and playing back the content.

Questions

1. What type of cable is used for the backbone networks of the Internet?

    A. Fiber optic

    B. Ethernet

    C. Telephone cord

    D. Power lines

2. What do routers do?

    A. Enable access to an ISP

    B. Store Web sites

    C. Store domain names

    D. Connect multiple networks

3. Which is the least expensive method of connecting to the Internet?

    A. Dial-up

    B. Ethernet

    C. ISDN

    D. DSL

4. What is the typical upload speed of a DSL connection?

    A. 6 Mbps

    B. 1.5 Mbps

    C. 10 Mbps

    D. 512 Kbps

5. What are the two components of an IP address? (Select two.)

    A. Protocol ID

    B. Network ID

    C. Host ID

    D. Domain ID

6. What is DHCP?

    A. A database of IP addresses and server names

    B. A pool of temporary IP addresses handed out to members of a network

    C. A high-speed connection to the Internet

    D. The three-letter extension at the end of a Web address

7. What are the ports used by the File Transfer Protocol (FTP)? (Select two.)

    A. 20

    B. 21

    C. 80

    D. 443

8. If a Web site uses the .org top-level domain, what kind of Web site is it?

    A. Academic

    B. Commercial

    C. Nonprofit organization

    D. International

9. What is an application used in your browser referred to as?

    A. Streaming content

    B. Social networking

    C. Web-delivered service

    D. Blog

10. What is the port number for HTTP?

    A. 80

    B. 443

    C. 20

    D. 21

Answers

1. **A.** The backbone of the Internet consists of fiber optic cable connections.

2. **D.** Routers connect multiple networks together to form wide area networks like the Internet.

3. **A.** Dial-up connections are the least expensive method of connecting to the Internet.

4. **D.** The typical upload speed of a DSL connection is 512 Kbps.

5. **B, C.** IP addresses consist of a network ID, which defines your network, and a host ID, which defines your node.

6. **B.** The Dynamic Host Configuration Protocol enables a pool of temporary IP addresses that are handed out to members of a network.

7. **A, B.** FTP uses ports 20 and 21.

8. **C.** The .org top-level domain is used by nonprofit and political organizations.

9. **C.** Applications used within a browser are considered Web-delivered services.

10. **A.** The port number for HTTP is 80.

Green Networking

In this chapter, you will learn how to
- Describe servers that offer substantial savings in electrical usage over traditional servers
- Explain methods for greening the workplace
- Discuss ways to reduce the power usage of workers

In the early days of personal computers, no one worried about how much electricity computers used. Most offices could afford only a few computers, anyway—the Internet didn't exist.

Today, just about every company has at least one computer per worker plus dedicated server computers for storing important data and running applications. Each of those computers has two or more fans, plus drives that spin and monitors that glow. All of these pieces use electricity.

Considering that most electricity generated in the world comes from nonrenewable fossil fuels, coming up with ways for devices to use less electricity makes a lot of sense. This chapter looks at three areas where companies and individuals can go green and use less energy:

- Green servers
- Green space
- Green workers

Green Servers

Companies use a variety of methods to lower the overall power consumption of server computers. All modern computers use power management techniques. Many companies have switched to new hardware that uses less electricity than older stuff. Plus, using powerful modern computers in new ways through a process called virtualization can save a lot of energy and money.

Power Management

Because server computers tend to be very powerful (and thus potentially power-hungry), you should implement good power management practices on them. Most servers run all the time, so having certain parts of them shut down when not in use can save a lot of electricity over time. If the server has a monitor, for example, set the server to shut the monitor off after 15 minutes if no one is using it. Clients accessing the server over the network—remotely—won't need the server's monitor anyway. They just use their own (Figure 16-1).

Many companies have specific procedures in place for servers that don't get accessed after regular business hours. They can have a policy, for example, for manual or even automatic shutdown of the server at the end of the day. The manual version requires a person to power it off. The automated version requires some sort of programming, called a *script*, to run (Figure 16-2). Windows and other server OSes come with this capability.

Low-Power Servers

Older servers looked a lot like a typical personal computer but offered more power and, consequently, higher electricity usage. Replacing that kind of server with a modern rack-mounted server can save a bundle of electricity. The rack-mounted servers are more efficient and take up less room (Figure 16-3).

Figure 16-1
Accessing a server
from a client

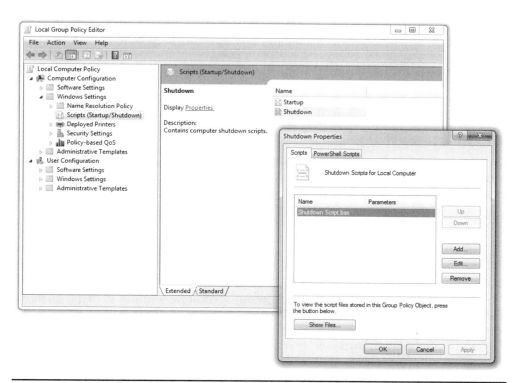

Figure 16-2   A shutdown script in automated tasks

Figure 16-3
Rack-mounted
servers

You can save even more electricity by replacing general-purpose servers used as file servers with specialized devices for serving. One such device is called *network attached storage (NAS)*. Figure 16-4 shows a NAS box. It's essentially a box of hard drives, a small motherboard, and electrical and network connections. Most are controlled with a highly customized version of Linux. You don't do anything on it except store and retrieve data.

Virtualization

The phenomenal power of today's computer hardware enables the creation of virtual computers so that a single machine can accomplish tasks that used to require multiple computers. That's a pretty bold statement, so let's break it up into pieces.

First off, what do servers do? They serve clients, for example, by making accessible stored data. That's a *file server*. Other servers can run programs that users across the network can access. These are *application servers*. Other servers host Web sites or enable users to send and receive e-mail or instant messages (Figure 16-5).

If you used multiple computers to handle each of these tasks, each computer would need to be plugged into the network and, more to the point, would require electricity. Considering how powerful modern hardware is, couldn't you use a single server to handle each of these separate duties? Of course you could, though it would require a computer much more powerful than a single-purpose computer (Figure 16-6).

Sometimes, though, it makes more sense to have unique servers handling special chores. Having a Web site accessible by people all over the network on the same server that handles all the security for a network, for example, seems like a disaster waiting to happen (Figure 16-7).

Figure 16-4
NAS (courtesy of
Data Robotics, Inc.)

Figure 16-5
Each server handles
a serving chore.

Figure 16-6
One server handling
multiple duties

That's where virtualization comes into play. *Virtualization* harnesses the power of modern hardware and operating systems to enable a single computer to be—for all intents—multiple computers. The operating system dedicates a portion of RAM to be a *virtual machine*, a computer within the computer. That virtual machine gets a piece of the hard drive, access to the CPU when needed, and a share of the network connection too. To anyone accessing the virtual machine from the network, it appears to be a stand-alone computer (Figure 16-8).

Virtualization offers a lot of benefits. First, and most obvious, you get the advantage and increased security of multiple dedicated computers, but you only have to buy one box. Second, that single box uses a lot less electricity than multiple boxes, again saving money. Finally, if you need to add a new server, you simply create another virtual machine. Easy!

Figure 16-7
Hmm . . . I wonder what would happen if I run this script on the Web site?

Figure 16-8
I am one, but many!

Green Space

Managing the space for servers and workers properly and using the right equipment can save a lot of electricity and money. This applies to setting up server rooms to make the cooling work efficiently, for example. Replacing traditional computers with centralized servers and specialized workstations can make a big difference too. Finally, paying a little extra up front for Energy Star–rated devices can pay off in the long term.

Setting Up the Server Room

Bigger companies devote rooms to nothing but rows of servers, powerful computers that people all over the organization use simultaneously. These powerful computers use electricity, naturally, and like all other computers, generate heat. Excessive heat kills computers and electronics, so keeping them cool matters a lot. A typical server room has rows and rows of computers, making the process of cooling complex. Let's look at both traditional and more efficient server room designs.

Traditional Server Rooms

A traditional server room keeps servers cool in a couple of ways. First, the room has very tight seals, so none of the cold air leaks out. Second, the servers sit on a raised floor and cold air is piped into that space. The hot air is pulled out at the top and recycled into the air conditioning units that cool the air and propel it back into the floor. The cool air is gradually pulled into the servers with the air flow. Figure 16-9 illustrates this process.

 EXAM TIP The first step in cooling a server room efficiently is to seal the room tightly. This optimizes the use of the air conditioning system.

The traditional server room system works well enough, though the more servers you put in the room, the bigger the air conditioning units need to be. The bigger they are, the more electricity they use.

In the earlier days of server rooms, this was no big deal. The rooms weren't that hot, and air conditioning them didn't cost much more than doing a normal room. Today, though, server rooms are literally packed with computers and the heat is tremendous.

Figure 16-9
Air flow in a traditional server room

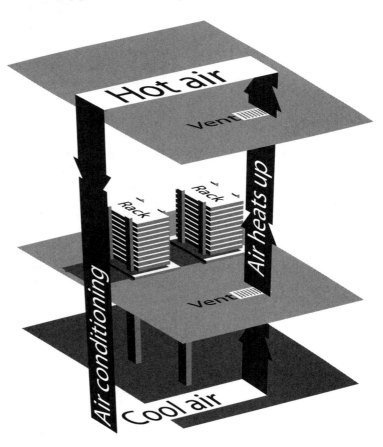

The problem with a traditional server room is that the cold air mingles with the hot air. This lessens the impact of the cold air and makes the system less efficient. Server room designers had to get serious about air flow.

Hot Aisle, Cool Aisle

Computers uniformly draw air in through the front of the box and expel air through the back. If you arrange the computers properly, you can create corridors that are uniformly hot or cool.

Figure 16-10 illustrates a hot and cool aisle layout. Note the computers face each other, creating an aisle that's only for intake. The two outer aisles are hot, because that's where the fans blow the hot air.

 EXAM TIP The fans inside a PC don't always need to run at the same speed. You can configure the BIOS to adjust the speed of the fans based on how hot or cool the system is, saving you even more on energy costs!

A proper cooling scenario with hot and cool aisles has all the cold air blown only to the floor in the cool aisle. The hot aisles have ducts at the top to draw the hot air away and send it back into the air conditioning unit. Figure 16-11 shows this ingenious method of efficiently cooling server rooms.

 EXAM TIP Arranging servers into hot and cool aisles helps keep server rooms cool efficiently.

Laptops, Terminal Servers, and Thin Clients

In a traditional office space, each worker has a personal computer that connects to a central network. The office has servers that hold important data that people throughout the organization access from the comfort of their desk (Figure 16-12).

Figure 16-10
Hot and cool aisles
in a server room

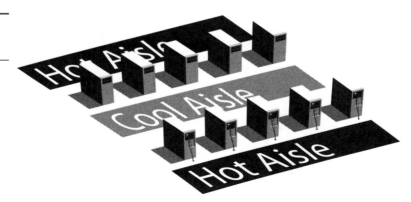

PART IV

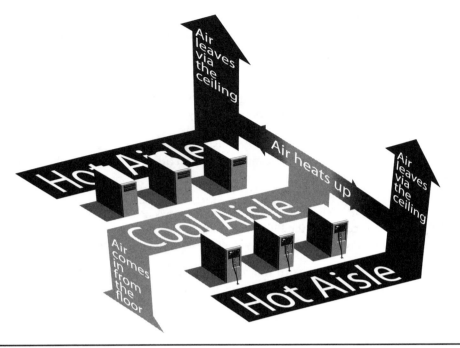

Figure 16-11 Air flow in a server room with hot and cool aisles

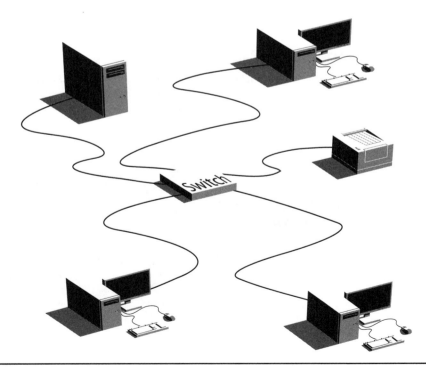

Figure 16-12 A traditional network

The computer that workers use to connect to the network is called a *fat client*, a not-so-flattering term for a powerful personal computer. The typical fat client has all its computing power built in (Figure 16-13). If unplugged from the network or the network goes down, the worker can still do a lot of work from his or her desk.

All that local computing power takes, well, power in the form of electricity. Plus, each computer must have copies of each application that the user needs to complete his or her work. That's expensive all around when you start factoring in multiple employees.

One solution to reduce electricity costs is to replace the desktop personal computer with laptops or portable PCs. This has two benefits and one detriment. First, laptops use less electricity than standard desktop computers. Second, laptops can go with the user. Issue an employee a laptop and he or she can work from anywhere (Figure 16-14).

 EXAM TIP Want to make that laptop even more energy-efficient? Switch that traditional hard drive for a solid state hard drive to extend your battery life and save on energy costs.

The drawback to laptops is that they are more expensive than desktop computers. This price difference has dropped a lot in recent years, but it's still big enough to factor into a company's equation when trying to offset energy costs. Oh, and you still need copies of applications for every laptop, so they don't solve that particular cost issue.

Figure 16-13
A fat client

Figure 16-14
Laptops replacing
desktops add a
degree of flexibility
and power savings.

A greener solution that works for many companies is to replace the standard server and workstation setup with terminal servers and thin clients. A *terminal server* offers a lot of centralized power, enabling users to log in and work directly with applications installed on the server. The *thin client* is not a standalone computer, but rather a keyboard, mouse, and monitor connected to a simple box that enables the client to log in to the terminal server. Figure 16-15 shows how this kind of network works.

A terminal server and thin client setup can work in many networks. You'll pay more for the server than for a standard data server, but the overall costs and electricity usage can be a lot less. Each client doesn't need a suite of applications. The severely limited computing power of the thin client requires a lot less electricity than a personal computer. And they're cheaper, too.

Energy Star Rating

Many computer component manufacturers submit their devices for testing by the United States Department of Energy to try to get Energy Star compliance. That means that the device uses electricity efficiently, at least in comparison with similar devices.

The most common items on the Energy Star bandwagon are monitors. Other big devices, such as printers and scanners, can have Energy Star ratings too. Look for the Energy Star logo (Figure 16-16).

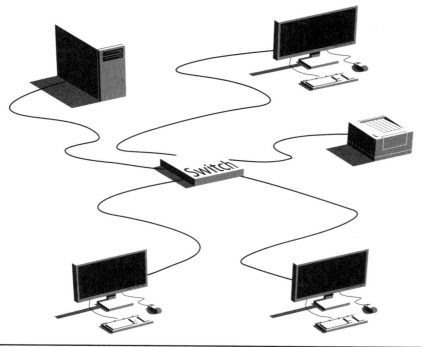

Figure 16-15   Network with terminal servers and thin clients

Figure 16-16
The Energy Star
monitor logo

Energy Star logo ——

Replacing an inefficient device with an Energy Star–compliant device can save a lot of electricity over the life of the device. Most monitors, for example, have useful life spans of five years or more. The cost of the monitor replacement can be offset by the energy savings.

 EXAM TIP   The best way to dispose of replaced computer components is to donate them to charity. The devices get recycled in the right way, not tossed in a landfill.

Green Workers

Today's tools enable companies to reimagine the way workers work. Figure 16-17 shows a standard office worker in his cube, a Dilbert moment. Here's what his company pays for:

- His work space
- His desk and chair
- His computer
- The air conditioning, heating, and lighting
- His Internet connection

Wait! Doesn't the local café have everything the worker needs except for a computer? If you issue him a laptop, do you need a centralized office space? In fact, most employees will have a PC and Internet connection at home. Couldn't you just have the employee log in from home and do work?

Welcome to the workforce of the twenty-first century. The power of the Internet and personal computers can, in many companies, reshape the way they work.

Figure 16-17
A typical worker

My team writes computer books—kind of an obvious statement, considering you're reading these words! Three different aspects of modern computing enable us to work from anywhere and still create great stuff:

- Telecommuting
- Voice over IP
- Cloud computing

Implementing all three means we save our company a huge amount of money in office space. Plus we optimize our own income, not having to shell out money for gas to commute to the office. It's a win-win situation all around. Here are the details.

Telecommuting

Telecommuting means not having to drive or take a bus or cab to the office. Instead, you do your work wherever is most convenient to you. This can be at your house, at a café, or at a public park. Whatever works, works. When you need company resources, you can log in to the company server over the Internet.

Telecommuting reduces the overall power usage of a company a lot. The employee doesn't burn fuel getting to the office, which also reduces emissions (like the exhaust from your car). The office doesn't need a dedicated space for the employee that needs to be heated and cooled.

Voice over IP

Using the Internet for traditional phone calls enables great savings, especially for jobs that live or die by the phone. Think "sales" and you'll be on target. The salesperson needs an Internet connection, computer, microphone, and headset. He or she can make calls all over the world for a fraction of the cost of a traditional telephone connection.

This process is called *Voice over IP*, or *VoIP*. The leading VoIP software is from a company called Skype. Figure 16-18 shows the author engaged in a Skype call to his buddy Michael.

You can use VoIP to communicate with people connected to the Internet. Plus, you can connect to the traditional phone network as well. The concept of a long-distance call goes right out the window when you use VoIP.

Cloud Computing

This chapter has explored all sorts of ways for companies and individuals to use a lot less electricity and power implementing green networking technologies. It's fitting that we save the killer app for last: cloud computing.

Every company needs a certain number of things to function:

- Centralized storage for data
- A good backup routine for that data
- Applications for employees to accomplish tasks

Figure 16-18
Skype call

Once you get to a certain level of complexity in an endeavor, it makes sense for people to start specializing. The same principle holds true for computing tasks. Why make every company learn all the tasks for success?

At its most basic level, *cloud computing* takes advantage of the power and speed of the Internet to move a lot of routine tasks into the hands of specialists. Companies can use those specialists to save money and concentrate on doing the job that they specialize in. We call it cloud computing because, for the end user, the location of the server that does the job he or she needs doesn't matter.

Here are some of the resources available through the cloud:

- Data storage (with full backup)
- E-mail
- Office applications, such as word processing and spreadsheets

Data Storage Example

The Web site Dropbox offers free and affordable plans for storage needs. Individual accounts enable you to put a file into a special Dropbox folder on your computer at the office. That file is quickly copied to your Dropbox folder somewhere out there in the cloud, plus it's copied to every other computer you have with Dropbox installed that's connected to the Internet (Figure 16-19). That includes your mobile phone, if you want. Plus, the transfers are secure and limited only by the speed of your Internet connection.

The free, individual accounts offer a nice service. You get two gigabytes of storage and peace of mind. For a small business, though, this can be huge.

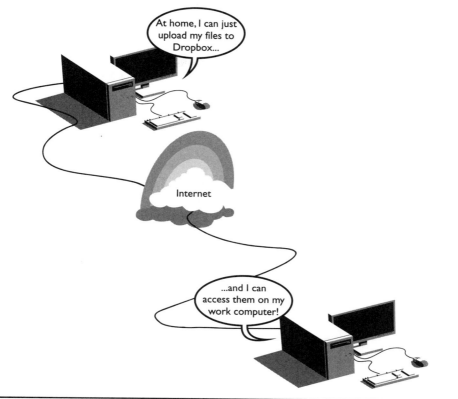

Figure 16-19   Data storage through the cloud

A low-end file server with a five-user license for Windows Server costs $1500+. Plus you need to do the backups and so on. The price for a Dropbox five-user license, including immediate backup and access from anywhere, is, at the time of this writing, US$795 per year. Dropbox does all the maintenance, backup, and so forth. That frees you up to do nothing more than create content.

Dropbox is just one service. Many other companies are in the game of providing storage for you.

NOTE   The Dropbox for Teams offers only 350GB of shared space. Small businesses that use a lot of storage space would need to look elsewhere for storage needs.

E-Mail Example

I have multiple e-mail accounts, including my work account, several personal accounts, and a junk mail account. In the past, having multiple accounts meant having multiple e-mail servers and multiple logins. These days, though, I just log in to my Gmail account—provided for free from Google—and link every other account to it. I can check my mail and respond to people; Gmail uses the proper "from" information, depending on which message I respond to, work or private.

Office Applications

By now, you might have noticed that cloud computing sounds a lot like something discussed in Chapter 15: Web-delivered services. While the two concepts are similar, they are not exactly the same thing. All Web-delivered services are a form of cloud computing, but not all cloud computing is a Web-delivered service.

Google Docs, a popular Web-delivered service containing a full suite of office applications, is a great tool for workers using the cloud. Figure 16-20 shows a document open in the word processing application of Google Docs.

I often use Google Docs when I start a new project. I can log in to my Gmail account from any computer attached to the Internet, switch over to Google Docs, and have access to my documents (Figure 16-21). In other words, it serves as a storage medium, too.

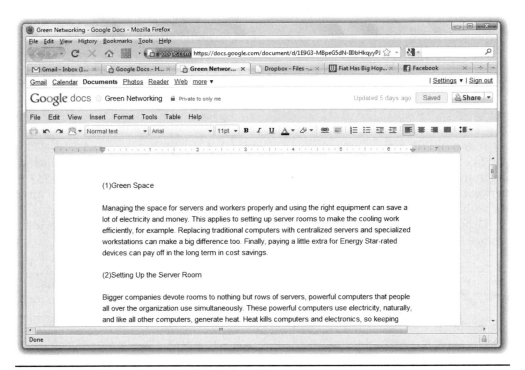

Figure 16-20 "Green Networking" open for editing

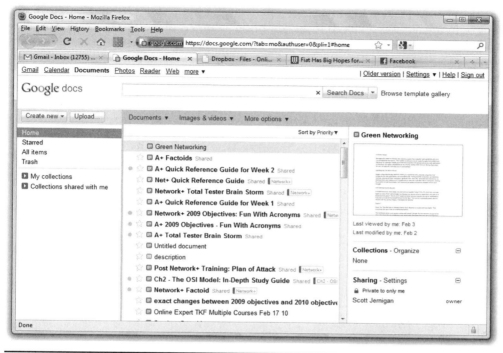

Figure 16-21   Listing of files in Google Docs

NOTE   I'm not sure if you can see the little "Network+" symbol next to some of the documents in Figure 16-21. Those refer to documents shared with me from one of our instructors. Google Docs can be shared among users of Gmail easily!

Chapter Review

This chapter examined the many ways companies and individuals can reduce their footprint, using less electricity and other resources, and saving money.

Servers can get a little greener by implementing good power management techniques and policies. Swapping out an older server for a low-power server, such as a NAS, is a good step too. Finally, the power of modern computers enables virtualization, creating computers within computers. This way you can use a single server to take the place—and do the jobs—of multiple computers.

You can make your work space more efficient by setting up the server room better. Make sure the server room seals are tight. Arrange servers into hot and cool aisles to optimize cooling. Switch out the old desktop computers for laptops, or go with a terminal server plus thin client arrangement to save even more. Finally, replace older devices with Energy Star devices. These save on energy use and cost in the long run.

People can make a big difference in energy consumption. Enabling employees to telecommute reduces the need to air condition an office, rent office space, or have multiple computers. The employee doesn't have to use time or fuel getting to and from the work space. Try replacing traditional phone lines with VoIP, using the power of the Internet for phone calls.

Go greenest of all by embracing cloud computing, moving some or all of your storage, e-mail, and office applications to specialized companies on the Internet. Documents can be accessed from anywhere you have access to the Internet.

Questions

1. Which technology enables a server to function as multiple computers at the same time?

    A. Duplication

    B. Multiplication

    C. Triplication

    D. Virtualization

2. Which of the following options would enable you to lower the electricity usage of your servers?

    A. Disable power management.

    B. Set them to low-power mode.

    C. Shut down servers at night when not in use.

    D. Replace a NAS with a file server.

3. How should you set up a server room to maximize the efficiency of the air conditioning and thus the cooling of the servers?

    A. Arrange the servers so that you create hot and cool aisles.

    B. Arrange the servers in rows, so that the air blown from one goes more quickly into the one behind.

    C. Place the cool vents in the ceiling, pulling the heated air into the floor.

    D. Place the servers directly onto the concrete floor, thus adding cooling from the earth.

4. What is the benefit of thin clients?

    A. Thin clients are more powerful than fat clients.

    B. Thin clients consume less electricity than fat clients.

    C. Thin clients offer more features than fat clients.

    D. Thin clients look better than fat clients.

5. What should you look for in a new computer monitor to optimize energy efficiency?

    A. Energy rating

    B. Energy Star rating

    C. Thinner screen

    D. Wider screen

6. John is in charge a group of salespeople. He wants to lower the overall energy usage of the workforce and also give his salespeople more flexibility in where they do their work. Which of the following helps him achieve those goals?

    A. Replace the traditional computers and servers with thin clients and terminal servers.

    B. Replace the file server with a NAS.

    C. Replace the traditional computers with laptop computers.

    D. Make the server room seal properly.

7. Which of the following best describes a NAS?

    A. A NAS is a hub that connects several computers together into a network.

    B. A NAS is a box containing hard drives, a motherboard, and network connections.

    C. A NAS connects multiple LANs together into a WAN like the Internet.

    D. A NAS is a collection of virtual machines that take the place of physical desktop systems.

8. Mary and Frank want to collaborate on a project for work. Mary is in New York and Frank is in London. Which of the following is the most cost-effective communication solution?

    A. Mary calls Frank long distance on his cell phone.

    B. Mary calls Frank long distance on his land-line telephone.

    C. Mary calls Frank over a VoIP service such as Skype.

    D. Mary flies to London.

9. Which of the following are examples of cloud computing? (Select two.)

    A. Microsoft Office

    B. Dropbox

    C. Thin client

    D. Google Docs

10. When attempting to create a greener office, which of the following is the biggest drawback for switching to laptops from desktops?

    A. Laptops are not as powerful or sophisticated.

    B. Laptops use more electricity.

    C. Laptops create more heat.

    D. Laptops cost more.

Answers

1. **D.** Virtualization enables you to create multiple virtual machines on a computer, making that one computer function like many computers.

2. **C.** The easiest way to have electronics use less electricity is to shut them down when not in use.

3. **A.** Arranging the servers in hot and cool aisles helps a lot. So does a raised floor with the cooling vents blowing into the cool aisles.

4. **B.** Switching to thin clients (and terminal servers) can save a lot of electricity.

5. **B.** Look for the Energy Star rating and logo to pick the most efficient monitor.

6. **C.** All of the options would lower overall electricity use, but the only way to give the salespeople flexibility is to let them unplug. Replace the traditional desktop computers with portable computers.

7. **B.** A Network Attached Storage device is just a box full of hard drives, a motherboard, and network connections. It is designed to take the place of full-blown server machines.

8. **C.** VoIP calls are much cheaper than traditional land-line or cell phone calls.

9. **B, D.** Dropbox and Google Docs are both examples of cloud computing because they operate entirely on the Internet (otherwise known as "the cloud").

10. **D.** While prices have come down over the years, a laptop still costs a lot more than a comparable desktop system.

PART V

Securing PCs

Local Security

In this chapter, you will learn how to
- Explain the threats to your computers and data
- Describe key security concepts and technologies

Your PC is under siege. Through your PC, a malicious person can gain valuable information about you and your habits. He can steal your files. He can run programs that log your keystrokes and thus gain account names and passwords, credit card information, and more. He can run software that takes over much of your computer processing time and use it to send spam or steal from others. The threat is real and right now. Worse, he's doing one or more of these things to your clients as I write these words. You need to secure your computer and your users from these attacks.

But what does computer security mean? Is it big, complex passwords? What about special programs that protect data from accidental deletion? Sure, it's both of these things, but what about the fact that your laptop can be stolen easily?

To secure computers, you need both a sound strategy and proper tactics. From a strategic sense, you need to understand the threat from unauthorized access to local machines as well as the big threats posed when computers go onto networks. Part of the big picture means to know what software and hardware to put in place to stop those threats. From a tactical, in-the-trenches standpoint, you need to master the details, to know how to implement and maintain the proper tools.

Analyzing Threats

Threats to your data and PC come from two directions: accidents and malicious people. All sorts of things can go wrong with your computer, from users getting access to folders they shouldn't see to a virus striking and deleting folders. Files can be deleted, renamed, or simply lost. Hard drives can die, and optical discs can get scratched and rendered unreadable. Accidents happen, and even well-meaning people can make mistakes.

Unfortunately, a lot of people out there intend to do you harm. Add that intent together with a talent for computers, and you have a deadly combination. Let's look at the following issues:

- Unauthorized access
- Social engineering

- Data destruction, accidental or deliberate
- Administrative access
- Catastrophic hardware failures
- Theft
- Viruses/spyware

Unauthorized Access

Unauthorized access occurs when a person accesses resources without permission. Resources in this case mean data, applications, and hardware. A user can alter or delete data; access sensitive information, such as financial data, personnel files, or e-mail messages; or use a computer for purposes the owner did not intend.

Not all unauthorized access is malicious—often this problem arises when users who are randomly poking around in a computer discover that they can access resources in a fashion the primary user did not intend. Unauthorized access becomes malicious when outsiders knowingly and intentionally take advantage of weaknesses in your security to gain information, use resources, or destroy data!

One of the ways to gain unauthorized access is through intrusion. You might imagine someone kicking in a door and hacking into a computer, but more often than not it's someone sitting at a home computer, trying various passwords over the Internet. Not quite as glamorous, but still. . . .

Dumpster diving is the generic term for anytime a hacker goes through your refuse, looking for information (Figure 17-1). This is also a form of intrusion. The amount of sensitive information that makes it into any organization's trash bin boggles the mind! Years ago, I worked with an IT security guru who gave me and a few other IT people a tour of our office's trash. In one 20-minute tour of the personal wastebaskets of one office area, we had enough information to access the network easily, as well as to embarrass seriously more than a few people. When it comes to getting information, the trash is the place to look!

Social Engineering

Although you're more likely to lose data by accident, the acts of malicious users get the vast majority of headlines. Most of these attacks come under the heading of *social engineering*—the process of using or manipulating people inside the networking environment to gain access to that network from the outside—which covers the many ways humans can use other humans to gain unauthorized information. This unauthorized information may be a network login, a credit card number, company customer data—almost anything you might imagine that one person or organization may not want a person outside of that organization to access.

Social engineering attacks aren't hacking—at least in the classic sense of the word—although the goals are the same. Social engineering means people attacking an organization through the people in the organization or physically accessing the organization to get the information they need. Following are a few of the more classic types of social engineering attacks.

Figure 17-1
Dumpster diving

 NOTE   It's common for social engineering attacks to be used together, so if you discover one of them being used against your organization, it's a good idea to look for others.

Infiltration

Hackers can physically enter your building under the guise of someone who might have a legitimate reason for being there, such as cleaning personnel, repair technicians, or messengers. They then snoop around desks, looking for whatever they can find. They might talk with people inside the organization, gathering names, office numbers, and department names—little things in and of themselves but powerful tools when combined later with other social engineering attacks. This is called *infiltration* (Figure 17-2).

Dressing the part of a legitimate user—with fake badge and everything—enables malicious people to gain access to locations and thus potentially your data. Following someone through the door, for example, as if you belong, is called *tailgating*. Tailgating is a common form of infiltration.

Figure 17-2
Not everyone
who comes to
your building is
trustworthy.

Telephone Scams

The *telephone scam* is a very common social engineering attack. In this case, the attacker makes a phone call to someone in the organization to gain information. The attacker attempts to come across as someone inside the organization and uses this to get the desired information (Figure 17-3). Probably the most famous of these scams is the "I forgot my username and password" scam. In this gambit, the attacker first learns the account name of a legitimate person in the organization, usually using the infiltration method. The attacker then calls someone in the organization, usually the help desk, in an attempt to gather information, in this case a password.

> **Hacker:** "Hi, this is John Anderson in accounting. I forgot my password. Can you reset it, please?"
>
> **Help Desk:** "Sure, what's your user name?"
>
> **Hacker:** "j_w_Anderson"
>
> **Help Desk:** "OK, I reset it to e34rd3."

Certainly telephone scams aren't limited to attempts to get network access. There are documented telephone scams against organizations aimed at getting cash, blackmail material, or other valuables.

Figure 17-3
Telephone scam

Phishing

Phishing is the act of trying to get people to give their usernames, passwords, or other security information by pretending to be someone else electronically. A classic example is when a bad guy sends you an e-mail that's supposed to be from your local credit card company asking you to send them your username and password. Phishing is by far the most common form of social engineering done today.

Data Destruction

Often an extension of unauthorized access, data destruction means more than just intentionally or accidentally erasing or corrupting data. It's easy to imagine some evil hacker accessing your network and deleting all your important files, but authorized users may also access certain data and then use that data beyond what they are authorized to do. A good example is the person who legitimately accesses a Microsoft Access product database to modify the product descriptions, only to discover that she can change the prices of the products, too (Figure 17-4).

This type of threat is particularly dangerous when users are not clearly informed about the extent to which they are authorized to make changes. A fellow tech once told me about a user who managed to mangle an important database when someone gave him incorrect access. When confronted, the user said: "If I wasn't allowed to change it, the system wouldn't let me do it!" Many users believe that systems are configured in a paternalistic way that wouldn't allow them to do anything inappropriate. As a result, users often assume they're authorized to make any changes they believe are necessary when working on a piece of data they know they're authorized to access.

Figure 17-4
Just because you *can* do something doesn't mean you should.

Administrative Access

Every operating system enables you to create user accounts and grant those accounts a certain level of access to files and folders in that computer. As an administrator, supervisor, or root user, you have full control over just about every aspect of the computer.

Windows XP, in particular, makes it entirely too easy to give users administrative access to the computer, especially Windows XP Home, which allows only two kinds of users: administrators and limited users. Because you can't do much as a limited user, most home and small office systems simply use multiple administrator accounts. If you need to control access, you really need to use non-Home versions of Windows.

System Crash/Hardware Failure

As with any technology, computers can and will fail—usually when you can least afford for it to happen. Hard drives crash, the power fails—it's all part of the joy of working in the computing business. You need to create redundancy in areas prone to failure (such as installing backup power in case of electrical failure) and perform those all-important data backups.

 EXAM TIP Keep track of where you store the discs or hard drives used to back up your computer. Loss of those materials through accident or theft could make a system crash truly catastrophic.

Theft

Thieves steal whatever you don't have locked down, either physically or electronically (Figure 17-5). When so many of us use computers in public spaces now, such as coffee

Figure 17-5
Always be sure
to lock up your
valuables; thieves
are lurking.

shops, theft has become a serious hazard. Be careful when you get up to buy another coffee or treat. Always keep an eye on your computer.

Another type of theft to worry about when computing in public is theft of your passwords. *Shoulder surfing* is when people spy on you from behind, watching what you type. Even though most passwords appear on the screen as dots rather than characters you typed, the thief could be watching your fingers and memorizing keys you press. The danger from shoulder surfing increases the more frequently you work in a specific place. Each day, an observant person of bad intent can get another keystroke or two. Eventually, you'll get hacked. Check before you type!

Virus/Spyware

Networks are without a doubt the fastest and most efficient vehicles for transferring computer viruses among systems. News reports focus attention on the many virus attacks from the Internet, but a huge number of viruses still come from users who bring in programs on floppy disks, writable optical discs, and USB drives.

 NOTE Chapter 18 describes the various methods of virus infection and what you need to do to prevent virus infection of your networked systems.

Security Concepts and Technologies

Once you've assessed the threats to your computers and networks, you need to take steps to protect those valuable resources. Depending on the complexity of your organization, this can be a small job encompassing some basic security concepts and procedures, or it can be exceedingly complex. The security needs for a three-person desktop publishing firm, for example, would differ wildly from those of a defense contractor supplying top-secret toys to the Pentagon.

Access Control

Access is the key. If you can control access to the data, programs, and other computing resources, you've secured your systems. *Access control* is composed of four interlinked areas that a good security-minded tech should think about: physical security, authentication, users and groups, and security policies. Much of this you know from previous chapters, but this section should help tie it all together as a security topic.

Secure Physical Area and Lock Down Your System

The first order of security is to block access to the physical hardware from people who shouldn't have access. This isn't rocket science. Lock the door. Don't leave a PC unattended when logged in. In fact, don't ever leave a system logged in, even as a limited user. Heaven help you if you walk away from a server still logged in as an administrator. You're tempting fate.

For that matter, when you see a user's computer logged in and unattended, do the user and your company a huge favor and lock the computer. Just walk up and press the WINDOWS LOGO KEY-L combination on the keyboard to lock the system. It works in all versions of Windows.

 EXAM TIP You can also set up your screensaver so that you are required to enter your password to return to the desktop.

Authentication

Security starts with properly implemented authentication, which is how the computer determines who can or should access it and once accessed, what that user can do. A computer can authenticate users through software or hardware, or a combination of both.

Software Authentication: Proper Passwords   It's still rather shocking to me to power up a friend's computer and go straight to his or her desktop, or with my married-with-kids friends, to click one of the parents' user account icons and not be prompted for a password. This is just wrong! I'm always tempted to assign passwords right then and there—and not tell them the passwords, of course—so they'll see the error of their ways when they try to log in next. I don't do it, but I always try to explain gently the importance of good passwords.

Make sure you and your users use *strong passwords:* at least eight characters in length, including letters, numbers, and punctuation symbols (Figure 17-6). Don't let them write passwords down or tape them to the underside of their mouse pads either! Try using a password generator Web site to guarantee a truly random password.

 EXAM TIP   A strong password has at least eight characters and a mix of letters, numbers, and symbols. Change your passwords often (at least once a month to be safe) and don't reuse old passwords.

Figure 17-6
Always use a strong
password.

If you forget a password and have to have it reset by an administrator, make sure you change it immediately after logging in. If you're an administrator, force the issue by requiring the user to change his or her password when logging in. This creates a *one-time password* that goes away, keeping the user safe from any potential mischief by an administrator.

Hardware Authentication   Smart cards and biometric devices enable modern systems to authenticate users with more authority than mere passwords. *Smart cards* are credit-card-sized cards with circuitry that can identify the bearer of the card. Smart cards are relatively common for such tasks as authenticating users for mass transit systems, for example, but are fairly uncommon in computers. Figure 17-7 shows a smart card and keyboard combination.

Figure 17-7
A keyboard-
mounted smart card
reader being used
for a commercial
application (photo
courtesy of Cherry
Corp.)

Figure 17-8
A Microsoft
keyboard with
fingerprint
accessibility

People can guess or discover passwords, but forging someone's fingerprints is a lot harder. The keyboard in Figure 17-8 authenticates users on a local machine by using fingerprints. Other devices that will do the trick are key fobs, retinal scanners, and PC cards for laptop computers. Devices that require some sort of physical, flesh-and-blood authentication are called *biometric devices*.

NOTE How's this for full disclosure? Microsoft does not claim that the keyboard in Figure 17-8 offers any security at all. In fact, the documentation specifically claims that the fingerprint reader is an accessibility tool, not a security device. Because it enables a person to log on to a local machine, though, I think it falls into the category of authentication devices.

Clever manufacturers have developed key fobs and smart cards that use radio frequency identification (RFID) to transmit authentication information so that users don't have to insert something into a computer or card reader. The Privaris plusID combines, for example, a biometric fingerprint fob with an RFID tag that makes security as easy as opening a garage door remotely! Figure 17-9 shows a plusID device.

Figure 17-9
plusID (photo
courtesy of
Privaris, Inc.)

plusID

PRIVARIS

NTFS, not FAT32!

The file system on a hard drive matters a lot when it comes to security. On a Windows machine with multiple users, you simply must use NTFS (as opposed to the older FAT32 file system) or you have no security at all. NTFS enables you to encrypt files and folders to better protect them from potential hackers. Primary drives and any secondary drives in computers in your care should be formatted as NTFS, with the exception of removable drives such as the one you use to back up your system.

Users and Groups

Windows uses user accounts and groups as the bedrock of access control. A user account is assigned to a group, such as Users, Power Users, or Administrators, and by association gets certain permissions on the computer. Using NTFS enables the highest level of control over data resources.

Assigning users to groups is a great first step in controlling a local machine, but this feature really shines once you go to a networked environment. Let's go there now.

User Account Control Through Groups

Access to user accounts should be restricted to the assigned individuals, and those who configure the permissions to those accounts must remember the Principle of Least Privilege: Accounts should have permission to access only the resources they need and no more. Tight control of user accounts is critical to preventing unauthorized access. Disabling unused accounts is an important part of this strategy, but good user account control goes far deeper than that. One of your best tools for user account control is groups.

Instead of giving permissions/rights to individual user accounts, give them to groups; this makes keeping track of the permissions assigned to individual user accounts much easier. Figure 17-10 shows me giving permissions to a group for a folder in Windows 7. Once a group is created and its permissions set, you can then add user accounts to that group as needed. Any user account that becomes a member of a group automatically gets the permissions assigned to that group. Figure 17-11 shows me adding a user to a newly created group in the same Windows 7 system.

Groups are a great way to achieve increased complexity without increasing the administrative burden on network administrators, because all network operating systems combine permissions. When a user is a member of more than one group, which permissions does that user have with respect to any particular resource?

In all network operating systems, the permissions of the groups are *combined*, and the result is what you call the *effective permissions* the user has to access the resource. As an example, if Rita is a member of the Sales group, which has List Folder Contents permission to a folder, and she is also a member of the Managers group, which has Read and Execute permissions to the same folder, Rita will have both List Folder Contents *and* Read and Execute permissions to that folder.

All of the default groups—Everyone, Guest, Users—define broad groups of users. Never use them unless you intend to permit all of those folks to access a resource. If you use one of the default groups, remember to configure it with the proper permissions to prevent users from doing things you don't want them to do with a shared resource!

Figure 17-10
Giving a group
permissions for a
folder in Windows 7

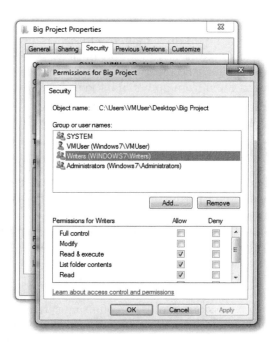

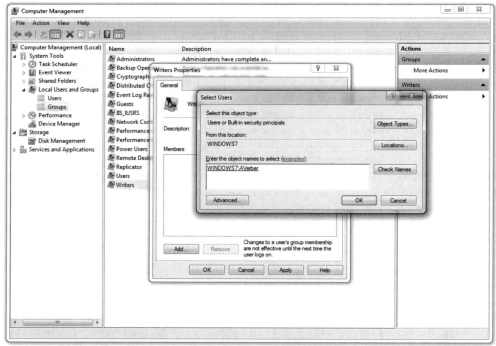

Figure 17-11   Adding a user to a newly created group in Windows 7

All of these groups and organizational units only do one thing for you: They let you keep track of your user accounts so you know they are only available for those who need them, and they can only access the resources you want them to use.

User Account Control

Windows XP made it too easy—and, in fact, almost necessary—to make your primary account on a computer an administrator account. Because limited users can't do common tasks, such as running certain programs, installing applications, updating applications, updating Windows, and so on, most users simply created an administrator-level account and logged in. Such accounts have full control over the computer, so any malware that slips in with that account could do a lot more harm.

Microsoft addressed this problem with the *User Account Control (UAC)*, a feature that enables standard users to do common tasks and provides a permissions dialog (Figure 17-12) when standard users *and* administrators do certain things that could potentially harm the computer (such as attempt to install a program). Windows Vista and Windows 7 user accounts function much more like user accounts in Linux and Macintosh OS X, with programs asking for administrative permission before making changes to the computer.

Parental Controls

With *Parental Controls*, you can monitor and limit the activities of any standard user in Windows Vista, a feature that gives parents and managers an excellent level of control over the content their children and employees can access (Figure 17-13). Activity Reporting logs applications run or attempted to run, Web sites visited or attempted to visit, any kind of files downloaded, and more. You can block various Web sites by type or specific URL, or you can allow only certain Web sites, a far more powerful option.

PART V

Figure 17-12
Prompting for
permission

Figure 17-13   Parental Controls

Parental Controls enable you to limit the time that standard users can spend logged in. You can specify acceptable and unacceptable times of day when standard users can log in. You can restrict access both to types of games and to specific applications. If you like playing rather gruesome games filled with monsters and blood that you don't want your kids to play, for example, you can simply block any games with certain ESRB (Entertainment Software Rating Board) ratings, such as *E* for Everyone, *T* for Teen, or *M* for Mature or Mature 17+.

Data Classification and Compliance

Larger organizations, such as government entities, benefit greatly from organizing their data according to its sensitivity—what's called *data classification*—and making certain that computer hardware and software stay as uniform as possible. In addition, many government and internal regulations apply fairly rigorously to the organizations.

Data classification systems vary by the organization, but a common scheme classifies documents as public, internal use only, highly confidential, top secret, and so on. Using a classification scheme enables employees such as techs to know very quickly what to do with documents, the drives containing documents, and more. Your strategy for recycling a computer system left from a migrated user, for example, will differ a lot if the data on the drive was classified as internal use only or top secret.

Compliance means, in a nutshell, that members of an organization or company must abide by or comply with all of the rules that apply to the organization or company. Statutes with funny names such as Sarbanes-Oxley impose certain behaviors or prohibitions on what people can and cannot do in the workplace.

From a technician's point of view, the most common compliance issue revolves around software, such as what sort of software users can be allowed to install on their computers or, conversely, why you have to tell a user that he can't install the latest application that may help him do the job more effectively because that software isn't on the approved list. This can lead to some uncomfortable confrontations, but it's part of a tech's job.

The concepts behind compliance in IT are not, as some might imagine at first blush, to stop you from being able to work effectively. Rather they're designed to stop users who don't have enough technical skill or knowledge from installing malicious programs or applications that will destabilize their systems. This keeps technical support calls down and enables techs to focus on more serious problems.

Reporting

As a final weapon in your security arsenal, you need to report any security issues so a network administrator or technician can take steps to make them go away. You can set up two tools within Windows so that the OS reports problems to you: Event Viewer and Auditing. You can then do your work and report those problems. Let's take a look.

Event Viewer

Event Viewer is Window's default tattletale program, spilling the beans about many things that happen on the system (Figure 17-14). You can find Event Viewer in Administrative Tools in the Control Panel. The most common use for Event Viewer is to view application or system errors for troubleshooting (Figure 17-15).

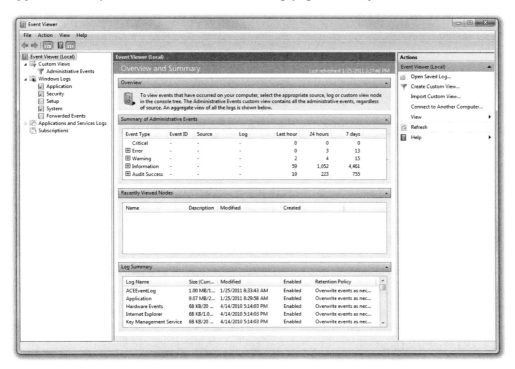

Figure 17-14 Event Viewer

Figure 17-15
A typical application
error message

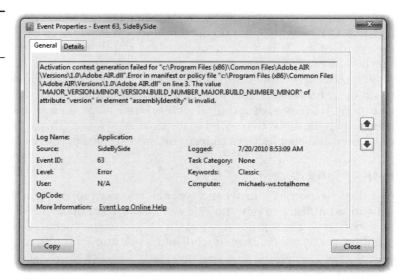

One very cool feature of Event Viewer is that you can click a link to take you to the online Help and Support Center at Microsoft.com, and the software reports your error (Figure 17-16), checks the online database, and comes back with a more or less useful explanation (Figure 17-17).

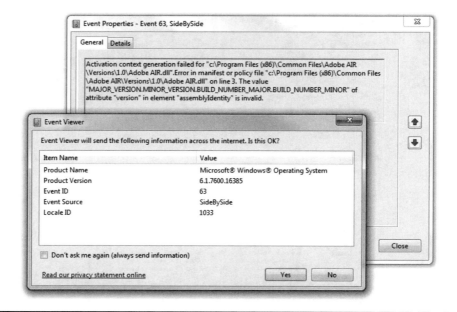

Figure 17-16   Details about to be sent

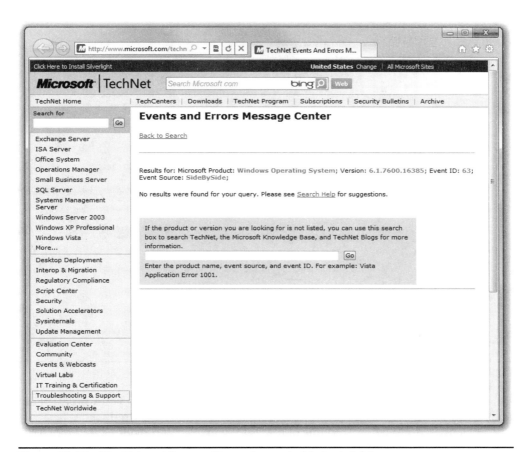

Figure 17-17   The Help and Support Center (somewhat) being helpful

Auditing

Event Viewer in Windows Vista and Windows 7 gives you all sorts of detail on events with the default configuration. Figure 17-18 shows the Security section in Windows 7. Unless you're in an unusual situation, you don't need to do much with the setup of the tool. That's not the case for Windows XP, though, so here's the scoop.

The Security section of Event Viewer in Windows XP doesn't show you anything by default. To unlock the full potential of Event Viewer, you need to set up auditing. *Auditing* in the security sense means to tell Windows to create an entry in the Security Log when certain events happen, for example, a user logs on—called *event auditing*—or tries to access a certain file or folder—called *object access auditing*. Figure 17-19 shows Event Viewer tracking logon and logoff events.

Incidence Reporting

Once you've gathered data about a particular system or you've dealt with a computer or network problem, you need to complete the mission by telling your supervisor. This is

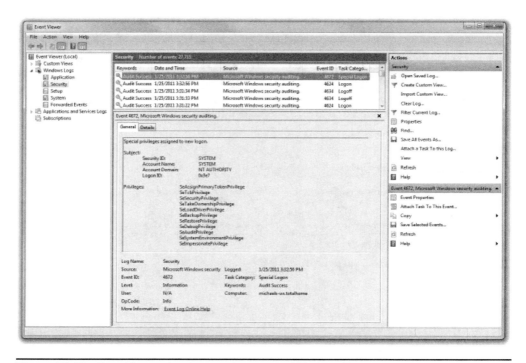

Figure 17-18   Event Viewer showing security events in Windows 7

called *incidence reporting*. Many companies have premade forms that you simply fill out and submit. Other places are less formal. Regardless, you need to do this!

Incidence reporting does a couple of things for you. First, it provides a record of work you've accomplished. Second, it provides a piece of information that, when combined with other information you might or might not know, reveals a pattern or bigger problem

Figure 17-19
Event Viewer
displaying
security alerts in
Windows XP

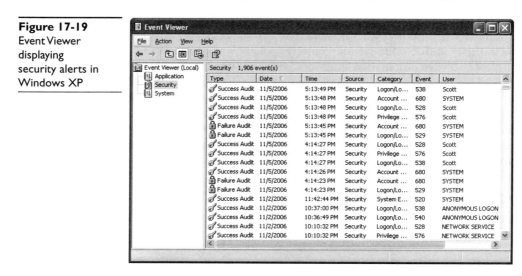

to someone higher up the chain. A seemingly innocuous security audit report, for example, might match other such events in numerous places in the building at the same time and thus show that conscious, coordinated action rather than a glitch was at work.

Chapter Review

Threats to your data and PC come from two directions: malicious people and accidents. People can gain unauthorized access to your computer in a variety of ways. One of the most important ways is through social engineering, using people on the inside to gain access. Hackers can infiltrate by pretending to be part of the company, for example. Calling up a gullible network administrator can get passwords reset and let bad people in.

Data destruction can be the result of unintended access, such as administrative privileges to a user not qualified to have those privileges. Hardware failures and theft can make for a very bad day. Keep your backed-up files someplace safe!

To maintain security, you must control access. You can control it in a variety of ways

- Secure the physical area.
- Put a lock on your laptop.
- Authenticate users with proper passwords.
- Use some kind of hardware authentication device, like a smart card or fingerprint reader.
- Lock down resources on a computer by using groups aggressively. Give access only to those users who need access.

Windows offers some specific tools for controlling access. User Account Control makes administrative permission necessary to make big changes to the computer, for example. Parental Controls enable you to restrict access to various resources for standard users.

Finally, follow the rules in your organization for data classification, compliance, and reporting. This means loading only approved software, for example, and following password guidelines. Access to resources is based on the group permissions, but the permissions are based on the classification of a document.

Event Viewer gives you a powerful tool for reviewing most things that happen on a computer, especially security. You can check for failed login attempts, for example. Write out a report to your supervisor if you discover any incidents that he or she needs to know about.

Questions

1. What is a person doing when accessing trash looking for useful information?

    A. Dumpster diving

    B. Garbage mining

    C. Sifting

    D. Trash talking

2. What is the process of using or manipulating people to gain access to network resources?

   A. Cracking

   B. Hacking

   C. Network engineering

   D. Social engineering

3. Which of the following might offer good hardware authentication?

   A. Strong passwords

   B. Encrypted passwords

   C. NTFS

   D. Smart cards

4. John dressed up in a fake security guard uniform that matched the uniforms of a company and then walked in with some legitimate employees in an attempt to gain access to company resources. What kind of attack is this?

   A. Administrative access

   B. Data destruction

   C. Spoofing

   D. Tailgating

5. Edward "works" at the local café, taking notes very carefully on what people type on their computers, especially at the login screens. What kind of theft does he practice?

   A. Café express

   B. Dumpster diving

   C. Infiltration

   D. Shoulder surfing

6. During her first day on the job, Jill received a spreadsheet that listed approved software for users and clear instructions not to allow any unapproved software. What kind of policy must she follow?

   A. Classification

   B. Compliance

   C. Group

   D. Security

7. Which Windows tool enables you to manage content accessed by users?

   A. Authentication

   B. Event Viewer

   C. Parental Controls

   D. User Account Control

8. Which tool in Windows enables you to view application errors?

   A. Application Viewer

   B. Event Viewer

   C. Performance Monitor

   D. System Monitor

9. How do Windows Vista and Windows 7 require administrative permission to make changes, such as install a new application?

   A. Application Control

   B. Event Viewer

   C. Parental Controls

   D. User Account Control

10. What term is used to describe the written report given to a supervisor about a particular computer or network problem?

   A. After-action reporting

   B. Auditing

   C. Incidence reporting

   D. Post-op

Answers

1. A. Digging through the trash looking for useful information is called dumpster diving.

2. D. Social engineering is the process of using or manipulating people to gain access to network resources.

3. D. Smart cards are an example of hardware authentication devices.

4. D. John just practiced tailgating on the unsuspecting company.

5. D. Edward uses shoulder surfing to gain access to people's accounts.

6. B. Jill needs to enforce compliance. This will help keep the tech support calls at a minimum and the uptime for users at a maximum.

7. C. Parental Controls enable you to control the content accessed by users.

8. B. Event Viewer enables you to see application errors, as well as system errors and security problems.

9. D. Windows Vista and Windows 7 use the User Account Control tool to require administrative permission to do anything major on the PC.

10. C. Incidence reporting is what you do when you make your supervisor aware of computer or network problems.

PART V

CHAPTER 18

Internet Security

In this chapter, you will learn how to
- Discuss different types of malicious software
- Protect against viruses
- Discuss browser configuration and firewalls

In Chapter 17, you learned about how to protect your local computer from unauthorized access and other attacks, but any computer attached to a network opens itself up to an entirely new set of dangers. Viruses and other malicious software can come from anywhere in the world and sneak onto your system to destroy your data. You need to know how to stop these infiltrators and recover from any successful intrusions.

This chapter looks at issues involving Internet-borne attacks and how to defend against them. This content is the security bread and butter for those seeking a CompTIA Strata certificate, so you need to understand the concepts and procedures and be able to implement them properly.

Malicious Software

The beauty of the Internet is the ease of accessing resources just about anywhere on the globe, all from the comfort of your favorite chair. This connection, however, runs both ways, and people can potentially access your computer from the comfort of their evil lairs. The Internet is awash with malicious software—*malware*—that is, even at this moment, trying to infect your systems.

Malware consists of computer programs designed to break into computers or cause havoc on computers. These programs are written by people known as *hackers*. Hacking refers to the circumvention of computer security, which malware is designed to do.

The most common types of malware are grayware, spam, viruses, Trojan horses, and worms. You need to understand the different types of malware so you can combat them for you and your users successfully.

 EXAM TIP While a lot of malicious software comes from the Internet or some type of storage device, it can also come from a local area network. Be careful when you connect to open (or free) wireless networks, like those at coffee shops and bookstores.

Grayware

Programs that intrude into your computing experience but don't actually do any damage to your systems or data—what's called *grayware*—can make that computing experience less than perfect.

On most systems, the Web browser is the most often used piece of software. Over the years, Web sites have come up with more and more ways to force you to see their advertising. In the early days of the Web, you only saw the occasional banner ad. In the past few years, Web site designers have become much more sophisticated, creating a number of intrusive and irritating ways to get you to part with your money in one form or another, all of which are considered grayware.

There are basically three irritating grayware types: pop-ups, spyware, and adware. Pop-ups are those surprise browser windows that appear automatically when you visit a Web site, proving themselves irritating and unwanted and nothing else. *Spyware*, meanwhile, defines a family of programs that run in the background on your PC, sending information about your browsing habits to the company that installed it on your system. *Adware* is not generally as malicious as spyware, but it works similarly to display ads on your system. Grayware programs download new ads and generate undesirable network traffic. Of the three, spyware is much less noticeable but far more nefarious.

Pop-Ups

At its worst, spyware can fire up pop-up windows of competing products on the Web site you're currently viewing. You might be perusing a bookseller's Web site, for example, only to have a pop-up from a competitor's site appear.

Getting rid of pop-ups is actually rather tricky. You've probably noticed that most pop-up browser windows don't look like browser windows at all. They have no menu bar, button bar, or address window, yet they are separate browser windows (Figure 18-1).

HTML coding permits Web site and advertising designers to remove the usual navigation aids from a browser window so that all you're left with is the content. In fact, as I'll describe in a minute, some pop-up browser windows are deliberately designed to mimic similar pop-up alerts from the Windows OS. They might even have buttons similar to Windows' own exit buttons, but you might find that when you click them, you wind up with more pop-up windows instead! What to do?

The first thing you need to know when dealing with pop-ups is how to close them without actually having to risk clicking them. As I said, most pop-ups have removed all navigation aids, and many are also configured to appear on your monitor screen in a position that places the browser window's exit button—the little X button in the upper-right corner—outside of your visible screen area. Some even pop up behind the active browser window and wait there in the background. Most annoying!

To remedy this, use alternate means to close the pop-up browser window. For instance, you can right-click the browser's icon in the taskbar to generate a pop-up menu of your own. Select Close, and the window should go away. You can also press ALT-TAB to bring the browser window in question to the forefront and then press ALT-F4 to close it.

Most Web browsers have features to prevent pop-up ads in the first place, but I've found that these types of applications are sometimes *too* thorough. That is, they tend to prevent all new browser windows from opening, even those you want to view. Still, they're free to try, so have a look to see if they suit your needs.

Figure 18-1   A pesky pop-up

Applications such as AdSubtract control a variety of Internet annoyances, including pop-up windows, cookies, and Java applets (which you will learn more about later in the chapter), and are more configurable. You can specify what you want to allow (pop-up windows, cookies, etc.) on any particular domain address. The fully functional versions usually cost at least something, but most are too confusing for novice-level users.

Spyware

Some types of spyware go considerably beyond the level of intrusion. They can use your computer's resources to run *distributed computing* applications, capture your keystrokes to steal passwords, reconfigure your dial-up settings to use a different phone number at a much higher connection charge, or even use your Internet connection and e-mail address contacts list to propagate itself to other computers in a virus-like fashion! Are you concerned yet?

Setting aside the legal and ethical issues—and there are many—you should at least appreciate that spyware can seriously impact your PC's performance and cause problems with your Internet connection. The threat is real, so what practical steps can you take to protect yourself? Let's look at how to prevent spyware installation and how to detect and remove any installed spyware.

How does this spyware get into your system in the first place? Obviously, sensible people don't download and install something that they know is going to compromise their computer (Figure 18-2). Makers of spyware know this, so they bundle their software with some other program or utility that purports to give you some benefit.

What kind of benefit? How about free access to MP3 music files? A popular program called Kazaa does that. How about a handy *e-wallet* utility that remembers your many screen names, passwords, and even your credit-card numbers to make online purchases easier and faster? A program called Gator does that and many other functions as well. How about browser enhancements, performance boosters, custom cursor effects, search utilities, buddy lists, file savers, or media players?

The list goes on and on, yet they all share one thing: they're simply window-dressing for the *real* purpose of the software. So you see, for the most part, spyware doesn't need to force its way into your PC. Instead, it saunters calmly through the front door.

Some spyware makers use more aggressive means to get you to install their software. Instead of offering you some sort of attractive utility, they instead use fear tactics and deception to try to trick you into installing their software. One popular method is to use pop-up browser windows crudely disguised as Windows' own system warnings. When clicked, these may trigger a flood of other browser windows, or may even start a file download.

The lesson here is simple: *Don't install these programs!* Careful reading of the software's license agreement before you install a program is a good idea, but realistically, it does little to protect your PC.

Figure 18-2 Windows Defender detecting spyware

Don't click *anywhere* inside of a pop-up browser window, even if it looks just like a Windows alert window or DOS command-line prompt—as I just mentioned, it's probably fake and the Close button is likely a hyperlink. Instead, use other means to close the window, such as pressing ALT-F4 or right-clicking the browser window's icon on the taskbar and selecting Close.

You can also install spyware detection and removal software on your system and run it regularly. Let's look at how to do that.

Some spyware makers are reputable enough to include a routine for uninstalling their software. Gator, for instance, makes it fairly easy to get rid of its programs; just use the Windows Programs and Features applet in the Control Panel (Figure 18-3). Others, however, aren't so cooperative. In fact, because spyware is so—well, *sneaky*—it's entirely possible that your system already has some installed that you don't even know about. How do you find out?

Windows comes with Windows Defender, a fine tool for catching most spyware, but it's not perfect. Another piece of software available for free from Microsoft is Security Essentials (Figure 18-4). It guards against viruses and spyware with active scans (scans you set up and run yourself) and passive detection (scans run in the background as you use the computer). Both of these applications work exactly as advertised. They detect and delete spyware of all sorts—hidden files and folders, cookies, and more.

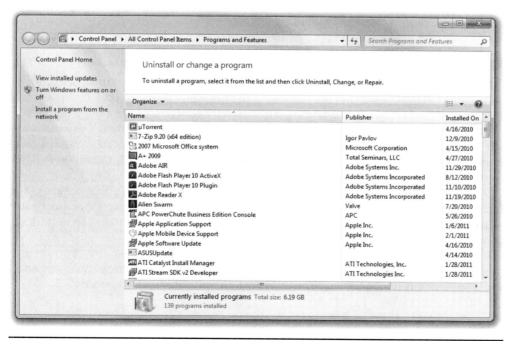

Figure 18-3 The Programs and Features applet

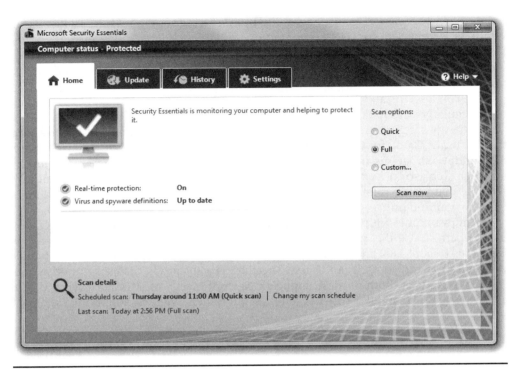

Figure 18-4 Microsoft Security Essentials

Spam

E-mail that comes into your Inbox from a source that's not a friend, family member, or colleague, and that you didn't ask for, can create huge problems for your computer and you (Figure 18-5). This unsolicited e-mail, called *spam*, accounts for a huge percentage of traffic on the Internet. Spam comes in many flavors, from legitimate businesses trying to sell you products to scammers who just want to take your money. Hoaxes, pornography, and get-rich-quick schemes pour into the Inboxes of most e-mail users. They waste your time and can easily offend.

You can use several options to cope with the flood of spam. The first option is defense. Never post your e-mail address on the Internet. One study tested this theory and found that *over 97 percent* of the spam received during the study went to e-mail addresses they had been posted on public Web sites.

Filters and filtering software can block spam at your mail server and at your computer. You can set most e-mail programs to block e-mail from specific people—good to use if someone is harassing you. You can block by subject line or keywords.

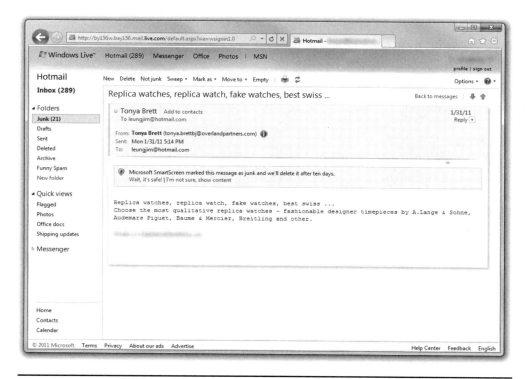

Figure 18-5   A spam message

Viruses

Just as a biological virus gets passed from person to person, a computer *virus* is a piece
of malicious software that gets passed from computer to computer. A computer virus is
designed to attach itself to a program on your computer. It could be your e-mail program, your word processor, or even a game. Whenever you use the infected program,
the virus goes into action and does whatever it was designed to do. It can wipe out your
e-mail or even erase your entire hard drive! Viruses are also sometimes used to steal
information or send spam e-mails to everyone in your address book.

EXAM TIP   Be sure to know the difference between viruses and spyware.
Too many people use the terms interchangeably, and they're very different
things.

Trojans

Trojans are true, freestanding programs that do something other than what the person who runs the program thinks they will do, much as the Trojan horse did in antiquity. An example of a Trojan horse is a program that a person thinks is an antivirus program but is actually a virus. Some Trojans are quite sophisticated. It might be a game that works perfectly well but causes some type of damage when the user quits the game.

Worms

Similar to a Trojan, a worm is a complete program that travels from machine to machine, usually through computer networks. Most worms are designed to take advantage of security problems in operating systems and install themselves on vulnerable machines. They can copy themselves over and over again on infected networks and can create so much activity that they overload the network by consuming bandwidth, in worst cases even bringing chunks of the entire Internet to a halt.

You can do several things to protect yourself and your data against these threats. First, make sure you are running up-to-date antivirus software—especially if you connect to the Internet via an always-on broadband connection. You should also be protected by a firewall, either as part of your network hardware or by means of a software program. (See the sections on antivirus programs and firewalls later in this chapter.)

Because worms most commonly infect systems through security flaws in operating systems, the next defense against them is to make sure you have the latest security patches installed on your version of Windows. A *security patch* is an addition to the operating system to patch a hole in the operating system code. You can download security patches from the Microsoft Update Web site.

Microsoft's Windows Update tool is handy for Windows users, as it provides a simple method to ensure that your version's security is up to date. The one downside is that not everyone remembers to run Windows Update. Don't wait until something goes wrong on your computer or you hear on the news that another nasty program is running rampant across the Internet. Set Windows Update to run automatically as a part of your normal system maintenance. Keeping your patches up to date is called patch *management*, and it goes a long way toward keeping your system safe.

Virus Prevention and Recovery

The only way to protect your PC permanently from getting a virus is to disconnect from the Internet and never permit any potentially infected software to touch your precious computer. Because neither scenario is likely these days, you need to use a specialized antivirus program to help stave off the inevitable virus assaults. When you discover infected systems, you need to know how to stop the spread of the virus to other computers and how to fix infected computers.

Antivirus Programs

An *antivirus program* protects your PC in two ways. It can be both sword and shield, working in an active seek-and-destroy mode and in a passive sentry mode. When ordered to seek and destroy, the program scans the computer's files for viruses and, if it finds any, presents you with the available options for removing or disabling them (Figure 18-6). Antivirus programs can also operate as *virus shields* that passively monitor your computer's activity, checking for viruses only when certain events occur, such as a program executing or a file being downloaded.

The antivirus program uses a library of signatures to detect viruses. A *signature* is the code pattern of a known virus. The antivirus program compares an executable file to its library of signatures. There have been instances where a perfectly clean program coincidentally held a virus signature. Usually the antivirus program's creator provides a patch to prevent further alarms.

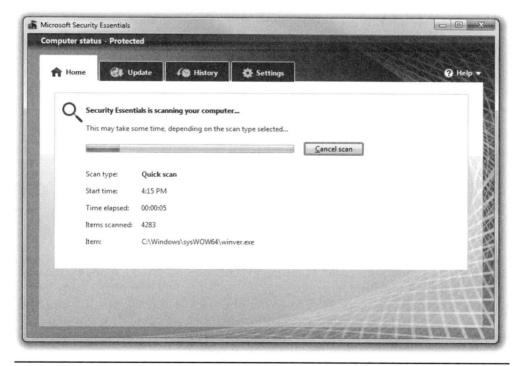

Figure 18-6　Microsoft Security Essentials scanning for viruses

Virus Prevention Tips

The secret to preventing damage from a malicious software attack is to keep from getting a virus in the first place. As discussed earlier, all good antivirus programs include a virus shield that scans e-mail, downloads, running programs, and so on automatically.

Use your antivirus shield. It is also a good idea to scan PCs daily for possible virus attacks. Know the source of any software before you load it. Although the chance of commercial, shrink-wrapped software having a virus is virtually nil (there have been a couple of well-publicized exceptions), that illegal copy of Modern Warfare 2 you borrowed from a local hacker should definitely be inspected with care.

Keep your antivirus program updated. New viruses appear daily, and your program needs to know about them. The list of virus signatures your antivirus program can recognize is called the *definition file,* and you must keep that definition file up to date so that your antivirus software has the latest signatures. Fortunately, most antivirus programs update themselves automatically. Further, you should periodically update the core antivirus software programming—called the *engine*—to employ the latest refinements the developers have included.

Virus Recovery Tips

When the inevitable happens and either your computer or one of your user's computers gets infected by a computer virus, you need to follow certain steps to stop the problem from spreading and get the computer back up safely into service. Try this five-step process:

1. Recognize
2. Quarantine
3. Search and destroy
4. Remediate
5. Educate

Recognize and Quarantine

The first step is to recognize that a potential virus outbreak has occurred. If you're monitoring network traffic and one computer starts spewing e-mail, that's a good sign. Or users might complain that a computer that was running snappily the day before seems very sluggish. You then need to quarantine—or cut off—the infected computer from the rest of the network. One easy method for doing this is to disconnect the network cable from the back of the system. Once you are sure the machine isn't capable of infecting others, you're ready to find the virus and get rid of it.

Search and Destroy

Once you've isolated the infected computer (or computers), you need to get to a safe boot environment like Windows Safe Mode and run your antivirus software.

Run your antivirus program's most comprehensive virus scan. Then check all removable media that were exposed to the system, as well as any other machine that might have received data from it or is networked to the cleaned machine.

E-mail is still a common source of viruses, and opening infected e-mails is a common way to get infected. Viewing an e-mail in a preview window opens the e-mail message and exposes your computer to some viruses. Download files only from sites you know to be safe, and of course the less reputable corners of the Internet are the most likely places to pick up computer infections.

Remediate

Virus infections can do a lot of damage to a system, especially to sensitive files needed to load Windows, so you might need to remediate formerly infected systems after cleaning off the drive or drives. *Remediation* simply means that you fix things the virus harmed. This usually means replacing corrupted or destroyed files with your backups— you did make backups, right? The Backup and Restore applet in the Windows Control Panel will walk you through restoring the backed-up files to your PC.

Educate

The best way to keep from having to deal with malware and grayware is education. It's your job as the IT person to talk to users, especially the ones whose systems you've just spent the last hour fixing, about how to avoid these programs. Show them samples of dangerous e-mails they should not open, Web sites to avoid, and the types of programs they should not install and use on the network. Any user who understands the risks of questionable actions on their computers will usually do the right thing and stay away from malware.

Finally, have your users run antivirus and antispyware programs regularly. Schedule them while interfacing with the user so you know it will happen.

 NOTE If, at any point, you don't think you can fix the problem or are unsure if you completely removed a virus, be sure to *escalate* the issue. Escalation is the process of handing off your task to someone else. This usually means calling your boss or someone else in the IT department.

Protecting Against Other Threats

Defending against viruses and malware is only half the battle. You need to also ensure that the software you already have is properly configured to keep the bad guys out. This includes setting up your browser and firewall.

Browser Configuration

You learned about browsers and the Internet back in Chapter 15, but you also need to know how to properly configure your browser to keep yourself safe from Internet intruders. Some of the settings for your browser are purely superficial; you can customize the size and type of fonts used on Web sites with your own styles. But you also have power over features such as cookies, the Internet cache, and add-ons that enhance the abilities of your browser. If these settings are configured improperly, you may be opening yourself up to outside attacks.

ActiveX and Java

ActiveX and *Java* are programming languages that can be integrated into Web sites. These tools allow Web developers to make Web pages more interactive. However, these tools can also be used to compromise your browser and run malicious code. If an unfamiliar Web site asks to run ActiveX or Java code, *don't do it*. ActiveX and Java can be deactivated entirely in most browsers.

 EXAM TIP ActiveX and Java can be disabled to prevent your browser from running malicious code found on an unsavory Web site.

Cookies and Internet Cache

When you go to a Web site, browsers store copies of the graphics and other items so the page will load more quickly the next time you access it. These are part of the *Internet cache* or *Temporary Internet Files*. A *cookie* is a small text file containing information about you.

The data stored in cookies is used to authenticate or identify you as a registered user of a Web site, so it will remember you next time you access that Web site. Cookies are also used to keep track of the shopping basket of goods you select to buy from a site. Cookies enable sites to present different looks and content to different users. They also track your access to Web sites, including what products you look at, even if you don't buy them.

Not all cookies (or Temporary Internet Files) are happy and friendly, though. Malicious cookies, installed by some type of malware, can track your Internet activities and report back to its creator. This information is often sold to advertisers so that they can better target you. The best way to defend against these bad cookies is to guard against all malware. Some browsers and browser add-ins can be set to partially or completely block cookies (Figure 18-7).

Plug-ins

Plug-ins are tiny pieces of software that add functionality to your browser. They often enable interactive and audio/visual content such as videos and games. Be careful when installing plug-ins. If you visit a Web site and are prompted to install a third-party application or plug-in that you've never heard of, *don't install it*. Well-known and reputable plug-ins such as *Adobe's Flash* or Microsoft's *Silverlight* are safe, but be suspicious of others.

Figure 18-7
Configuring cookies
in Mozilla Firefox

 EXAM TIP Many Web browsers also include antiphishing features that will warn you if you attempt to visit a potentially hazardous Web site. A dialog box or other window will appear asking you to confirm that you want to visit that particular Web site. Unless you are absolutely sure it is safe, turn around and find a secure Web site.

Firewalls

Firewalls are devices or software that protect an internal network from unauthorized access to and from the Internet at large. Hardware firewalls use a number of methods to protect networks, such as hiding IP addresses and blocking TCP/IP ports. Most small office/home office networks use a hardware firewall, such as a Linksys router. Many routers use access control lists (ACLs) that can filter by port number, IP address, or several other attributes.

Windows XP and later come with an excellent software firewall called the Windows Firewall (Figure 18-8). It can also handle the heavy lifting of port blocking, security logging, and more. You can access the Windows Firewall by opening the Windows Firewall applet in the Control Panel.

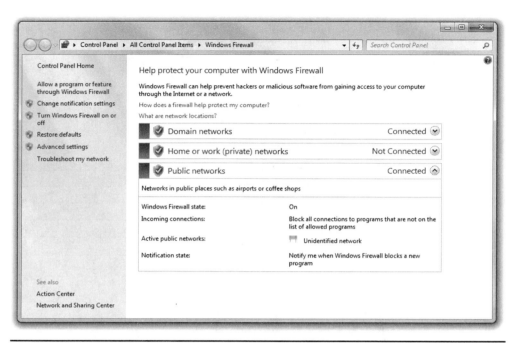

Figure 18-8 Windows Firewall

Chapter Review

You need to defend your computer from Internet-based attacks. Malicious software can destroy your data or report your personal information back to the hacker who wrote the program. Viruses, Trojans, and worms can all infiltrate your system, often posing as something more legitimate, like a downloadable screen saver. These bad programs also have a habit of growing worse over time, as they destroy more data or infect more systems.

Grayware, including pop-ups, spyware, and adware, do not necessarily do harm to your PC, but they can make using it a pain by causing ads to pop up in front of your browser or slowing down your computer. Spam is any unwanted e-mail that appears in your inbox. These are usually scams for money. Don't reply to them—delete them.

There are tools for all of these that scan for any malware currently on your system and defend against any future infiltration. If your system becomes infected with a virus (or other malware), be sure you know what to do to get rid of it: recognize that there is a virus, quarantine the virus or the entire PC, search for and destroy the virus using antivirus software, remediate by restoring your PC with previously made backups, and educate yourself and anyone else who may have allowed the infection to occur. Also, be sure to escalate the problem to a boss or coworker if you are unable to fix it yourself.

Proper browser configuration can often prevent malware from getting onto your PC. You can disable things like ActiveX and Java that, though rarely, may be used to run malicious code on your computer. You can also disable the use of cookies and Temporary Internet Files, which can be used to track your movements across the Internet. Only download plug-ins from reputable companies, such as Adobe and Microsoft.

Make sure you are using a firewall to keep prying eyes out of your computer. You should use both a hardware firewall, such as a router, and the software firewall that is included with Windows.

Questions

1. What is the name for programs that are bothersome but not necessarily malicious?

    A. Malware

    B. Grayware

    C. Spyware

    D. Software

2. Which of the following are alternative methods of closing a pop-up window? (Select two.)

    A. Click the pop-up.

    B. Press ALT-F4.

    C. Right-click the window's taskbar icon and select Close.

    D. Run your antivirus software.

3. What is spam?

    A. Unwanted e-mail messages

    B. A type of virus

    C. An antivirus program

    D. A type of firewall

4. Even if you don't have antivirus software, what two things can you do to protect your Windows machine from intruders? (Select two.)

    A. Run Windows Update regularly.

    B. Use only Internet Explorer.

    C. Back up your data.

    D. Use a firewall.

5. After you have recognized that there is a virus on your PC, what is the next step to removing the virus?

    A. Educate

    B. Search and destroy

    C. Quarantine

    D. Remediate

6. How can you defend against viruses delivered by e-mail?

   A. Delete old messages regularly.

   B. Don't open messages from unknown senders.

   C. Only use the preview window.

   D. Only use Mozilla Thunderbird.

7. Which type of file tracks your activities on the Internet?

   A. Spam

   B. Java

   C. Pop-up

   D. Cookie

8. Which of the following can be disabled in a Web browser to avoid any malicious code being run on your system? (Select two.)

   A. HTML

   B. Java

   C. ActiveX

   D. Firewalls

9. Which of the following devices is a kind of firewall?

   A. Modem

   B. Router

   C. Switch

   D. Ethernet cable

10. Which of the following types of malware is the least malicious?

    A. Trojan

    B. Worm

    C. Spyware

    D. Adware

Answers

1. **B.** Grayware is unwanted software like pop-ups and adware that can cause headaches but don't actually attack your PC.

2. **B, C.** To safely close a pop-up window, you can either press ALT-F4 or right-click the window's taskbar icon and select Close.

3. **A.** Spam is the name for the unwanted e-mail messages that can clog your inbox.

4. **A, D.** Updating your operating system and using a firewall are two things that will help protect you from hackers.

5. **C.** After you recognize that there is a virus on your machine, you need to quarantine, either by using antivirus software or disconnecting the infected machine from the network.

6. **B.** The best defense against virus-filled e-mails is to not open e-mails from unknown senders.

7. **D.** Web browsers use cookies to track certain things you do on the Internet.

8. **B, C.** Disabling ActiveX and Java can help prevent malicious code from being run on your PC.

9. **B.** A router acts as a hardware firewall by hiding your PC's IP address from the Internet.

10. **D.** Adware is the least malicious—most adware just gathers information about your browsing habits to display more targeted ads on your PC.

PART VI

Appendixes

About the CD

We have put together a bunch of resources that will help you prepare for the CompTIA Strata IT Fundamentals exam(s) and that you will find invaluable in your career as a PC tech. The CD-ROM included with this book comes complete with the following:

- An introductory video featuring Scott Jernigan
- A sample version of the Total Tester practice exam software with two full practice exams
- A searchable electronic copy of the book
- A document from CompTIA with a list of acronyms that you should know for the CompTIA Strata exams
- A complete list of the objectives for three of the CompTIA Strata exams, including IT Fundamentals, PC Functionality, and Technology
- A sample of LearnKey's video training

To use the practice tests and video software, they must be installed on a Windows 2000/XP/Vista/7 computer. The eBook and CompTIA Strata acronyms and objectives lists are Adobe Acrobat files. If you don't have Adobe Reader, you can use the link provided on the CD-ROM to download it.

System Requirements

The software on the CD-ROM requires Windows XP or higher and 100 MB of hard disk space for full installation. Learn more about the system requirements for the LearnKey video training by visiting www.learnkey.com/Customer_support.

Installing and Running Total Tester

If your computer's optical drive is configured to autorun, the CD-ROM will automatically start upon inserting the disk. If the autorun feature does not launch the CD-ROM's splash screen, browse to the CD-ROM and double-click the Launch.exe icon.

From the splash screen, click the Install Strata Practice Exams button to install Total Tester. This will begin the installation process, create a program group named Total Seminars, and put an icon on your desktop. To run Total Tester, go to Start | Programs or All Programs | Total Seminars or just double-click the icon on your desktop.

To uninstall the Total Tester software, go to Start | Settings | Control Panel | Add/ Remove Programs in Windows 2000/XP or Start | Control Panel | Uninstall a program in Windows Vista/7 and select the Strata Total Tester program. Select Remove, and Windows will completely uninstall the software.

About Total Tester

The best way to prepare for the CompTIA Strata exams is to read the book and then test your knowledge and review. The CD-ROM includes a sample of Total Seminars' practice exam software to help you test your knowledge as you study. Total Tester provides you with a simulation of the actual exam. These exams can be taken in either practice or final mode. Practice mode provides an assistance window with hints, references to the book, and the ability to check your answer as you take the test. Both practice and final modes provide an overall grade and a grade broken down by certification objective. To launch a test, select Suites from the menu at the top and then select an exam.

Additional practice exams are available. Visit our Web site at www.totalsem.com or call 800-446-6004 for more information.

Accessing the eBook, CompTIA Strata Acronyms List, and CompTIA Strata Exam Objectives

You will find the eBook, CompTIA Strata acronyms list, and CompTIA Strata exam objectives useful in your preparation for the exams. To access these PDF documents, first be sure you have a copy of Adobe Reader installed. If you don't have Adobe Reader installed on your system, you can follow the link on the CD-ROM to download it from Adobe's Web page. Once you have installed Acrobat Reader, simply select the document you want to view from the CD-ROM's splash screen to open the document.

LearnKey Video Training

If you like Scott's writing style, you will love watching LearnKey's video training series. The CD-ROM includes sample videos covering several different topics. If you like them, you can purchase the set of interactive videos by contacting Scott's company, Total Seminars, at www.totalsem.com or 800-446-6004.

To check out the video training, click Install LearnKey Demo to launch a wizard to install the software on your computer. Follow the instructions in the wizard to complete the installation. To run the LearnKey demo, go to Start | (All) Programs | LearnKey or just double-click the icon on your desktop. Enter a user name and password to begin your video training.

Technical Support

For questions regarding the Total Tester software, visit www.totalsem.com or e-mail support@totalsem.com.

LearnKey Technical Support

For technical problems with the LearnKey video training software (installation, operation, or uninstalling the software) and for questions regarding LearnKey video training, e-mail techsupport@learnkey.com.

Exam Objective Reference

IT Fundamentals

The CompTIA Strata IT Fundamentals exam is designed to show that the successful candidate has the knowledge to identify and explain PC components, set up a basic PC workstation, conduct basic software installation, identify compatibility issues, and recognize/prevent basic security risks. Further, this test will assess the candidate's knowledge in the areas of Green IT and preventative maintenance of computers. This test is intended for candidates who are advanced home users or are considering the pursuit of a CompTIA A+ certification.

 NOTE The lists under each objective are not exhaustive. Even though they are not included in this document, other examples of technologies, processes, or tasks pertaining to each objective may also be included on the exam.

Domain	% of Examination
1.0 Technology and Computer Hardware Basics	40%
2.0 Compatibility Issues and Common Errors	13%
3.0 Software Installation and Functions	11%
4.0 Security	16%
5.0 Green IT and Preventative Maintenance	20%
Total	100%

Topic	Chapter
1.0 Technology and Computer Hardware Basics	
1.1 Identify basic IT vocabulary	
Processor speed/cores	2
Single/Dual/Quad core	2
Intel based/Cell based/AMD based	2
GHz vs. MHz	2
Processor cache size	2

Topic	Chapter
Bus speed (as it relates to motherboards, memory, etc.)	2
RAM	1, 2
DDR, DDR2, DDR3	2
DIMMS vs. SODIMMS	2
Hard drives	1, 4
RPMs	4
Cache size	4
Flash based vs. traditional hard drives	4, 10
SATA, SCSI, IDE	4, 10
Internal vs. external	10
Local vs. network shares	13
Networking	13, 14, 15, 18
Wireless networking terms	14
802.11a/b/g/n	14
Bluetooth	14
RF (Radio Frequency)	14
Interference	14
WAP (Wireless Access Point)	14
SSID	14
Wireless router	15
Ethernet technologies	13
CAT5 connections and cables	13
Home plug (Ethernet over Power)	13
Broadband router	15
DSL and cable modems	15
Standard vs. crossover cables	13
Auto-negotiating (speed and duplex)	13
Internet	15, 18
Protocols	15
HTTP vs. HTTPS	15
FTP	15
SSL	15
POP3	15
SMTP	15

Topic	Chapter
IMAP	15
DNS	15
DHCP	15
TCP/IP (IPv4 address, IPv6 address)	15
Browser features	18
Plug-ins	18
Customization (text sizes, text styles, etc.)	18
Anti-phishing features	18
ActiveX and Java	18
Cookies	18
Internet Cache	18

1.2 Demonstrate the proper use of the following devices

Monitors	1, 3
Adjust monitor settings (brightness, contrast, etc.)	3
Desktop	12
Server	13
Portable	12
Laptop	12
PDA	12
Smartphone	1, 12
Netbook	12

1.3 Explain the characteristics and functions of internal and external storage devices

CD/CD-RW Drive	4
DVD/DVD-RW Drive	4
Blu-Ray Disk Drive	4
USB storage (solid state vs. magnetic disk)	10
Multi-card reader and writer	10
Hard drives	1, 4, 10
Mobile media devices (e.g. MP3 player or PDAs)	12

1.4 Explain the characteristics and functions of peripheral devices

Digital camera	1, 9
Web camera	9
Speaker	1, 9
Tuner	9

Topic	Chapter
Microphone	9
Printer/scanner	1, 9, 11
1.5 Explain the characteristics and functions of core input devices	
Keyboard	1, 3
Mouse	1, 3
Tablet (touch screen)	1
Numeric keypad	3
Gamepad	9
1.6 Identify the risks associated with upgrading the following technologies and equipment	
Operating systems (open source and commercial)	7
Compatibility issues	7, 8
Upgrade issues	7, 8
Data loss	7
PC Speed/storage capability	2, 4, 10
Compatibility issues	7, 8
Upgrade issues	7, 8
Bus differences	8
Hardware failure	8
Application	7
Minimum requirements	7
Compatibility issues	7
Bandwidth and contention	15
VoIP	15
Streaming	15
Web delivered services	15
Automatic application and operating system updates	7
Risks of automatic updates	7
Risks of not using automatic updates	7
Risks of not using manufacturer websites	7
1.7 Demonstrate the ability to set up a basic PC workstation	
Identify differences between connector types	2
DVI, VGA, HDMI	3, 8, 9
USB, PS/2	8
FireWire	8

Topic	Chapter
Bluetooth and Wireless	8
Serial	8
Network connectors	13
PCMCIA	12
ExpressCard	12
3.5mm audio jack	9
Power connectors	2, 3, 4, 9
Monitor types	3
Computer (desktop, tower, laptop, custom cases)	8, 12
Keyboard (keyboard layout: regionalization)	3
Mouse (touchpad, optical, trackball)	3
Printer (USB, wireless, networked)	11
Voltage and power requirements	2, 3, 4
Turn on and use the PC and peripherals	1
2.0 Compatibility Issues and Common Errors	
2.1 Identify basic compatibility issues between:	
Processor performance	8
RAM memory	8
USB (1.1, 2.0)	8
FireWire	8
PS/2	8
Ethernet	13
Wireless networks	14
2.2 Recognize common operational problems caused by hardware	
Critical error message or crash	8
System lockup (freeze)	8
Application will not start or load	8
Cannot logon to network	8
Driver/hardware compatibility	8
Input device will not function	8
2.3 Demonstrate the ability to minimize risks	
Data loss	8, 17
Loss of service	15
Damage to equipment	8

Topic	Chapter
3.0 Software Installation and Functions	
3.1 Conduct basic software installation, removal, and/or upgrading	
Follow basic installation/upgrade procedures	7
Check PC meets minimum requirements	7
Administrative Rights	7
Firewall access (unblocking ports for proper functionality)	7, 15
Configure the Operating System	5
Adjust basic settings (e.g. volume, date, time, time zone)	8, 12
User accounts	5
Power settings (power save, sleep mode, etc.)	8, 12
Screen resolutions	5
Documentation	7
Licensing (Commercial, Freeware, Shareware)	7
Software registration	7
Digital Rights Management	7
Software removal (clean un-installation)	7
Re-installation (clean installation)	7
3.2 Identify issues related to folder and file management	
Create, delete, rename, and move folders	5
Assign folder structure during installation	5
Create, delete, rename, move, and print files	5
Importance of following back-up guidelines and procedures	6
3.3 Explain the function and purpose of software tools	
Performance and error correction tools	7, 8
Activity or event logging	17
Back-up tools	6
Disk clean-up tools	6
File compression tools	6
4.0 Security	
4.1 Recognize basic security risks and procedures to prevent them	
Identify Risks	17
Social Engineering	17
Viruses	17
Worms	17, 18
Trojan Horses	18

Topic	Chapter
Unauthorized Access	17
Hackers	17
Phishing	17
Spyware	17
Adware	18
Malware	18
Identity Fraud	15
File and folder sharing	13
Web browser risks	18
Operating System vulnerability	18
Service packs	7
Security updates	7
Theft	17
Open or free networks	18
Identify prevention methods	18
User awareness/education	18
Anti-virus software	18
Ensure proper security certificate are used (SSL)	15
Wireless encryption (WPA/WEP)	14
Anti-spyware	18
File encryption	17
Firewalls	18
Anti-spam software	18
Password best practice	17
Complexity (password construction)	17
Password confidentiality	17
Change frequency	17
Re-use	17
Utilization	17
Identify access control methods	17
Passwords and User ID	17
Screensavers	17
Physical security of hardware	17
Locks	17
Parental controls	17

Topic	Chapter
Smart card	17
Fingerprint reader	17
One time password	17
Identify security threats related to the following:	17
Media used for backup (theft or loss)	17
Screen visibility (shoulder surfing)	17
Cookies (can be stolen, stores passwords, browser tracking)	18
Pop-ups (automatic installations, click on links to malware)	18
Accidental mis-configuration	17
4.2 Recognize security breaches and ways to resolve them	
Recognize the proper diagnostic procedures when infected with a virus	18
Run anti-virus scan	18
Quarantine virus when possible	18
Escalate to IT professional when needed	18
Recognize the proper procedures to maintain a secure environment	17
Regular antivirus and malware scans	18
Application/operating system updates	17
5.0 Green IT and Preventative Maintenance	
5.1 Identify environmentally sound techniques to preserve power and dispose of materials	
Environmentally hazardous substance disposal	8, 11
Battery disposal	12
CRT disposal—replace with LCDs	8
Recycling of computers for reuse or parts	8
Toner disposal	11
Cleaning supply disposal	6
Materials that meet RoHS guidelines	16
Power management (Power saving features)	12
Shutdown/power off procedures/policies at end of day	16
Automatic power off after 15 minutes of non-use	16
Shutdown scripts	15
Power management PCs and lower power servers replace large desktops with energy efficient laptops and thin clients	16

Topic	Chapter
5.2 Identify green techniques, equipment, and procedures	
Define Cloud computing	16
Define Virtualization (Have more than one server running on a single piece of hardware)	16
Reduced power and cooling consumption	16
Duplex printing and use lower cost per page network printers	11
Terminal Servers	16
Energy Star rating	16
Use low power NAS (network attached storage) instead of file servers	16
Employee telecommuting	16
Reduced emissions	16
Reduced office space heating, lighting, etc.	16
Solid State drives	10
Define VoIP and how it relates to Green IT	16
Green building infrastructure	16
Eliminate cool air leaks in server rooms	16
Proper spacing for cooling IT equipment	16
Energy efficient cooling fans—BIOS adjustable	16
5.3 Identify preventative maintenance products, techniques, and how to use them	
Liquid cleaning compounds	6
Types of materials to clean contacts and connections	12
Compressed air	6
Cleaning monitors	6
Cleaning removable media devices	6
Ventilation, dust, and moisture control on the PC hardware interior	6
Surge suppressors	6
Use of ESD equipment	6
Wire placement and safety	6

PART VI

U.K. Strata Exams

The CompTIA Strata Fundamentals of Technology and Fundamentals of PC Functionality exams cover the same material as the U.S. version of the exam, but the specific objectives are arranged differently, as outlined here.

Fundamentals of Technology

Topic	Chapter
1.0 Computer Hardware	
1.1 Demonstrate the proper use of the following devices	
Monitors	1, 3
Adjust monitor settings (brightness, contrast, etc.)	3
Desktop	12
Server	13
Portable	12
Laptop	12
PDA	12
Smartphone	1, 12
Netbook	12
1.2 Explain the characteristics and functions of internal and external storage devices	
CD/CD-RW Drive	4
DVD/DVD-RW Drive	4
Blu-Ray Disk Drive	4
USB storage (solid state vs. magnetic disk)	10
Multi-card reader and writer	10
Hard drives	1, 4, 10
Mobile media devices (e.g. MP3 player or PDAs)	12
1.3 Explain the characteristics and functions of peripheral devices	
Digital camera	1, 9
Web camera	9
Tuner	9
Microphone	9
Printer/scanner	1, 9, 11
1.4 Explain the characteristics and functions of core input devices	
Keyboard	1, 3
Mouse	1, 3
Tablet (touch screen)	1
Numeric keypad	3
Gamepad	9

Topic	Chapter
2.0 Compatibility Issues and Common Errors	
2.1 Identify basic compatibility issues between:	
Processor performance	8
RAM memory	8
USB (1.1, 2.0)	8
FireWire	8
PS/2	8
Ethernet	13
Wireless networks	14
2.2 Recognize common operational problems caused by hardware	
Critical error message or crash	8
System lockup (freeze)	8
Application will not start or load	8
Cannot logon to network	8
Driver/hardware compatibility	8
Input device will not function	8
2.3 Demonstrate the ability to minimize risks	
Data loss	8, 17
Loss of service	15
Damage to equipment	8
3.0 Health, Safety, and Preventative Maintenance	
3.1 Recognize safety hazards and identify corresponding guidelines	
Hazards	6
Fire	6
Flood	6
Electrical Surges	6
Extreme storms	6
Environmental hazards	6
Guidelines	6
Use of ESD equipment	6
Use of tools and equipment	6
Electricity and safety	6
Hazardous substances	6

Topic	Chapter
Wire placement and safety	6
Environmental legislation and regulations (e.g. disposal of materials)	6, 11
3.2 Identify preventative maintenance products, techniques, and how to use them	
Liquid cleaning compounds	6
Types of materials to clean contacts and connections	12
Compressed air	6
Cleaning monitors	6
Cleaning removable media devices	6
Ventilation, dust, and moisture control on the PC hardware interior	6
Surge suppressors	6
Replacing printer consumables	11

Fundamentals of PC Functionality

Topic	Chapter
1.0 Technology	
1.1 Identify basic IT vocabulary	
Processor speed/cores	2
Single/Dual/Quad core	2
Intel based/Cell based/AMD based	2
GHz vs. MHz	2
Processor cache size	2
Bus speed (as it relates to motherboards, memory, etc.)	2
RAM	1, 2
DDR, DDR2, DDR3	2
DIMMS vs. SODIMMS	2
Hard drives	1, 4
RPMs	4
Cache size	4
Flash based vs. traditional hard drives	4, 10
SATA, SCSI, IDE	4, 10
Internal vs. external	10
Local vs. network shares	13
Networking	13, 14, 15, 18

PART VI

Topic	Chapter
1.2 Identify the risks associated with upgrading the following technologies and equipment	
Operating systems (open source and commercial)	7
Compatibility issues	7, 8
Upgrade issues	7, 8
Data loss	7
PC Speed/storage capability	2, 4, 10
Compatibility issues	7, 8
Upgrade issues	7, 8
Bus differences	8
Hardware failure	8
Application	7
Minimum requirements	7
Compatibility issues	7
Bandwidth and contention	15
VoIP	15
Streaming	15
Web delivered services	15
Automatic application and operating system updates	7
Risks of automatic updates	7
Risks of not using automatic updates	7
Risks of not using manufacturer websites	7
1.3 Demonstrate the ability to set up a basic PC workstation	
Identify differences between connector types	2
DVI, VGA, HDMI	3, 8, 9
USB, PS/2	8
FireWire	8
Bluetooth and Wireless	8
Serial	8
Network connectors	13
PCMCIA	12
ExpressCard	12
3.5mm audio jack	9
Power connectors	2, 3, 4, 9

Topic	Chapter
Monitor types	3
Computer (desktop, tower, laptop, custom cases)	8, 12
Keyboard (keyboard layout: regionalization)	3
Mouse (touchpad, optical, trackball)	3
Printer (USB, wireless, networked)	11
Voltage and power requirements	2, 3, 4
Turn on and use the PC and peripherals	1
2.0 Software Installation and Functions	
2.1 Conduct basic software installation, removal, and/or upgrading.	
Follow basic installation/upgrade procedures	7
Check PC meets minimum requirements	7
Administrative Rights	7
Firewall access (unblocking ports for proper functionality)	7, 15
Configure the Operating System	5
Adjust basic settings (e.g. volume, date, time, time zone)	8, 12
User accounts	5
Power settings (power save, sleep mode, etc.)	8, 12
Screen resolutions	5
Documentation	7
Licensing (Commercial, Freeware, Shareware)	7
Software registration	7
Digital Rights Management	7
Software removal (clean un-installation)	7
2.2 Identify issues related to folder and file management	
Create, delete, rename, and move folders	5
Assign folder structure during installation	5
Create, delete, rename, move, and print files	5
Importance of following back-up guidelines and procedures	6
2.3 Explain the function and purpose of software tools	
Performance and error correction tools	7, 8
Activity or event logging	17
Back-up tools	6
Disk clean-up tools	6
File compression tools	6

PART VI

Topic	Chapter
3.0 Security	
3.1 Recognize basic security risks and procedures to prevent them	
Identify Risks	17
Social Engineering	17
Viruses	17
Worms	17, 18
Trojan Horses	18
Unauthorized Access	17
Hackers	17
Phishing	17
Spyware	17
Adware	18
Malware	18
Identity Fraud	15
File and folder sharing	13
Web browser risks	18
Operating System vulnerability	18
Service packs	7
Security updates	7
Theft	17
Open or free networks	18
Identify prevention methods	18
User awareness/education	18
Anti-virus software	18
Ensure proper security certificate are used (SSL)	15
Wireless encryption (WPA/WEP)	14
Anti-spyware	18
File encryption	17
Firewalls	18
Anti-spam software	18
Password best practice	17
Complexity (password construction)	17
Password confidentiality	17
Change frequency	17
Re-use	17
Utilization	17

Topic	Chapter
Identify access control methods	17
Passwords and User ID	17
Screensavers	17
Physical security of hardware	17
Locks	17
Parental controls	17
Smart card	17
Fingerprint reader	17
One time password	17
Identify security threats related to the following	17
Media used for backup (theft or loss)	17
Screen visibility (shoulder surfing)	17
Cookies (can be stolen, stores passwords, browser tracking)	18
Pop-ups (automatic installations, click on links to malware)	18
Accidental mis-configuration	17
3.2 Recognize security breaches and ways to resolve them	
Recognize the proper diagnostic procedures when infected with a virus	18
Run anti-virus scan	18
Quarantine virus when possible	18
Escalate to IT professional when needed	18
Recognize the proper procedures to maintain a secure environment	17
Regular antivirus and malware scans	18
Application/operating system updates	17
3.3 Recognize IT related laws and guidelines	
Data Protection Act	Not covered
Copyright Act	Not covered
Computer Misuse Act	Not covered
Freedom of Information Act	Not covered

PART VI

10BaseT   Ethernet LAN designed to run on UTP cabling. 10BaseT runs at 10 megabits per second. The maximum length for the cabling between the NIC and the hub (or switch, repeater, etc.) is 100 meters. It uses baseband signaling. No industry standard spelling exists, so sometimes written 10BASE-T or 10Base-T.

100BaseT   Generic term for an Ethernet cabling system designed to run at 100 megabits per second on UTP cabling. It uses baseband signaling. No industry standard spelling exists, so sometimes written 100BASE-T or 100Base-T.

1000BaseT   Gigabit Ethernet on UTP.

16-bit   Able to process 16 bits of data at a time.

2.1   Speaker setup consisting of two stereo speakers combined with a subwoofer.

3.5-inch floppy drive   All modern floppy disk drives are of this size; the format was introduced in 1986 and is one of the longest surviving pieces of computer hardware.

32-bit architecture   A CPU that can handle data that is 32 bits in complexity.

34-pin ribbon cable   Type of cable used by floppy disk drives.

3-D graphics   Video technology that attempts to create images with the same depth and texture as objects seen in the real world.

40-pin ribbon cable   Type of cable used to attach EIDE devices (such as hard drives) or ATAPI devices (such as CD-ROMs) to a system.

5.1 speaker system   Four satellite speakers plus a center speaker and a subwoofer.

8.3 naming system   File-naming convention that specified a maximum of eight characters for a filename, followed by a three-character file extension. Has been replaced by LFN (long filename) support.

80-wire ribbon cable   Type of cable used to attach EIDE devices (such as hard drives) or ATAPI devices (such as CD-ROMs) to a system.

802.11a   Wireless networking standard that operates in the 5-GHz band with a theoretical maximum throughput of 54 Mbps.

802.11b   Wireless networking standard that operates in the 2.4-GHz band with a theoretical maximum throughput of 11 Mbps.

802.11g   Wireless networking standard that operates in the 2.4-GHz band with a theoretical maximum throughput of 54 Mbps and is backward compatible with 802.11b.

802.11n   Wireless networking standard that can operate in both the 2.4-GHz and 5-GHz bands and uses MIMO to achieve a theoretical maximum throughput of 100+ Mbps.

A/V sync   Process of synchronizing audio and video.

AC (alternating current)   Type of electricity in which the flow of electrons alternates direction, back and forth, in a circuit.

AC'97   Sound card standard for lower-end audio devices; created when most folks listened to stereo sound at best.

access control   Security concept using physical security, authentication, users and groups, and security policies.

ACPI (Advanced Configuration and Power Interface)   Power management specification that far surpasses its predecessor, APM, by providing support for hot-swappable devices and better control of power modes.

activation   Process of confirming that an installed copy of a Microsoft product (most commonly Windows or a Microsoft Office application) is legitimate. Usually done at the end of software installation.

active matrix   Type of liquid crystal display that replaced the passive matrix technology used in most portable computer displays. Also called TFT (thin film transistor).

active partition   On a hard drive, primary partition that contains an operating system.

active PFC (power factor correction)   Circuitry built into PC power supplies to reduce harmonics.

ActiveX   Programming language incorporated into some Web sites.

ad hoc mode   Decentralized wireless network mode, otherwise known as peer-to-peer mode, where each wireless node is in direct contact with every other node.

Add or Remove Programs   Applet allowing users to manually add or remove a program from the system.

address bus   Wires leading from the CPU to the memory controller chip (usually the Northbridge) that enable the CPU to address RAM. Also used by the CPU for I/O addressing. An internal electronic channel from the microprocessor to random access memory, along which the addresses of memory storage locations are transmitted. Like a post office box, each memory location has a distinct number or address; the address bus provides the means by which the microprocessor can access every location in memory.

address space   Total amount of memory addresses that an address bus can contain.

administrative rights   Permission to install software and modify system settings.

administrative shares   Administrator tool to give local admins access to hard drives and system root folders.

Administrative Tools   Group of Control Panel applets, including Computer Management, Event Viewer, and Performance.

Administrator account   User account, created when the OS is first installed, that is allowed complete, unfettered access to the system without restriction.

Administrators group   List of members with complete administrator privileges.

ADSL (Asymmetric Digital Subscriber Line)   Fully digital, dedicated connection to the telephone system that provides download speeds of up to 9 Mbps and upload speeds of up to 1 Mbps.

Advanced Micro Devices (AMD)   CPU and chipset manufacturer that competes with Intel. Produces the popular Phenom, Athlon, Sempron, and Duron processors.

Advanced Startup Options menu   Menu that can be reached during the boot process that offers advanced OS startup options, such as boot in Safe mode or boot into Last Known Good Configuration.

adware   Type of malicious program that downloads ads to a user's computer, generating undesirable network traffic.

Aero   The Windows Vista desktop environment. Aero adds some interesting aesthetic effects such as window transparency and Flip 3D.

AGP (accelerated graphics port)   32/64-bit expansion slot designed by Intel specifically for video that runs at 66 MHz and yields a throughput of at least 254 Mbps. Later versions (2×, 4×, 8×) give substantially higher throughput.

algorithm   Set of rules for solving a problem in a given number of steps.

ALU (arithmetic logic unit) CPU logic circuits that perform basic arithmetic (add, subtract, multiply, and divide).

AMI (American Megatrends, Inc.) Major producer of BIOS software for motherboards, as well as many other computer-related components and software.

amperes (amps or A) Unit of measure for amperage, or electrical current.

amplitude Loudness of a sound card.

AMR (audio/modem riser) Proprietary slot used on some motherboards to provide a sound interference–free connection for modems, sound cards, and NICs.

analog Device that uses a physical quantity, such as length or voltage, to represent the value of a number. By contrast, digital storage relies on a coding system of numeric units.

anti-aliasing In computer imaging, blending effect that smoothes sharp contrasts between two regions—e.g., jagged lines or different colors. Reduces jagged edges of text or objects. In voice signal processing, process of removing or smoothing out spurious frequencies from waveforms produced by converting digital signals back to analog.

anti-static bag Bag made of anti-static plastic into which electronics are placed for temporary or long-term storage. Used to prevent electrostatic discharge.

anti-static mat Special surface on which to lay electronics. These mats come with a grounding connection designed to equalize electrical potential between a workbench and one or more electronic devices. Used to prevent electrostatic discharge.

anti-static vacuum A vacuum that doesn't create a static electricity charge as dust flows through the nozzle, used to clean the insides of computers.

anti-static wrist strap Special device worn around the wrist with a grounding connection designed to equalize electrical potential between a technician and an electronic device. Used to prevent electrostatic discharge.

antivirus program Software designed to combat viruses by either seeking out and destroying them or passively guarding against them.

API (application programming interface) Software definition that describes operating system calls for application software; conventions defining how a service is invoked.

APIPA (Automatic Private IP Addressing) Feature of Windows that automatically assigns an IP address to the system when the client cannot obtain an IP address automatically.

APM (advanced power management)   BIOS routines that enable the CPU to turn on and off selected peripherals.

applet   Generic term for a program in the Windows Control Panel.

application   Software that enables you to do a specialized task on a computer.

application server   Computer that hosts applications for clients.

archive   To copy programs and data onto a relatively inexpensive storage medium (disk, tape, etc.) for long-term retention.

archive attribute   Attribute of a file that shows whether the file has been backed up since the last change. Each time a file is opened, changed, or saved, the archive bit is turned on. Some types of backups turn off this archive bit to indicate that a good back-up of the file exists on tape.

ARP (Address Resolution Protocol)   Protocol in the TCP/IP suite used with the command-line utility of the same name to determine the MAC address that corresponds to a particular IP address.

ASCII (American Standard Code for Information Interchange)   Industry-standard 8-bit characters used to define text characters, consisting of 96 upper- and lowercase letters, plus 32 nonprinting control characters, each of which is numbered. These numbers were designed to achieve uniformity among computer devices for printing and the exchange of simple text documents.

aspect ratio   Ratio of width to height of an object. Standard television has a 4:3 aspect ratio.

ASR (Automated System Recovery)   Windows XP tool designed to recover a badly corrupted Windows system; similar to ERD.

assertive communication   Means of communication that is not pushy or bossy but is also not soft. Useful in dealing with upset customers, as it both defuses their anger and gives them confidence that you know what you're doing.

AT (Advanced Technology)   Model name of the second-generation, 80286-based IBM computer. Many aspects of the AT, such as the BIOS, CMOS, and expansion bus, have become de facto standards in the PC industry. The physical organization of the components on the motherboard is called the AT form factor.

ATA (AT attachment)   Type of hard drive and controller designed to replace the earlier ST506 and ESDI drives without requiring replacement of the AT BIOS—hence, AT attachment. These drives are more popularly known as IDE drives. (*See* IDE.) The **ATA/33** standard has drive transfer speeds up to 33 MBps; the **ATA/66** up to 66 MBps; the **ATA/100** up to 100 MBps; and the **ATA/133** up to 133 MBps. (*See* Ultra DMA.)

ATA/ATAPI-6 Also known as ATA-6 or "big drive." Replaced the INT13 extensions and allowed for hard drives as large as 144 petabytes (144 million gigabytes).

ATAPI (ATA packet interface) Series of standards that enable mass storage devices other than hard drives to use the IDE/ATA controllers. Extremely popular with CD-ROM drives and removable media drives such as the Iomega Zip drive. (*See* EIDE.)

ATAPI-compliant Devices that utilize the ATAPI standard. (*See* ATAPI.)

Athlon Name used for a popular series of CPUs manufactured by AMD.

ATTRIB.EXE Command used to view the specific properties of a file; can also be used to modify or remove file properties, such as Read-Only, System, or Archive.

attributes Values in a file that determine the hidden, read-only, system, and archive status of the file.

ATX (Advanced Technology Extended) Popular motherboard form factor that generally replaced the AT form factor.

auditing Creating entries in a log when certain events occur.

authentication Any method a computer uses to determine who can access it and what that user can do.

autodetection Process through which new disks are automatically recognized by the BIOS.

auto-negotiation Feature that senses both the duplex mode and the speed of network cables and devices.

Automatic Updates Feature allowing updates to Windows to be retrieved automatically over the Internet.

AutoPlay Windows 2000/XP/Vista/7 setting, along with autorun.inf, enabling Windows to automatically detect media files and begin using them. (*See* AUTORUN.INF.)

AUTORUN.INF File included on some media that automatically launches a program or installation routine when the media is inserted/attached to a system.

autosensing Better-quality sound cards use autosensing to detect a device plugged into a port and to adapt the features of that port.

auto-switching power supply Type of power supply able to detect the voltage of a particular outlet and adjust accordingly.

Award Software   Major producer of BIOS software for motherboards.

backbone   Central heart of the Internet consisting of many university, corporate, and government networks connected together via thick bundles of fiber optic cabling.

backlight   One of three main components used in LCDs to illuminate an image.

backside bus   Set of wires that connect the CPU to Level 2 cache. Most modern CPUs have a special backside bus, which first appeared in the Pentium Pro. Some buses, such as that in the later Celeron processors (300A and beyond), run at the full speed of the CPU, whereas others run at a fraction. Earlier Pentium IIs, for example, had backside buses running at half the speed of the processor. (*See also* frontside bus *and* external data bus.)

Backup or Restore Wizard   Utility contained within Windows that allows users to create system backups and set system restore points.

ball mouse   Input device that enables users to manipulate a cursor on the screen by using a ball and sensors that detect the movement and direction of the ball.

bandwidth   Piece of the spectrum occupied by some form of signal, such as television, voice, fax data. Signals require a certain size and location of bandwidth to be transmitted. The higher the bandwidth, the faster the signal transmission, allowing for a more complex signal such as audio or video. Because bandwidth is a limited space, when one user is occupying it, others must wait their turn. Bandwidth is also the capacity of a network to transmit a given amount of data during a given period.

bank   Total number of SIMMs or DIMMs that can be accessed simultaneously by the chipset. The "width" of the external data bus divided by the "width" of the SIMM or DIMM sticks.

bar code reader   Tool to read Universal Product Code (UPC) bar codes.

basic disks   Hard drive partitioned in the "classic" way with a master boot record (MBR) and partition table. (*See also* dynamic disks.)

baud   One analog cycle on a telephone line. In the early days of telephone data transmission, the baud rate was often analogous to bits per second. Due to advanced modulation of baud cycles as well as data compression, this is no longer true.

BD-RE (Blu-ray Disc-REwritable)   Blu-ray equivalent of the rewritable DVD, allows writing and rewriting several times on the same BD. (*See* Blu-ray Disc.)

BD-ROM   Blu-ray equivalent of a DVD-ROM or CD-ROM. (*See* Blu-ray Disc.)

beaming   Term used to describe transferring data from one PDA to another by means of IrDA.

beep codes Series of audible tones produced by a motherboard during the POST. These tones identify whether the POST has completed successfully or whether some piece of system hardware is not working properly. Consult the manual for your particular motherboard for a specific list of beep codes.

binary numbers Number system with a base of 2, unlike the number systems most of us use that have bases of 10 (decimal numbers), 12 (measurement in feet and inches), and 60 (time). Binary numbers are preferred for computers for precision and economy. An electronic circuit that can detect the difference between two states (on–off, 0–1) is easier and more inexpensive to build than one that could detect the differences among ten states (0–9).

biometric device Hardware device used to support authentication; works by scanning and remembering unique aspects of a user's various body parts (e.g., retina, iris, face, or fingerprint) by using some form of sensing device such as a retinal scanner.

BIOS (basic input/output system) Classically, software routines burned onto the system ROM of a PC. More commonly seen as any software that directly controls a particular piece of hardware. A set of programs encoded in read-only memory (ROM) on computers. These programs handle startup operations and low-level control of hardware such as disk drives, the keyboard, and monitor.

bit Single binary digit. Also, any device that can be in an on or off state.

bit depth Number of colors a video card is capable of producing. Common bit depths are 16-bit and 32-bit, representing 65,536 colors and 16.7 million colors, respectively.

BitLocker Drive Encryption Drive encryption software offered in Windows Vista/7 Ultimate and Enterprise editions. BitLocker utilizes a special chip to validate hardware status and that the computer hasn't been hacked.

Bluetooth Wireless technology designed to create small wireless networks preconfigured to do specific jobs, but not meant to replace full-function networks or Wi-Fi.

Blu-ray Disc (BD) Optical disc format that stores 25 GB or 50 GB of data, designed to be the replacement media for DVD. Competed with HD DVD.

boot To initiate an automatic routine that clears the memory, loads the operating system, and prepares the computer for use. Term is derived from "pull yourself up by your bootstraps." PCs must do that because RAM doesn't retain program instructions when power is turned off. A cold boot occurs when the PC is physically switched on. A warm boot loads a fresh OS without turning off the computer, lessening the strain on the electronic circuitry.

BOOT.INI   Text file used during the boot process that provides a list of all OSs currently installed and available for NTLDR. Also tells where each OS is located on the system.

bootable disk   Disk that contains a functional operating system; can also be a floppy disk, USB thumb drive, or CD-ROM.

boot sector   First sector on a PC hard drive or floppy disk, track 0. The boot-up software in ROM tells the computer to load whatever program is found there. If a system disk is read, the program in the boot record directs the computer to the root directory to load the operating system.

bootstrap loader   Segment of code in a system's BIOS that scans for an operating system, looks specifically for a valid boot sector, and, when one is found, hands control over to the boot sector; then the bootstrap loader removes itself from memory.

bps (bits per second)   Measurement of how fast data is moved from one place to another. A 56K modem can move 56,000 bits per second.

broadband   Commonly understood as a reference to high-speed, always-on communication links that can move large files much more quickly than a regular phone line.

browser   Program specifically designed to retrieve, interpret, and display Web pages.

BSoD (Blue Screen of Death)   Infamous error screen that appears when Windows encounters an unrecoverable error. Officially known as a Windows stop error.

BTX (Balanced Technology eXtended)   Motherboard form factor designed as an improvement over ATX.

buffered/registered DRAM   Usually seen in motherboards supporting more than four sticks of RAM, it is required to address interference issues caused by the additional sticks.

buffer underrun   Inability of a source device to provide a CD-burner with a constant stream of data while burning a CD-R or CD-RW.

bug   Programming error that causes a program or a computer system to perform erratically, produce incorrect results, or crash. The term was coined when a real bug was found in one of the circuits of one of the first ENIAC computers.

burn   Process of writing data to a writable CD or DVD.

burn-in failure   Critical failure usually associated with manufacturing defects.

bus Series of wires connecting two or more separate electronic devices, enabling those devices to communicate.

bus mastering Circuitry allowing devices to avoid conflicts on the external data bus.

bus speed The speed at which motherboards operate.

bus topology Network configuration wherein all computers connect to the network via a central bus cable.

byte Unit of eight bits; fundamental data unit of personal computers. Storing the equivalent of one character, the byte is also the basic unit of measurement for computer storage.

CAB files Short for cabinet files. These files are compressed and most commonly used during OS installation to store many smaller files, such as device drivers.

cable modem Device that uses regular cable TV cables to connect a PC to the Internet.

cache (disk) Special area of RAM that stores the data most frequently accessed from the hard drive. Cache memory can optimize the use of your systems.

cache (L1, L2, L3, etc.) Special section of fast memory, usually built into the CPU, used by the onboard logic to store information most frequently accessed by the CPU.

calibration Process of matching the print output of a printer to the visual output of a monitor.

card reader Device with which you can read data from one of several types of flash memory.

card services Uppermost level of PCMCIA services. The card services level recognizes the function of a particular PC Card and provides the specialized drivers necessary to make the card work.

CardBus 32-bit PC cards that can support up to eight devices on each card. Electrically incompatible with earlier PC cards (3.3 V versus 5 V).

CAT 5 Category 5 wire; a TIA/EIA standard for UTP wiring that can operate up to 100 megabits per second.

CAT 5e Category 5e wire; TIA/EIA standard for UTP wiring that can operate up to 1 gigabit per second.

CAT 6 Category 6 wire; TIA/EIA standard for UTP wiring that can operate up to 10 gigabits per second.

catastrophic failure   Occurs when a component or whole system will not boot; usually related to a manufacturing defect of a component. Could also be caused by overheating and physical damage to computer components.

CCFL (cold-cathode fluorescent lamp)   Light technology used in LCDs and flatbed scanners. CCFLs use relatively little power for the amount of light they provide.

CD (CHDIR)   DOS shorthand for "Change Directory." Allows you to change the focus of the command prompt from one directory to another.

CD (compact disc)   Originally designed as the replacement for vinyl records, CDs have become the primary method of long-term storage of music and data.

CD quality   CD-quality audio has a sample rate of 44.4 KHz and a bit rate of 128 bits.

CD-DA (CD-digital audio)   Special format used for early CD-ROMs and all audio CDs; divides data into variable length tracks. A good format to use for audio tracks but terrible for data because of lack of error checking.

CD-R (compact disc recordable)   CD technology that accepts a single "burn" but cannot be erased after that one burn.

CD-ROM (compact disc/read only memory)   Read-only compact storage disk for audio or video data. Recordable devices, such as CD-Rs, are updated versions of the older CD-ROM players. CD-ROMs are read by using CD-ROM drives.

CD-RW (compact disc rewritable)   CD technology that accepts multiple reads/ writes like a hard drive.

Celeron   Lower-cost CPU based on Intel's older CPUs.

Cell   A CPU created by IBM and partners which powers the PlayStation 3, among other devices.

cellular WAN   Technology that allows laptops and other mobile devices to access the Internet over a cell phone network.

cellular wireless networks   Networks that enable cell phones, PDAs, and other mobile devices to connect to the Internet.

Centrino   Marketing name for an Intel laptop solution including the mobile processor, support chips, and wireless networking.

Centronics connector   Connector commonly used with printers.

certification   License that demonstrates competency in some specialized skill.

Certified Cisco Network Associate (CCNA) One of the certifications demonstrating a knowledge of Cisco networking products.

CHAP (Challenge Handshake Authentication Protocol) Common remote access protocol; serving system challenges the remote client, usually by means of asking for a password.

chassis intrusion detection Feature offered in some chassis that trips a switch when the chassis is opened.

chat room Place on the Internet that provides real-time communication with multiple people at the same time.

chipset Electronic chips, specially designed to work together, that handle all of the low-level functions of a PC. In the original PC, the chipset consisted of close to 30 different chips; today, chipsets usually consist of one, two, or three separate chips embedded into a motherboard.

CHKDSK (Checkdisk) Hard drive error detection and, to a certain extent, correction utility in Windows. Originally a DOS command (chkdsk.exe).

clean installation Operating system installed on a fresh drive, following a reformat of that drive. Often the only way to correct a problem with a system when many of the crucial operating system files have become corrupted.

client Computer program that uses the services of another computer program. Software that extracts information from a server; your auto-dial phone is a client, and the phone company is its server. Also, a machine that accesses shared resources on a server.

client/server Relationship in which client software obtains services from a server on behalf of a person.

client/server network Network that has dedicated server machines and client machines.

clock cycle Single charge to the clock wire of a CPU.

clock-multiplying CPU CPU that takes the incoming clock signal and multiples it inside the CPU to let the internal circuitry of the CPU run faster.

clock speed Speed at which a CPU executes instructions, measured in MHz or GHz. In modern CPUs, the internal speed is generally a multiple of the external speed. (*See also* clock-multiplying CPU.)

clock (CLK) wire Charge on the CLK wire to tell the CPU that another piece of information is waiting to be processed.

cloud computing Specialized services found online that handle a certain task without the user knowing where the server that does the job is.

cluster Basic unit of storage on a floppy or hard disk. Two or more sectors are contained in a cluster. When Windows stores a file on a disk, it writes those files into dozens or even hundreds of contiguous clusters. If there aren't enough contiguous open clusters available, the operating system finds the next open cluster and writes there, continuing this process until the entire file is saved. The FAT tracks how the files are distributed among the clusters on the disk.

CMOS (complementary metal-oxide semiconductor) Originally, the type of nonvolatile RAM that held information about the most basic parts of your PC, such as hard drives, floppies, and amount of DRAM. Today, actual CMOS chips have been replaced by flash-type nonvolatile RAM. The information is the same, however, and is still called CMOS—even though it is now almost always stored on flash RAM.

CMOS setup program Program enabling you to access and update CMOS data.

CNR (Communications and Network Riser) Proprietary slot used on some motherboards to provide a sound interference-free connection for modems, sound cards, and NICs.

coaxial cable Cabling in which an internal conductor is surrounded by another, outer conductor, thus sharing the same axis.

code Set of symbols representing characters (e.g., ASCII code) or instructions in a computer program (a programmer writes source code, which must be translated into executable or machine code for the computer to use).

codebook *See* instruction set.

Codec (compressor/decompressor) Software that compresses or decompresses media streams.

color depth Term to define a scanner's ability to produce color, hue, and shade.

COM port(s) Serial communications ports available on your computer. When used as a program extension, .COM indicates an executable program file limited to 64 KB.

command A request, typed from a terminal or embedded in a file, to perform an operation or to execute a particular program.

command-line interface User interface for an OS devoid of all graphical trappings; interfaces directly with the OS.

command prompt Text prompt for entering commands.

commercial license Software license that gives permission to install a program on one computer.

CompactFlash (CF) One of the older but still popular flash media formats. Its interface uses a simplified PC Card bus, so it also supports I/O devices.

compatibility modes Feature of Windows 2000 and beyond to allow software written for previous versions of Windows to operate in newer operating systems.

compliance Concept that members of an organization must abide by the rules of that organization. For a technician, this often revolves around what software can or cannot be installed on an organization's computer.

component failure Occurs when a system device fails due to manufacturing or some other type of defect.

compression Process of squeezing data to eliminate redundancies, allowing files to use less space when stored or transmitted.

compressed air A small aerosol can used to clean dust out of a computer case.

CompTIA A+ Certification Industry-wide, vendor-neutral computer certification program that demonstrates competency as a computer technician.

CompTIA Network+ Certification Certification for network technicians, covering network hardware, installation, and troubleshooting.

Computer (Vista/7) Renamed from My Computer for Windows Vista and 7. (*See* My Computer.)

Computer Administrator One of three types of user accounts, the Administrator account has access to all resources on the computer.

Computer Management Applet in Windows' Administrative Tools that contains several useful snap-ins, such as Device Manager and Disk Management.

computing process Four parts of a computer's operation: input, processing, output, and storage.

Computing Technology Industry Association (CompTIA) Nonprofit IT trade association that administers the Strata exams.

conditioning charger Battery charger that contains intelligent circuitry that prevents portable computer batteries from being overcharged and damaged.

connectors Small receptacles used to attach cables to a system. Common types of connectors include USB, PS/2, and DB-25.

consumables   Materials used up by printers, including paper, ink, ribbons, and toner cartridges.

container file   File containing two or more separate, compressed tracks, typically an audio track and a moving picture track. Also known as a wrapper.

context menu   Small menu brought up by right-clicking objects in Windows.

Control Panel   Collection of Windows applets, or small programs, that can be used to configure various pieces of hardware and software in a system.

controller card   Card adapter that connects devices, such as a disk drive, to the main computer bus/motherboard.

convergence   Measure of how sharply a single pixel appears on a CRT; a monitor with poor convergence produces images that are not sharply defined.

cookie   Small text file containing information about a user.

copy backup   Type of backup similar to Normal or Full, in that all selected files on a system are backed up. This type of backup does not change the archive bit of the files being backed up.

Copy command   Command in the command-line interface for making a copy of a file and pasting it in another location.

Core   Name used for the family of Intel CPUs that succeeded the Pentium 4.

counter   Used to track data about a particular object when using the Performance console.

CPU (central processing unit)   "Brain" of the computer. Microprocessor that handles primary calculations for the computer. CPUs are known by names such as Pentium 4 and Athlon.

CRC (cyclic redundancy check)   Very accurate mathematical method used to check for errors in long streams of transmitted data. Before data is sent, the main computer uses the data to calculate a CRC value from the data's contents. If the receiver calculates a CRC value different from the received data, the data was corrupted during transmission and is resent. Ethernet packets have a CRC code.

C-RIMM or CRIMM (continuity RIMM)   Passive device added to populate unused banks in a system that uses Rambus RIMMs.

crossover cable   Special UTP cable used to connect hubs or to connect network cards without a hub. Crossover cables reverse the sending and receiving wire pairs from one end to the other.

CRT (cathode ray tube)   Tube of a monitor in which rays of electrons are beamed onto a phosphorescent screen to produce images. Also a shorthand way to describe a monitor that uses CRT rather than LCD technology.

CSMA/CA (carrier sense multiple access with collision avoidance)   Networking scheme used by wireless devices to transmit data while avoiding data collisions, which wireless nodes have difficulty detecting.

cylinder   Single track on all the platters in a hard drive. Imagine a hard drive as a series of metal cans, nested one inside another; a single can would represent a cylinder.

daily backup   Backup of all files that have been changed on that day without changing the archive bits of those files. Also called *daily copy backup*.

daisy-chaining   Method of connecting several devices along a bus and managing the signals for each device.

data classification   System of organizing data according to its sensitivity. Common classifications include public, highly confidential, and top secret.

data storage   Saving a permanent copy of your work onto a storage device (such as a hard drive or DVD-RW) so that you can come back to it later.

data structure   Scheme that directs how an OS stores and retrieves data on and off a drive. Used interchangeably with the term file system. (*See also* file system.)

DB connectors   D-shaped connectors used for a variety of connections in the PC and networking world. Can be male (with prongs) or female (with holes) and have a varying number of pins or sockets. Also called D-sub or D-subminiature connectors.

DB-9   DB connector with nine pins. Also known as a serial port connector.

DB-15   A two- or three-row DB connector (female) used for 10Base5 networks, MIDI/joysticks, and analog video.

DB-25 connector   DB connector (female), commonly referred to as a parallel port connector.

DC (direct current)   Type of electricity in which the flow of electrons is in a complete circle in one direction.

DDR SDRAM (double data rate SDRAM)   Type of DRAM that makes two processes for every clock cycle. (*See also* DRAM.)

DDR2 SDRAM   Type of SDRAM that sends four bits of data in every clock cycle. (*See also* DDR SDRAM.)

DDR3 SDRAM   Type of SDRAM that transfers data at twice the rate of DDR2 SDRAM.

dead spot   Area where radio signals are blocked; often caused by large electrical appliances, fuse boxes, metal plumbing, and air conditioning units.

debug   To detect, trace, and eliminate errors in computer programs.

decibels   Unit of measurement typically associated with sound. The higher the number of decibels, the louder the sound.

dedicated server   Machine that is not used for any client functions, only server functions.

default gateway   In a TCP/IP network, the nearest router to a particular host. This router's IP address is part of the necessary TCP/IP configuration for communicating with multiple networks using IP.

definition file   List of virus signatures that an antivirus program can recognize.

defragmentation (DEFRAG)   Procedure in which all the files on a hard disk are rewritten on disk so that all parts of each file reside in contiguous clusters. The result is an improvement of up to 75 percent of the disk's speed during retrieval operations.

degauss   Procedure used to break up the electromagnetic fields that can build up on the cathode ray tube of a monitor; involves running a current through a wire loop. Most monitors feature a manual degaussing tool.

DEL (Erase) command   Command in the command-line interface used to delete/ erase files.

desktop   User's primary interface to the Windows operating system.

desktop extender   Portable computer that offers some of the features of a full-fledged desktop computer but with a much smaller footprint and lower weight.

desktop replacement   Portable computer that offers the same performance as a full-fledged desktop computer; these systems are normally very heavy to carry and often cost much more than the desktop systems they replace.

Device Manager   Utility that allows techs to examine and configure all the hardware and drivers in a Windows PC.

DHCP (Dynamic Host Configuration Protocol)   Protocol that enables a DHCP server to set TCP/IP settings automatically for a DHCP client.

differential backup Similar to an incremental backup. Backs up the files that have been changed since the last backup. This type of backup does not change the state of the archive bit.

digital camcorder Video camera that simulates film technology electronically.

digital camera Camera that simulates film technology electronically.

digital certificate Form in which a public key is sent from a Web server to a Web browser so that the browser can decrypt the data sent by the server.

digital zoom Software tool to enhance the optical zoom capabilities of a digital camera.

digitally signed driver All drivers designed specifically for Windows are digitally signed, meaning they are tested to work stably with these operating systems.

DIMM (dual inline memory module) 32- or 64-bit type of DRAM packaging, similar to SIMMs, with the distinction that each side of each tab inserted into the system performs a separate function. DIMMs come in a variety of sizes, with 184- and 240-pin being the most common on desktop computers.

dipole antennae Standard straight-wire antennae that provide the most omnidirectional function.

DIR command Command used in the command-line interface to display the entire contents of the current working directory.

directory Another name for a folder.

directory service Centralized index that each PC accesses to locate resources in the domain.

DirectX Set of APIs enabling programs to control multimedia, such as sound, video, and graphics. Used in Windows Vista to draw the Aero desktop.

Disk Cleanup Series of utilities, built into Windows, that can help users clean up their disks by removing temporary Internet files, deleting unused program files, and more.

disk cloning Taking a PC and making duplicates of the hard drive, including all data, software, and configuration files, and transferring it to another PC. (*See* image installation.)

disk compression A process that makes data on a drive occupy less space. Compressed data has to be uncompressed for the computer to use it.

disk duplexing Type of disk mirroring using two separate controllers rather than one; faster than traditional mirroring.

Disk Management Snap-in available with the Microsoft Management Console that allows users to configure the various disks installed in a system; available from the Administrative Tools area of the Control Panel.

disk mirroring Process by which data is written simultaneously to two or more disk drives. Read and write speed is decreased, but redundancy in case of catastrophe is increased.

disk quota Application allowing network administrators to limit hard drive space usage.

disk striping Process by which data is spread among multiple (at least two) drives. Increases speed for both reads and writes of data. Considered RAID level 0 because it does not provide fault tolerance.

disk striping with parity Method for providing fault tolerance by writing data across multiple drives and then including an additional drive, called a parity drive, that stores information to rebuild the data contained on the other drives. Requires at least three physical disks: two for the data and a third for the parity drive. This provides data redundancy at RAID levels 3–5 with different options.

disk thrashing Hard drive that is constantly being accessed due to lack of available system memory. When system memory runs low, a Windows system will utilize hard disk space as "virtual" memory, thus causing an unusual amount of hard drive access.

display adapter Handles all the communication between the CPU and the monitor. Also known as a video card.

Display applet Tool used to adjust display settings, including resolution, refresh rate, driver information, and color depth.

distributed computing Using multiple computers to carry out a single resource-intensive task.

DMA (direct memory access) modes Technique that some PC hardware devices use to transfer data to and from the memory without using the CPU.

DMA controller Resides between the RAM and the devices and handles DMA requests.

DNS (Domain Name System) TCP/IP name resolution system that translates a host name into an IP address.

430

DNS domain   Specific branch of the DNS name space. First-level DNS domains include .COM, .GOV, and .EDU.

docking station   Includes extra features such as a DVD drive or PC Card, in addition to legacy and modern ports. Similar to a port replicator.

document   Steps a technician uses to a solve a problem: To record the relevant information. For a technician, this would be recording each troubleshooting job: what the problem was, how it was fixed, and other helpful information.

Documents folder   Windows Vista/7 folder for storing user-created files. Replaces the My Documents folder previously used in Windows 2000/XP. (*See* My Documents.)

Dolby Digital   Technology for sound reductions and channeling methods used for digital audio.

domain   Groupings of users, computers, or networks. In Microsoft networking, a domain is a group of computers and users that share a common account database, called a SAM, and a common security policy. On the Internet, a domain is a group of computers that share a common element in their hierarchical name. Other types of domains exist—e.g., collision domain, etc.

domain-based network   Network that eliminates the need for logging in to multiple servers by using domain controllers to hold the security database for all systems.

domain name   Name used in place of an IP address to describe a Web site; for example, www.totalsem.com. Also known as a Web address.

DOS (Disk Operating System)   First popular operating system available for PCs. A text-based, single-tasking operating system that was not completely replaced until the introduction of Windows 95.

dot-matrix printer   Printer that creates each character from an array of dots. Pins striking a ribbon against the paper, one pin for each dot position, form the dots. May be a serial printer (printing one character at a time) or a line printer.

dot pitch   Value relating to CRTs, showing the diagonal distance between phosphors measured in millimeters.

double-click   Clicking twice very quickly.

double-sided DVD   A DVD with information written to both sides.

double-sided RAM   RAM stick with RAM chips soldered to both sides of the stick. May only be used with motherboards designed to accept double-sided RAM. Very common.

DPI (dots per inch)   Measure of printer resolution that counts the dots the device can produce per linear (horizontal) inch.

DPMS (Display Power-Management Signaling)   Specification that can reduce CRT power consumption by 75 percent by reducing/eliminating video signals during idle periods.

DRAM (dynamic random access memory or dynamic RAM)   Memory used to store data in most personal computers. DRAM stores each bit in a "cell" composed of a transistor and a capacitor. Because the capacitor in a DRAM cell can only hold a charge for a few milliseconds, DRAM must be continually refreshed, or rewritten, to retain its data.

DriveLock   CMOS program enabling you to control the ATA security mode feature set. Also known as drive lock.

driver   Program used by the operating system to control communications between the computer and peripherals.

driver signing   Digital signature for drivers used by Windows to protect against potentially bad drivers.

DS3D (DirectSound3D)   Introduced with DirectX 3.0, DS3D is a command set used to create positional audio, or sounds that appear to come from in front, in back, or to the side of a user. (*See also* DirectX.)

DSL (Digital Subscriber Line)   High-speed Internet connection technology that uses a regular telephone line for connectivity. DSL comes in several varieties, including asynchronous (ADSL) and synchronous (SDSL), and many speeds. Typical home-user DSL connections are ADSL with a download speed of up to 3 Mbps and an upload speed of 512 Kbps.

DSL receiver   Device that uses telephone lines to connect a PC to the Internet.

D-subminiature   *See* DB connectors.

DTS (Digital Theatre Systems)   Technology for sound reductions and channeling methods, similar to Dolby Digital.

dual boot   Refers to a computer with two operating systems installed, enabling users to choose which operating system to load on boot. Can also refer to kicking a device a second time just in case the first time didn't work.

dual-channel architecture   Using two sticks of RAM (either RDRAM or DDR) to increase throughput.

dual-channel memory Form of DDR, DDR2, and DDR3 memory access used by many motherboards that requires two identical sticks of DDR, DDR2, or DDR3 RAM.

dual-core architecture Dual-core CPUs have two execution units on the same physical chip but share caches and RAM.

dual-scan passive matrix Manufacturing technique for increasing display updates by refreshing two lines at a time.

DualView Microsoft feature to utilize two monitors as one large monitor.

dumpster diving To go through someone's trash in search of information.

DUN (Dial-Up Networking) Software used by Windows to govern the connection between the modem and the ISP.

duplexing Similar to mirroring in that data is written to and read from two physical drives, for fault tolerance. Separate controllers are used for each drive, both for additional fault tolerance and additional speed. Considered RAID level 1. Also called *disk duplexing* or *drive duplexing*.

duplex printing Technology that enables printing on both sides of a paper page, either by an internal print mechanism or add-on tray device.

Duron Lower-cost version of AMD's Athlon series of CPUs.

DVD (digital versatile disc) Optical disc format that provides for 4–17 GB of video or data storage.

DVD-ROM DVD equivalent of the standard CD-ROM.

DVD-RW Rewritable DVD media.

DVD-Video DVD format used exclusively to store digital video; capable of storing over two hours of high-quality video on a single DVD.

DVI (Digital Video Interface) Special video connector designed for digital-to-digital connections; most commonly seen on PC video cards and LCD monitors. Some versions also support analog signals with a special adapter.

Dxdiag (DirectX Diagnostics) Diagnostic tool for getting information about and testing a computer's DirectX version.

dye-sublimation printers Printer that uses a roll of heat-sensitive plastic film embedded with dyes, which are vaporized and then solidified onto specially coated paper to create a high-quality image.

dynamic disks Special feature of Windows that allows users to span a single volume across two or more drives. Dynamic disks do not have partitions; they have volumes. Dynamic disks can be striped, mirrored, and striped or mirrored with parity.

EAP (Extensible Authentication Protocol) Industry standard for wireless security that enables and improves encryption key integrity-checking and user authentication.

EAX (Environment Audio eXtensions) 3-D sound technology developed by Creative Labs but now supported by most sound cards.

ECC (error correction code) Special software, embedded on hard drives, that constantly scans the drives for bad sectors.

ECC RAM/DRAM (error correction code DRAM) RAM that uses special chips to detect and fix memory errors. Commonly used in high-end servers where data integrity is crucial.

e-commerce site Web site used to buy or sell goods over the Internet.

effective permissions User's combined permissions granted by multiple groups.

EFI (Extensible Firmware Interface) Firmware created by Intel and HP that replaced traditional 16-bit BIOS and added several new enhancements.

EFS (Encrypting File System) Encryption tool found in NTFS 5.

EIDE (Enhanced IDE) Marketing concept of hard drive maker Western Digital, encompassing four improvements for IDE drives, including drives larger than 528 MB, four devices, increase in drive throughput, and non–hard drive devices. (*See* ATAPI, PIO mode.)

electromagnetic interference (EMI) Electrical interference from one device to another, resulting in poor performance of the device being interfered with. Examples: Static on your TV while running a blow dryer, or placing two monitors too close together and getting a "shaky" screen.

electronic book (e-book) reader Single-purpose handheld computer that stores and displays electronic book files.

electrostatic discharge (ESD) Movement of electrons from one body to another. A real menace to PCs, as it can cause permanent damage to semiconductors.

eliciting answers Communication strategy designed to help techs understand a user's problems better. Works by listening to a user's description of a problem and then asking cogent questions.

e-mail (electronic mail)   Messages, usually text, sent from one person to another via computer. Can also be sent automatically to a group of addresses (mailing list).

emergency repair disk (ERD)   Saves critical boot files and partition information and is the main tool for fixing boot problems in Windows 2000.

enclosure   Case for containing an external hard drive.

encryption   Making data unreadable by those who do not possess a key or password.

erase lamp   Component inside laser printers that uses light to make the coating of the photosensitive drum conductive.

error-checking   Windows XP/Vista/7 name for the Checkdisk and ScanDisk tools.

eSATA   Serial ATA-based connector for external hard drives and optical drives.

escalate   Process used when person assigned to repair a problem is not able to get the job done, such as sending the problem to someone else.

Ethernet   Name coined by Xerox for the first standard of network cabling and protocols. Based on a bus topology.

Ethernet over Power   Technology that enables a network signal to be transmitted through existing power outlets. Also known as HomePlug.

Ethic of Reciprocity   Golden Rule: Do unto others as you would have them do unto you.

EULA (end-user license agreement)   Agreement that accompanies a piece of software, to which user must agree before using the software. Outlines the terms of use for the software and also lists any actions on the part of the user that violate the agreement.

event auditing   Feature of Event Viewer's Security section that creates an entry in the Security Log when certain events happen, such as a user logging on.

Event Viewer   Utility made available as an MMC snap-in that allows users to monitor various system events, including network bandwidth usage and CPU utilization.

e-wallet   Utility that tracks usernames, passwords, and even credit card information to make online purchases easier and faster.

EXPAND   CAB file utility program included with Windows. Similar to EXTRACT.

expansion bus   Set of wires going to the CPU, governed by the expansion bus crystal, directly connected to expansion slots of varying types (PCI, AGP, PCIe, etc.). Depending on the type of slots, the expansion bus runs at a percentage of the main system speed (8.33–133 MHz).

expansion bus crystal   Controls the speed of the expansion bus.

expansion card   Device that is inserted into an expansion slot to add more functionality to a PC.

expansion slots   Connectors on a motherboard that enable users to add optional components to a system. (*See also* AGP and PCI.)

ExpressCard   Serial PC Card designed to replace CardBus PC Cards. ExpressCards connect to either a Hi-Speed USB (480 Mbps) or PCI Express (2.5 Gbps) bus.

extended display   Using a second monitor to display more of your desktop.

extended partition   Type of non-bootable hard disk partition. May only have one extended partition per disk. Purpose is to divide a large disk into smaller partitions, each with a separate drive letter.

extension   Three or four letters that follow a filename and identify the type of file. Common file extensions are .ZIP, .EXE, and .DOC.

external data bus (EDB)   Primary data highway of all computers. Everything in your computer is tied either directly or indirectly to the external data bus. (*See also* frontside bus and backside bus.)

extranet   Private intranet that is made accessible to a select group of outsiders using the Internet.

fast user switching   Account option that is useful when multiple users share a system; allows users to switch without logging off.

FAT (file allocation table)   Hidden table that records how files on a hard disk are stored in distinct clusters; the only way DOS knows where to access files. Address of first cluster of a file is stored in the directory file. FAT entry for the first cluster is the address of the second cluster used to store that file. In the entry for the second cluster for that file is the address for the third cluster, and so on until the final cluster, which gets a special end-of-file code. There are two FATs, mirror images of each other, in case one is destroyed or damaged.

fat client   Standard personal computer.

FAT32   File allocation table that uses 32 bits for addressing clusters. Commonly used with Windows 98 and Windows Me systems. Some Windows 2000 Professional and Windows XP systems also use FAT32, although most modern Windows systems use the more robust NTFS.

FDISK   Disk-partitioning utility included with Windows.

feedback   Responses, both good and bad, that software developers use to make better products.

fiber optics   High-speed channel for transmitting data, made of high-purity glass sealed within an opaque tube. Much faster than conventional copper wire such as co-axial cable.

file   Collection of any form of data that is stored beyond the time of execution of a single job. A file may contain program instructions or data, which may be numerical, textual, or graphical information.

file allocation unit   Another term for cluster. (*See also* cluster.)

file association   Windows term for the proper program to open a particular file; for example, file association for opening .MP3 programs might be Winamp.

file extension   How information is encoded in a file. Two primary types are binary (pictures) and ASCII (text), but within those are many formats, such as BMP and GIF for pictures. Commonly represented by a suffix at the end of the filename; for example, .txt for a text file or .exe for an executable.

file server   Computer designated to store software, courseware, administrative tools, and other data on a local- or wide-area network. It "serves" this information to other computers via the network when users enter their personal access codes.

file system   Scheme that directs how an OS stores and retrieves data on and off a drive; FAT32 and NTFS are both file systems. Used interchangeably with the term "data structure." (*See also* data structure.)

filename   Name assigned to a file when the file is first written on a disk. Every file on a disk within the same folder must have a unique name. Filenames can contain any character (including spaces), except the following: \ / : * ? " < > |

firewall   Device that restricts traffic between a local network and the Internet.

FireWire (IEEE 1394)   Interconnection standard to send wide-band signals over a serialized, physically thin connector system. Serial bus developed by Apple and Texas Instruments; enables connection of 60 devices at speeds up to 800 megabits per second.

firmware   Embedded programs or code stored on a ROM chip. Generally OS-independent, thus allowing devices to operate in a wide variety of circumstances without direct OS support. The system BIOS is firmware.

flash-based storage   Storage type that uses small memory chips to store data.

flash ROM   ROM technology that can be electrically reprogrammed while still in the PC. Overwhelmingly the most common storage medium of BIOS in PCs today, as it can be upgraded without a need to open the computer on most systems.

flatbed scanner   Most popular form of consumer scanner; runs a bright light along the length of the tray to capture an image.

FlexATX   Motherboard form factor. Motherboards built in accordance with the FlexATX form factor are very small, much smaller than microATX motherboards.

Flip 3D   In the Aero desktop environment, a three-dimensional replacement for ALT-TAB. Accessed by pressing the WINDOWS KEY-TAB key combination.

floppy disk   Removable storage medium that can hold between 720 KB and 1.44 MB of data.

floppy drive (FDD)   System hardware that uses removable 3.5-inch disks as storage media.

flux reversal   Point at which a read/write head detects a change in magnetic polarity.

FM synthesis   Producing sound by electronic emulation of various instruments to more-or-less produce music and other sound effects.

folder   Where files are stored in a computer.

folders list   Toggle button in Windows Explorer for Windows 2000 and XP that displays the file structure on the left side of the window. In Windows Vista and 7, the folders list is active by default.

force feedback   Technology that shakes a game controller in time with what is happening on the monitor.

form factor   Standard for the physical organization of motherboard components and motherboard size. Most common form factors are ATX, BTX, and NLX.

FORMAT command   Command in the command-line interface used to format a storage device.

formatting   Magnetically mapping a disk to provide a structure for storing data; can be done to any type of disk, including a floppy disk, hard disk, or other type of removable disk.

forum   Web site used by people with similar interests to post and respond to messages accessible to everyone in the group. Also known as a message board or newsgroup.

FPU (floating point unit) Formal term for math coprocessor (also called a numeric processor) circuitry inside a CPU. A math coprocessor calculates by using a floating point math (which allows for decimals). Before the Intel 80486, FPUs were separate chips from the CPU.

fragmentation Occurs when files and directories get jumbled on a fixed disk and are no longer contiguous. Can significantly slow down hard drive access times and can be repaired by using the DEFRAG utility included with each version of Windows. (*See also* defragmentation (DEFRAG).)

freeware Software that is distributed for free, with no license fee.

frequency Measure of a sound's tone, either high or low.

frontside bus Wires that connect the CPU to the main system RAM. Generally running at speeds of 66–133 MHz. Distinct from the expansion bus and the backside bus, though it shares wires with the former.

front-view projector Shoots the image out the front and counts on you to put a screen in front at the proper distance.

FRU (field replaceable unit) Any part of a PC that is considered to be replaceable "in the field," i.e., a customer location. There is no official list of FRUs—it is usually a matter of policy by the repair center.

FTP (File Transfer Protocol) Rules that enable two computers to talk to one another during a file transfer. Protocol used when you transfer a file from one computer to another across the Internet.

fuel cells Power source that uses chemical reactions to produce electricity. Lightweight, compact, and stable devices expected to replace batteries as the primary power source for portable PCs.

full-duplex Any device that can send and receive data simultaneously.

Full-speed USB USB standard that runs at 12 Mbps.

function keys Keys along the top of a keyboard that enable additional functions.

fuser assembly Mechanism in laser printers that uses two rollers to fuse toner to paper during the print process.

gain Ratio of increase of radio frequency output provided by an antenna, measured in decibels (dB).

game pad Game controller used for playing some video games on a PC.

GDI (graphical device interface)   Component of Windows that utilizes the CPU rather than the printer to process a print job as a bitmapped image of each page.

general protection fault (GPF)   Error code usually seen when separate active programs conflict on resources or data.

geometry   Numbers representing three values: heads, cylinders, and sectors per track; define where a hard drives stores data.

giga   Prefix for the quantity 1,073,741,824 or for 1 billion. One gigabyte would be 1,073,741,824 bytes, except with hard drive labeling, where it means 1 billion bytes. One gigahertz is 1 billion hertz.

gigahertz (GHz)   One billion cycles per second.

GPU (graphics processing unit)   Specialized processor that helps CPU by taking over all of the 3-D rendering duties.

grayscale depth   Number that defines how many shades of gray the scanner can save per dot.

grayware   Program that intrudes into a user's computer experience without damaging any systems or data.

group   Collection of user accounts that share the same access capabilities.

Group Policy   Means of easily controlling the settings of multiple network clients with policies such as setting minimum password length or preventing Registry edits.

Guest/Guest account   Very limited built-in account type for Windows.

GUI (graphical user interface)   Interface that enables user to interact with computer graphically, by using a mouse or other pointing device to manipulate icons that represent programs or documents, instead of with text as in early interfaces. Pronounced "gooey."

hacker   Person who circumvents computer security.

HAL (hardware abstraction layer)   Part of the Windows OS that separates system-specific device drivers from the rest of the NT system.

half-duplex   Device that sends and receives data, but not at the same time.

handheld computer   *See* PDA (personal digital assistant).

handshaking   Procedure performed by modems, terminals, and computers to verify that communication has been correctly established.

hang   When a computer freezes so it does not respond to keyboard commands, it is said to "hang" or to have "hung."

hang time   Number of seconds a too-often-hung computer is airborne after you have thrown it out a second-story window.

hardware   Physical computer equipment such as electrical, electronic, magnetic, and mechanical devices. Anything in the computer world that you can hold in your hand. A floppy drive is hardware; Microsoft Word is not.

hardware protocol   Defines many aspects of a network, from the packet type to the cabling and connectors used.

HBA (host bus adapter)   Connects SATA devices to the expansion bus. Also known as the SATA controller.

HD (Hi-Definition)   Multimedia transmission standard that defines high-resolution images and 5.1, 6.1, and 7.1 sound.

HDA (High-Definition Audio)   Intel-designed standard to support features such as true surround sound with many discrete speakers.

HDD (hard disk drive)   Data-recording system using solid disks of magnetic material turning at high speeds to store and retrieve programs and data in a computer.

HDMI (high-definition multimedia interface)   Single multimedia connection that includes both high-definition video and audio. One of the best connections for outputting to television. Also contains copy protection features.

heads   Short for read/write heads used by hard drives to store data.

heat dope   *See* thermal compound.

hertz (Hz)   A measurement of frequency. A hertz equals one cycle per second.

hex (hexadecimal)   Base-16 numbering system using 10 digits (0 through 9) and six letters (A through F). In the computer world, shorthand way to write binary numbers by substituting one hex digit for a four-digit binary number (e.g., hex 9 = binary 1001).

hibernation   Power management setting in which all data from RAM is written to the hard drive before going to sleep. Upon waking up, all information is retrieved from the hard drive and returned to RAM.

hidden attribute   File attribute that, when used, does not allow DIR command to show a file.

hierarchical directory tree   Method by which Windows organizes files into a series of folders, called directories, under the root directory. (*See also* root directory.)

high gloss   Laptop screen finish that offers sharper contrast, richer colors, and wider viewing angles than a matte finish, but is also much more reflective.

high-level formatting   Format that sets up a file system on a drive.

high-voltage anode   Component in a CRT monitor that has very high voltages of electricity flowing through it.

Hi-speed USB   USB standard that runs at 480 Mbps.

HomePlug   Technology that enables a network signal to be transmitted through existing power outlets. Also known as Ethernet over Power.

honesty   Telling the truth—a very important thing for a tech to do.

host   On a TCP/IP network, single device that has an IP address—any device (usually a computer) that can be the source or destination of a data packet. In the mainframe world, computer that is made available for use by multiple people simultaneously.

host ID   Part of an IP address that defines the node.

hot-swappable   Hardware that may be attached to or removed from a PC without interrupting the PC's normal processing. Also known as hot-pluggable.

HotSync (synchronization)   Program used by PalmOS-based PDAs to synchronize files between a PDA and a desktop computer.

HRR (horizontal refresh rate)   Amount of time it takes for a CRT to draw one horizontal line of pixels on a display.

HTML (Hypertext Markup Language)   ASCII-based, script-like language for creating hypertext documents such as those on the World Wide Web.

HTTP (Hypertext Transfer Protocol)   Extremely fast protocol used for network file transfers in the WWW environment.

HTTPS (HTTP over Secure Sockets Layer)   Secure form of HTTP used commonly for Internet business transactions or any time when a secure connection is required. (*See also* HTTP.)

hub   Electronic device that sits at the center of a star topology network, providing a common point for the connection of network devices. Hubs repeat all information out to all ports and have been replaced by switches, although the term is still commonly used.

hyperthreading   CPU feature that enables a single pipeline to run more than one thread at once.

I/O (input/output)   General term for reading and writing data to a computer. "Input" includes data from a keyboard, pointing device (such as a mouse), or loaded from a disk. "Output" includes writing information to a disk, viewing it on a CRT, or printing it to a printer.

I/O addressing   Using the address bus to talk to system devices.

I/O advanced programmable interrupt controller (IOAPIC)   Typically located in the southbridge, the IOAPIC acts as the traffic cop for interrupt requests to the CPU.

I/O base address   First value in an I/O address range.

ICH (I/O controller hub)   Official name for southbridge chip found in Intel's chipsets.

icon   Small image or graphic, most commonly found on a system's desktop, that launches a program when selected.

ICS (Internet Connection Sharing)   Allowing a single network connection to be shared among several machines. ICS was first introduced with Windows 98.

IDE (intelligent drive electronics)   PC specification for small- to medium-sized hard drives in which the controlling electronics for the drive are part of the drive itself, speeding up transfer rates and leaving only a simple adapter (or "paddle"). IDE only supported two drives per system of no more than 504 megabytes each, and has been completely supplanted by Enhanced IDE. EIDE supports four drives of over 8 gigabytes each and more than doubles the transfer rate. The more common name for PATA drives. Also known as *integrated drive electronics*. (*See* PATA.)

Identify the problem.   Question the user and find out what has been changed recently or is no longer working properly. (One of the steps a technician uses to a solve a problem.)

IEC-320   Connects the cable supplying AC power from a wall outlet into the power supply.

IEEE (Institute of Electronic and Electrical Engineers)   Leading standards-setting group in the United States.

IEEE 1284   IEEE standard governing parallel communication.

IEEE 1394   IEEE standard governing FireWire communication. (*See also* FireWire.)

IEEE 1394a   FireWire standard that runs at 400 Mbps.

IEEE 1394b   FireWire standard that runs at 800 Mbps

IEEE 802.11 Wireless Ethernet standard more commonly known as Wi-Fi.

image file Bit-by-bit image of data to be burned on CD or DVD—from one file to an entire disc—stored as a single file on a hard drive. Particularly handy when copying from CD to CD or DVD to DVD.

image installation Operating system installation that uses a complete image of a hard drive as an installation media. Helpful when installing an operating system on a large number of identical PCs.

IMAP (Internet Message Access Protocol) Protocol used to handle incoming e-mail messages.

impact printer Uses pins and inked ribbons to print text or images on a piece of paper.

impedance Amount of resistance to an electrical signal on a wire. Relative measure of the amount of data a cable can handle.

incident report Record of the details of an accident, including what happened and where it happened.

incremental backup Backs up all files that have their archive bits turned on, meaning that they have been changed since the last backup. Turns the archive bits off after the files have been backed up.

Information Technology (IT) Field of computers, their operation, and their maintenance.

infrastructure mode Wireless networking mode that uses one or more WAPs to connect the wireless network nodes to a wired network segment.

inheritance Feature that passes on the same permissions in any subfolders/files resident in the original folder.

ink cartridge Small container of ink for inkjet printers.

inkjet printer Uses liquid ink, sprayed through a series of tiny jets, to print text or images on a piece of paper.

installation disc Typically a CD-ROM or DVD that holds all the necessary device drivers.

instruction set All of the machine-language commands that a particular CPU is designed to understand.

integrated video Video processor built into the motherboard.

integrity   Always doing the right thing.

Intel   One of the two major CPU manufacturers. Designer of the Pentium and Core series of CPUs. (*See also* Advanced Micro Devices (AMD).)

interface   Means by which a user interacts with a piece of software.

Internet   Worldwide network that connects millions of computers and networks.

Interrupt 13 (INT13) extensions   Improved type of BIOS that accepts EIDE drives up to 137 GB.

interrupt/interruption   Suspension of a process, such as the execution of a computer program, caused by an event external to the computer and performed in such a way that the process can be resumed. Events of this kind include sensors monitoring laboratory equipment or a user pressing an interrupt key.

intranet   Private network similar to the Internet, but scaled down.

inverter   Device used to convert DC current into AC. Commonly used with CCFLs in laptops and flatbed scanners.

IP (Internet Protocol)   Internet standard protocol that provides a common layer over dissimilar networks; used to move packets among host computers and through gateways if necessary. Part of the TCP/IP protocol suite.

IP address   Numeric address of a computer connected to the Internet. An IPv4 address is made up of 4 octets of 8-bit binary numbers translated into their shorthand numeric values. An IPv6 address is 128 bits long. The IP address can be broken down into a network ID and a host ID. Also called Internet address.

IPCONFIG   Command-line utility for Windows servers and workstations that displays the current TCP/IP configuration of the machine. Similar to WINIPCFG and IFCONFIG.

IPSec (Internet Protocol Security)   Microsoft's encryption method of choice for networks consisting of multiple networks linked by a private connection, providing transparent encryption between the server and the client.

IrDA (Infrared Data Association)   Protocol that enables communication through infrared devices, with speeds of up to 4 Mbps.

IRQ (interrupt request)   Signal from a hardware device, such as a modem or a mouse, indicating that it needs the CPU's attention. In PCs, IRQs are sent along specific IRQ channels associated with a particular device. IRQ conflicts were a common problem in the past when adding expansion boards, but the plug-and-play specification has removed this headache in most cases.

ISA (Industry Standard Architecture) Industry Standard Architecture design was found in the original IBM PC for the slots that allowed additional hardware to be connected to the computer's motherboard. An 8-bit, 8.33-MHz expansion bus was designed by IBM for its AT computer and released to the public domain. An improved 16-bit bus was also released to the public domain. Replaced by PCI in the mid-1990s.

ISDN (Integrated Services Digital Network) CCITT (Comité Consultatif Internationale de Télégraphie et Téléphonie) standard that defines a digital method for communications to replace the current analog telephone system. ISDN is superior to POTS telephone lines because it supports up to 128 Kbps transfer rate for sending information from computer to computer. It also allows data and voice to share a common phone line. DSL reduced demand for ISDN substantially.

ISO 9660 CD format to support PC file systems on CD media. Supplanted by the Joliet format.

ISO file Complete copy (or image) of a storage media device, typically used for optical discs.

ISP (Internet service provider) Company that provides access to the Internet, usually for money.

jack (physical connection) Part of a connector into which a plug is inserted. Also referred to as a port.

Java Programming language that is used on some Web sites.

Joliet Extension of the ISO 9660 format. Most popular CD format to support PC file systems on CD media.

joule Unit of energy describing (in this book) how much energy a surge suppressor can handle before it fails.

joystick Peripheral often used while playing computer games; originally intended as a multipurpose input device.

jumper Pair of small pins that can be shorted with a shunt to configure many aspects of PCs. Typically used in configurations that are rarely changed, such as master/slave settings on IDE drives.

Kerberos Authentication encryption developed by MIT to enable multiple brands of servers to authenticate multiple brands of clients.

kernel Core portion of program that resides in memory and performs the most essential operating system tasks.

keyboard Input device. Three common types of keyboards: those that use a mini-DIN (PS/2) connection, those that use a USB connection, and those that use wireless technology.

keying The small notches on the bottom of RAM sticks that prevent you from installing incorrect RAM in your system.

Knowledge Base Large collection of documents and FAQs that is maintained by Microsoft. Found on Microsoft's Web site, the Knowledge Base is an excellent place to search for assistance on most operating system problems.

KVM (keyboard, video, mouse switch) Hardware device that enables multiple computers to be viewed and controlled by a single mouse, keyboard, and screen.

LAN (local area network) Group of PCs connected via cabling, radio, or infrared that use this connectivity to share resources such as printers and mass storage.

lane Connection used by PCIe cards to communicate with the rest of the PC.

laptop Traditional clamshell portable computing device with built-in LCD monitor, keyboard, and trackpad.

laser Single-wavelength, in-phase light source that is sometimes strapped to the head of sharks by bad guys. Note to henchmen: Lasers should never be used with sea bass, no matter how ill-tempered they might be.

laser printer Electro-photographic printer in which a laser is used as the light source.

Last Known Good Configuration Option on the Advanced Startup Options menu that allows your system to revert to a previous configuration to troubleshoot and repair any major system problems.

latency Amount of delay before a device may respond to a request; most commonly used in reference to RAM.

LBA (logical block addressing) Translation (algorithm) of IDE drives promoted by Western Digital as a standardized method for breaking the 504-MB limit in IDE drives. Subsequently universally adopted by the PC industry and now standard on all EIDE drives.

LCD (liquid crystal display) Type of display commonly used on portable PCs. Also have mostly replaced CRTs as the display of choice for most desktop computer users, due in large part to rapidly falling prices and increasing quality. LCDs use liquid crystals and electricity to produce images on the screen.

LED (light-emitting diode) Solid-state device that vibrates at luminous frequencies when current is applied.

Level 1 (L1) cache First RAM cache accessed by the CPU, which stores only the absolute most-accessed programming and data used by currently running threads. Always the smallest and fastest cache on the CPU.

Level 2 (L2) cache Second RAM cache accessed by the CPU. Much larger and often slower than the L1 cache, and accessed only if the requested program/data is not in the L1 cache.

Level 3 (L3) cache Third RAM cache accessed by the CPU. Much larger and slower than the L1 and L2 caches, and accessed only if the requested program/data is not in the L2 cache. Seen only on high-end CPUs.

libraries A collection of folders whose contents are all displayed in one location. Libraries were introduced in Windows 7.

Li-Ion (lithium-ion) Battery commonly used in portable PCs. Li-Ion batteries don't suffer from the memory effects of NiCd batteries and provide much more power for a greater length of time.

limited account/user User account in Windows XP that has limited access to a system. Accounts of this type cannot alter system files, cannot install new programs, and cannot edit settings by using the Control Panel.

Linux Open-source UNIX-clone operating system.

Local Security Settings Windows tool used to set local security policies on an individual system.

local share Files shared with other accounts on a single PC.

local user account List of users allowed access to a system.

Local Users and Groups Tool enabling creation and changing of group memberships and accounts for users.

localization Setting up a computer for a specific location using the Clock, Language, and Region applet in the Control Panel.

log files Files created in Windows to track the progress of certain processes.

logical drives Sections of a hard drive that are formatted and assigned a drive letter, each of which is presented to the user as if it were a separate drive.

login screen First screen of the Windows interface, used to log in to the computer system.

loopback plug Device used during loopback tests to check the female connector on a NIC.

Low-speed USB   USB standard that runs at 1.5 Mbps.

LPT port   Commonly referred to as a printer port; usually associated with a local parallel port.

LPX   First slimline form factor; replaced by NLX form factor.

lumens   Unit of measure for amount of brightness on a projector or other light source.

Mac   (Also Macintosh.) Apple Computers' flagship operating system, currently up to OS v10.6 "Snow Leopard" and running on Intel-based hardware.

MAC (Media Access Control) address   Unique 48-bit address assigned to each network card. IEEE assigns blocks of possible addresses to various NIC manufacturers to help ensure that the address is always unique. The Data Link layer of the OSI model uses MAC addresses for locating machines.

MAC address filtering   Method of limiting wireless network access based on the physical, hard-wired address of the units' wireless NIC.

machine language   Binary instruction code that is understood by the CPU.

maintenance kits   Commonly replaced printer components provided by many manufacturers.

malware   Computer programs designed to break into computers and cause trouble.

mass storage   Hard drives, CD-ROMs, removable media drives, etc.

matte   Laptop screen finish that offers a good balance between richness of colors and reflections, but washes out in bright light.

MBR (master boot record)   Tiny bit of code that takes control of the boot process from the system BIOS.

MCC (memory controller chip)   Chip that handles memory requests from the CPU. Although once a special chip, it has been integrated into the chipset on all PCs today.

MCH (memory controller hub)   Intel-coined name for what is now commonly called the northbridge.

MD (MKDIR) command   Command in the command-line interface used to create directories.

mega-   Prefix that usually stands for the binary quantity 1,048,576 (2^{20}). One megabyte is 1,048,576 bytes. One megahertz, however, is a million hertz. Sometimes shortened to *Meg*, as in "a 286 has an address space of 16 Megs."

megahertz (MHz)   One million cycles per second.

megapixel   Term used typically in reference to digital cameras and their ability to capture data.

memory   Device or medium for temporary storage of programs and data during program execution. Synonymous with storage, although it most frequently refers to the internal storage of a computer that can be directly addressed by operating instructions. A computer's temporary storage capacity is measured in kilobytes (KB), megabytes (MB), or gigabytes (GB) of RAM (random-access memory). Long-term data storage on disks is also measured in kilobytes, megabytes, gigabytes, and terabytes.

memory addressing   Taking memory address from system RAM and using it to address nonsystem RAM or ROM so that the CPU can access it.

Memory Stick   Sony's flash memory card format; rarely seen outside of Sony devices.

mesh topology   Network topology where each computer has a dedicated line to every other computer, most often used in wireless networks.

MFT (master file table)   Enhanced file allocation table used by NTFS. (*See also* FAT.)

microATX   Variation of the ATX form factor, which uses the ATX power supply. MicroATX motherboards are generally smaller than their ATX counterparts but retain all the same functionality.

microBTX   Variation of the BTX form factor. MicroBTX motherboards are generally smaller than their BTX counterparts but retain all the same functionality.

microprocessor   "Brain" of a computer. Primary computer chip that determines relative speed and capabilities of the computer. Also called CPU.

Microsoft Windows Logo Program   Testing program for hardware manufacturers, designed to ensure compatibility with the Windows OS.

MIDI (Musical Instrument Digital Interface)   Interface between a computer and a device for simulating musical instruments. Rather than sending large sound samples, a computer can simply send "instructions" to the instrument describing pitch, tone, and duration of a sound. MIDI files are therefore very efficient. Because a MIDI file is made up of a set of instructions rather than a copy of the sound, modifying each component of the file is easy. Additionally, it is possible to program many channels, or "voices" of music to be played simultaneously, creating symphonic sound.

migration   Moving users from one operating system or hard drive to another.

MIMO (multiple in/multiple out)   Feature of 802.11n devices that enables the simultaneous connection of up to four antennae, allowing for increased throughput.

mini-audio connector   Very popular, 1/8-inch diameter connector used to transmit two audio signals; perfect for stereo sound.

mini connector   One type of power connector from a PC power supply unit. Supplies 5 and 12 volts to peripherals. Also known as a floppy connector.

mini-DIN   Small connection most commonly used for keyboards and mice. Most modern systems implement USB in place of mini-DIN connections. (*See also* PS/2.)

MiniDisc   Small, obsolete CD-R form factor designed for portable music players.

mini-PCI   Specialized form of PCI designed for use in laptops.

mini-power connector   Connector used to provide power to floppy disk drives.

mirrored display   Showing the same screen on two monitors.

mirrored volume   Volume that is mirrored on another volume. (*See also* mirroring.)

mirroring   Reading and writing data at the same time to two drives for fault tolerance purposes. Considered RAID level 1. Also called drive mirroring.

MMC (Microsoft Management Console)   Means of managing a system, introduced by Microsoft with Windows 2000. The MMC allows an Administrator to customize management tools by picking and choosing from a list of snap-ins. Available snap-ins include Device Manager, Users and Groups, and Computer Management.

MMX (multimedia extensions)   Specific CPU instructions that enable a CPU to handle many multimedia functions, such as digital signal processing. Introduced with the Pentium CPU, these instructions are used on all ×86 CPUs.

mode   Any single combination of resolution and color depth set for a system.

modem (modulator/demodulator)   Device that converts a digital bit stream into an analog signal (modulation) and converts incoming analog signals back into digital signals (demodulation). The analog communications channel is typically a telephone line, and analog signals are typically sounds.

module   Small circuit board that DRAM chips are attached to. Also known as a "stick."

Molex connector   Computer power connector used by CD-ROM drives, hard drives, and case fans. Keyed to prevent it from being inserted into a power port improperly.

monaural Describes recording tracks from one source (microphone) as opposed to stereo, which uses two sources.

monitor Screen that displays data from a PC. Can use either a cathode ray tube (CRT) or a liquid crystal display (LCD) to display images. Also called a display.

motherboard Flat piece of circuit board that resides inside your computer case and has a number of connectors on it. You can use these connectors to attach a variety of devices to your system, including hard drives, CD-ROM drives, floppy disk drives, and sound cards.

motherboard manual Valuable resource when installing a new motherboard. Normally lists all the specifications about a motherboard, including the type of memory and type of CPU that should be used with the motherboard.

mount point Drive that functions like a folder mounted into another drive.

mouse Input device that enables users to manipulate a cursor on the screen to select items.

MOVE command Command in the command-line interface used to move a file from one location to another.

MP3 Short for MPEG, Layer 3. MP3 is a type of compression used specifically for turning high-quality digital audio files into much smaller, yet similar sounding, files.

MPA (Microsoft Product Activation) Introduced by Microsoft with the release of Windows XP, Microsoft Product Activation prevents unauthorized use of Microsoft's software by requiring users to activate the software.

MPEG-2 (Moving Pictures Experts Group) Standard of video and audio compression offering resolutions up to 1280 × 720 at 60 frames per second.

MPEG-4 (Moving Pictures Experts Group) Standard of video and audio compression offering improved compression over MPEG-2.

MS-CHAP Microsoft's variation of the CHAP protocol, which uses a slightly more advanced encryption protocol. Windows Vista uses MS-CHAP v2 (version 2) and does not support MS-CHAP v1 (version 1).

MSCONFIG (System Configuration Utility) Executable file that runs the Windows System Configuration Utility, which enables users to configure a system's boot files and critical system files. Often used for the name of the utility, as in "just run MSCONFIG."

MSDS (material safety data sheet) Standardized form that provides detailed information about potential environmental hazards and proper disposal methods associated with various PC components.

MSINFO32 Provides information about hardware resources, components, and the software environment. Also known as System Information.

multiboot OS installation in which multiple operating systems are installed on a single machine. Can also refer to kicking a device several times in frustration.

multi-card reader and writer Peripheral capable of reading to and writing from several different memory card formats.

multicore A CPU with more than one execution core.

multimedia extensions Originally an Intel CPU enhancement designed for graphics-intensive applications (such as games). It was never embraced but eventually led to improvements in how CPUs handle graphics.

multimeter Device used to measure voltage, amperage, and resistance.

multisession drive Recordable CD drive capable of burning multiple sessions onto a single recordable disc. Also can close a CD-R so that no further tracks can be written to it.

multitasking Process of running multiple programs or tasks on the same computer at the same time.

Music-CD-R CD using a special format for home recorders. Music CD-R makers pay a small royalty to avoid illegal music duplication.

My Computer Applet that allows users to access a complete list of all fixed and removable drives contained within a system.

My Documents Introduced with Windows 98 and used in Windows 2000 and Windows XP, the My Documents folder provides a convenient place for users to store their documents, log files, and any other type of files.

My Network Places Folder in Windows XP that enables users to view other computers on their network or workgroup.

NAS (network attached storage) Device containing hard drives, a small motherboard, and electrical and network connections that is used as a file server.

native resolution Resolution on an LCD monitor that matches the physical pixels on the screen. CRTs do not have fixed pixels and therefore do not have a native resolution.

Navigation pane A graphical, hierarchical view of a folder's contents in Windows Explorer.

NET   Command in Windows that allows users to view a network without knowing the names of the other computers on that network.

NetBIOS (Network Basic Input/Output System)   Protocol that operates at the Session layer of the OSI seven-layer model. This protocol creates and manages connections based on the names of the computers involved.

netbook   Smaller, cheaper portable computer with limited capabilities designed specifically for browsing the Internet.

network   Collection of two or more computers interconnected by telephone lines, coaxial cables, satellite links, radio, and/or some other communication technique. Group of computers that are connected and that communicate with one another for a common purpose. Also, the name of Vista's version of the My Network Places folder.

network frame   Wrapping around a packet of data that enables it to be transmitted.

network ID   Number that identifies the network on which a device or machine exists. This number exists in both IP and IPX protocol suites.

network printer   Printer that connects directly to a network.

network resources   Files, printers, and anything else that is shared over a network.

network share   Files shared with users on other PCs.

newsgroup   Web site used by people with similar interests to post and respond to messages accessible to everyone in the group. Also known as a forum or message board.

NIC (network interface card)   Expansion card that enables a PC to physically link to a network.

NiCd (nickel-cadmium)   Battery that was used in the first portable PCs. Heavy and inefficient, these batteries also suffered from a memory effect that could drastically shorten the overall life of the battery. (*See also* NiMH, Li-Ion.)

NiMH (nickel metal hydride)   Battery used in portable PCs. NiMH batteries had fewer issues with the memory effect than NiCd batteries. NiMH batteries have been replaced by lithium-ion batteries. (*See also* NiCd, Li-Ion.)

nit   Value used to measure the brightness of an LCD display. A typical LCD display has a brightness of between 100 and 400 nits.

NLQ (near-letter quality)   Designation for dot-matrix printers that use 24-pin printheads.

NLX   Second form factor for slimline systems. Replaced the earlier LPX form factor. (NLX apparently stands for nothing; it's just a cool grouping of letters.)

NMI (non-maskable interrupt)   Interrupt code sent to the processor that cannot be ignored. Typically manifested as a BSOD.

NNTP (Network News Transfer Protocol)   Protocol run by news servers that enable newsgroups.

node   Any machine attached to a network.

non-system disk or disk error   Error that occurs during the boot process. Common causes for this error are leaving a non-bootable floppy disk, CD, or other medium in the drive while the computer is booting.

nonvolatile   Memory that retains data even if power is removed.

normal backup   Full backup of every selected file on a system. Turns off the archive bit after the backup.

northbridge   Chip that connects a CPU to memory, the PCI bus, Level 2 cache, and AGP activities. Communicates with the CPU through the frontside bus. Newer Athlon 64-bit CPUs feature an integrated northbridge.

NOS (network operating system)   Standalone operating system or part of an operating system that provides basic file and supervisory services over a network. Although each computer attached to the network has its own OS, the NOS describes which actions are allowed by each user and coordinates distribution of networked files to the user who requests them.

notification area   Contains icons representing background processes, the system clock and volume control. Located by default at the right edge of the Windows taskbar. Most users call this area the system tray.

NSLOOKUP   Command-line program in Windows used to determine exactly what information the DNS server is providing about a specific host name.

NTDETECT.COM   One of the critical Windows NT/2000/XP startup files.

NTFS (NT file system)   Robust and secure file system introduced by Microsoft with Windows NT. NTFS provides an amazing array of configuration options for user access and security. Users can be granted access to data on a file-by-file basis. NTFS enables object-level security, long filename support, compression, and encryption.

NTFS permissions   Restrictions that determine the amount of access given to a particular user on a system using NTFS.

NTLDR Windows NT/2000/XP boot file. Launched by the MBR or MFT, NTLDR looks at the BOOT.INI configuration file for any installed operating systems.

number pad A portion of the keyboard that lays out the numbers 0–9 along with various math symbols (plus, minus, and so on) like a calculator. (*See also* numeric keypad.)

numeric keypad A portion of the keyboard that lays out the numbers 0–9 along with various math symbols (plus, minus, and so on) like a calculator. (*See also* number pad.)

NVIDIA One of the foremost manufacturers of graphics cards and chipsets.

object System component that is given a set of characteristics and can be managed by the operating system as a single entity.

object access auditing Feature of Event Viewer's Security section that creates an entry in the Security Log when certain objects are accessed, such as a file or folder.

OCR (optical character recognition) Scanner technology used to scan a document as text rather than an image.

ohm(s) Electronic measurement of a cable's impedance.

OpenGL One of two popular APIs used today for video cards. Originally written for UNIX systems but now ported to Windows and Apple systems. (*See also* DirectX.)

optical disc/media Types of data discs (such as DVDs, CDs, Blu-ray Discs, etc.) that are read by a laser.

optical drive Drive used to read/write to optical discs, typically CDs or DVDs.

optical mouse Pointing device that uses light rather than electronic sensors to determine movement and direction the mouse is being moved.

optical resolution Resolution a scanner can achieve mechanically. Most scanners use software to enhance this ability.

optical zoom Mechanical ability of most cameras to "zoom" in as opposed to the digital ability.

option ROM Alternative way of telling the system how to talk to a piece of hardware. Option ROM stores BIOS for the card onboard a chip on the card itself.

OS (operating system) Series of programs and code that create an interface so that users can interact with a system's hardware, for example, DOS, Windows, and Linux.

OSI seven-layer model Architecture model based on the OSI protocol suite that defines and standardizes the flow of data between computers. The seven layers are:

Layer 1, The Physical layer Defines hardware connections and turns binary into physical pulses (electrical or light). Repeaters and hubs operate at the Physical layer.

Layer 2, The Data Link layer Identifies devices on the Physical layer. MAC addresses are part of the Data Link layer. Bridges operate at the Data Link layer.

Layer 3, The Network layer Moves packets between computers on different networks. Routers operate at the Network layer. IP and IPX operate at the Network layer.

Layer 4, The Transport layer Breaks data down into manageable chunks. TCP, UDP, SPX, and NetBEUI operate at the Transport layer.

Layer 5, The Session layer Manages connections between machines. NetBIOS and Sockets operate at the Session layer.

Layer 6, The Presentation layer Can also manage data encryption; hides the differences between various types of computer systems.

Layer 7, The Application layer Provides tools for programs to use to access the network (and the lower layers). HTTP, FTP, SMTP, and POP3 are all examples of protocols that operate at the Application layer.

OS X Current operating system on Apple Macintosh computers. Based on a UNIX core, early versions of OS X ran on Motorola-based hardware; current versions run on Intel-based hardware. Pronounced "ten" rather than "ex."

overclocking To run a CPU or video processor faster than its rated speed.

P1 power connector Provides power to ATX motherboards.

P4 12V connector Provides additional 12-volt power to motherboards that support Pentium 4 and later processors.

P8 and P9 connectors Provides power to AT-style motherboards.

packet Basic component of communication over a network. Group of bits of fixed maximum size and well-defined format that is switched and transmitted as a single entity through a network. Contains source and destination address, data, and control information.

page fault Minor memory-addressing error.

page file Portion of the hard drive set aside by Windows to act like RAM. Also known as virtual memory or swap file.

PAN (personal area network) Small wireless network created with Bluetooth technology and intended to link PCs and other peripheral devices.

parallel port Connection for the synchronous, high-speed flow of data along parallel lines to a device, usually a printer.

parallel processing When a multicore CPU processes more than one thread.

parental controls Tool to allow monitoring and limiting of user activities; designed for parents to control the content their children can access.

parity Method of error detection where a small group of bits being transferred is compared to a single parity bit set to make the total bits odd or even. Receiving device reads the parity bit and determines if the data is valid, based on the oddness or evenness of the parity bit.

parity RAM Earliest form of error-detecting RAM; stored an extra bit (called the parity bit) to verify the data.

partition Section of the storage area of a hard disk. Created during initial preparation of the hard disk, before the disk is formatted.

partition table Table located in the boot sector of a hard drive that lists every partition on the disk that contains a valid operating system.

partitioning Electronically subdividing a physical hard drive into groups called partitions (or volumes).

passive matrix Technology for producing colors in LCD monitors by varying voltages across wire matrices to produce red, green, or blue dots.

password Key used to verify a user's identity on a secure computer or network.

Password Authentication Protocol (PAP) Oldest and most basic form of authentication. Also the least safe, because it sends all passwords in clear text.

password reset disk Special type of floppy disk with which users can recover a lost password without losing access to any encrypted, or password-protected, data.

PATA (parallel ATA) Implementation that integrates the controller on the disk drive itself. (*See also* ATA, IDE, SATA.)

patch Small piece of software released by a software manufacturer to correct a flaw or problem with a particular piece of software.

patch management Keeping patches up to date.

path   Route the operating system must follow to find an executable program stored in a subdirectory.

PC bus   Original 8-bit expansion bus developed by IBM for PCs; ran at a top speed of 4.77 MHz. Also known as the XT bus.

PC Card   Credit card–sized adapter card that adds functionality in many notebook computers, PDAs, and other computer devices. Comes in 16-bit and CardBus parallel format and ExpressCard serial format. (*See also* PCMCIA.)

PC tech   Someone with computer skills who works on computers.

PCI (peripheral component interconnect)   Design architecture for the expansion bus on the computer motherboard, which enables system components to be added to the computer. Local bus standard, meaning that devices added to a computer through this port will use the processor at the motherboard's full speed (up to 33 MHz) rather than at the slower 8 MHz speed of the regular bus. Moves data 32 or 64 bits at a time rather than the 8 or 16 bits the older ISA buses supported.

PCIe (PCI Express)   Serialized successor to PCI and AGP, which uses the concept of individual data paths called lanes. May use any number of lanes, although single lanes (×1) and 16 lanes (×16) are the most common on motherboards.

PCI-X (PCI Extended)   Enhanced version of PCI; 64 bits wide. Typically seen in servers and high-end systems.

PCL   Printer control language created by Hewlett-Packard and used on a broad cross-section of printers.

PCM (Pulse Code Modulation)   Sound format developed in the 1960s to carry telephone calls over the first digital lines.

PCMCIA (Personal Computer Memory Card International Association)   Consortium of computer manufacturers who devised the PC Card standard for credit card–sized adapter cards that add functionality in many notebook computers, PDAs, and other computer devices. (*See also* PC Card.)

PDA (personal digital assistant)   Handheld computer that blurs the line between calculators and computers.

Pearson VUE   One of the two companies that administers the CompTIA Strata exams, along with Prometric.

peer-to-peer networks   Network in which each machine can act as both a client and a server.

Pentium   Name given to the fifth and later generations of Intel microprocessors; has a 32-bit address bus, 64-bit external data bus, and dual pipelining. Also used for subsequent generations of Intel processors—the Pentium Pro, Pentium II, Pentium III, and Pentium 4. Pentium name was retired after the introduction of the Intel Core CPUs.

pen-based computing   Input method used by many PDAs that combines handwriting recognition with modified mouse functions, usually in the form of a pen-like stylus.

performance console   Windows tool used to log resource usage over time.

Performance Logs and Alerts   Snap-in enabling the creation of a written record of most everything that happens on the system.

Performance Options   Tool allowing users to configure CPU, RAM, and virtual memory settings.

peripheral   Any device that connects to the system unit.

permission propagation   Term to describe what happens to permissions on an object when you move or copy it.

persistence   Phosphors used in CRT screens continuing to glow after being struck by electrons, long enough for the human eye to register the glowing effect. Glowing too long makes the images smeary, and too little makes them flicker.

Personalization applet   Windows Vista/7 applet with which users can change display settings such as resolution, refresh rate, color depth, and also desktop features.

PGA (pin grid array)   Arrangement of a large number of pins extending from the bottom of the CPU package. There are many variations on PGA.

Phillips-head screwdriver   Most important part of a PC tech's toolkit.

phishing   Trying to get people to give their usernames, passwords, or other security information by pretending to be someone else electronically.

Phoenix Technologies   Major producer of BIOS software for motherboards.

phosphor   Electro-fluorescent material that coats the inside face of a cathode ray tube (CRT). After being hit with an electron, it glows for a fraction of a second.

photosensitive drum   Aluminum cylinder coated with particles of photosensitive compounds. Used in a laser printer and usually contained within the toner cartridge.

photosite   Name for the photosensitive pixels that cover a digital camera's sensor.

picoBTX   Variation of the BTX form factor. picoBTX motherboards are generally smaller than their BTX or microBTX counterparts but retain the same functionality.

pin 1   Designator used to ensure proper alignment of floppy disk drive and hard drive connectors.

ping (packet Internet groper)   Slang term for a small network message (ICMP ECHO) sent by a computer to check for the presence and aliveness of another. Used to verify the presence of another system. Also the command used at a prompt to ping a computer.

PIO mode   Series of speed standards created by the Small Form Factor Committee for the use of PIO by hard drives. Modes range from PIO mode 0 to PIO mode 4.

pipeline   Processing methodology where multiple calculations take place simultaneously by being broken into a series of steps. Often used in CPUs and video processors.

pixel (picture element)   In computer graphics, smallest element of a display space that can be independently assigned color or intensity.

platter   Magnetic metal disk inside a hard drive where the data is stored.

plug   Hardware connection with some sort of projection that connects to a port.

plug and play (PnP)   Combination of smart PCs, smart devices, and smart operating systems that automatically configure all necessary system resources and ports when you install a new peripheral device.

plug-in   Tiny piece of software that adds functionality to a Web browser.

polygons   Multi-sided shapes used in 3-D rendering of objects. In computers, video cards draw large numbers of triangles and connect them to form polygons.

polymorph virus   Virus that attempts to change its signature to prevent detection by antivirus programs, usually by continually scrambling a bit of useless code.

polyphony   Number of instruments a sound card can play at once.

POP3 (Post Office Protocol)   Refers to the way e-mail software such as Eudora gets mail from a mail server. When you obtain a SLIP, PPP, or shell account, you almost always get a POP account with it. It is this POP account that you tell your e-mail software to use to get your mail.

pop-up   Irritating browser window that appears automatically when you visit a Web site.

port (networking)   In networking, the number used to identify the requested service (such as SMTP or FTP) when connecting to a TCP/IP host. Examples: 80 (HTTP), 20 (FTP), 69 (TFTP), 25 (SMTP), and 110 (POP3).

port (physical connection)   Part of a connector into which a plug is inserted. Physical ports are also referred to as jacks.

port replicator   Device that plugs into a USB port or other specialized port and offers common PC ports, such as serial, parallel, USB, network, and PS/2. By plugging your notebook computer into the port replicator, you can instantly connect the computer to nonportable components such as a printer, scanner, monitor, or full-sized keyboard. Port replicators are typically used at home or in the office with the non-portable equipment already connected.

portable digital music/media player   Single-purpose handheld computer designed to store and play back digital media files. Also known as an MP3 player.

positional audio   Range of commands for a sound card to place a sound anywhere in 3-D space.

POST (power-on self test)   Basic diagnostic routine completed by a system at the beginning of the boot process to make sure a display adapter and the system's memory are installed; it then searches for an operating system. If it finds one, it hands over control of the machine to the OS.

PostScript   Language defined by Adobe Systems, Inc., for describing how to create an image on a page. The description is independent of the resolution of the device that will actually create the image. It includes a technology for defining the shape of a font and creating a raster image at many different resolutions and sizes.

potential   Amount of static electricity stored by an object.

power conditioning   Ensuring and adjusting incoming AC wall power to as close to standard as possible. Most UPS devices provide power conditioning.

power good wire   Used to wake up the CPU after the power supply has tested for proper voltage.

power management   Specialized software and hardware that enables a PC to conserve power and save on battery life.

power supply fan   Small fan located in a system power supply that draws warm air from inside the power supply and exhausts it to the outside.

power supply unit   Provides the electrical power for a PC. Converts standard AC power into various voltages of DC electricity in a PC.

Power User(s) Group   Second most powerful account and group type in Windows after Administrator/Administrators.

ppm (pages per minute)   Speed of a printer.

PPP (Point-to-Point Protocol)   Enables a computer to connect to the Internet through a dial-in connection and enjoy most of the benefits of a direct connection.

primary corona   Wire located near the photosensitive drum in a laser printer that is charged with extremely high voltage to form an electric field, enabling voltage to pass to the photosensitive drum, thus charging the photosensitive particles on the surface of the drum.

primary partition   Partition on a Windows hard drive designated to store the operating system.

print resolution   Quality of a print image.

print spooler   Area of memory that queues up print jobs that the printer will handle sequentially.

printer   Output device that can print text or illustrations on paper. Microsoft uses the term to refer to the software that controls the physical print device.

printed circuit boards   Copper etched onto a nonconductive material and then coated with some sort of epoxy for strength.

printhead   Case that holds the printwires in a dot-matrix printer.

printwires   Grid of tiny pins in a dot-matrix printer that strike an inked printer ribbon to produce images on paper.

PRML (Partial Response Maximum Likelihood)   Advanced method of RLL that uses powerful, intelligent circuitry to analyze each flux reversal on a hard drive and to make a best guess as to what type of flux reversal it just read. This allows a dramatic increase in the amount of data a hard drive can store.

processing   When the components inside your computer (especially the CPU) work on completing a task.

product key   Code used during installation to verify legitimacy of the software.

program/programming   Series of binary electronic commands sent to a CPU to get work done.

Programs and Features   Windows Vista/7 replacement for the Add or Remove Programs applet.

projector   Device for projecting video images from PCs or other video sources, usually for audience presentations. Available in front and rear view displays.

Prometric   One of the two companies that administers the CompTIA Strata exams, along with Pearson VUE.

prompt   A character or message provided by an operating system or program to indicate that it is ready to accept input.

proprietary   Technology unique to a particular vendor.

protocol   Agreement that governs the procedures used to exchange information between cooperating entities. Usually includes how much information is to be sent, how often it is sent, how to recover from transmission errors, and who is to receive the information.

proxy server   Device that fetches Internet resources for a client without exposing that client directly to the Internet. Usually accepts requests for HTTP, FTP, POP3, and SMTP resources. Often caches, or stores, a copy of the requested resource for later use. Common security feature in the corporate world.

PS/2   Connector for attaching keyboards and mice. (*See also* mini-DIN.)

public folder   Folder that all users can access and share with all other users on the system or network.

queue   Area where objects wait their turn to be processed. Example: the printer queue, where print jobs wait until it is their turn to be printed.

Quick Launch toolbar   Enables you to launch commonly used programs with a single click.

QVGA   Video display mode of 320 × 240.

QWERTY   Most common layout for English-language keyboards. The name refers to the first six letters on the top row.

RAID (redundant array of inexpensive devices)   Six-level (0–5) way of creating a fault-tolerant storage system:

Level 0   Uses byte-level striping and provides no fault tolerance.

Level 1   Uses mirroring or duplexing.

Level 2   Uses bit-level striping.

Level 3   Stores error-correcting information (such as parity) on a separate disk, and uses data striping on the remaining drives.

Level 4   Level 3 with block-level striping.

Level 5   Uses block-level and parity data striping.

RAID-5 volume   Striped set with parity. (*See also* RAID).

rails   Separate DC paths within an ATX power supply.

RAM (random access memory)   Memory that can be accessed at random, that is, memory that you can write to or read from without touching the preceding address. This term is often used to mean a computer's main memory.

RAMDAC (random access memory digital-to-analog converter)   Circuitry used on video cards that support analog monitors to convert the digital video data to analog.

RAM stick   The circuit board that RAM comes on. (*See also* DIMM (dual inline memory module) *and* SODIMM (small outline DIMM).)

raster image   Pattern of dots representing what the final product should look like.

raster line   Horizontal pattern of lines that form an image on the monitor screen.

RD (RMDIR)   Command in the command-line interface used to remove directories.

RDRAM (Rambus DRAM)   Patented RAM technology that uses accelerated clocks to provide very high-speed memory.

read-only attribute   File attribute that does not allow a file to be altered or modified. Helpful when protecting system files that should not be edited.

read-only memory (ROM)   Generic term for nonvolatile memory that can be read from but not written to. This means that code and data stored in ROM cannot be corrupted by accidental erasure. Additionally, ROM retains its data when power is removed, which makes it the perfect medium for storing BIOS data or information such as scientific constants.

rear-view projector   Projector that shoots an image onto a screen from the rear. Rearview projectors are always self-enclosed and very popular for TVs but are virtually unheard of in the PC world.

Recovery Console   Command-line interface boot mode for Windows used to repair a Windows 2000 or Windows XP system suffering from massive OS corruption or other problems.

Recycle Bin   When files are deleted from a modern Windows system, they are moved to the Recycle Bin. To permanently remove files from a system, they must be emptied from the Recycle Bin.

REGEDIT.EXE   Program used to edit the Windows Registry.

regionalization Act of modifying a device or piece of software for different geographic areas. For example, would add accented characters such as *é* and Spanish-only characters such as *ñ*.

register Storage area inside the CPU used by the onboard logic to perform calculations. CPUs have many registers to perform different functions.

registration Usually optional process that identifies the legal owner/user of the product to the supplier.

Registry Complex binary file used to store configuration data about a particular system. To edit the Registry, users can use the applets found in the Control Panel or REGEDIT.EXE or REGEDT32.EXE.

Reliability and Performance Monitor Windows Vista's extended Performance applet.

remediation Repairing damage caused by a virus.

remnant Potentially recoverable data on a hard drive that remains despite formatting or deleting.

Remote Assistance Feature of Windows that enables users to give anyone control of his or her desktop over the Internet.

Remote Desktop Connection Windows tool used to enable a local system to graphically access the desktop of a remote system.

removable storage media Any type of data storage that can be removed.

REN (RENAME) command Command in the command-line interface used to rename directories.

resistance Difficulty in making electricity flow through a material, measured in ohms.

resistor Any material or device that impedes the flow of electrons. Electronic resistors measure their resistance (impedance) in ohms. (*See* ohm(s).)

resolution Measurement for CRTs and printers expressed in horizontal and vertical dots or pixels. Higher resolutions provide sharper details and thus display better-looking images.

resources Data and services of a PC.

respect What all techs should feel for their customers.

response rate Time it takes for all of the sub-pixels on the panel to go from pure black to pure white and back again.

restore point System snapshot created by the System Restore utility that is used to restore a malfunctioning system. (*See also* System Restore.)

Restriction of Hazardous Substances (ROHS) A European Union (EU) standard that regulates toxic substances such as lead, mercury, and cadmium.

RET (resolution enhancement technology) Technology that uses small dots to smooth out jagged edges that are typical of printers without RET, producing a higher-quality print job.

RFI (radio frequency interference) Another form of electrical interference, caused by radio-wave emitting devices, such as cell phones, wireless network cards, and microwave ovens.

RG-58 Coaxial cabling used for 10Base2 networks.

ribbon cable A flat cable used to connect floppy drives and PATA devices.

RIMM Individual stick of Rambus RAM. The letters don't actually stand for anything; they just rhyme with SIMM and DIMM.

RIP (raster image processor) Component in a printer that translates the raster image into commands for the printer.

riser card Special adapter card, usually inserted into a special slot on a motherboard, that changes the orientation of expansion cards relative to the motherboard. Riser cards are used extensively in slimline computers to keep total depth and height of the system to a minimum. Sometimes called a daughterboard.

RJ (registered jack) connector UTP cable connector, used for both telephone and network connections. RJ-11 is a connector for four-wire UTP; usually found in telephone connections. RJ-45 is a connector for eight-wire UTP; usually found in network connections.

RJ-11 *See* RJ (registered jack) connector.

RJ-45 *See* RJ (registered jack) connector.

ROM (read-only memory) Generic term for nonvolatile memory that can be read from but not written to. This means that code and data stored in ROM cannot be corrupted by accidental erasure. Additionally, ROM retains its data when power is removed, which makes it the perfect medium for storing BIOS data or information such as scientific constants.

root directory Directory that contains all other directories.

root keys   Five main categories in the Windows Registry:

HKEY_CLASSES_ROOT

HKEY_CURRENT_USER

HKEY_USERS

HKEY_LOCAL_MACHINE

HKEY_CURRENT_CONFIG

rotation speed   How fast a hard drive's platters spin. Measured in rotations per minute (RPMs).

router   Device connecting separate networks. Forwards a packet from one network to another based on the network address for the protocol being used. For example, an IP router looks only at the IP network number. Routers operate at Layer 3 (Network) of the OSI seven-layer model.

RS-232C   Standard port recommended by the Electronics Industry Association for serial devices.

Run dialog box   Command box in which users can enter the name of a particular program to run; an alternative to locating the icon in Windows.

Safe mode   Important diagnostic boot mode for Windows that only runs very basic drivers and turns off virtual memory.

sampling   Capturing sound waves in electronic format.

SATA (serial ATA)   Serialized version of the ATA standard that offers many advantages over PATA (parallel ATA) technology, including thinner cabling, keyed connectors, and lower power requirements.

SATA bridge   Adapter that allows PATA devices to be connected to a SATA controller.

SATA power connector   15-pin, L-shaped connector used by SATA devices that support the hot-swappable feature.

satellites   Two or more standard stereo speakers to be combined with a subwoofer for a speaker system (i.e. 2.1, 5.1, etc.).

scan code   Unique code corresponding to each key on the keyboard sent from the keyboard controller to the CPU.

script   Small piece of programming.

SCSI (Small Computer System Interface)   Powerful and flexible peripheral interface popularized on the Macintosh and used to connect hard drives, CD-ROM drives, tape drives, scanners, and other devices to PCs of all kinds. Normal SCSI enables up to seven devices to be connected through a single bus connection, whereas Wide SCSI can handle 15 devices attached to a single controller.

SCSI chain   Series of SCSI devices working together through a host adapter.

SCSI host adapter   Device that enables SCSI peripherals and drives to connect to a PC.

SCSI ID   Unique identifier used by SCSI devices. No two SCSI devices may have the same SCSI ID.

SD (secure digital)   Very popular format for flash media cards; also supports I/O devices.

SDRAM (synchronous DRAM)   DRAM that is synchronous, or tied to the system clock, and thus runs much faster than traditional FPM and EDO RAM. This type of RAM is used in all modern systems.

SEC (single-edge cartridge)   Radical CPU package where the CPU was contained in a cartridge that snapped into a special slot on the motherboard called Slot 1.

sector   Segment of one of the concentric tracks encoded on the disk during a low-level format. A sector holds 512 bytes of data.

sector translation   Translation of logical geometry into physical geometry by the onboard circuitry of a hard drive.

sectors per track (sectors/track)   Combined with the number of cylinders and heads, defines the disk geometry.

security patch   Fix to the operating system that prevents hackers from breaking through holes in the code.

serial port   Common connector on a PC. Connects input devices (such as a mouse) or communications devices (such as a modem).

server   Computer that shares its resources, such as printers and files, with other computers on a network. Example: Network File System server that shares its disk space with a workstation that does not have a disk drive of its own.

service pack   Collection of software patches released at one time by a software manufacturer.

SetupAPI.log   Log file that tracks the installation of all hardware on a system.

Setuplog.txt   Log file that tracks the complete installation process, logging the success or failure of file copying, Registry updates, and reboots.

SFC (system file checker)   Scans, detects, and restores Windows system files, folders, and paths.

shadow mask   CRT screen that allows only the proper electron gun to light the proper phosphors.

shared documents   Windows pre-made folder accessible by all users on the computer.

shared memory   Means of reducing the amount of memory needed on a video card by borrowing from the regular system RAM, which reduces costs but also decreases performance.

share-level security   Security system in which each resource has a password assigned to it; access to the resource is based on knowing the password.

shareware   Program protected by copyright; holder allows (encourages!) you to make and distribute copies under the condition that those who adopt the software after preview pay a fee to the holder of the copyright. Derivative works are not allowed, although you may make an archival copy.

shoulder surfing   Someone spying on you from behind, watching what you type.

shunt   Tiny connector of metal enclosed in plastic that creates an electrical connection between two posts of a jumper.

SID (security identifier)   Unique identifier for every PC that must be changed when cloning.

sidebanding   Second data bus for AGP video cards; enables the video card to send more commands to the northbridge while receiving other commands at the same time.

signal-to-noise ratio   Measure that describes the relative quality of an input port.

signature   Code pattern of a known virus; used by antivirus software to detect viruses.

SIMM (single in-line memory module)   DRAM packaging distinguished by having a number of small tabs that install into a special connector. Each side of each tab is the same signal. SIMMs come in two common sizes: 30-pin and 72-pin.

simple file sharing   Allows users to share locally or across the network but gives no control over what others do with shared files.

simple volume   Volume created when setting up dynamic disks. Acts like a primary partition on a dynamic disk.

single-core architecture   Design of a CPU with only one execution core.

single-sided RAM   Has chips on only one side, as opposed to double-sided RAM.

single inline memory module (SIMM)   The form factor on which RAM used to be installed. Now outdated in favor of DIMMs and SODIMMs.

slimline   Motherboard form factor used to create PCs that were very thin. NLX and LPX were two examples of this form factor.

slot covers   Metal plates that cover up unused expansion slots on the back of a PC. Useful in maintaining proper airflow through a computer case.

S.M.A.R.T. (Self-Monitoring, Analysis, and Reporting Technology) Monitoring system built into hard drives.

smart battery   Portable PC battery that tells the computer when it needs to be charged, conditioned, or replaced.

smart card   Hardware authentication involving a credit-card-sized card with circuitry that can be used to identify the bearer of that card.

SmartMedia   Format for flash media cards; no longer used with new devices.

smartphone   Handheld computer with built-in cell phone and Internet connectivity.

SMM (System Management Mode)   Special CPU mode that enables the CPU to reduce power consumption by selectively shutting down peripherals.

SMTP (Simple Mail Transport Protocol)   Main protocol used to send electronic mail on the Internet.

snap-ins   Small utilities that can be used with the Microsoft Management Console.

social engineering   Using or manipulating people inside the networking environment to gain access to that network from the outside.

social network   Connecting and interacting online with friends, colleagues, and people with similar interests.

socket services   Device drivers that support the PC Card socket, enabling the system to detect when a PC Card has been inserted or removed, and providing the necessary I/O to the device.

SODIMM (small outline DIMM)   Memory used in portable PCs because of its small size.

soft power   Characteristic of ATX motherboards, which can use software to turn the PC on and off. The physical manifestation of soft power is the power switch. Instead of the thick power cord used in AT systems, an ATX power switch is little more than a pair of small wires leading to the motherboard.

software   Single group of programs designed to do a particular job; always stored on mass storage devices.

solid ink printers   Printer that uses solid sticks of nontoxic "ink" that produce more vibrant color than other print methods.

sound card   Expansion card that can produce audible tones when connected to a set of speakers.

southbridge   Part of a motherboard chipset; handles all the inputs and outputs to the many devices in the PC.

spam   Unsolicited e-mails from both legitimate businesses and scammers that account for a huge percentage of traffic on the Internet.

spanned volume   Volume that uses space on multiple dynamic disks.

SPD (serial presence detect)   Information stored on a RAM chip that describes the speed, capacity, and other aspects of the RAM chip.

S/PDIF (Sony/Philips Digital Interface Format)   Digital audio connector found on many high-end sound cards. Users can connect their computers directly to a 5.1 speaker system or receiver. S/PDIF comes in both coaxial and optical versions.

speaker   Device that outputs sound by using a magnetically driven diaphragm.

spread-spectrum   Radio wave that broadcasts data in small, discrete chunks over different frequencies in a certain range.

sprite   Bitmapped graphic such as a BMP file used by early 3-D games to create the 3-D world.

spyware   Grayware that runs in the background of a user's PC, sending information about browsing habits back to the company that installed it onto the system.

SRAM (static RAM)   RAM that uses a flip-flop circuit rather than the typical transistor/capacitor of DRAM to hold a bit of information. SRAM does not need to be refreshed and is faster than regular DRAM. Used primarily for cache.

SSD (solid-state drive)   Data storage device that uses solid-state memory to store data.

SSH (Secure Shell)   Terminal emulation program similar to Telnet, except that the entire connection is encrypted.

SSID (service set identifier)   Parameter used to define a wireless network, otherwise known as the network name.

SSL (Secure Sockets Layer)   Security protocol used by a browser to create secure Web sites.

standard account/user   User account in Windows Vista/7 that has limited access to a system. Accounts of this type cannot alter system files, cannot install new programs, and cannot edit some settings by using the Control Panel without supplying an administrator password. Replaces the Limited accounts in Windows XP.

Standard Definition   Low-resolution video format with 4:3 aspect ratio.

standouts   Small connectors that screw into a computer case. A motherboard is then placed on top of the standouts, and small screws are used to secure it to the standouts.

Start button   Button on the Windows taskbar that enables access to the Start menu.

Start menu   Menu that can be accessed by clicking the Start button on the Windows taskbar. Enables you to see all programs loaded on the system and to start them.

star topology   Network topology where the computers on the network connect to a central wiring point, usually called a hub.

static charge eliminator   Device used to remove a static charge.

static IP address   Manually set IP address that will not change.

stealth virus   Virus that uses various methods to hide from antivirus software.

stepper motor   One of two methods used to move actuator arms in a hard drive. (*See also* voice coil motor.)

stereo   Describes recording tracks from two sources (microphones) as opposed to monaural, which uses one source.

stick   Generic name for a single physical SIMM, RIMM, or DIMM.

Sticky Keys   Accessibility feature for users unable to press multiple keys at once.

STP (shielded twisted pair)   Popular cabling for networks, composed of pairs of wires twisted around each other at specific intervals. Twists serve to reduce interference (also called crosstalk)—the more twists, the less interference. Cable has metallic shielding to protect the wires from external interference. Token Ring networks are the only common network technology that uses STP, although Token Ring now uses UTP more often.

streaming media   Broadcast of data that is played on your computer and immediately discarded.

stream loading Process a program uses to constantly download updated information.

stripe set Two or more drives in a group that are used for a striped volume.

strong password Password containing at least eight characters, including letters, numbers, and punctuation symbols.

stylus Pen-like input device used for pen-based computing.

subnet mask Value used in TCP/IP settings to divide the IP address of a host into its component parts: network ID and host ID.

sub-pixel Tiny liquid crystal molecules arranged in rows and columns between polarizing filters used in LCDs.

subwoofer Powerful speaker capable of producing extremely low-frequency sounds.

super I/O chip Chip specially designed to control low-speed, legacy devices such as the keyboard, mouse, and serial and parallel ports.

supercomputer Large, extremely powerful computers used to do complex math very, very quickly.

SuperSpeed USB USB standard that runs at up to 5 Gbps.

surge suppressor Inexpensive device that protects your computer from voltage spikes (or, in Strata terms, that mitigates electrical issues). Also called a surge protector.

SVGA (super video graphics array) Video display mode of 800 × 600.

swap file Large file used by virtual memory. More commonly known as a page file.

switch Device that filters and forwards traffic based on some criteria. A bridge and a router are both examples of switches.

SXGA Video display mode of 1280 × 1024.

SXGA+ Video display mode of 1400 × 1050.

syntax The proper way to write a command-line command so that it functions and does what it's supposed to do.

Sysprep Windows tool that makes cloning of systems easier by making it possible to undo portions of the installation.

System BIOS   Primary set of BIOS stored on an EPROM or flash chip on the motherboard. Defines the BIOS for all the assumed hardware on the motherboard, such as keyboard controller, floppy drive, basic video, and RAM.

system bus speed   Speed at which the CPU and the rest of the PC operates; set by the system crystal.

system crystal   Crystal that provides the speed signals for the CPU and the rest of the system.

system disk   Any device with a functional operating system.

system fan   Any fan controlled by the motherboard but not directly attached to the CPU.

System Management Mode (SMM)   Provided CPUs the ability to turn off high-power devices (monitors, hard drives, etc.). Originally for laptops; later versions are incorporated in all AMD and Intel CPUs.

System Monitor   Utility that can evaluate and monitor system resources, such as CPU usage and memory usage.

system resources   In classic terms, the I/O addresses, IRQs, DMA channels, and memory addresses. Also refers to other computer essentials such as hard drive space, system RAM, and the processor speed.

System Restore   Utility in Windows that enables you to return your PC to a recent working configuration when something goes wrong. System Restore returns your computer's system settings to the way they were the last time you remember your system working correctly—all without affecting your personal files or e-mail.

System ROM   ROM chip that stores the system BIOS.

System Tools   Menu containing tools such as System Information and Disk Defragmenter, accessed by selecting Start | Accessories | System Tools.

system tray   Contains icons representing background processes and the system clock. Located by default at the right edge of the Windows taskbar. Accurately called the notification area.

system unit   Main component of the PC, in which the CPU, RAM, CD-ROM, and hard drive reside. All other devices—the keyboard, mouse, and monitor—connect to the system unit.

SystemRoot   The tech name given to the folder in which Windows has been installed.

tablet PC Small portable computer distinguished by the use of a touch screen with stylus and handwriting recognition as the primary modes of input. Also the name of the Windows XP–based operating system designed to run on such systems.

tailgating Form of infiltration and social engineering that involves following someone else through a door as if you belong.

take ownership Special permission allowing users to seize control of a file or folder and potentially preventing others from accessing the file/folder.

Task Manager Shows all running programs, including hidden ones, accessed by pressing CTRL-ALT-DEL. Able to shut down an unresponsive application that refuses to close normally.

taskbar Contains the Start button, the system tray, the Quick Launch bar, and buttons for running applications. Located by default at the bottom of the desktop.

TCP/IP (Transmission Control Protocol/Internet Protocol) Communication protocols developed by the U.S. Department of Defense to enable dissimilar computers to share information over a network.

Tech Toolkit Tools a PC tech should never be without, including a Phillips-head screwdriver, a pair of tweezers, a flat-head screwdriver, a hemostat, a Torx wrench, a parts retriever, and a nut driver or two.

telecommuting Working from home and over the phone or Internet.

telephone scams Social engineering attack in which the attacker makes a phone call to someone in an organization to gain information.

Telnet Terminal emulation program for TCP/IP networks that allows one machine to control another as if the user were sitting in front of it.

Temporary Internet Files Web files stored on a PC to speed up browsing.

tera- Prefix that usually stands for the binary number 1,099,511,627,776 (2^{40}). When used for mass storage, it's often shorthand for a trillion bytes.

terminal Dumb device connected to a mainframe or computer network that acts as a point for entry or retrieval of information.

terminal emulation Software that enables a PC to communicate with another computer or network as if the PC were a specific type of hardware terminal.

terminal server Central computer that hosts files and applications for terminals.

termination Using terminating resistors to prevent packet reflection on a network cable.

terminator   Resistor that is plugged into the end of a bus cable to absorb the excess electrical signal, preventing it from bouncing back when it reaches the end of the wire. Terminators are used with coaxial cable and on the ends of SCSI chains. RG-58 coaxial cable requires resistors with a 50-ohm impedance.

Test the theory   Attempt to resolve the issue by either confirming the theory and learning what needs to be done to fix the problem, or by not confirming the theory and forming a new one or escalating. (One of the steps a technician uses to a solve a problem.)

texture   Small picture that is tiled over and over again on walls, floors, and other surfaces to create the 3-D world.

TFT (thin film transistor)   Type of LCD screen. (*See also* active matrix.)

theory of probable cause   One possible reason why something is not working; a guess.

thermal compound   Paste-like material with very high heat-transfer properties. Applied between the CPU and the cooling device, it ensures the best possible dispersal of heat from the CPU. Also called heat dope.

thermal printer   Printers that use heated printheads to create high-quality images on special or plain paper.

thermal unit   Combination heat sink and fan designed for BTX motherboards; blows hot air out the back of the case instead of just into the case.

thin client   Keyboard, mouse, and monitor connected to a simple box that enables the client to log in to the terminal server.

thread   Smallest logical division of a single program.

throttling   Power reduction/thermal control capability allowing CPUs to slow down during low activity or high heat build-up situations. Intel's version is known as SpeedStep, AMD's as PowerNow!

throughput   Amount of data being moved.

throw   Size of the image a projector displays at a certain distance from the screen.

tiers   Levels of Internet providers, ranging from the Tier 1 backbones to Tier 3 regional networks.

timbre   Qualities that differentiate the same note played on different instruments.

toner A fine powder made up of plastic particles bonded to iron particles, used to create the text and images for a laser printer.

toner cartridge Object used to store the toner in a laser printer. (*See also* laser printer, toner.)

top-level domain End piece of a domain name; for example, .com. Also known as the extension.

touchpad Flat, touch-sensitive pad that serves as a pointing device for most laptops.

touch screen Monitor with a type of sensing device across its face that detects the location and duration of contact, usually by a finger or stylus.

TRACERT Command-line utility used to follow the path a packet takes between two hosts. Also called TRACEROUTE.

traces Small electrical connections embedded in a circuit board.

track Area on a hard drive platter where data is stored. A group of tracks with the same diameter is called a cylinder.

trackball Pointing device distinguished by a ball that is rolled with the fingers.

TrackPoint IBM's pencil eraser–sized joystick used in place of a mouse on laptops.

transfer corona Thin wire, usually protected by other thin wires, that applies a positive charge to the paper during the laser printing process, drawing the negatively charged toner particles off of the drum and onto the paper.

transparency (Windows Vista Aero) Effect in the Aero desktop environment that makes the edges of windows transparent.

triad Group of three phosphors—red, green, blue—in a CRT.

Trojan Program that does something other than what the user who runs the program thinks it will do.

troubleshooting theory Steps a technician uses to solve a problem: identify the problem, establish a theory of probable cause, test the theory, establish a plan of action, verify functionality, and document findings.

TV tuner Typically an add-on device that allows users to watch television on a computer.

TWAIN (technology without an interesting name)   Programming interface that enables a graphics application, such as a desktop publishing program, to activate a scanner, frame grabber, or other image-capturing device.

UAC (User Account Control)   Windows Vista/7 feature that enables Standard accounts to do common tasks and provides a permissions dialog when Standard and Administrator accounts do certain things that could potentially harm the computer (such as attempt to install a program).

UART (universal asynchronous receiver/transmitter)   Device that turns serial data into parallel data. The cornerstone of serial ports and modems.

UDF (universal data format)   Replaced the ISO-9660 formats, allowing any operating system and optical drive to read UDF formatted disks.

UEFI (Unified Extensible Firmware Interface)   Consortium of companies that established the UEFI standard that replaced the original EFI standard.

Ultra DMA   Hard drive technology that enables drives to use direct memory addressing. Ultra DMA mode 3 drives—called ATA/33—have data transfer speeds up to 33 MBps. Mode 4 and 5 drives—called ATA/66 and ATA/100, respectively—transfer data at up to 66 MBps for mode 4 and 100 MBps for mode 5. Both modes 4 and 5 require an 80-wire cable and a compatible controller to achieve these data transfer rates.

unauthorized access   Anytime a person accesses resources in an unauthorized way. This access may or may not be malicious.

Unicode   16-bit code that covers every character of the most common languages, plus several thousand symbols.

unsigned driver   Driver that has not gone through the Windows Hardware Quality Labs or Microsoft Windows Logo Program to ensure compatibility.

UPC (Universal Product Code)   Bar code used to track inventory.

upgrade   Going from an old version of a piece of software or hardware to a newer version. For example, going from Windows XP to Windows 7.

Upgrade Advisor   The first process that runs on the XP installation CD. It examines your hardware and installed software (in the case of an upgrade) and provides a list of devices and software that are known to have issues with XP. It can also be run separately from the Windows XP installation, from the Windows XP CD. The Upgrade Advisor is also available for Windows Vista and Windows 7.

upgrade installation   Installation of Windows on top of an earlier installed version, thus inheriting all previous hardware and software settings.

UPS (uninterruptible power supply)   Device that supplies continuous clean power to a computer system the whole time the computer is on. Protects against power outages and sags.

URL (uniform resource locator)   An address that defines the location of a resource on the Internet. URLs are used most often in conjunction with HTML and the World Wide Web.

USB (universal serial bus)   General-purpose serial interconnect for keyboards, printers, joysticks, and many other devices. Enables hot-swapping and daisy-chaining devices.

USB host controller   Integrated circuit that is usually built into the chipset and controls every USB device that connects to it.

USB hub   Device that extends a single USB connection to two or more USB ports, almost always directly from one of the USB ports connected to the root hub.

USB root hub   Part of the host controller that makes the physical connection to the USB ports.

USB thumb drive   Flash memory device that uses the standard USB connection.

USENET   Collection of thousands of unregulated newsgroups that contain posts on every topic imaginable.

User account   Container that identifies a user to an application, operating system, or network, including name, password, user name, groups to which the user belongs, and other information based on the user and the OS or NOS being used. Usually defines the rights and roles a user plays on a system.

User Accounts applet   Windows XP (and later versions) applet that replaced the Users and Passwords applet of Windows 2000.

user interface   Visual representation of the computer on the monitor that makes sense to the people using the computer, through which the user can interact with the computer.

user profiles   Settings that correspond to a specific user account and may follow users regardless of the computers where they log on. These settings enable the user to have customized environment and security settings.

User's Files   Windows Vista's redux of the My Documents folder structure. It is divided into several folders such as Documents, Pictures, Music, and Video.

Users and Passwords applet   Windows 2000 application that allowed management of user accounts and passwords.

Users group   List of local users not allowed, among other things, to edit the Registry or access critical system files. They can create groups, but can only manage the groups they create.

USMT (User State Migration Tool)   Advanced application for file and settings transfer of multiple users.

UTP (unshielded twisted pair)   Popular type of cabling for telephone and networks, composed of pairs of wires twisted around each other at specific intervals. The twists serve to reduce interference (also called crosstalk). The more twists, the less interference. Unlike its cousin, STP, UTP cable has no metallic shielding to protect the wires from external interference. 10BaseT uses UTP, as do many other networking technologies. UTP is available in a variety of grades, called categories, as follows:

Category 1 UTP   Regular analog phone lines—not used for data communications.

Category 2 UTP   Supports speeds up to 4 megabits per second.

Category 3 UTP   Supports speeds up to 16 megabits per second.

Category 4 UTP   Supports speeds up to 20 megabits per second.

Category 5 UTP   Supports speeds up to 100 megabits per second.

Category 5e UTP   Supports speeds up to 1000 megabits per second.

Category 6 UTP   Supports speeds up to 10 gigabits per second.

V standards   Standards established by CCITT for modem manufacturers to follow (voluntarily) to ensure compatible speeds, compression, and error correction.

Verify   Make sure that a problem has been resolved and will not return. (One of the steps a technician uses to a solve a problem.)

vertices   Used in the second generation of 3-D rendering, vertices have a defined X, Y, and Z position in a 3-D world.

VESA (Video Electronics Standards Association)   Consortium of computer manufacturers that standardized improvements to common IBM PC components. VESA is responsible for the Super VGA video standard and the VLB bus architecture.

VGA (Video Graphics Array)   Standard for the video graphics adapter that was built into IBM's PS/2 computer. It supports 16 colors in a 640 × 480 pixel video display and quickly replaced the older CGA (Color Graphics Adapter) and EGA (Extended Graphics Adapter) standards.

video capture   Computer jargon for the recording of video information, such as TV shows or movies.

video card Expansion card that works with the CPU to produce the images displayed on your computer's display. Also called GPU.

video display *See* monitor.

virtual machine A software "computer" within another computer.

virtualization Technology that enables a single computer to act as multiple computers.

virus Program that can make a copy of itself without your necessarily being aware of it. Some viruses can destroy or damage files. The best protection is to always maintain backups of your files.

virus definition or data file Files that enable the virus protection software to recognize the viruses on your system and clean them. These files should be updated often. They are also called signature files, depending on the virus protection software in use.

virus shield Passive monitoring of a computer's activity, checking for viruses only when certain events occur.

VIS (viewable image size) Measurement of the viewable image that is displayed by a CRT rather than a measurement of the CRT itself.

voice coil motor One of two methods used to move actuator arms in a hard drive. (*See also* stepper motor.)

VoIP (Voice over Internet Protocol) Collection of protocols that make voice calls over a data network possible.

volatile Memory that must have constant electricity to retain data. Alternatively, any programmer six hours before deadline after a nonstop, 48-hour coding session, running on nothing but caffeine and sugar.

volts (V) Measurement of the pressure of the electrons passing through a wire, or voltage.

volume Physical unit of a storage medium, such as tape reel or disk pack, that is capable of having data recorded on it and subsequently read. Also refers to a contiguous collection of cylinders or blocks on a disk that are treated as a separate unit.

volume boot sector First sector of the first cylinder of each partition; stores information important to its partition, such as the location of the operating system boot files.

voucher Means of getting a discount on the CompTIA Strata exams.

VPN (virtual private network) Encrypted connection over the Internet between a computer or remote network and a private network.

VRM (voltage regulator module) Small card supplied with some CPUs to ensure that the CPU gets correct voltage. This type of card, which must be used with a motherboard specially designed to accept it, is not commonly seen today.

VRR (vertical refresh rate) The amount of time it takes for a CRT to draw a complete screen. This value is measured in hertz, or cycles per second. Most modern CRTs have a VRR of 60 Hz or better.

wait state Occurs when the CPU has to wait for RAM to provide code. Also known as a pipeline stall.

WAN (wide area network) Network that covers a large area; usually composed of two or more interconnected local area networks.

WAP (wireless access point) Device that centrally connects wireless network nodes.

wattage (watts or W) Measurement of the amps and volts needed for a particular device to function.

wave table synthesis Technique that supplanted FM synthesis, wherein recordings of actual instruments or other sounds are embedded in the sound card as WAV files. When a particular note from a particular instrument or voice is requested, the sound processor grabs the appropriate prerecorded WAV file from its memory and adjusts it to match the specific sound and timing requested.

Web browser Program designed to retrieve, interpret, and display Web pages.

webcam PC camera most commonly used for Internet video.

Web-delivered services Desktop software recreated for use in a Web browser.

Weblog Type of Web site that enables a user to share his or her thoughts, personal ideas, and so on.

Web server Server that runs specialized software for hosting Web sites.

Welcome screen Login screen for Windows XP. Enables users to select their particular user account by clicking on their user picture.

WEP (Wired Equivalent Privacy) Wireless security protocol that uses a standard 40-bit encryption to scramble data packets. Does not provide complete end-to-end encryption and is vulnerable to attack.

Wi-Fi Common name for the IEEE 802.11 wireless Ethernet standard.

wildcard   Character used during a search to represent search criteria. For instance, searching for *.doc will return a list of all files with a .doc extension, regardless of the filename. The * is the wildcard in that search.

Windows 2000   Windows version that succeeded Windows NT; it came in both Professional and Server versions.

Windows 9x   Term used collectively for Windows 95, Windows 98, and Windows Me.

Windows Explorer   Windows utility that enables you to manipulate files and folders stored on the drives in your computer.

Windows Logo'd Products List   List of products that have passed the Microsoft Windows Logo Program and are compatible with the Windows operating system. Formerly called the Hardware Compatibility List (or HCL).

Windows NT   Precursor to Windows 2000, XP, and Vista, which introduced many important features (such as HAL and NTFS) used in all later versions of Windows.

Windows sidebar   User interface feature in Windows Vista that enables users to place various gadgets, such as clocks, calendars, and other utilities, on the right side of their desktop.

Windows Update   Microsoft application used to keep Windows operating systems up to date with the latest patches or enhancements. (*See* Automatic Updates.)

Windows Vista   Pre–Windows 7 version of Windows; comes in many different editions for home and office use but does not have a Server edition.

Windows XP   Version of Windows that replaced both the entire Windows 9x line and Windows 2000; does not have a Server version.

wireless   Name sometimes used for the technology used with cordless mice and keyboards.

worm   Very special form of virus. Unlike other viruses, a worm does not infect other files on the computer. Instead, it replicates by making copies of itself on other systems on a network by taking advantage of security weaknesses in networking protocols.

WPA (Wi-Fi Protected Access)   Wireless security protocol that uses encryption key integrity-checking and EAP and is designed to improve on WEP's weaknesses.

WPA2 (Wi-Fi Protected Access 2)   Wireless security protocol, also known as IEEE 802.11i. Uses the Advanced Encryption standard and replaces WPA.

WQUXGA   Video display mode of 2560 × 1600.

wrapper   *See* container file.

WSXGA   Video display mode of 1440 × 900.

WSXGA+   Video display mode of 1680 × 1050.

WUXGA   Video display mode of 1920 × 1200.

WVGA   Video display mode of 800 × 480.

WWW (World Wide Web)   System of Internet servers that support documents formatted in HTML and related protocols. Can be accessed by using Gopher, FTP, HTTP, Telnet, and other tools.

www.comptia.org   CompTIA's Web site.

WXGA   Video display mode of 1280 × 800.

x64   Describes 64-bit operating systems and software.

x86   Describes 32-bit operating systems and software.

XCOPY command   Command in the command-line interface used to copy multiple directories at once, which the COPY command could not do.

xD (Extreme Digital) picture card   Very small flash media card format.

Xeon   Line of Intel CPUs designed for servers.

XGA (extended graphics array)   Video display mode of 1024 × 768.

XPS (XML Paper Specification) print path   Improved printing subsystem included in Windows Vista. Has enhanced color management and better print layout fidelity.

XT bus   *See* PC bus.

ZIF (zero insertion force) socket   Socket for CPUs that enables insertion of a chip without the need to apply pressure. Intel promoted this socket with its overdrive upgrades. The chip drops effortlessly into the socket's holes, and a small lever locks it in.

INDEX

F

F2 key, renaming files, 108
Facebook, 316–317
failure, burn-in, 178
families, optical disc, 83
fat client, 333
FAT (File Allocation Table), 218
FAT32 (File Allocation Table), 218
FDDs (floppy disk drives), 75–78, 86–88
feedback, to software developers, 134
fiber-optic
    Ethernet, 265
    Internet backbone connected via, 291
File Allocation Table (FAT), 218
File Allocation Table (FAT32), 218
file extensions, 101
file servers, 326
file systems, formatting hard drives with, 217–218
File Transfer Protocol (FTP), 304–306
files and folders
    backing up, 129
    creating, 105
    deleting, 106
    Documents, 102–103
    in each user account, 96–97
    hard drive organization, 108–110
    moving/copying/cutting/pasting, 105–106
    Navigation pane, 103–104
    operating system folders, 110–111
    overview of, 101–102
    program folders, 111
    renaming files, 108
    review Q & A, 112–114
    securing using NTFS, 357
    selecting multiple targets, 106–107
    sharing, 267–271
    viewing contents, 104
    Windows Explorer handling, 102
FileZilla, 305–306
filters, spam blocking, 374
Finder, OS X, 157

fingerprint reader, 356
firewalls
    enabling access after upgrades, 155–157
    for Internet security, 381–382
    protecting against worms, 376
FireWire
    connection speeds, 177
    port and connector, 173
    ports for camcorders, 201
    ports on back of typical PCs, 167–168
flash-based storage
    hard disk drives vs., 219–220
    HDD vs., 219
    implementations of, 220
    memory card formats, 220–221
    multi-card readers and writers, 221
    solid state drives, 222–223
    USB flash drives, 222
    why SSDs rule, 223–224
flatbed scanners, 194
floppy disk drives (FDDs), 75–78, 86–88
floppy diskettes, 75–76
fonts, adjusting size on screen, 94
force feedback game controllers, 210
form factor
    digital cameras, 202–203
    motherboards, 44, 48
formats
    creating file system for hard drive, 217–219
    memory card, 220–221
    optical disc and drive, 82
    optical disc families, 83
forums, 313–314
Foxit Reader, 154
fragmentation, advantages of SSDs, 224
frame rate, webcam issues, 203–204
freeware licensing, 150
FTP (File Transfer Protocol), 304–306
full-duplex mode, NICs, 265
function keys, standard keyboard layout, 54–55

The Best in Security Certification Prep

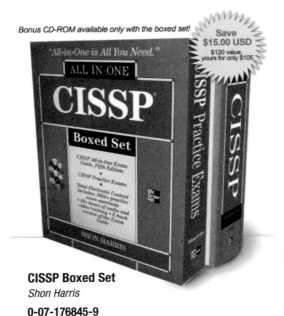

Bonus CD-ROM available only with the boxed set!

Save $15.00 USD
$120 value, yours for only $105.

CISSP Boxed Set
Shon Harris
0-07-176845-9

CISSP All-in-One Exam Guide, Fifth Edition
Shon Harris
0-07-160217-8

CISSP Practice Exams
Shon Harris
0-07-170139-7

CSSLP Certification All-in-One Exam Guide
Wm. Arthur Conklin and Daniel Shoemaker
0-07-176026-1

CISA Certified Information Systems Auditor All-in-One Exam Guide, Second Edition
Peter Gregory
0-07-176910-2

 Learn more. Do more.
MHPROFESSIONAL.COM

Available in print and ebook formats.

 Follow us @MHComputing

New Online Resources for IT Professionals!

Certification Shows You Know IT—Now Share IT

Join the IT Pro Community to network and engage with professionals from around the world. You can also post your resume on the CompTIA IT Job Board—an employment website designed for CompTIA certified professionals. Highlight your certification status so you'll come up first when employers search for qualified candidates.

Get Involved. Get Smart.
Get on the Path to Success.

CompTIA.

JOIN TODAY!

IT Pro Community http://itpro.comptia.org

CompTIA IT Job Board http://itcareers.comptia.org

LICENSE AGREEMENT

THIS PRODUCT (THE "PRODUCT") CONTAINS PROPRIETARY SOFTWARE, DATA AND INFORMATION (INCLUDING DOCUMENTATION) OWNED BY THE McGRAW-HILL COMPANIES, INC. ("McGRAW-HILL") AND ITS LICENSORS. YOUR RIGHT TO USE THE PRODUCT IS GOVERNED BY THE TERMS AND CONDITIONS OF THIS AGREEMENT.

LICENSE: Throughout this License Agreement, "you" shall mean either the individual or the entity whose agent opens this package. You are granted a non-exclusive and non-transferable license to use the Product subject to the following terms:

(i) If you have licensed a single user version of the Product, the Product may only be used on a single computer (i.e., a single CPU). If you licensed and paid the fee applicable to a local area network or wide area network version of the Product, you are subject to the terms of the following subparagraph (ii).

(ii) If you have licensed a local area network version, you may use the Product on unlimited workstations located in one single building selected by you that is served by such local area network. If you have licensed a wide area network version, you may use the Product on unlimited workstations located in multiple buildings on the same site selected by you that is served by such wide area network; provided, however, that any building will not be considered located in the same site if it is more than five (5) miles away from any building included in such site. In addition, you may only use a local area or wide area network version of the Product on one single server. If you wish to use the Product on more than one server, you must obtain written authorization from McGraw-Hill and pay additional fees.

(iii) You may make one copy of the Product for back-up purposes only and you must maintain an accurate record as to the location of the back-up at all times.

COPYRIGHT; RESTRICTIONS ON USE AND TRANSFER: All rights (including copyright) in and to the Product are owned by McGraw-Hill and its licensors. You are the owner of the enclosed disc on which the Product is recorded. You may not use, copy, decompile, disassemble, reverse engineer, modify, reproduce, create derivative works, transmit, distribute, sublicense, store in a database or retrieval system of any kind, rent or transfer the Product, or any portion thereof, in any form or by any means (including electronically or otherwise) except as expressly provided for in this License Agreement. You must reproduce the copyright notices, trademark notices, legends and logos of McGraw-Hill and its licensors that appear on the Product on the back-up copy of the Product which you are permitted to make hereunder. All rights in the Product not expressly granted herein are reserved by McGraw-Hill and its licensors.

TERM: This License Agreement is effective until terminated. It will terminate if you fail to comply with any term or condition of this License Agreement. Upon termination, you are obligated to return to McGraw-Hill the Product together with all copies thereof and to purge all copies of the Product included in any and all servers and computer facilities.

DISCLAIMER OF WARRANTY: THE PRODUCT AND THE BACK-UP COPY ARE LICENSED "AS IS." McGRAW-HILL, ITS LICENSORS AND THE AUTHORS MAKE NO WARRANTIES, EXPRESS OR IMPLIED, AS TO THE RESULTS TO BE OBTAINED BY ANY PERSON OR ENTITY FROM USE OF THE PRODUCT, ANY INFORMATION OR DATA INCLUDED THEREIN AND/OR ANY TECHNICAL SUPPORT SERVICES PROVIDED HEREUNDER, IF ANY ("TECHNICAL SUPPORT SERVICES"). McGRAW-HILL, ITS LICENSORS AND THE AUTHORS MAKE NO EXPRESS OR IMPLIED WARRANTIES OF MERCHANTABILITY OR FITNESS FOR A PARTICULAR PURPOSE OR USE WITH RESPECT TO THE PRODUCT. McGRAW-HILL, ITS LICENSORS, AND THE AUTHORS MAKE NO GUARANTEE THAT YOU WILL PASS ANY CERTIFICATION EXAM WHATSOEVER BY USING THIS PRODUCT. NEITHER McGRAW-HILL, ANY OF ITS LICENSORS NOR THE AUTHORS WARRANT THAT THE FUNCTIONS CONTAINED IN THE PRODUCT WILL MEET YOUR REQUIREMENTS OR THAT THE OPERATION OF THE PRODUCT WILL BE UNINTERRUPTED OR ERROR FREE. YOU ASSUME THE ENTIRE RISK WITH RESPECT TO THE QUALITY AND PERFORMANCE OF THE PRODUCT.

LIMITED WARRANTY FOR DISC: To the original licensee only, McGraw-Hill warrants that the enclosed disc on which the Product is recorded is free from defects in materials and workmanship under normal use and service for a period of ninety (90) days from the date of purchase. In the event of a defect in the disc covered by the foregoing warranty, McGraw-Hill will replace the disc.

LIMITATION OF LIABILITY: NEITHER McGRAW-HILL, ITS LICENSORS NOR THE AUTHORS SHALL BE LIABLE FOR ANY INDIRECT, SPECIAL OR CONSEQUENTIAL DAMAGES, SUCH AS BUT NOT LIMITED TO, LOSS OF ANTICIPATED PROFITS OR BENEFITS, RESULTING FROM THE USE OR INABILITY TO USE THE PRODUCT EVEN IF ANY OF THEM HAS BEEN ADVISED OF THE POSSIBILITY OF SUCH DAMAGES. THIS LIMITATION OF LIABILITY SHALL APPLY TO ANY CLAIM OR CAUSE WHATSOEVER WHETHER SUCH CLAIM OR CAUSE ARISES IN CONTRACT, TORT, OR OTHERWISE. Some states do not allow the exclusion or limitation of indirect, special or consequential damages, so the above limitation may not apply to you.

U.S. GOVERNMENT RESTRICTED RIGHTS: Any software included in the Product is provided with restricted rights subject to subparagraphs (c), (1) and (2) of the Commercial Computer Software-Restricted Rights clause at 48 C.F.R. 52.227-19. The terms of this Agreement applicable to the use of the data in the Product are those under which the data are generally made available to the general public by McGraw-Hill. Except as provided herein, no reproduction, use, or disclosure rights are granted with respect to the data included in the Product and no right to modify or create derivative works from any such data is hereby granted.

GENERAL: This License Agreement constitutes the entire agreement between the parties relating to the Product. The terms of any Purchase Order shall have no effect on the terms of this License Agreement. Failure of McGraw-Hill to insist at any time on strict compliance with this License Agreement shall not constitute a waiver of any rights under this License Agreement. This License Agreement shall be construed and governed in accordance with the laws of the State of New York. If any provision of this License Agreement is held to be contrary to law, that provision will be enforced to the maximum extent permissible and the remaining provisions will remain in full force and effect.